PRAISE FOR *DEFENDING THE FAITH AGAINST PRESENT HERESIES*

"Fidelity to Christ and His Church requires fidelity to the Deposit of Faith that Christ entrusted to the Apostles and to their successors to propagate and safeguard. The faithful, whether clerics or laymen, share a responsibility to make known to their pastors, especially the chief shepherd, the Roman Pontiff, whenever they have moral certainty that novel teachings that contradict the doctrine of the Church have been authoritatively proposed for belief, even by the Supreme Pontiff himself. Well-reasoned pleas to uphold the Church's plain and constant teaching in the face of deviations are acts of charity, not of sinful defiance. This book is an invaluable compilation of such efforts."
—**FR. GERALD E. MURRAY, JCD**, New York, NY

"With admirable lucidity and a wealth of evidence and argument, this timely book collects the main published documents making the case that heresies designedly put about by Pope Francis are today a primary cause and manifestation of Christianity's worst crisis ever. A valuable and enlightening resource for understanding the state of the battle."
—**JOHN FINNIS**, Biolchini Family Emeritus Professor of Law at Notre Dame Law School and Permanent Senior Distinguished Research Fellow at the Notre Dame Center for Ethics and Culture

"A great saint wrote as regards the turmoil surrounding Vatican II: 'In the Church of Christ, everyone is obliged to make a tenacious effort to remain loyal to the teaching of Christ. No one is exempt.' And what if it seems, to some knowledgeable and conscientious Catholics, that their efforts and their loyalty are contradicted, not assisted, by the Holy Father? What if, in such baffling circumstances, some of these brothers and sisters of ours, being scholars—other alternatives apparently fruitless—draw up a formal and public expression of their concerns? These deserve our respectful attention, I believe, and in charity should not be dismissed."
—**MICHAEL PAKALUK**, Professor of Ethics and Social Philosophy, The Catholic University of America

"This book is an extraordinary document in the history of the Church. It bears witness to a struggle within the Church comparable only to that of St. Athanasius in the fourth century. Since Jorge Bergoglio was elected supreme Pontiff, it has become necessary for priests and laymen alike to reprimand him over and over again, in order to make him gear up to the standards of his high office in both doctrine and acts, according to his capacity as *cultor orthodoxae, catholicae, et apostolicae fidei.*

These efforts have not proven to be in vain, for they address not only the ruling Pontiff but also his successors, as a witness for all time."
— **MARTIN MOSEBACH**, author of *The Heresy of Formlessness*

"Confusion reigns in the Church, and many questions put to Pope Francis remain unanswered. In the resulting jungle of darkness and division for want of truth, the number of papal texts, acts, and declarations accused of error or heresy is overwhelming. Where to begin? John R. T. Lamont and Claudio Pierantoni have edited a much-needed compendium of the most serious and scholarly documents addressing these problems since *Amoris Laetitia*. In so doing, *Defending the Faith against Present Heresies* offers a complete and intelligible sequence of reflections on the doctrinal ills faced by our beloved Church. This book is a testimony for history. But even more, it brings answers to Catholics wounded in their very faith."
— **JEANNE SMITS**

"This book presents the case that Pope Francis has shown himself a heretic, in a collection of very able and highly readable essays. It is well worth reading by anyone with an open mind on the present upheaval in the Church."
— **HENRY SIRE**, author of *Phoenix from the Ashes* and *The Dictator Pope*

"As Christ tells us, we cannot follow two masters. We must choose between God or Mammon; we must choose between the *Heiliger Geist* and the *Zeitgeist*, between the Holy Spirit and the Spirit of the Age. This opportune volume helps us to focus on the Magisterium's timeless truth in uncertain times."
— **JOSEPH PEARCE**, Editor, *St. Austin Review* and Senior Contributor at the *Imaginative Conservative*

Defending the Faith against Present Heresies

Defending the Faith against Present Heresies

Letters & Statements Addressed to Pope Francis, the Cardinals, and the Bishops

WITH A COLLECTION OF
RELATED ARTICLES & INTERVIEWS

Edited by
JOHN R.T. LAMONT
and
CLAUDIO PIERANTONI

With a Foreword by
Archbishop Carlo Maria Viganò

Copyright © John R.T. Lamont and Claudio Pierantoni
Foreword © Carlo Maria Viganò

All rights reserved:
No part of this book may be reproduced or transmitted,
in any form or by any means, without permission

ISBN: 978-1-989905-40-1 (pbk)
ISBN: 978-1-989905-41-8 (hardcover)

Arouca Press
PO Box 55003
Bridgeport PO
Waterloo, ON N2J3G0
Canada
www.aroucapress.com
Send inquiries to info@aroucapress.com

Book and cover design by
Michael Schrauzer
Cover photo modified from www.flickr.com/
photos/governortomwolf/21748736366/

TABLE OF CONTENTS

FOREWORD by Archbishop Carlo Maria Viganò xi
PUBLISHER'S NOTE xv

INTRODUCTION by John Lamont 1
ADDITIONAL NOTE 1:
Reflections on a New Dialogue Between Traditionalist and Conservative Catholics by Claudio Pierantoni 21
ADDITIONAL NOTE 2:
The Documents Collected Here Do Not Attempt a Moral Judgement on the Person of the Pope
by Claudio Pierantoni. 31

I   THE *DUBIA* OF THE FOUR CARDINALS 35

II   LETTERS AND STATEMENTS TO THE POPE OR THE BISHOPS. 47

   A   *Theological Censures of* Amoris Laetitia. 49
   B   Correctio filialis de haeresibus propagatis *(Filial Correction concerning the Propagation of Heresies)* . . . 75
   C   *Open Letter to the Bishops of the Catholic Church* 125
   D   *An Appeal to the Cardinals of the Catholic Church* 161
   E   Contra recentia sacrilegia *(Protest against Pope Francis's Sacrilegious Acts)* 167

III   ARTICLES AND INTERVIEWS. 177

   1   ANNA M. SILVAS
       Some Concerns about Amoris Laetitia 179
   2   "Chaos was raised to a principle by the stroke of a pen":
       Interview with Robert Spaemann. 193
   3   FR JOHN HUNWICKE
       The Holy Spirit Guides the Pope? 199
   4   CLAIRE CHRETIEN
       Forty-five Catholic Academics Urge Cardinals to Ask Pope Francis to Fix Exhortation's Errors. 211

5 JOHN R.T. LAMONT
   The Meaning of Amoris Laetitia
   According to Pope Francis 215

6 CLAUDIO PIERANTONI
   *The Need for Consistency between Magisterium
   and Tradition: Examples from History* 235

7 ANNA M. SILVAS
   A Year After Amoris Laetitia: *A Timely Word* 253

8 "By far the worst document that has ever
   come out with a papal signature":
   *Interview with Claudio Pierantoni
   on the* Filial Correction 265

9 CLAUDIO PIERANTONI
   Response to Rocco Buttiglione's Latest Interview 277

10 ROBERTO DE MATTEI
   *The Worldwide Impact and Significance
   of the* Correctio filialis 283

11 ROBERTO DE MATTEI
   Correctio filialis: *A First Appraisal* 287

12 "True love may justly express itself
   in the form of a correction":
   Interview with Joseph Shaw on the Filial Correction 291

13 ROBERT FASTIGGI AND DAWN EDEN GOLDSTEIN
   Ratzinger's Rules for Faithful Theological Discourse 299

14 JOSEPH SHAW
   A Challenge for Fastiggi and Goldstein 305

15 *Fastiggi and Goldstein versus Shaw: Responses* 309

16 MICHAEL SIRILLA
   On the Moral Liceity of Publicly Correcting the Pope 315

17 MAIKE HICKSON
   *Before Pope Francis Was Accused of Heresy,
   Catholics Reached Out to Him Numerous Times* 323

18 EDWARD PETERS
   *The Heresy Letter Is Intelligent,
   But Doesn't Quite Convince* 333

19 EDWARD FESER
   *The Right and the Not-so-right in the Open Letter
   Accusing Pope Francis of Heresy* 335

20 "Why I Signed the Papal Heresy Open Letter":
   Interview with John Rist. 341

21 PETER KWASNIEWSKI
   *Why I Signed the Open Letter Accusing
   Pope Francis of Heresy* 347

22 FR BRIAN W. HARRISON, O.S.
   *Why I Didn't Sign the Open Letter
   Accusing the Pope of Heresy* 351

23 JOHN R.T. LAMONT
   *Theologian Responds to Criticisms of Letter to Bishops
   Concerning Heresies of Pope Francis* 355

24 THOMAS WEINANDY, O.F.M. CAP.
   Is Pope Francis a Heretic? 363

25 "We uphold the dignity of the Apostolic See
   by desiring that its occupant be free of heresy":
   Interview with Claudio Pierantoni on the Open Letter . . . 367

26 PETER A. KWASNIEWSKI
   When Creeping Normalcy Bias Protects a Chaotic Pope . . . 379

27 MAIKE HICKSON
   *Cardinal Müller: Open Letter Accusing Pope
   of Heresy Deserves a Response* 385

28 THOMAS G. WEINANDY, O.F.M. CAP.
   Pope Francis and Schism 389

29 JOHN R.T. LAMONT
   *The SSPX, the Open Letter,
   and the Heresies of Pope Francis* 393

30 CLAUDIO PIERANTONI
   On Bishop Voderholzer's Dissociation from the "Protest" . . . 409

31 PAUPER PEREGRINUS
   Papal Infallibility After One Hundred and Fifty Years . . . 415

CONTRIBUTORS 421

INDEX 427

FOREWORD

ARCHBISHOP CARLO MARIA VIGANÒ

> *My sheep hear my voice,*
> *and I know them, and they follow me;*
> *and I give them eternal life, and they shall never perish,*
> *and no one shall snatch them out of my hand.*
> *My Father, who has given them to me, is greater than all,*
> *and no one is able to snatch them out of the Father's hand.*
> Jn 10: 27–30

WHEN WE CONSIDER HOW INCREDIBLE IT would have been, eighty years ago, to even contemplate that it might be necessary for laymen and prelates to defend the Faith against doctrinal deviations promoted by the Vicar of Christ, we must painfully acknowledge that what has happened since then has severely compromised the Holy Church and the Papacy.

Today we find ourselves once again defending the Faith against the highest echelons of the Church, after decades of having to defend it against the errors formulated by no less heterodox cardinals, bishops, and priests. Those who have denounced their errors have often found themselves alone, and rarely has the Holy See intervened to condemn the "false christs and false prophets" (Mt 24:24). And those who, certain of the impunity guaranteed to them, have advanced their careers and been promoted, are today among the staunchest supporters of Jorge Mario Bergoglio, who in turn has risen to the highest throne. Some proudly boast of being the architects of his election at the 2013 Conclave, after a failed attempt at the previous Conclave.

We must therefore ask ourselves, after having read the errors denounced in this volume and the entire conglomeration of official and unofficial interventions, whether the "demythologization of the papacy" desired by the proponents of the "synodal path" is not materializing in the 2013 election and unstoppable demolition project of the Argentinean cardinal. Certainly those who wanted him at the summit of the hierarchy now see some of their most daring plans already implemented: some explicitly and formally, such as the admission of public adulterers to the sacraments and the condemnation of capital punishment; others implicitly or informally, such as the legitimation of sodomy; and, finally, others such as the ordination of women and the abolition of clerical celibacy, for which the discussion has resumed as if the definitive acts of the Magisterium had no value. This demonstrates, if proof were needed, that the infallible Magisterium of the Church is not seen as having the authority that seems instead to apply absolutely to the controversial documents of the so-called "Conciliar Magisterium."

In this race towards the abyss, we are faced with what social psychology calls "cognitive dissonance," i.e., the tension or discomfort we feel when faced with two opposing and incompatible ideas. The American social psychologist Leon Festinger (1919–1989) demonstrated that such discomfort leads us to process these beliefs in three ways, in order to reduce the psychological incongruity that this dissonance causes: we change our *attitude*, change the *context*, or change *behavior*.

This phenomenon is also evident in the religious sphere, starting with the Council, which for the first time in the Church's history introduced elements into doctrine, morals, and the liturgy that were objectively discordant, or at least deliberately highly ambiguous, with respect to what the Magisterium had always taught. These elements—an ecumenism in contradiction with the uniqueness of the one true Religion, the theorization of the secular nature of the State in contradiction with the Social Kingship of Christ, collegiality and synodality in contradiction with the hierarchical and monarchical structure of the Church, the common priesthood of the faithful in contradiction with the ordained ministerial priesthood, the imposition of Communion in the hand in contradiction with faith in the Real Presence, etc.—have almost instinctively led the faithful to come up with solutions to reduce this cognitive dissonance. This happened—to a much greater extent, yet in a perfectly consistent manner—after the abdication of Benedict XVI and the election of his successor.

On the one hand, as Catholics we believe that the Holy Spirit guarantees the Supreme Pontiff a special assistance, which is expressed in infallibility when, as supreme Pastor of the universal Church, he defines a truth concerning faith or morals and teaches that it is to be believed with religious assent by all the faithful. On the other hand, as people endowed with reason, we note that the holder of the papacy uses his authority for a purpose opposite to that which legitimizes it and for which the special assistance of the Paraclete is guaranteed. The dissonance consists in not being able to explain two opposing and divergent representations—a dissonance the layman tends to eliminate or reduce because it undermines his certainties. Thus, not being able to admit that the pope can assert heresies, the layman is inclined to deny that they are heresies in the name of a changed understanding of doctrine (thus adapting his *attitude*); to reduce the gravity of the heresy, for example by distinguishing between material and formal heresies (changing the *context*); or to deny that Bergoglio is pope and that obedience is due to him (changing his *behavior*).

However, I would like to stress that Catholics have already experienced this cognitive dissonance with the Second Vatican Council and the liturgical reform. After sixty years of unresolved conflicts, the faithful are now used to coming up with their own solutions to a reality that seems impossible to accept in its contradictory nature. And if social psychology detects the behavior of the individual, Catholic moral theology—and even before that, philosophy and the fundamental principle of non-contradiction—allows us to detect the inconsistency between two opposing concepts and to reject what is manifestly unacceptable, adhering to what is certainly true because it is guaranteed by God's authority. In essence, a Catholic must understand that this dissonance reveals a real and concrete problem that can be resolved not so much by reformulating or attenuating it to one's liking, but rather by analyzing it according to the infallible criterion that Saint Vincent of Lérins in his *Commonitorium* summed up in the adage: *Quod ubique, quod semper, quod ab omnibus creditum est* [that which is believed everywhere, always, and by all].

Yet we need only read a commentary on the Book of Revelation or some of the writings of the Church Fathers on the end of the world to understand that the present crisis cannot and must not be interpreted as part of a normal situation, but on the contrary as confirmation of the extraordinary nature of the end times. From this supernatural perspective, and instructed by the words of Sacred Scripture and the messages of the Blessed Virgin and the mystics, we can understand the spiritual dimension of the present events and the reasons for the crisis in the Church and the papacy.

This volume has the merit of drawing together the evidence of apostasy, like the burning coals of which Saint Paul speaks in his Epistle to the Romans (12:19–20). And whoever, for love of the Apostolic See and for the honor of Holy Mother Church, has the courage to denounce false shepherds, will have the consolation of hearing the divine Master call to him: "Well done, good and faithful servant, enter into the joy of your Lord" (Mt 25:21). I dare not think of the words that the just Judge will address to those who have betrayed their mandate by deceiving the flock entrusted to them. May this sobering reflection spur us on to beseech from the Holy Spirit the gift of repentance and conversion for those who today seem to want to bring to pass in Rome the terrible visions of the prophet Daniel.

Let us not forget one of the cornerstones of our Faith: the papacy is the infallible garrison against which the gates of hell can never prevail. The horrors and scandals we are witnessing must not cause this certainty to crumble but rather strengthen it, for it is easy to recognize the provident hand of God in crushing victories over the enemy, but it requires Faith and Hope to understand that, in adversity, the Church is tested like gold in the crucible.

✠ Carlo Maria Viganò, Archbishop
29 November 2020
Dominica I Adventus

PUBLISHER'S NOTE

THE WRITINGS CONTAINED IN THIS book should be taken *singulatim* as the expression of the opinions of their immediate authors or groups of signatories, and should not be construed as necessarily the opinions of other authors or signatories included in the book, or of Arouca Press.

In this volume, scriptural references are taken from the Vulgate or from the neo-Vulgate. References to Denzinger are taken from the forty-third edition.

INTRODUCTION

DR JOHN LAMONT

THIS BOOK HAS THE OBJECT OF RECORDING the efforts of a number of Catholic scholars and ecclesiastics in defence of the Catholic faith. The occasion for these efforts is an extraordinary and unprecedented development in the history of the Catholic Church; a prolonged campaign by the regnant bishop of Rome against central truths of this faith. A group of Catholic scholars has sought to resist this attack through a series of documents addressing it. This book publishes these documents, and a selection from the discussions and debates that they provoked when originally published.

Part I of the book reproduces the *dubia* of the four cardinals, since the content of this document is relevant to much that came afterwards.

The first document of Part II is entitled "Theological Censures of *Amoris Laetitia*." A copy of this document was sent privately to each of the cardinals of the Church, and to each of the Eastern Catholic patriarchs during the summer of 2016. The authors mentioned a series of passages in *Amoris Laetitia* which, understood in their natural meaning, imply a deviation from orthodoxy in different degrees. They asked the dean of the College of Cardinals, Cardinal Angelo Sodano, to petition the pope to correct or clarify such passages, so that they could be amended or understood in an orthodox sense. This document was placed into the public domain by an unknown person at the end of July 2016. No answer was ever received from Cardinal Sodano.

The second document, the *Correctio filialis de haeresibus propagatis* ("Filial Correction concerning the Propagation of Heresies") goes a step beyond the Theological Censures. It synthesizes seven heresies that Pope Francis is accused of spreading through his public statements, as well as through his acts and omissions. However, it passes no judgement about the degree of awareness that the pope might have of the heretical nature of these statements, and of the fact that he is so propagating them. This *Correctio filialis* was delivered to the pope on August 11, 2017, with sixty signatures. After more than one month, it had received no answer, and so it was published on the internet at a specifically created website and signed by two hundred and fifty Catholic clergy and scholars.

Given his persistent silence about the *Correctio filialis*, a formal accusation of the canonical delict of heresy was levelled against the pope, in the form of an Open Letter to the Bishops of the Catholic Church, published on April 30, 2019. This Open Letter accuses the pope not only of propagating, but also of himself knowingly upholding seven heresies. These heresies were synthesized from statements of his contained in public documents, and this synthesis was shown to be confirmed both by other relevant words of Pope Francis and by his governance of the Church, in particular by his appointment of prelates who openly uphold unorthodox beliefs.

In the Open Letter, the bishops of the Catholic Church were formally requested to "take the steps necessary to deal with the grave situation of a heretical pope." They were thus requested, first, "publicly to admonish Pope Francis to abjure the heresies that he has professed." Secondly, the signatories made this appeal to the bishops if the pope should not abjure after such an admonition: "We request that you carry out your duty of office to declare that he has committed the canonical delict of heresy and that he must suffer the canonical consequences of this crime." These canonical consequences are not specified in the body of the letter, but a document is attached after the signatures, with the title "Canon law and Catholic theology concerning the situation of a heretical pope." Here, the authors explain the theological and canonical consensus that the final "canonical consequence" of such a verification of papal heresy must necessarily be the declaration of a pope's fall from office. Finally, the Open Letter includes a select bibliography that contains the full demonstration of the heretical character of the pope's positions, and refutations of the main defences that have been presented in his favor. First issued with nineteen signatures, the Open Letter later gathered ninety-four signatures in total.

The fourth document is "An Appeal to the Cardinals of the Catholic Church," published online at *First Things* on August 15, 2018. This appeal responds to Pope Francis's attempt to change the Church's bimillennial teaching on capital punishment, asking the cardinals to advise the pope that it is his duty to withdraw the new number 2267 from the *Catechism* as contradicting and adulterating the word of God. The appeal was published with the signatures of forty-five scholars and pastors. The same document was subsequently published at *LifeSiteNews* where it garnered several dozen more signatures of scholars and pastors.

The fifth document is *Contra recentia sacrilegia*, "Protest against Pope Francis's Sacrilegious Acts." This document was issued on November 9, 2019 in response to the veneration of the idols of Pachamama, a South American fertility goddess, during the Amazonian Synod in Rome in 2019. The document condemned Pope Francis's involvement in these idolatrous acts and asked him to repent and do penance for them.

The detailed assertions and criticisms made by these documents not unnaturally provoked a good deal of public discussion. A selection of these discussions has therefore been included in the book as Part III. This selection contains both attacks and defences of the documents. The goal of the selections was to give the most substantial criticisms of the documents, to provide responses to these criticisms from signatories and sympathetic observers, and to provide useful reflections on or background for the issues raised by the documents. It should be emphasized that these selections express only the views of the authors of the pieces included, who do not speak for all the signatories of the documents. The same assertion must be made about the editors of this volume, who speak only for themselves.

The principal genesis of these efforts was the Synod on the Family in Rome in 2015. During the preparatory session for this Synod in 2014, it became apparent that many of the participants were opposed to fundamental Catholic teachings on faith and morals, and that they intended to use the Synod on the Family to undermine or reject these teachings. The prolonged struggle over doctrine that took place during the preparatory session and the Synod itself helped to clarify the issues at stake, and to reveal the identity of the participants on opposing sides in this struggle.

These issues were not new ones. Most of the doctrines at stake were ones that had been hotly disputed since at least the 1960s, and that had been the subjects of magisterial interventions by or at the behest of Pope John Paul II—most notably in the Encyclical *Veritatis Splendor*, the Apostolic Exhortation *Familiaris Consortio*, the Declaration *Dominus Iesus*, and the *Catechism of the Catholic Church*. Adherents of errors that had been rejected in these interventions tried to get the Synod on the Family to rehabilitate their favoured positions, and even to impose them as compulsory on the whole Church. The most significant fact about the Synod and its preparation was that Pope Francis revealed himself as being one of these adherents. This was a departure from his public statements before his election to the papacy. During the reign of John Paul II, he had been generally supportive of the teachings of that pontiff. Pope Francis may have changed his views on this subject over time, or he may have dissimulated his real views before his election in order to protect his advancement in the Church. However, Pope Francis's record of protecting sexual offenders as Archbishop of Buenos Aires—some details of which are provided in the Letter to the Bishops—suggests that dissimulation is the more likely explanation for his change of tune after his accession to the pontificate. The history of the Synod and its preparation indicate that Pope Francis launched this synod precisely in order to advance his heretical views, and to consign the contrary positions to the rubbish heap of history.

On March 19, 2016, Pope Francis released the Post-synodal Apostolic Exhortation *Amoris Laetitia*. On a natural interpretation, many of the texts in this Apostolic Exhortation expressed meanings that contradicted Catholic teachings. In consequence, these texts posed a grave danger to the faith of Catholics. A group of concerned Catholic scholars and ecclesiastics, recognizing this danger, decided to request the cardinals and patriarchs of the Church to take action against it.

Some remarks should be made about the membership of this group. The group that produced the theological censures and the *Correctio filialis* was substantially the same. The group that produced the Open Letter to the bishops was a subset of the previous groups. The group that produced the Protest against Sacrilege was a subset of the previous groups, with some new members. It has been alleged that these groups were tools of wealthy American neoconservative interests, who funded them in order to undermine the papacy of Pope Francis. No funding was received or needed for any of the five documents in this book. For all of the documents except the one that appeared in *First Things*, none of the drafters could be described as neoconservatives. Although the members of these groups belonged to a number of different nationalities, no Americans took part in drafting the first three documents. The principal link between the drafters of the first three documents is the adherence of many to liturgical traditionalism and the opposition of all to theological modernism. Some connection to Oxford

University, rather than to any American institution, was common to most of the Anglophone drafters of those documents. A number of signatories of these documents have suffered severe reprisals as a consequence of their signature; laymen have been dismissed from their employment, and religious have been penalized. For this reason, the scholars involved in drafting the documents must largely remain anonymous. It can be said that the original initiative for the theological censures came from Dr John Lamont, one of the editors of this volume, and from a member of the Order of Preachers (who was not, it should be mentioned, Aidan Nichols, O. P.). Lamont's initiative stemmed from his academic work on revelation, faith, theology, and Church teaching.

Some background should also be given for the documents themselves.

The theological censures of *Amoris Laetitia* contained in the document sent to the cardinals and patriarchs are technical theological terms that in many cases require scholarly elucidation in order to be fully explained. As a result, the complete meaning of the document is not readily accessible to the general Catholic public. This lack of accessibility was not considered by the drafters to be a shortcoming of the document. As with the other documents in this volume, the theological censures were not written to get across a message to the general public, but to address the problems raised by the statements and actions of Pope Francis. An explanation of each censure would overburden this work, and do no more than repeat the explanations given by standard theological sources. The reader is referred to these sources for analyses of the individual censures. (It should be noted however that the meaning of the censure of heresy is given in the *Correctio filialis*, and more prominently in the Letter to the Bishops.) The correctness of each censure in the document is subject to examination and debate by theologians, and to the future judgement of the magisterium of the Church. Hopefully this examination and debate will take place in future discussion of *Amoris Laetitia* and the pontificate of Pope Francis, and an authoritative and final magisterial judgement will eventually determine whether or how far these censures are accurate.

It will be helpful nonetheless to give some explanations of theological censures in general, and to explain why these censures were thought to be a suitable means of dealing with the problems raised by *Amoris Laetitia*.

The theological censures of *Amoris Laetitia* were a return to an old practice in the Church. Theological censures were first developed and applied by the theology faculties of medieval universities, most notably the University of Paris. These censures had the function of identifying certain propositions as contrary to the faith. This identification was a normal part of the disputations that were central to the activities of medieval universities. In the context of these disputations, the identification of heresy was simply a function of the search for knowledge and the teaching activity that were proper to these universities. If a proposition could be identified with confidence as heretical, however, this had consequences for what could be taught and maintained in a university. As a result, the faculties of theology as a whole began to censure propositions as heretical. The consequence of such a censure was that the members of the university were forbidden to put forward these propositions as possible or true. This activity of the universities was welcomed by the Holy See, and was incorporated into the teaching function of the Church. The procedure was for a suspect proposition to be debated in the theology faculties, and for the faculties to decide on its status and to censure it if it was considered heterodox. After such a pronouncement by the theology faculty, the issue would be referred to the Roman authorities, who would then make their own pronouncement on the status of the proposition in question. Unlike the university censures, this pronouncement had juridical force and was final. During the second half of the sixteenth century, however, the Holy See ceased to depend on the input of universities in its formulation of theological censures. The Roman Inquisition and special congregations charged by the pope with the task of reporting on some theological question carried out theological investigations independently, and these investigations furnished the basis for theological censures issued by the Holy See.[1]

The infliction of theological censures was not limited to heretical propositions. Censures were developed that specified categories of propositions that offended against the faith without directly contradicting divinely revealed truths. These censures distinguished both the degree to which a proposition offended against the faith, and

---

1 See Bruno Neveu, *L'erreur et son juge: remarques sur les censures doctrinales à l'époque moderne* (Naples: Bibliopolis, 1993), 81–128.

the character of the harm that it caused to believers. The meanings of the censures were debated by theologians in the sixteenth and seventeenth centuries. Theological investigation of the censures culminated in the *Scrutinium doctrinarum qualificandis assertionibus thesibusque atque libris conducentium*, published in 1709 by the Franciscan Antonius Panormitanus (Antonio de Panormo). Subsequent theologians largely followed the views of Panormitanus on the interpretation of theological censures.[2]

The assignment of theological censures to propositions became the normal way in which the papal magisterium was exercised from the sixteenth to the eighteenth centuries. When applied to individual propositions, this form of teaching held many advantages, and can indeed be considered the most valuable way in which the papal magisterium has been exercised outside of ecumenical councils. Such censures defined precisely the sense of the propositions being censured and the fault that led to the censure. There was no doubt about the certainty of the censure or the assent that was required to it. All censures were understood to have the highest level of certainty possessed by the papal teaching office. In the case of propositions censured as heretical, the censure was understood as requiring the assent of faith. However, the practice of issuing theological censures was abandoned by the papacy in the nineteenth century. The last important instance of the censuring of propositions by the Holy See was Pius VI's apostolic constitution *Auctorem Fidei* (1794), censuring the errors of the Synod of Pistoia.

It may be freely admitted that most Catholics, and even most Catholic priests, have never heard of theological censures and could not explain them if they were asked about them. But this situation is part of the wider problem that is responsible for the evils addressed by the documents reproduced in this book. This is the problem of a steady decay of knowledge and belief in Catholic teaching and tradition. The programme of Pope Francis and the lamentable failure of most Catholics to effectively oppose this programme are both results of this decay.

---

2 Theological censures should not be confused with the system of theological notes developed by theologians. Theological notes give positive evaluations of the extent to which propositions are connected to divine revelation and magisterial teaching. They were developed much later than theological censures. They are not used in magisterial teaching, and cannot be simply mapped onto theological censures.

In addition to this general decay, there is also a more specific link between the abandonment of theological censures by nineteenth-century popes and the way that the Church has responded to the heterodoxy of Pope Francis. Instead of issuing teachings whose binding nature was clearly defined, and then proceeding legally against those who offended against these teachings, the nineteenth- and twentieth-century popes chose to enforce adherence to Catholic teachings by broader utterances conformity to which was based on a general appeal to papal authority, and to deal with opposition to these utterances by administrative punishments. This approach relied on an ultramontane exaltation of the papacy and an appeal to blind obedience. It also helped to inculcate and reinforce these ultramontane positions. A theological censure requires the faithful to accept a specific, clearly delimited exercise of papal authority because it is an official act of the required kind. Such an act of acceptance involves a reference to a higher law that confers authority on papal actions, and to the rational justification that warrants the pope in taking the action in question. It also limits the acceptance demanded of the faithful to the precise scope of the action as indicated by the law. This is very different from believing what the pope says because the pope says it and because the pope cannot do any wrong. The latter attitude is the one inculcated by the demotic version of ultramontanism that has shaped Catholic attitudes to the papacy since the time of Lamennais. It is allied to a conception of papal authority also inculcated by this demotic ultramontanism, which sees the pope as the source of all law and authority in the Church, and hence considers the pope to be above the law.[3]

---

[3] Lest this description of ultramontane conceptions of papal authority seem a caricature, we can cite an example of such a conception from a criticism of the *Open Letter:* "Disons d'abord qu'accuser le pape d'adhésion à certaines hérésies est objectivement une faute très grave. Pourquoi? La réponse est simple, mais dirimante: le canon 1404 du *Code* de 1983 nous dit: 'Le Premier Siège n'est jugé par personne.'... Juger signifie ici accuser au for externe d'une faute qui relève de son pouvoir suprême et non d'une faute morale personnelle.... Juger signifie accuser le pape dans sa charge suprême d'enseigner et de gouverner l'Église. Juger le pape comme hérétique, c'est l'accuser au for externe dans son pouvoir d'enseigner et de gouverner. Ce que personne n'a le droit de faire! ... Ainsi, on n'a pas le droit de dire que le pape enseigne l'erreur ou qu'il est incompétent dans les décisions qu'il prend. Pourquoi cela? Parce que le pape, quand il

Introduction

These ultramontane positions explain much of the lack of resistance by believing Catholics to Pope Francis's attacks on the faith and the Church. A substantial part of the laity and clergy reject the heterodox views that he expresses, but practice doublethink when presented with incontrovertible evidence that he is expressing them. They refuse to accept that he holds, states, and promotes heresies, no matter how clear the evidence. In the opinions of the editors, some of the criticisms of the *Correctio filialis* and the Open Letter reproduced below provide examples of this phenomenon. Even those Catholics who are quite aware that he holds and expresses heretical theses almost all decline to publicly state that this is the case. His morally scabrous protection and promotion of criminal bishops and priests is treated by most Catholics as if it does not exist.

The ultramontanism that was a factor in the eclipse of theological censures thus also played a role in producing the situation in which it was thought necessary to revive them. The drafters of the censures and the filial correction were well aware that the responsibility of correcting papal utterances that stray from the faith belongs primarily to the bishops of the Church. Such a correction should have been made after *Amoris Laetitia* was issued. Pope

---

enseigne ou gouverne selon son pouvoir suprême et universel sur toute l'Église, ne remplit pas cette charge en vertu d'un simple pouvoir humain, comme le fait toute autorité humaine, mais en vertu d'une assistance spéciale et personnelle promise par le Christ lui-même, chef indéfectible et éternellement présent à son Église jusqu'à la fin des temps." Aline Lizotte, "Non, le pape n'est pas hérétique!," *Smart Reading Press*, May 10, 2019. [*Translation:* Let us say, first of all, that accusing the Pope of adhering to certain heresies is objectively a very serious fault. Why is this so? The answer is simple but decisive: Canon 1404 of the 1983 *Code* tells us: "The First See is judged by no one".... To judge here means to accuse the Pope in the external forum of a fault connected with his supreme power and not of a personal moral fault.... To judge means to accuse the Pope in his supreme office of teaching and governing the Church. To judge the pope as a heretic is to accuse him, in the external forum, in his power to teach and govern. No one has the right to do this!... Thus, one has no right to say that the Pope teaches error or is incompetent in the decisions he makes. Why not? Because the Pope, when he teaches or governs according to his supreme and universal power over the whole Church, does not fulfill this office by virtue of mere human power, as every human authority does, but by virtue of the special and personal assistance promised by Christ himself, the unfailing and eternal Head of his Church until the end of time.]

Francis had already made his views clear during the Synod on the Family, and there was little doubt about the meaning and purpose that he had in mind for the Apostolic Exhortation. However, no such correction occurred, and there seemed no reason to expect that one would take place. This was partly because many bishops agreed with the views of Pope Francis, and indeed manifested their agreement in unmistakable terms. But those bishops who still kept the faith said nothing, in some cases no doubt out of cowardice, but also because of the faulty ultramontanism described above.

This situation posed a grave and pressing danger to souls. The Catholic scholars involved in drafting the theological censures thought that in the absence of episcopal action, it was incumbent on them to do something about this danger. Recognizing the primary responsibility of the ecclesiastical hierarchy in this matter, it was thought right to first request that the College of Cardinals and the patriarchs of the Church petition the pope to condemn any interpretations of *Amoris Laetitia* that are contrary to the Catholic faith. The College of Cardinals was chosen because it has the task of advising the pope, and the patriarchs were chosen as being the most senior members of the episcopate. The decision of using theological censures to make this request was taken for several reasons. Theological criticism of a papal document is a very grave act. It demands the highest level of accuracy and precision. Assigning theological censures to the suspect passages of *Amoris Laetitia* met this demand for accuracy better than any other approach. This criticism had to warn of the dangers to the faith posed by the document, and theological censures define this danger with the greatest possible precision. The use of theological censures is a rejection of any form of modernism or neo-modernism, which deny the conceptions of divine revelation and magisterial teaching that such censures assert or imply. Since the censures reject propositions because of their incompatibility with divine revelation rather than their disagreement with papal utterances, they are also a departure from the sort of ultramontanism that has silenced criticism of Pope Francis. The practice of theologians issuing censures of propositions on their own initiative is a traditional one that has been recognized as legitimate by the Church. The only restriction that has been imposed on this practice by ecclesiastical authority is the interdiction of censuring propositions that have never been condemned by magisterial teaching and are matters of free debate among Catholic schools; none of the propositions at issue in this book falls into this category.[4]

The identification and formulation of the propositions censured and the choice of the censures to be applied to them was the most intellectually substantial and difficult part of the composition of any of the five documents. All these questions were intensively debated by a large international group of Catholic scholars. Invaluable contributions were made to this process by scholars who did not agree with the censures, and did not end up signing any of the documents. Their criticisms identified many errors, and the work of responding to them led to important revisions and new insights. This theological work laid the foundations for the *Correctio filialis* and the Open Letter as well as for the theological censures, since the later documents incorporated some of the censures and based their arguments on them. The drafting of the censures was almost entirely the work of John Lamont, but since this drafting was based on the intense collective work and debate of many theologians, the censures cannot be attributed to a single person.

An important event occurred shortly after the despatch to Cardinal Sodano of the document containing the theological censures and its accompanying letter. This was the submission in September 2016 to Pope Francis and to Cardinal Gerhard Müller, then Prefect of the Congregation of the Doctrine of the Faith, of *dubia* asking for a clarification of the meaning of *Amoris Laetitia* (included in this volume as Part I). Cardinals Walter Brandmüller, Raymond L. Burke, Carlo Caffarra, and Joachim Meisner asked Pope Francis if *Amoris Laetitia* was to be taken as teaching five propositions that substantially corresponded to assertions censured in the document sent to the cardinals and patriarchs. The cardinals made these *dubia* public on November 14 along with an explanation when no immediate response to them was received. It should be said that as far as the editors of this volume are aware, none of the persons involved in the drafting of the censures knew about the *dubia* or were consulted in their formulation. The *dubia* and the censures were independent initiatives. When the existence of the *dubia* was made public, Cardinal Burke asserted that a formal correction of

---

4 See H. Quilliet, "Censures théologiques," *Dictionnaire de théologie catholique*, vol. 2, Baader-Cisterciens (Paris: Letouzey et Ané, 1905), cols. 2102–13.

Pope Francis would be necessary if it became clear that no reply to them was to be expected.

> LifeSiteNews: *You have spoken about a potential upcoming formal correction of Pope Francis, should he continue to refuse to answer the* dubia *expressed by you and the other cardinals—with the vocal support of numerous theologians and tens of thousands of faithful. When would such an action take place, and what would it look like? Can you describe that for us?*
>
> *Cardinal Burke*: Well, the *dubia* have to have a response because they have to do with the very foundations of the moral life and of the Church's constant teaching with regard to good and evil, with regard to various sacred realities like marriage and Holy Communion and so forth. What format it would take is very simple; namely, it would be direct, even as the *dubia* are, only in this case there would no longer be raising questions, but confronting the confusing statements in *Amoris Laetitia* with what has been the Church's constant teaching and practice, and thereby correcting *Amoris Laetitia*. It's an old institute in the Church, the correction of the pope. This has not happened in recent centuries, but there are examples and it's carried out with the absolute respect for the office of the Successor of Saint Peter. In fact, the correction of the pope is actually a way of safeguarding that office and its exercise.[5]

No direct reply to the *dubia* was ever provided. It could be argued that Pope Francis effectively replied to the *dubia* by making public in September 2016 his letter to the bishops of the Buenos Aires area concerning *Amoris Laetitia*, and then ordering that this letter be published in the *Acta Apostolicae Sedis* with a note stating that it constituted magisterial teaching. In this letter Pope Francis confirmed that the heterodox interpretation given to *Amoris Laetitia* by the Argentine bishops was the only correct one (these texts are reproduced in the *Correctio filialis* below). A reply of this kind of course was not a reason for Cardinal Burke to refrain from a

---

5   Cardinal Raymond Burke, interview with *LifeSiteNews*, December 19, 2016.

formal correction of Pope Francis; it made such a correction more necessary than ever. However, no formal correction has been made.

These developments were decisive in leading to the *Correctio filialis*. The *dubia* meant that there was no doubt that Pope Francis had been apprised of the heretical meanings that could plausibly be attributed to *Amoris Laetitia*. His letter to the Argentinian bishops was a public confirmation on his part that the Apostolic Exhortation contained heresy. It had become clear with time that Cardinal Burke was never going to make his promised formal correction of Pope Francis. The people involved in the theological censures agreed with Cardinal Burke that a formal correction of Pope Francis was now necessary, but it again became clear that if something was to be done about this correction, they would have to do it themselves. In addition to these decisive factors, there was the consideration that Pope Francis had not only failed to withdraw the seemingly heterodox passages of *Amoris Laetitia* or explain them in an orthodox sense, but had gone on with further heterodox actions and statements.

The *Correctio filialis* was the work of a team of several laymen and clerics. It differed from the theological censures in that it was not addressing the contents of a document, but the words and deeds of a man. In order to better understand and respond to the situation of a pope promoting heresy, it attempted to identify the theological outlook that had led Pope Francis to espouse the heresies in question. There were many other protests, requests for clarification, and reaffirmations of Catholic teaching in response to *Amoris Laetitia*. The *Correctio filialis*, however, seems to have been the only one that addressed Pope Francis directly and told him that he was promoting heresy and that he had to stop doing this and recant. As such, it was an essential preliminary for the Open Letter.

Pope Francis indicated that he was aware of the existence of the *Correctio filialis* by referring to accusations of heresy against himself.[6] His support of heresy became if anything more flagrant after

---

6   During his apostolic voyage to Colombia in September 2017, Pope Francis visited the city of Cartagena de Indias, where he met privately with sixty-five religious of the Society of Jesus for an informal conversation. A transcript of much of this conversation was published in *La Civiltà Cattolica* on September 28. At one point the pope is reported as saying: "I hear many comments—they are respectable for they come from children of God, but wrong—concerning the post-synod apostolic

the *Correctio* was issued, and it entered into a new dimension: the advocacy of religious indifferentism. Here again it is the bishops of the Church who should have corrected him; here, again, no proper correction was made. As a result, some of the people involved in the *Correctio filialis* again decided that something had to be done, and that it was up to them to do it, because no one else would. The content of the Open Letter was tougher than that of the preceding documents, and as a result fewer people were willing to sign it. The process of getting it drafted and made public was a difficult struggle. The difficulties resembled those that had arisen with the earlier documents, but with an increase in intensity. All honour is due to those who were willing to take the risks and face the consequences of signing. The charges of heresy made against Pope Francis in the Open Letter were largely taken from the *Correctio filialis*, with some new material. The new feature of the Open Letter was its raising the issue of the loss of papal office as a result of heresy. This issue is thoroughly debated in the letter and the discussions given below, and it will not be further addressed in this introduction. Its practical importance may however be mentioned. Francis is a catastrophic pope, who is devastating the Church. The only way to stop him is to get rid of him; and the only way to get rid of him is on account of his being a heretic. The case made in the Open Letter is thus of the first importance for any Catholic bishop, because it establishes that Pope Francis can and must be removed from office. As the Dogmatic Constitution *Lumen Gentium* asserts, "each of [the individual bishops], as a member of the episcopal college and legitimate successor of the apostles, is obliged by Christ's institution

---

exhortation. To understand *Amoris Laetitia* you need to read it from the start to the end. Beginning with the first chapter, and to continue to the second and then on... and reflect. And read what was said in the Synod. A second thing: some maintain that there is no Catholic morality underlying *Amoris Laetitia*, or at least, no sure morality. I want to repeat clearly that the morality of *Amoris Laetitia* is Thomist, the morality of the great Thomas. You can speak of it with a great theologian, one of the best today and one of the most mature, Cardinal Schönborn. I want to say this so that you can help those who believe that morality is purely casuistic. Help them understand that the great Thomas possesses the greatest richness, which is still able to inspire us today. But on your knees, always on your knees..." Cardinal Pietro Parolin also mentioned the *Correctio*: see Pete Baklinski, "Vatican Cardinal wants to 'dialogue' with signers of Filial Correction to Pope," *LifeSiteNews*, September 28, 2017.

and command to be solicitous for the whole Church" (*Lumen Gentium* 23). Taking action to remove Pope Francis is a necessity for any Catholic bishop who intends to carry out his responsibility of protecting the Church and saving souls.

The fourth document in part II, "An Appeal to the Cardinals of the Catholic Church," concerns the attempt of Pope Francis to alter Catholic teaching on the legitimacy of capital punishment. Although the pope's manifestly erroneous beliefs on this subject did not play a particularly large role in the other documents, these beliefs, as well as his actions to enforce them on the entire Church, are undoubtedly harmful, confusing, and scandalous. It was therefore thought suitable to include a document that, although originating outside of the groups of scholars discussed in this introduction, reflects and complements their concerns, and furnishes another witness to the growing awareness of the pope's heterodoxy.

It is not really possible to go farther in the way of protest than calling for Pope Francis to be removed from office because of heresy. Pope Francis's involvement with the idolatrous worship of the demon Pachamama was nonetheless so scandalous that a new public statement was thought to be required. The preparation of this statement involved less difficulty than that of any of the previous documents, and it received wider and more immediate support. Its content provides further support for the case against Pope Francis made in the Open Letter, and for the measures against him that the Open Letter proposes.

The various discussions included in this book range from scholarly reflections to polemical accusations. This partly reflects the sort of reactions that the documents produced, but the range of these discussions is also intended to do justice to the reality that they are addressing. The pontificate of Pope Francis is a many-sided event. Its different aspects call for reactions of different kinds, which include both scholarly discussion and more popular communications. The polemical and condemnatory nature of some of the contributions may lead to charges of a lack of objectivity. In some cases this may perhaps be admitted as being true, but not as necessarily being grounds for criticism. Objectivity is not always required to make a statement valuable. It is not however the case that any of the documents themselves, or all or even most of the discussions, lack objectivity. Of course, anger and condemnation can be found in them, but that does not mean that they are not objective. To be objective, one must not let one's interests, emotions, or preconceptions bias or distort one's account of the facts or the inferences one draws from the facts. This does not exclude anger or condemnation, when these are subsequent to an objective determination. On the contrary, to refrain from anger or condemnation when the facts are shown to warrant these reactions itself shows a lack of objectivity. In such a case, cowardice, passivity, human respect, and indifference, rather than anger and indignation, are the dangers that threaten an objective response.

What are we to make of the man who is the subject of this book? The evidence about him presented here gives a clear picture from one angle, the angle of his goals and strategy as Supreme Pontiff. He has been criticised for ruling in an arbitrary and tyrannical fashion as pope.[7] Whatever the justice of these criticisms, it would be wrong to portray him as a petty dictator concerned above all with his own power and self-aggrandizement. He is not simply an ecclesiastical Juan Perón. He has an objective for his papacy that goes beyond himself, and his methods of rule are selected with this objective in mind. This objective is to establish, as the norm for belief for Catholics, the religious conception containing the propositions that are the subject of the theological censures, and to reshape the Church into a form that will correspond to this conception. A complete portrait of the man would have to give an account of how he came to adopt this objective, tracing his religious goals and dispositions to their origins in his past experiences and choices. Painting an accurate portrait of this kind is intrinsically difficult to achieve, since its subject is the inner spiritual life. We do not attempt to anticipate the divine judgment by offering a full portrait of the spiritual state of Pope Francis.

It is nonetheless possible to offer some moral evaluation of a person's character on the basis of his actions. If this were not the case, there would be no connection between human actions and moral character, and the notions of virtue and vice would lack any content. The morally salient features of the actions of Pope Francis are his sustained attacks on basic truths of the divine and natural law, and his protection and promotion of the vilest criminals. His protection of the pedophile Fr Julio Grassi, mentioned in the Open Letter, is particularly worthy of examination for those wishing to

---

7   See, e.g., *The Dictator Pope*, Marcantonio Colonna [Henry Sire], 2nd rev. ed. (Washington, DC: Regnery, 2018).

understand his character. He not only attempted to shield Fr Grassi from the consequences of his crimes after the existence of these crimes had been firmly established, but also carried on a campaign of slander against Fr Grassi's victims, who had already suffered terribly at the hands of the clergy. The actions of Pope Francis are planned and deliberate. There are no indications that he suffers from mental disorders or intellectual handicaps that could dispense him of responsibility for these actions, if indeed it is possible for mental illness or invincible ignorance to fully dispense anyone of responsibility for the knowing and deliberate actions of the kind that he has taken. There may be factors that partially excuse him for what he has done—or aggravating factors; there generally are both in any human life. In his case, the fact of being pope, and thus of having both the strictest standards of required conduct of any human being in the world and the graces of state needed to attain these standards, is an aggravating factor that should not be overlooked. We must therefore conclude that his actions are those of a deeply corrupt, indeed of an evil, man.

The nature and extent of this corruption are displayed by the character of his religious programme. The Scriptures draw a close connection between adultery, fornication, and idolatry. In Ezekiel 3:36–41, God condemns Jerusalem for idolatry in the following terms:

> Thus saith the Lord God: Because thy money hath been poured out, and thy shame discovered through thy fornications with thy lovers, and with the idols of thy abominations, by the blood of thy children whom thou gavest them: Behold, I will gather together all thy lovers with whom thou hast taken pleasure, and all whom thou hast loved, with all whom thou hast hated: and I will gather them together against thee on every side, and will discover thy shame in their sight, and they shall see all thy nakedness. And I will judge thee as adulteresses and they that shed blood are judged: and I will give thee blood in fury and jealousy. And I will deliver thee into their hands, and they shall destroy thy brothel house, and throw down thy stews: and they shall strip thee of thy garments, and shall take away the vessels of thy beauty: and leave thee naked, and full of disgrace. And they shall bring upon thee a multitude, and they shall

stone thee with stones, and shall slay thee with their swords. And they shall burn thy houses with fire, and shall execute judgments upon thee in the sight of many women: and thou shalt cease from fornication, and shalt give no hire any more.[8]

This portrays idolatry as a form of adultery and sexual immorality. Conversely, sexual immorality is associated in the Scriptures with lack of knowledge of God and seen as characteristic of idolaters (cf. 1 Thessalonians 4:3–5). St. Paul asserts that sexual immorality among idolaters is a consequence of their idolatry (Romans 1:18–32). According to the Scriptures, idolatry, adultery, and other forms of sexual immorality are all connected parts of a particular human condition. This condition involves rejection of God, complete human degradation, and eventual condemnation by divine justice to eternal punishment. It is the condition that Our Lord Jesus Christ died to save us from.

Promotion of this complex whole of idolatry and sexual immorality is the goal of the religious programme of Pope Francis. The most obvious goal of *Amoris Laetitia* was to legitimize adultery. That document also rejected the commandments of God and the moral law by denying the existence of absolute moral norms, and denied the existence of divine punishment for violation of these norms by asserting that eternal damnation does not exist. From the legitimation of adultery against an earthly spouse, Pope Francis proceeded to the legitimation of false religions in his Joint Declaration with Ahmad Al-Tayyeb, the Grand Imam of Al-Azhar Mosque. This was followed by actual involvement in idolatrous ceremonies venerating the Pachamama idols in the Vatican Gardens. Pope Francis has dedicated his pontificate to bringing it about that Christ died in vain.

What was the importance and impact of the documents collected in this work? Certainly none of them achieved its immediate object. The cardinals and patriarchs did not petition the pope to condemn the censured propositions, Pope Francis did not withdraw any of his words or actions or repent of his misdeeds, and the bishops of the Church have taken no action to deal with the heresies of the pope. The failure to achieve these objects did not come as a great surprise to the drafters of the documents. The era that has produced Pope Francis has also produced an episcopate that lacks

---

8 Cf. Ezek 23:37, Jer 13:27, Rev 21:8.

the fidelity and courage needed to take the actions requested by the documents, and this was known to the scholars who produced them. These ventures were all undertaken in the belief that they would achieve important results, even if no one acted on them.

One important result achieved was to put on record the fact that Pope Francis's heresy and idolatry did not pass unchallenged by Catholics. If they had passed unchallenged, future generations of Catholics might reasonably conclude that they were legitimate. How could they be considered at odds with the faith, if no one in the entire Church had raised any objection to them during Francis's pontificate? By putting these objections on record, the documents forestall this possibility. This result was one of the goals of the drafters of the documents. Pursuit of this goal had an impact on the formulation of the documents, since it ruled out the more tactful and indirect approaches adopted by other protests against Pope Francis's heresies. It required that the falsehoods in Pope Francis's words, the sin and sacrilege in his actions, and his own personal responsibility, be stated clearly and without compromise. Since the tactful and indirect approaches have had no more success than the blunt ones collected in this volume, the direct approach of these documents does not seem to have been a disadvantage.

Another good result of the documents was simply to place their theological content in the public domain. Ultimately, the value of the documents will depend on whether or not their content is true. If it is, the publication of the documents will prove to have been an important contribution.

Finally, we may observe that the Open Letter requested both that Pope Francis be condemned as a heretic and that he be removed from office if he does not recant. No steps have been taken towards the goal of removing him from office, and it is unlikely that such steps will be taken before his death. But a failure to remove him from office does not exclude his condemnation for heresy. No pope has been condemned as a heretic by the Church during his lifetime; Pope Honorius was condemned for heresy only after his death. If the documents collected in this book make a contribution to the pope's repentance or to the concerted action of the hierarchy, or (if so it must be) to a future *damnatio memoriae* of Pope Francis and a solemn anathematizing of his errors, they will have abundantly proven their worth.

ADDITIONAL NOTE 1

Reflections on a New Dialogue Between Traditionalist and Conservative Catholics

CLAUDIO PIERANTONI

THE MAIN PURPOSE OF THIS NOTE IS TO OFFER a brief reflection on the fact that the two editors of this book, Dr John Lamont and myself, do not come from exactly the same theological and ecclesiastical background. This is certainly no coincidence and it is a significant example of an important phenomenon that has been appearing in the present controversy.

Dr Lamont, together with other principal actors among the original drafters of these documents, comes from what may be termed "Catholic Traditionalism," whereas other theologians and philosophers who in different ways have contributed to the discussions and revisions that gave the same documents their final shape, among whom I count myself, come from what could be referred to as "mainstream conservative Catholicism." We mostly grew up under, and were shaped through the guidelines given by, John Paul II and Cardinal Ratzinger, later Benedict XVI.

In a rough simplification, we can say that the first kind of theologian, although able to appreciate important qualities and merits of the last two pontiffs, possesses a strong sense of being a minority in opposition to and resistance within a Church afflicted by the profound theological, liturgical, and pastoral crisis that exploded in the Sixties, the origins of which can be traced back to Liberalism and above all Modernism in the second half of the nineteenth century. The second kind, on the other hand, although sharing essentially the same faith and the same love for orthodoxy, has tended to have the opposite perception: although he has been ready to admit that the Church was confronting a profound crisis, and also to recognize that the last pontiffs made some serious mistakes, he has generally perceived himself as part of a majority that shares the same faith and the same doctrine, in a Church that has gone more or less in the right direction under the wise guidance of John Paul and Benedict. He knew that there were heretics in theological faculties and religious congregations, as well as among the episcopate, but he tended to perceive them as a minority (albeit an expanding one), and he just thought that they should receive a bit more attention and correction from the hierarchy and the popes.

To give a concrete example of the second kind, I will rapidly sketch my own experience as a conservative Catholic and professor in a theological faculty. My case has indeed some peculiarities, for I did not start my career studying theology, but classical philology in Rome State University; only in the latter part of my college career did I discover Latin and Greek *Christian* literature, and for some years followed the Master courses in Patristics at the Institute *Augustinianum* also in Rome (my native city). Back at the State university, I worked on a doctoral thesis about an ancient Christological heresy (Apollinarism). At the same time, I became friends with a Chilean priest and patrologist, who afterwards invited me to teach the History of the Ancient Church at the Faculty of Theology of Santiago: there I worked for a decade.

Having dedicated myself mostly to the study of the Fathers and the ancient Church, I had the advantage of not having been so much influenced by contemporary theologians, but neither did I have a clear idea of the exact nature and extent of the "new" heresies. During those years, however, I grew increasingly aware of the extent to which heresy had been propagated at all levels among professors and students, both religious and lay people, and especially among prominent religious Orders. Trying to fight heresy in that context is very insidious and apparently hopeless: it was like fighting the mythical hydra with seven heads. As soon as you cut off one head, another comes out where you do not expect it. I found myself increasingly in conflict with some colleagues, and gradually also with students. Conservative colleagues, in those discussions, tended to be silent, in order to avoid conflict. Finally, a letter of protest was sent by a group of "liberal" students (mainly young Jesuits), denouncing to the dean that I not only dared to teach that in the ancient Church a strange thing existed, called "heresy," which the Fathers and the Councils had correctly identified and condemned, but also that one could find, under different forms, the very same errors in contemporary times too. Of course, I already knew that speaking of "heresy" was not politically correct, but I was not a little surprised when I realized that, for a substantial part of my students, that way of speaking was itself the worst heresy! The culprit of such a grave ideological sin was not to be tolerated, and they refused to have me as a professor the following semester. My full contract was *ipso facto* reduced to half, with no possibility of defence, and the following year I was asked to resign from the faculty. I thought the faculty was doubtless in a great theological crisis, and besides, I had not been particularly prudent and astute. Still, my optimism as a mainstream conservative Catholic was not seriously shaken; I went on opposing heresies from outside the faculty in the way I could; as a consolation in those years, one could still hear a word of authentic faith and genuine Christian teaching from the reigning pope.

From then on (2011), I dedicated myself to teaching Medieval Philosophy, Latin Literature, and Dante. I thought I had left theological quarrels behind, when the Synods on the Family, and then *Amoris Laetitia*, suddenly appeared. I had not dedicated so much attention to Bergoglio up to that moment, and therefore I had no clear idea about him. I was only sad that Benedict had "renounced" the papacy. But when *Amoris Laetitia* was published, I providentially came across an article by Prof. Roberto de Mattei in his online review, *Corrispondenza Romana*: "First Impressions on a Disastrous Document." (A layman, Prof. de Mattei is a Church historian and theologian, certainly the most prominent intellectual figure in Catholic traditionalism in Italy; but I did not know him at that time.) I found the article was a bit strong in its title but extremely lucid in its analysis and it obliged me to read the infamous Chapter VIII of *Amoris Laetitia*. Then I knew that the adjective "disastrous" was in no way exaggerated: the situation was even worse than I had been prepared to expect. I was truly shocked. Never in my life had I suspected I would think so badly of a document issued from the Holy See of Peter.

Then, through other providential circumstances, during a family visit to Rome I was able to meet Prof. de Mattei and discuss the situation with him. He soon put me in contact with John Lamont and the little group of British theologians who were then preparing the *Theological Censures*. I came to meet more people interested in this discussion at the congress organized near Florence by Prof. de Mattei in September 2016, where Lamont and other important participants in this "resistance" could exchange their points of view and discuss the situation. In turn, I introduced to the group Austrian philosopher Josef Seifert, also a conservative and a good friend of John Paul II, a permanent member of the Pontifical Academy of Life and founder of the "International Academy of Philosophy" of Liechtenstein under that Pope's auspices (I had become friends with him in Santiago at the Chilean branch of the same Academy), and Venezuelan lawyer and philosopher Carlos Casanova (an exile from the régime for his anti-Chávez activities), who also worked in Santiago at the IAP. After this, many others joined the discussion, like American theologian Fr Brian Harrison, Italian priest and theologian Giovanni Scalese (Ordinary of the Catholic Mission in Afghanistan), British scholar of ancient philosophy and patrology John Rist (who was later even forbidden physical entrance to the *Augustinianum* Institute for signing the *Open letter*) and the young Italian scholar Luca Gili, who teaches in Canada, among others. So, we started long email discussions in various groups, which continued during the drafting and subsequent discussion of the documents that were addressed to the Pope. It is impossible to mention all the people that in some way or other contributed to this enterprise.

Back to the main point: by now, I was definitely waking up from the "relative optimism" of the mainstream conservative Catholic, and grew aware that many other people — not just scholars and intellectuals, but thousands of "mid-culture" orthodox Catholics — were similarly waking up: what we had thought to be a heretical or liberal *minority* (although an increasingly vocal one) had suddenly taken hold of the power in the Church. The terrible prophecy contained in Pope Leo XIII's exorcism seemed to come true:

> The most astute enemies filled the Church, the Immaculate Bride of the Lamb, with their bitterness, intoxicated her with absinthe; they got their impious hands on every beauty of hers. Where the See of the most blessed Peter and the Chair of Truth has been constituted to be light for the people, there they put the throne of their abomination and impiety; so that, having struck the Shepherd, they could disperse the flock.[9]

---

9   *Ecclesiam, Agni immaculati sponsam, faverrimi hostes repleverunt amaritudinibus, inebriarunt absinthio; ad omnia desiderabilia eius impias miserunt manus. Ubi sedes beatissimi Petri et Cathedra veritatis ad lucem gentium constituta est, ibi thronum posuerunt abominationis et impietatis suae; ut percusso Pastore, et gregem disperdere valeant.* (Text from *Acta*

Most conservatives kept silent as the new régime went on revealing itself, and those who dared to speak up, got fired, like the same Prof. Seifert and Prof. Rist. This explains why there are relatively few conservatives among the signatories of our statements, and why many that appeared in the first documents cease to appear in the following ones. This gives the false impression that "orthodox" or "true" conservatives are not so many, whereas it only means that there are not many who are willing to speak up. (Here in Chile alone, I could mention at least a hundred conservative scholars that would have signed most of our documents, if it had not been clear that they would get fired. Only three scholars from Chile, including me, signed the first document, the *Theological Censures*; but from the *Correctio* onwards, only one did.)

At the same time, it is easy to understand that conservatives who could not tolerate keeping silent started to join traditionalists, who were the only other people willing to speak (traditionalists having often made their careers outside the Catholic "establishment" or, in some cases, having already been fired in previous situations of theological conflict). On the other hand, it quickly became clear that many had been faithful only in appearance to the lines of John Paul II and Benedict XVI in order to advance in their careers, but their real convictions were different. In many cases, people—even scholars—founded their convictions on the teaching of recent popes, but possessed no solid foundation for these beliefs in Scripture and Tradition, and so, based on a distorted idea of papal authority (well described by Dr Lamont in the Introduction), honestly believed they had to change their mind if the pope did so. In short, the orthodox were now, at least apparently, a minority in the Church, and an openly persecuted one.

Now, it must be stressed that this encounter between traditionalists and "true conservatives" that came about for the motives described, is an historical and providential fact within the Church, which in my opinion is highly positive and can bear excellent fruits. It somehow broke the ice between two categories of Catholic intellectuals that, at a certain point, started to work almost independently of one another. We probably always knew that our respective positions were not so far away, but as it sometimes

---

Sanctae Sedis, ed. Victorii Piazzesi, vol. XXIII [Rome: Ex Typographia Polyglotta, 1890–91], p. 744.)

happens between groups that are close enough ideologically, some specific differences tend to harden up, on questions that, though important, are not strictly essential, and they perpetuate through lack of dialogue. For example, the differences on the interpretation of Vatican II came to be considered unsurpassable and have also deeply influenced the present controversy. From the point of view of many traditionalists, the Bergoglio catastrophe tends to be interpreted as a logical and necessary consequence of Vatican II. On the other hand, for most conservatives there is a possibility of interpreting the Council without contradicting the basic doctrine of the Church, through a "hermeneutics of continuity"; as a result, the conservative sees the Bergoglio phenomenon as the temporary triumph of the wrong *interpretation* of Vatican II, the "Spirit of the Council" that certainly was already present in the *minds* of the "liberal" or "modernist" conciliar Fathers, but did not succeed in being accepted and formulated as such in the *documents*. This is because traditionalists tend to think that the texts of Vatican II contain, together with ambiguous formulations, also *positive errors* that are irreconcilable with sound doctrine, whereas conservatives think that they only contain *ambiguous formulations* that can be interpreted in accordance with Tradition, as well as against it. Now, the Bergoglio crisis has stimulated new conversations and reciprocal knowledge between traditionalists and conservatives: together with the discussions that gave birth to the documents here presented, I wish to mention the more recent debate about the Council, started in the summer of 2020 by Archbishop Viganò and Bishop Schneider, in which many eminent theologians participated, both traditionalist and conservative, such as Archbishop Pozzo, Fr Weinandy, Fr de Souza, Fr Lanzetta, Fr Cavalcoli, Dr Cavadini, Dr Kwasniewski, Prof. Morselli, and Prof. Radaelli, authors Eric Sammons and Anthony Esolen, and eminent vaticanists like Sandro Magister and Aldo Maria Valli. I wish to express here my gratitude to all participants in this discussion, which has already been fruitful, and, if continued, may really open a new season of clarification of Church doctrine.

In this short note I cannot delve more deeply into this question: I merely wish to suggest here that it is possible to think of a way to get out of this half-century-long opposition. Certainly, Bergoglio proves, if contrasted to Wojtyła and Ratzinger, that there can be very different interpretations of the Council: this seems to support the thesis of ambiguity. One person who accepts the Council can be fundamentally orthodox, while another who accepts it can be a heretic. The startling actions and words of this pontificate make most criticisms leveled against former pontiffs look almost trivial, and this, it seems to me, can help to correct an excessive pessimism about the whole postconciliar era.

At the same time, Bergoglio proves that a mere hermeneutic of continuity is not sufficient to correct the problems posed both by the conciliar texts and by the other theological errors that have been emerging, unless the correction is carried out through new *solemn* Church documents that bear at least the same dogmatic weight as the conciliar texts. It has become evident that the problem cannot be solved by an eternal discussion about texts that are, at very least, ambiguous: what we need, then, is a new ecumenical council. But, to achieve such a correction, a new ecumenical council should go back to the traditional method of solemnly *excluding* a given proposition as erroneous. It is certainly not possible, as some prelates have proposed, to condemn any propositions of the dogmatic constitutions of the Council, let alone to annul the Council itself, as some have also suggested, for they constitute solemn teaching of a valid ecumenical council confirmed by the Pope. What can be done is to solemnly condemn a list of errors that can be, and have been, propagated on the basis of ambiguous texts or "half-truths," as they have been called. I am glad to quote here a passage by a priest and theologian who wishes to remain anonymous, but has actively participated in the redaction of our documents as well as in the aforementioned debate about Vatican II:

> What is the way forward? I do not think it is to write scholarly commentaries showing how all the documents promulgated by the Second Vatican Council, and everything in the new liturgy promulgated afterward, can be read in an orthodox fashion. That has been done, and it has not succeeded in exorcising the evil. Something else must be tried. The way up and the way down are one and the same, said an ancient sage. It does not seem likely that the evil spirit will be expunged until the bishops shall *have assembled again in council and anathematized by name each of the errors circulating in the Church.* [...] It would seem also wise to join to these

definitions a further anathema against those who would use any of the documents of the last council to support the errors that this new one would condemn. After the poison had thus been drawn, theologians could consider at their leisure whether there were statements within those earlier documents that could not in any way be reconciled with orthodoxy. On this point, I believe I am more sanguine than Archbishop Viganò and Bishop Schneider.[10]

Then, reflecting on what can be done in the meantime, the same theologian suggests possible lines of resistance both by diocesan bishops and by the laity. I quote from his reflection on the laity, which can be equally applied to the clergy:

> What of the laity? They can assist the Church greatly by pursuing holiness according to the duties of their state in life. But in past years, it sometimes happened that laymen took the initiative in resisting some heresy. In the 5th century, when the patriarch of Constantinople preached against calling Mary the mother of God, a layman called Eusebius interrupted him and protested, and thus began the movement that led to the great Council of Ephesus. Of course, one has to be sure of one's ground, *but the grace of Confirmation gives everyone the right and duty to witness to the Faith whenever silence would mean consent to error. If a bishop, even a bishop in some great patriarchal see, has taught heresy, the faithful need not take it lying down.*[11]

Now this witness and collaboration of the laity, and also of many clergy, in the present defence of the faith has been a characteristic of the movement that gave birth to the present resistance and the documents it produced.

For the purpose of excluding errors, I think in the end the present experience will prove of invaluable benefit, for Bergoglio has given formal or informal expression to many deviations that had been previously present in the Church only by way of ambiguity

---

10   https://www.lifesitenews.com/opinion/time-to-stop-making-excuses-for-vatican-ii-and-the-new-mass; emphasis added.
11   Ibid., emphasis added.

in Church documents, or of "infiltration" in pastoral actions and declarations of bishops or popes. (Two examples: it is one thing for Bergoglio as a bishop to give Holy Communion to unmarried couples in Buenos Aires; it is quite a different thing for him as pope to publish *Amoris Laetitia*; it is one thing for Pope John Paul II to kiss the Koran — as shocking and scandalous as it is — and quite another for a pope to sign a formal declaration where *all* religions are declared, without any qualification, to be "willed by God.") So, Bergoglio's formulations are likely to provide an almost complete repertory of errors that could and should be formally condemned in a future council.

But this will be possible only if a new and more compact front of orthodoxy is formed and organized to work together. To this end it is indispensable that the dialogue that has now started among all orthodox thinkers to react to the present crisis should continue and develop more and more. Of course, it will not be possible to solve all problems or to reach a complete uniformity among the orthodox, and it would not even be desirable. The important thing is to clarify the essential points of orthodoxy that need urgent correction, through a negative formulation, i.e., the formal exclusion of the corresponding error: in short, the traditional condemnation of *heresies*. That is the very thing that Vatican II and postconciliar popes all too optimistically *avoided* doing, and probably the principal reason for the problems we are confronting nowadays.

Together with this collection of documents I offer my humble prayers that Bergoglio and the bishops and theologians who are supporting him may finally retract their errors before it is too late for them; and that all orthodox forces may go on communicating, uniting, and organizing themselves in the difficult struggle that we will confront in the immediate future. May this book be a testimony and an example of the joint effort that has been carried on in the last four years, and an encouragement for the years to come.

ADDITIONAL NOTE 2

The Documents Collected Here Do Not Attempt a Moral Judgement on the Person of the Pope

CLAUDIO PIERANTONI

IT IS IMPORTANT TO BEAR IN MIND THAT THE documents and articles included in this collection do not attempt a general moral judgement about Pope Francis. Not certainly in the *Theological Censures*, nor in the *Correctio filialis*, where only material heresy is contemplated. Not even in the *Open Letter*, where the pope is directly accused of heresy, nor in *Contra recentia sacrilegia*, "Protest against Pope Francis's Sacrilegious Acts," which denounced Pope Francis's involvement in idolatrous acts during the Amazonian synod. (In the *Open Letter*, the relationships of the Pope with controversial prelates accused of sexual abuse or other crimes, such as Cardinal Rodríguez Maradiaga or Cardinal McCarrick, are not mentioned to prove or suggest the pope's complicity in their actions, but only as indications about his theological ideas.) All these documents of course are aimed at denouncing objective faults against the Faith, but do not have the pretension of assessing the subjective gravity of these faults, that is, the internal forum of the pope's conscience, which only God can penetrate. In other words, all these questionings, complaints, and denunciations have in no way the pretension of bearing the prophetic charisma of scrutinizing the conscience of another person.

They also do not have the pretension of making what could be called an "historical judgement" of someone's moral character, which can be made only in the presence of two essential conditions, which are not present in our case: (1) a thorough analysis and discussion of all the biographical evidence at our disposal, with an exhaustive debate of all the circumstances available to the historian, and (2) the fact that the person's life has already come to an end, and no more events can happen that could modify the picture that is being drawn. It goes without saying that a historical moral judgement is also limited to objective indications, and cannot enter the realm of internal conscience, for it can attain only a very limited portion of the facts and circumstances, and above all, of secret intentions accessible to God alone: "Judge nothing before the appointed time; wait until the Lord comes. He will bring to light what is hidden in darkness and will expose the motives of the heart" (1 Cor 4:5).

Finally, to judge, or rather to propose that the pope be judged, in a juridical sense, is also not attempted here, except for the delict of heresy. As it has been argued in the *Open Letter*, given that the pope is the highest authority on earth, the only cause for which he can be judged, according to tradition, is heresy alone, as the Appendix to the *Open Letter* explains ("Canon law and Catholic theology concerning the situation of a heretical pope").[12] I quote here the relevant passage from the Appendix:

> Distinction XL, canon 6 of the *Decretum* states that the pope can be judged by no one, unless he is found to have deviated from the faith: "Cunctos ipse iudicaturus a nemine est iudicandus, nisi deprehendatur a fide devius."[13]
>
> The wording of this statement seems to have been influenced by Cardinal Humbert's *De sancta Romana ecclesia* (1053), which stated that the pope is immune from judgment by anyone except in questions of faith: "a nemine est iudicandus nisi forte deprehendatur a fide devius." The claim made in the canon is a development of Pope Gregory the Great's statement that evil prelates

---

12 See below, pp. 155–56. Of course, this would not hold true for those who deny that Bergoglio is truly the pope, either for the invalidity of his election or for the invalidity of Pope Benedict's renunciation. But this problem is also not discussed in these documents and articles, although of course it has been the subject of private conversations among the different authors. The reference to Jorge Mario Bergoglio as "Pope Francis," however, must not be taken as a proof that a certain author necessarily thinks he is the true pope, although this holds true for the majority of them.

13 "He, the one who is to judge all, is to be judged by none, unless he be found straying from the faith."

Additional Note 2

must be tolerated by their subjects if this can be done while saving the faith.[14]

The canonical assertion that the pope can be judged for heresy came into being as an explication of the canonical principle that the pope is judged by no one. The statement in this canon is an enunciation of a privilege; its object is to assert that the pope has the widest possible exemption from judgement by others.

This canon was included, along with the rest of the *Decretum* of Gratian, in the *Corpus iuris canonici*, which formed the basis of canon law in the Latin Church until 1917. Its authority is supported by papal authority itself, since the canon law of the Church is upheld by papal authority. It was taught by Pope Innocent III, who asserted in his sermon on the consecration of the Supreme Pontiff that "God was his sole judge for other sins, and that he could be judged by the Church only for sins committed against the faith."[15] Rejection of the canon in the *Decretum* would undermine the canonical foundation for papal primacy itself, since this canon forms part of the legal basis for the principle that the pope is judged by no one.

The canon was universally accepted by the Church after the compilation and publication of the *Decretum*. The heresy referred to in this canon is understood by virtually all authors to mean externally manifested heresy (the thesis that a pope loses his office for purely internal heresy was advanced by Juan de Torquemada, O. P., but it has been conclusively refuted and has been rejected by all canonists and theologians ever since). Neither the 1917 *Code of Canon Law* nor the 1983 *Code of Canon Law* abrogates the principle that a heretical pope loses the papal office. This is agreed by all commentators on these codes, who state that this principle is correct.[16]

---

14   *Moralia in Iob* XXV, c. 16: "Subditi praelatos etiam malos tolerant, si salva fide possint..."
15   "In tantum enim fides mihi necessaria est, ut cum de caeteris peccatis solum Deum iudicium habeam, propter solum peccatum quod in fide committitur possem ab Ecclesia judicari."
16   See, e.g., *Jus Canonicum ad Codicis Normam Exactum*, Franciscus

The objections that have been raised against this position have been convincingly answered by John Lamont, "The SSPX, the Open Letter, and the Heresies of Pope Francis," found below in Part III, chapter 29.

Wernz and Petrus Vidal (Gregorianum, 1924–1949), II (1928), n. 453; *Introductio in Codicem*, 3rd ed., Udalricus Beste (Collegeville: St. John's Abbey Press, 1946), can. 221; *New Commentary on the Code of Canon Law*, John P. Beal, James A. Coriden, and Thomas J. Green, eds. (New York: Paulist, 2000), p. 1618.

PART I

The Dubia *of the Four Cardinals*

The Dubia *of the Four Cardinals*[1]

I. A NECESSARY FOREWORD

The sending of the letter to His Holiness Pope Francis by four cardinals has its origin in a deep pastoral concern. We have noted a grave disorientation and great confusion of many faithful regarding extremely important matters for the life of the Church. We have noted that even within the episcopal college there are contrasting interpretations of Chapter 8 of *Amoris Laetitia*.

The great Tradition of the Church teaches us that the way out of situations like this is recourse to the Holy Father, asking the Apostolic See to resolve those doubts which are the cause of disorientation and confusion.

Ours is therefore an act of justice and charity. Of justice: with our initiative we profess that the Petrine ministry is the ministry of unity, and that to Peter, to the Pope, belongs the service of confirming in the faith. Of charity: we want to help the Pope to prevent divisions and conflicts in the Church, asking him to dispel all ambiguity.

We have also carried out a specific duty. According to the *Code of Canon Law* (can. 349) the cardinals, even taken individually, are entrusted with the task of helping the Pope to care for the universal Church.

The Holy Father has decided not to respond. We have interpreted his sovereign decision as an invitation to continue the reflection, and the discussion, calmly and with respect. And so we are informing the entire people of God about our initiative, offering all of the documentation.

We hope that no one will choose to interpret the matter according to a "progressive/conservative" paradigm. That would be completely off the mark. We are deeply concerned about the true good of souls, the supreme law of the Church, and not about promoting any form of politics in the Church. We hope that no one will judge us, unjustly, as adversaries of the Holy Father and people devoid

---

[1] Translated by Matthew Sherry. Published under the title "Full text of 4 cardinals' letter to Pope Francis with explanatory notes and 5 questions," *LifeSiteNews*, November 14, 2016.

of mercy. What we have done and are doing has its origin in the deep collegial affection that unites us to the Pope, and from an impassioned concern for the good of the faithful.

Card. Walter Brandmüller
Card. Raymond L. Burke
Card. Carlo Caffarra
Card. Joachim Meisner

2. THE LETTER OF THE FOUR CARDINALS TO THE POPE

Rome, September 19, 2016

To His Holiness Pope Francis
and for the attention of
His Eminence Cardinal Gerhard L. Müller

Most Holy Father,

Following the publication of your Apostolic Exhortation *Amoris Laetitia*, theologians and scholars have proposed interpretations that are not only divergent, but also conflicting, above all in regard to Chapter VIII. Moreover, the media have emphasized this dispute, thereby provoking uncertainty, confusion, and disorientation among many of the faithful.

Because of this, we the undersigned, but also many Bishops and Priests, have received numerous requests from the faithful of various social strata on the correct interpretation to give to Chapter VIII of the Exhortation.

Now, compelled in conscience by our pastoral responsibility and desiring to implement ever more that synodality to which Your Holiness urges us, we, with profound respect, permit ourselves to ask you, Holy Father, as Supreme Teacher of the Faith, called by the Risen One to confirm his brothers in the faith, to resolve the uncertainties and bring clarity, benevolently giving a response to the *Dubia* that we attach to the present letter.

May Your Holiness wish to bless us, as we promise constantly to remember you in prayer.

Card. Walter Brandmüller
Card. Raymond L. Burke
Card. Carlo Caffarra
Card. Joachim Meisner

3. THE DUBIA

1. It is asked whether, following the affirmations of *Amoris Laetitia* (nn. 300–305), it has now become possible to grant absolution in the Sacrament of Penance and thus to admit to Holy Communion a person who, while bound by a valid marital bond, lives together with a different person *more uxorio* (in a marital way) without fulfilling the conditions provided for by *Familiaris Consortio* n. 84 and subsequently reaffirmed by *Reconciliatio et Paenitentia* n. 34 and *Sacramentum Caritatis* n. 29. Can the expression "in certain cases" found in note 351 (n. 305) of the exhortation *Amoris Laetitia* be applied to divorced persons who are in a new union and who continue to live *more uxorio*?

2. After the publication of the Post-synodal Apostolic Exhortation *Amoris Laetitia* (cf. n. 304), does one still need to regard as valid the teaching of St. John Paul II's Encyclical *Veritatis Splendor* n. 79, based on Sacred Scripture and on the Tradition of the Church, on the existence of absolute moral norms that prohibit intrinsically evil acts and that are binding without exceptions?

3. After *Amoris Laetitia* (n. 301) is it still possible to affirm that a person who habitually lives in contradiction to a commandment of God's law, as for instance the one that prohibits adultery (cf. Mt 19:3–9), finds him- or herself in an objective situation of grave habitual sin (cf. Pontifical Council for Legislative Texts, Declaration, June 24, 2000)?

4. After the affirmations of *Amoris Laetitia* (n. 302) on "circumstances which mitigate moral responsibility," does one still need to regard as valid the teaching of St. John Paul II's Encyclical *Veritatis Splendor* n. 81, based on Sacred Scripture and on the Tradition of the Church, according to which "circumstances or intentions can never transform an act intrinsically evil by virtue of its object into an act 'subjectively' good or defensible as a choice"?

5. After *Amoris Laetitia* (n. 303), does one still need to regard as valid the teaching of St. John Paul II's encyclical *Veritatis Splendor* n. 56, based on Sacred Scripture and on the Tradition of the Church, that excludes a creative interpretation of the role of conscience and that emphasizes that conscience can never be authorized to legitimate exceptions to absolute moral norms that prohibit intrinsically evil acts by virtue of their object?

4. EXPLANATORY NOTE OF THE FOUR CARDINALS

Dubia (from the Latin: "doubts") are formal questions brought before the Pope and to the Congregation for the Doctrine of the Faith asking for clarifications on particular issues concerning doctrine or practice. What is peculiar about these inquiries is that they are worded in a way that requires a "yes" or "no" answer, without theological argumentation. This way of addressing the Apostolic See is not an invention of our own; it is an age-old practice.

Let's get to what is concretely at stake. Upon the publication of the Post-synodal Apostolic Exhortation *Amoris Laetitia* on love in the family, a debate has arisen particularly around its eighth chapter. Here, specifically paragraphs 300–305 have been the object of divergent interpretations.

For many—bishops, priests, faithful—these paragraphs allude to or even explicitly teach a change in the discipline of the Church with respect to the divorced who are living in a new union, while others, admitting the lack of clarity or even the ambiguity of the passages in question, nonetheless argue that these same pages can be read in continuity with the previous magisterium and do not contain a modification in the Church's practice and teaching.

Motivated by a pastoral concern for the faithful, four cardinals have sent a letter to the Holy Father under the form of *Dubia*, hoping to receive clarity, given that doubt and uncertainty are always highly detrimental to pastoral care.

The fact that interpreters come to different conclusions is also due to divergent ways of understanding the Christian moral life. In this sense, what is at stake in *Amoris Laetitia* is not only the question of whether or not the divorced who have entered into a new union can—under certain circumstances—be readmitted to the sacraments. Rather, the interpretation of the document also implies different, contrasting approaches to the Christian way of life. Thus, while the first question of the *Dubia* concerns a practical question regarding the divorced and civilly remarried, the other four questions touch on fundamental issues of the Christian life.

DOUBT NUMBER 1

It is asked whether, following the affirmations of *Amoris Laetitia* (nn. 300–305), it has now become possible to grant absolution in the sacrament of penance and thus to admit to Holy Communion a person who, while bound by a valid marital bond, lives together with a different person *more uxorio* (in a marital way) without fulfilling the conditions provided for by *Familiaris Consortio* n. 84 and subsequently reaffirmed by *Reconciliatio et Paenitentia* n. 34 and *Sacramentum Caritatis* n. 29. Can the expression "in certain cases" found in note 351 (n. 305) of the exhortation *Amoris Laetitia* be applied to divorced persons who are in a new union and who continue to live *more uxorio*?

Question 1 makes particular reference to *Amoris Laetitia* n. 305 and to footnote 351. While note 351 specifically speaks of the sacraments of penance and communion, it does not mention the divorced and civilly remarried in this context, nor does the main text.

Pope John Paul II's Apostolic Exhortation *Familiaris Consortio*, n. 84, already contemplated the possibility of admitting the divorced and civilly remarried to the sacraments. It mentions three conditions:

— The persons concerned cannot separate without committing new injustices (for instance, they may be responsible for the upbringing of their children);

— They take upon themselves the commitment to live according to the truth of their situation, that is, to cease living together as if they were husband and wife ("more uxorio"), abstaining from those acts that are proper to spouses;

— They avoid giving scandal (that is, they avoid giving the appearance of sin so as to avoid the danger of leading others into sin).

The conditions mentioned by *Familiaris Consortio* n. 84 and by the subsequent documents recalled will immediately appear reasonable once we remember that the marital union is not just based on mutual affection and that sexual acts are not just one activity among others that couples engage in. Sexual relations are for marital love. They are something so important, so good and so precious, that they require a particular context, the context of marital love. Hence, not only the divorced living in a new union need to abstain, but also everyone who is not married. For the Church, the sixth commandment "Do not commit adultery" has always covered any exercise of human sexuality that is not marital, i.e., any kind of sexual acts other than those engaged in with one's rightful spouse. It would seem that admitting to communion those of the faithful who are separated or divorced from their rightful spouse and who have entered a new union in which they live with someone else as if they were husband and wife would mean for the Church to teach by her practice one of the following affirmations about marriage, human sexuality, and the nature of the sacraments:

— A divorce does not dissolve the marriage bond, and the partners to the new union are not married. However, people who are not married can under certain circumstances legitimately engage in acts of sexual intimacy.

— A divorce dissolves the marriage bond. People who are not married cannot legitimately engage in sexual acts. The divorced and remarried are legitimate spouses and their sexual acts are lawful marital acts.

— A divorce does not dissolve the marriage bond, and the partners to the new union are not married. People who are not married cannot legitimately engage in sexual acts, so that the divorced and civilly remarried live in a situation of habitual, public, objective and grave sin. However, admitting persons to the Eucharist does not mean for the Church to approve their public state of life; the faithful can approach the Eucharistic table even with consciousness of grave sin, and receiving absolution in the sacrament of penance does not always require the purpose of amending one's life. The sacraments, therefore, are detached from life: Christian rites and worship are in a completely different sphere than the Christian moral life.

DOUBT NUMBER 2

After the publication of the Post-synodal Exhortation *Amoris Laetitia* (cf. n. 304), does one still need to regard as valid the teaching of St. John Paul II's Encyclical *Veritatis Splendor* n. 79, based on Sacred Scripture and on the Tradition of the Church, on the existence of absolute moral norms that prohibit intrinsically evil acts and that are binding without exceptions?

The second question regards the existence of so-called intrinsically evil acts. John Paul II's Encyclical *Veritatis Splendor* n. 79 claims that one can "qualify as morally evil according to its species...the deliberate choice of certain kinds of behavior or specific acts, apart from a consideration of the intention for which the choice is made or the totality of the foreseeable consequences of that act for all persons concerned."

Thus, the encyclical teaches that there are acts that are always evil, which are forbidden by moral norms that bind without exception ("moral absolutes"). These moral absolutes are always negative, that is, they tell us what we should not do: "Do not kill"; "Do not commit adultery." Only negative norms can bind without exception.

According to *Veritatis Splendor*, with intrinsically evil acts no discernment of circumstances or intentions is necessary. Uniting oneself to a woman who is married to another is and remains an act of adultery that as such is never to be done, even if by doing so an agent could possibly extract precious secrets from a villain's wife so as to save the kingdom (what sounds like an example from a James Bond movie has already been contemplated by St. Thomas Aquinas, *De Malo*, q. 15, a. 1). John Paul II argues that the intention (say, "saving the kingdom") does not change the species of the act (here: "committing adultery"), and that it is enough to know the species of the act ("adultery") to know that one must not do it.

DOUBT NUMBER 3

After *Amoris Laetitia* (n. 301), is it still possible to affirm that a person who habitually lives in contradiction to a commandment of God's law, as for instance the one that prohibits adultery (cf. Mt 19:3–9), finds him- or herself in an objective situation of grave habitual sin (cf. Pontifical Council for Legislative Texts, Declaration, June 24, 2000)?

In paragraph 301, *Amoris Laetitia* recalls that: "The Church possesses a solid body of reflection concerning mitigating factors and situations." And it concludes that "hence it can no longer simply be said that all those in any 'irregular' situation are living in a state of mortal sin and are deprived of sanctifying grace."

In its Declaration of June 24, 2000, the Pontifical Council for Legislative Texts seeks to clarify Canon 915 of the *Code of Canon Law*, which states that those who "obstinately persist in manifest grave sin, are not to be admitted to Holy Communion." The Pontifical Council's Declaration argues that this canon is applicable also to faithful who are divorced and civilly remarried. It spells out that "grave sin" has to be understood objectively, given that the minister of the Eucharist has no means of judging another person's subjective imputability. Thus, for the Declaration, the question of the admission to the sacraments is about judging a person's objective life situation and not about judging that this person is in a state of mortal sin. Indeed subjectively he or she may not be fully imputable or not be imputable at all.

Along the same lines, in his encyclical *Ecclesia de Eucharistia*, n. 37, Saint John Paul II recalls that "the judgment of one's state of grace obviously belongs only to the person involved, since it is a question of examining one's conscience." Hence, the distinction referred to by *Amoris Laetitia* between the subjective situation of mortal sin and the objective situation of grave sin is indeed well established in the Church's teaching. John Paul II continues however by insisting that "in cases of outward conduct which is seriously, clearly and steadfastly contrary to the moral norm, the Church, in her pastoral concern for the good order of the community and out of respect for the sacrament, cannot fail to feel directly involved." He then reiterates the teaching of Canon 915 mentioned above.

Question 3 of the *Dubia* hence would like to clarify whether, even after *Amoris Laetitia*, it is still possible to say that persons who habitually live in contradiction to a commandment of God's law, such as the commandment against adultery, theft, murder, or perjury, live in objective situations of grave habitual sin, even if, for whatever reasons, it is not certain that they are subjectively imputable for their habitual transgressions.

DOUBT NUMBER 4

After the affirmations of *Amoris Laetitia* (n. 302) on "circumstances which mitigate moral responsibility," does one still need to regard as valid the teaching of St. John Paul II's encyclical *Veritatis Splendor*, n. 81, based on Sacred Scripture and on the Tradition of the Church, according to which "circumstances or intentions can never transform an act intrinsically evil by virtue of its object into an act 'subjectively' good or defensible as a choice"?

In paragraph 302, *Amoris Laetitia* stresses that on account of mitigating circumstances "a negative judgment about an objective situation does not imply a judgment about the imputability or culpability of the person involved." The *Dubia* point to the Church's teaching as expressed in John Paul II's *Veritatis Splendor* according to which circumstances or good intentions can never turn an intrinsically evil act into one that is excusable or even good.

The question arises whether *Amoris Laetitia*, too, is agreed that any act that transgresses against God's commandments, such as adultery, murder, theft, or perjury, can never, on account of circumstances that mitigate personal responsibility, become excusable or even good. Do these acts, which the Church's Tradition has called bad in themselves and grave sins, continue to be destructive and harmful for anyone committing them, in whatever subjective state of moral responsibility he may be? Or could these acts, depending on a person's subjective state and depending on the circumstances and intentions, cease to be injurious and become commendable or at least excusable?

DOUBT NUMBER 5

After *Amoris Laetitia* n. 303, does one still need to regard as valid the teaching of St. John Paul II's encyclical *Veritatis Splendor* n. 56, based on Sacred Scripture and on the Tradition of the Church, that excludes a creative interpretation of the role of conscience and that emphasizes that conscience can never be authorized to legitimate exceptions to absolute moral norms that prohibit intrinsically evil acts by virtue of their object?

Amoris Laetitia n. 303 states that "conscience can do more than recognize that a given situation does not correspond objectively to the overall demands of the Gospel. It can also recognize with sincerity and honesty what for now is the most generous response which can be given to God." The *Dubia* ask for a clarification of these affirmations, given that they are susceptible to divergent interpretations.

For those proposing the creative idea of conscience, the precepts of God's law and the norm of the individual conscience can be in tension or even in opposition, while the final word should always go to conscience that ultimately decides about good and evil. According to *Veritatis Splendor* n. 56, "on this basis, an attempt is made to legitimize so-called 'pastoral' solutions contrary to the teaching of the Magisterium, and to justify a 'creative' hermeneutic according to which the moral conscience is in no way obliged, in every case, by a particular negative precept." In this perspective, it will never be enough for moral conscience to know "this is adultery," or "this is murder," in order to know that this is something one cannot and must not do. Rather, one would also need to look at the circumstances or the intentions to know if this act could not, after all, be excusable or even obligatory (cf. question 4 of the *Dubia*). For these theories, conscience could indeed rightfully decide that in a given case, God's will for me consists in an act by which I transgress one of his commandments. "Do not commit adultery" is seen as just a general norm. In the here and now, and given my good intentions, committing adultery is what God really requires of me. Under these terms, cases of virtuous adultery, lawful murder, and obligatory perjury are at least conceivable. This would mean to conceive of conscience as a faculty for autonomously deciding about good and evil and to conceive of God's law as a burden that is arbitrarily imposed and that could at times be opposed to our true happiness.

However, conscience does not decide about good and evil. The whole idea of a "decision of conscience" is misleading. The proper act of conscience is to *judge* and not to *decide*. It says, "This is good," "This is bad." This goodness or badness does not depend on it. It acknowledges and recognizes the goodness or badness of an action, and for doing so, that is, for judging, conscience needs criteria; it is inherently dependent on truth. God's commandments are a most welcome help for conscience to get to know the truth and hence to judge verily. God's commandments are the expression of the truth about our good, about our very being, disclosing something crucial about how to live life well. Pope Francis, too, expresses himself in these terms in *Amoris Laetitia* 295: "The law is itself a gift of God which points out the way, a gift for everyone without exception."

PART II

Letters and Statements to the Pope or the Bishops

A

Theological Censures *of* Amoris Laetitia

I. LETTER TO CARDINAL ANGELO SODANO, DEAN OF THE COLLEGE OF CARDINALS

June 29, 2016

Your Eminence,

As Catholic theologians and philosophers, church historians and pastors of souls, we are writing to you in your capacity as Dean of the College of Cardinals to request that the College of Cardinals and the Patriarchs of the Catholic Church take collective action to respond to the dangers to Catholic faith and morals posed by the Apostolic Exhortation *Amoris Laetitia* issued by Pope Francis on March 19, 2016. This Apostolic Exhortation contains a number of statements that can be understood in a sense that is contrary to Catholic faith and morals. We have specified the nature and degree of the errors that could be attributed to *Amoris Laetitia* in the accompanying document. We request that the Cardinals and Patriarchs petition the Holy Father to condemn the errors listed in the document in a definitive and final manner, and to authoritatively state that *Amoris Laetitia* does not require any of them to be believed or considered as possibly true. For the convenience of the Patriarchs and members of the College of Cardinals, we shall send each of them a copy of this letter and its accompanying document.

Requesting your blessing, we are
Yours faithfully,

Dr José Tomás Alvarado
 Associate Professor, Institute of Philosophy, Pontifical Catholic University of Chile

Rev. Fr Scott Anthony Armstrong, PhD
 Brisbane Oratory in formation

Rev. Claude Barthe

Part II: Letters and Statements to the Pope or the Bishops

Rev. Ray Blake
Parish priest, Diocese of Arundel and Brighton

Fr Louis-Marie de Blignières FSVF
Doctor of Philosophy

Dr Philip Blosser
Professor of Philosophy, Sacred Heart Major Seminary, Archdiocese of Detroit

Msgr. Ignacio Barreiro Carambula, STD, JD
Chaplain and Faculty Member of the Roman Forum

Rev. Fr Thomas Crean OP, STD
Holy Cross parish, Leicester

Fr Albert-Marie Crignion FSVF
Doctor designatus of Theology

Robert de Mattei
Professor of History of Christianity, European University of Rome

Cyrille Dounot, JCL
Professor of Law, University of Auvergne
Ecclesiastical advocate, Archdiocese of Lyon

Fr Neil Ferguson OP, MA, BD
Lecturer in Sacred Scripture, Blackfriars Hall, University of Oxford

Dr Alan Fimister STL, PhD
Assistant Professor of Theology, St. John Vianney Seminary, Archdiocese of Denver

Luke Gormally
Director Emeritus, The Linacre Centre for Healthcare Ethics
Sometime Research Professor, Ave Maria School of Law, Ann Arbor, Michigan
Ordinary Member, The Pontifical Academy for Life

Carlos A. Casanova Guerra
Doctor of Philosophy, Full Professor of Universidad Santo Tomás de Chile

Rev. Brian W. Harrison OS, MA, STD
Associate Professor of Theology (retired), Pontifical University of Puerto Rico
Scholar-in-Residence, Oblates of Wisdom Study Center, St. Louis, Missouri
Chaplain, St. Mary of Victories Chapel, St. Louis, Missouri

Rev. Simon Henry, BA (Hons), MA
Parish priest of the archdiocese of Liverpool

Rev. John Hunwicke
Former Senior Research Fellow, Pusey House, Oxford
Priest of the Ordinariate of Our Lady of Walsingham

Peter A. Kwasniewski, PhD, Philosophy
Professor, Wyoming Catholic College

Dr John R. T. Lamont, STL, D. Phil

Fr Serafino M. Lanzetta, PhD
Lecturer in Dogmatic Theology, Theological Faculty of Lugano, Switzerland
Priest in charge of St. Mary's, Gosport, in the diocese of Portsmouth

Dr Anthony McCarthy
Visiting Lecturer in Moral Philosophy, International Theological Institute, Austria

Rev. Stephen Morgan, D.Phil (Oxon)
Lecturer & Tutor in Theology, Maryvale Higher Institute of Religious Sciences

Don Alfredo Morselli, STL
Parish priest of the archdiocese of Bologna

Rev. Richard A. Munkelt, PhD
Chaplain and Faculty Member, Roman Forum

Don Reto Nay, STD

Fr Aidan Nichols OP, PhD
Formerly John Paul II Lecturer in Roman Catholic Theology, University of Oxford
Prior of the Convent of St. Michael, Cambridge

Fr Robert Nortz MMA, STL
Director of Studies, Monastery of the Most Holy Trinity, Massachusetts (Maronite)

Rev. John Osman MA, STL
Parish priest in the archdiocese of Birmingham, former Catholic chaplain to the University of Cambridge

Christopher D. Owens, STL (cand.)
Adjunct Instructor, Faculty of Theology and Religious Studies, St. John's University (NYC)
Director, St. Albert the Great Center for Scholastic Studies

Dr Paolo Pasqualucci
Professor of Philosophy (retired), University of Perugia

Dr Claudio Pierantoni
Professor of Medieval Philosophy in the Philosophy Faculty of the University of Chile
Former Professor of Church History and Patrology at the Faculty of Theology of the Pontificia Universidad Católica de Chile
Member of the International Association of Patristic Studies

Fr Anthony Pillari, JCL (cand.)
Priest of the archdiocese of San Antonio, chaplain to Carmelite nuns

Prof. Enrico Maria Radaelli
International Science and Commonsense Association (ISCA), Department of Metaphysics of Beauty and Philosophy of Arts, Research Director

Dr John C. Rao, D.Phil (Oxford)
Associate Professor of History, St. John's University (NYC)
Chairman, Roman Forum

Fr Reginald-Marie Rivoire FSVF
Doctor designatus of canon law

Rt. Rev. Giovanni Scalese CRSP, SThL, DPhil
Ordinary of Afghanistan

Dr Joseph Shaw
Fellow and Tutor in Philosophy at St. Benet's Hall, Oxford University

Dr Anna M. Silvas FAHA
Adjunct research fellow, University of New England, NSW, Australia

Michael G. Sirilla, PhD
Professor of Systematic and Dogmatic Theology, Franciscan University of Steubenville

Professor Dr Thomas Stark
Phil.-Theol. Hochschule Benedikt XVI, Heiligenkreuz

Rev. Glen Tattersall
Parish priest, Parish of Bl. John Henry Newman, archdiocese of Melbourne
Rector, St. Aloysius' Church

Giovanni Turco
Professor of the Philosophy of Public Law, University of Udine

Nicolas Warembourg
Professeur agrégé des facultés de droit, École de Droit de la Sorbonne, Université Paris

II. THE APOSTOLIC EXHORTATION *AMORIS LAETITIA*: A THEOLOGICAL CRITIQUE

The Apostolic Exhortation *Amoris Laetitia*, issued by Pope Francis on March 19, 2016 and addressed to bishops, priests, deacons, consecrated persons, Christian married couples, and all the lay faithful, has caused grief and confusion to many Catholics on account of its apparent disagreement with a number of teachings of the Catholic Church on faith and morals. This situation poses a grave danger to souls. Since, as St. Thomas Aquinas teaches, inferiors are bound to correct their superiors publicly when there is an imminent danger to the faith,[1] and the Catholic faithful have the right and at times the duty, in keeping with their knowledge, competence, and position, to make known their views on matters which concern the good of the Church,[2] Catholic theologians have a strict duty to speak out against the apparent errors in the document. This statement on *Amoris Laetitia* is intended to fulfil that duty, and to assist the hierarchy of the Church in addressing this situation.

---

1 *Summa theologiae* II-II, q. 33, a. 4, ad 2; a. 7 co.
2 *Code of Canon Law* (1983), can. 212 §3.

THE AUTHORITY OF *AMORIS LAETITIA*

The official character of *Amoris Laetitia* enables it to pose a grave danger to the faith and morals of Catholics. Although an apostolic exhortation pertains normally or principally to the purely pastoral governing power, nevertheless, on account of the interconnection of the powers of teaching and of government, it also pertains indirectly to the magisterial power. It can also contain directly magisterial passages, which are then clearly indicated as being such. This was the case for previous apostolic exhortations such as *Evangelii Nuntiandi, Familiaris Consortio,* and *Reconciliatio et Paenitentia.*

There is no obstacle as such to the pope's using an apostolic exhortation to teach infallibly on faith and morals, but no infallible teaching is contained in *Amoris Laetitia,* since none of its statements satisfy the strict requirements for an infallible definition. It is thus a non-infallible exercise of the papal magisterium.

Some commentators have asserted that the document does not contain magisterial teaching as such, but only the personal reflections of the pope on the subjects it addresses. This assertion if true would not remove the danger to faith and morals posed by the document. If the Supreme Pontiff expresses a personal opinion in a magisterial document, this expression of opinion implicitly presents the opinion in question as one that it is legitimate for Catholics to hold. As a result, many Catholics will come to believe that the opinion is indeed compatible with Catholic faith and morals. Some Catholics out of respect for a judgment expressed by the Supreme Pontiff will come to believe that the opinion is not only permissible but true. If the opinion in question is not in fact compatible with Catholic faith or morals, these Catholics will thus reject the faith and moral teaching of the Catholic Church as it applies to this opinion. If the opinion relates to questions of morals, the practical result for the actions of Catholics will be the same whether they come to hold that the opinion is legitimate or actually true. An opinion on moral questions that is in truth legitimate for the Supreme Pontiff to hold is one that it is legitimate for Catholics to follow. Belief in the legitimacy of a moral position will thus lead Catholics to believe that it is legitimate to act as if it is true. If there is a strong motivation to act in this way, as there is with the questions being addressed here for the faithful to whose situations these questions are pertinent, most Catholics will act accordingly. This is an important factor in an evaluation of *Amoris Laetitia*, because that document addresses concrete moral questions.

It is however not the case that *Amoris Laetitia* is intended to do no more than express the personal views of the pope. The document contains statements about the personal positions of the current Holy Father, but such statements are not incompatible with these positions being presented as teachings of the Church by the document. Much of the document consists of straightforward assertoric and imperative statements that make no reference to the personal views of the Holy Father, and that thus have the form of magisterial teachings. This form will cause Catholics to believe that these statements are not simply permissible, but are teachings of the authentic magisterium which call for religious submission of mind and will; teachings to which they must yield not a respectful silence accompanied by inner disagreement, but actual inner assent.[3]

THE DANGERS OF *AMORIS LAETITIA*

The following analysis does not deny or question the personal faith of Pope Francis. It is not justifiable or legitimate to deny the faith of any author on the basis of a single text, and this is especially true in the case of the Supreme Pontiff. There are further reasons why the text of *Amoris Laetitia* cannot be used as a sufficient reason for holding that the pope has fallen into heresy. The document is extremely long, and it is probable that much of its original text was produced by an author or authors who are not Pope Francis, as is normal with papal documents. Those statements in it that on the face of them contradict the faith could be due to simple error on Pope Francis's part, rather than to a voluntary rejection of the faith.

When it comes to the document itself, however, there is no doubt that it constitutes a grave danger to Catholic faith and morals. It contains many statements whose vagueness or ambiguity permit interpretations that are contrary to faith or morals, or that suggest a claim that is contrary to faith and morals without actually

---

3   Cf. Lucien Choupin, *Valeur des décisions doctrinales et disciplinaires du Saint-Siège*, 2nd ed. (Paris: Beauchesne, 1913), 52–55; A.-M. Aubry, *Obéir ou assentir? De la «soumission religieuse» au magistère simplement authentique*, Collection «Sed Contra» (Paris: DDB, 2015).

stating it. It also contains statements whose natural meaning would seem to be contrary to faith or morals.

The statements made by *Amoris Laetitia* are not expressed with scientific accuracy. This can be advantageous for the very small proportion of Catholics who have a scientific training in theology, because such Catholics will be able to discern that the assertions of *Amoris Laetitia* do not demand their religious submission of mind and will, or even a respectful silence in regard to them. Accurate formulation and proper legal form are needed in order to make a magisterial utterance binding in this fashion, and these are for the most part lacking in the document. It is however harmful for the vast majority of Catholics who do not have a theological training and are not well informed about Catholic teachings on the topics that the Apostolic Exhortation discusses. The lack of precision in the document's statements makes it easier to interpret them as contradicting the real teachings of the Catholic Church and of divine revelation, and as justifying or requiring the abandonment of these teachings by Catholics in theory and in practice. Some cardinals, bishops, and priests, betraying their duty to Jesus Christ and to the care of souls, are already offering interpretations of this sort.

The problem with *Amoris Laetitia* is not that it has imposed legally binding rules that are intrinsically unjust or authoritatively taught binding teachings that are false. The document does not have the authority to promulgate unjust laws or to require assent to false teachings, because the pope does not have the power to do these things. The problem with the document is that it can mislead Catholics into believing what is false and doing what is forbidden by divine law. The document is formulated in terms that are not legally or theologically exact, but this does not matter for the evaluation of its contents, because the most precise formulation cannot give legal and doctrinal status to decrees that are contrary to divine law and divine revelation. What is important about the document is the damaging effect it can have on the belief and moral life of Catholics. The character of this effect will be determined by the meaning that most Catholics will take it to have, not by its meaning when evaluated by precise theological criteria, and it is this meaning that will be addressed here. The propositions of *Amoris Laetitia* that require censure must thus be condemned in the sense that the average reader is liable to attribute to their words. The average reader here is understood to be one who is not trying to twist the words of the document in any direction, but who will take the natural or the immediate impression of the meaning of the words to be correct.

It is acknowledged that some of the censured propositions are contradicted elsewhere in the document, and that *Amoris Laetitia* contains many valuable teachings. Some of the passages of *Amoris Laetitia* make an important contribution to the defence and preaching of the faith. The criticism of *Amoris Laetitia* offered here permits these valuable elements to have their true effect, by distinguishing them from the problematic elements in the document and neutralising the threat to the faith posed by them.

For the sake of theological clarity and justice, this criticism of the harmful parts of *Amoris Laetitia* will take the form of a theological censure of the individual passages that are deficient. These censures are to be understood in the sense traditionally held by the Church,[4] and are applied to the passages *prout iacent*, as they lie. The propositions censured are so damaging that a complete listing of the censures that apply to them is not attempted. Most if not all of them fall under the censures of *aequivoca, ambigua, obscura, praesumptuosa, anxia, dubia, captiosa, male sonans, piarum aurium offensiva*,[5] as well as the ones listed. The censures list i) the censures that bear upon the content of the statements censured, and ii) those that bear upon the damaging effects of the statements. The censures are not intended to be an exhaustive list of the errors that *Amoris Laetitia* on a plausible reading contains; they seek to identify the worst threats to Catholic faith and morals in the document. The propositions censured are divided into those that

---

4   See H. Quilliet, "Censures doctrinales," *DTC* II, 2101–13, and the Sacred Congregation for the Doctrine of the Faith, "Doctrinal commentary on the concluding formula of the *Professio fidei*," June 29, 1998.

5   Note by editors: The statement that some of the propositions censured might also be censured as *piarum aurium offensiva* contradicts the other censures applied to these propositions. In the usual understanding of *piarum aurium offensiva*, this censure applies to propositions that are true as stated but that are expressed in such a way as to be offensive to a well-judging and pious person; an example would be the prayer "St. Peter, coward and traitor, pray for us." The propositions censured in the letter are all however considered to be false, and the censures applied to the propositions either imply or state that they are false. So it would be contrary to the intention of the letter to describe any of them as *piarum aurium offensiva*. This mistake has not been corrected, since the intention of this book is to record the documents and debates as they originally happened.

are heretical and those that fall under a lesser censure. Heretical propositions, censured as *haeretica*, are ones that contradict propositions that are contained in divine revelation and are defined with a solemn judgment as divinely revealed truths either by the Roman Pontiff when he speaks *ex cathedra*, or by the College of Bishops gathered in council, or infallibly proposed for belief by the ordinary and universal Magisterium. The propositions that fall under a lesser censure than heresy are included as posing an especially grave danger to faith and morals.

The censures of these propositions are not censures of administrative, legislative, or doctrinal acts of the Supreme Pontiff, since the propositions censured do not and cannot constitute such acts. The censures are the subject of a filial request to the Supreme Pontiff, which asks him to make a definitive and final juridical and doctrinal act condemning the propositions censured.

Finally, some of the theologians who are signatories to this letter reserve the right to make minor adjustments to some of the censures attached to some of the propositions: their signatures should be taken as indicating their belief that all the propositions should be censured, and a general agreement with the censures here proposed.

III. THEOLOGICAL CENSURES OF PROPOSITIONS DRAWN FROM THE APOSTOLIC EXHORTATION *AMORIS LAETITIA*

A) HERETICAL PROPOSITIONS

— I —

| The Church ... firmly rejects the death penalty. (*AL* 83)

If understood as meaning that the death penalty is always and everywhere unjust in itself and therefore cannot ever be rightly inflicted by the state:

    i) *Haeretica, sacrae Scripturae contraria.*
    ii) *Perniciosa.*

Gen. 9:63: "Whoever sheds the blood of man, by man shall his blood be shed; for God made man in his own image."

See also: Lev. 20–21; Deut. 13, 21–22; Matt. 15:4; Mk. 7:10; Jn. 19:11; Rom. 13:4; Heb. 10:28; Innocent I, *Letter to Exsuperius*, PL 120: 499A–B; Innocent III, *Profession of Faith* prescribed for the Waldensians, DH 7954; *Catechism of the Council of Trent*, commentary on the fifth commandment; Pope Pius XII, *Address to the First International Congress of Histopathology of the Nervous System*, *AAS* 44 (1952): 787; *Catechism of the Catholic Church*, 2267.

— 2 —

> Every form of sexual submission must be clearly rejected. (*AL* 156)

If understood not simply as denying that a wife owes servile obedience to her husband or that the husband has authority over his wife that is the same as parental authority, but as also denying that the husband has any form of authority over his wife, or as denying that the wife has any duty to obey the legitimate commands of her husband in virtue of his authority as husband:

i) *Haeretica, sacrae Scripturae contraria.*
ii) *Prava, perniciosa.*

Eph. 5:24: "As the Church is subject to Christ, so also let wives be to their husbands in all things."

See also: 1 Cor. 11:3; Col. 3:18; Tit. 2:3–5; 1 Pet. 3:1–5; *Catechism of the Council of Trent*, commentary on the sacrament of matrimony; Leo XIII, *Arcanum*, *ASS* 12 (1879): 389; Pius XI, *Casti Connubii*, *AAS* 22 (1930): 549 (DH 3708–9); John XXIII, *Ad Petri Cathedram*, *AAS* 51 (1959): 509–10.

— 3 —

> Saint Paul recommended virginity because he expected Jesus's imminent return and he wanted everyone to concentrate only on spreading the Gospel: "the appointed time has grown very short" (1 Cor. 7:29)... Rather than speak absolutely of the superiority of virginity, it should be enough to point out that the different states of life complement one another, and consequently that some can be more perfect in one way and others in another. (*AL* 159)

Understood as denying that a virginal state of life consecrated to Christ is superior considered in itself to the state of Christian marriage:

i) *Haeretica, sacrae Scripturae contraria.*
ii) *Perniciosa, suspensiva gravis resolutionis.*

Council of Trent, Session 24, canon 10: "If anyone says that the married state surpasses that of virginity or celibacy, and that it is not better and more blessed to remain in virginity or celibacy than to be united in matrimony, let him be anathema" (DH 1810).

See also: Mt. 19:12, 21; 1 Cor. 7:7–8, 38; 2 Thess. 2:1–2; Rev. 14:4; Council of Florence, *Decree for the Jacobites*, DH 1353; Pius X, *Response of the Biblical Commission*, DH 3629; Pius XII, *Sacra Virginitas*, *AAS* 46 (1954): 174; Second Vatican Council, Decree *Optatam Totius* 10.

— 4 —

> Saint John Paul II proposed the so-called "law of gradualness" in the knowledge that the human being "knows, loves and accomplishes moral good by different stages of growth." This is not a "gradualness of law" but rather a gradualness in the prudential exercise of free acts on the part of subjects who are not in a position to understand, appreciate, or fully carry out the objective demands of the law. (*AL* 295)
>
> It is [sic] can no longer simply be said that all those in any "irregular" situation are living in a state of mortal sin and are deprived of sanctifying grace. More is involved here than mere ignorance of the rule. A subject may know full well the rule, yet have great difficulty in understanding "its inherent values," or be in a concrete situation which does not allow him or her to act differently and decide otherwise without further sin. (*AL* 301)

Understood as meaning that a justified person has not the strength with God's grace to carry out the objective demands of the divine law, as though any of the commandments of God are impossible for the justified; or as meaning that God's grace, when it produces justification in an individual, does not invariably and of its nature produce conversion from all serious sin, or is not sufficient for conversion from all serious sin:

i) *Haeretica, sacrae Scripturae contraria.*
ii) *Impia, blasphema.*

Council of Trent, Session 6, canon 18: "If anyone says that the commandments of God are impossible to observe even for a man who is justified and established in grace, let him be anathema" (DH 1568).

See also: Gen. 4:7; Deut. 30:11–19; Ecclesiasticus 15:11–22; Mk. 8:38; Lk. 9:26; Heb. 10:26–29; 1 Jn. 5:17; Zosimus, 15th (or 16th) Synod of Carthage, canon 3 on grace, DH 225; Felix III, Second Synod of Orange, DH 397; Council of Trent, Session 5, canon 5; Session 6, canons 18–20, 22, 27 and 29; Pius V, Bull *Ex Omnibus Afflictionibus*, on the errors of Michael du Bay, 54 (DH 1954); Innocent X, Constitution *Cum Occasione*, on the errors of Cornelius Jansen, 1 (DH 2001); Clement XI, Constitution *Unigenitus*, on the errors of Pasquier Quesnel, 71 (DH 2471); John Paul II, Apostolic Exhortation *Reconciliatio et Paenitentia* 17, *AAS* 77 (1985): 222; *Veritatis Splendor* 65–70, *AAS* 85 (1993): 1185–89 (DH 4964–67).

— 5 —

No one can be condemned for ever, because that is not the logic of the Gospel! (*AL* 297)

If understood as meaning that no human being can or will be condemned to eternal punishment in hell:

i) *Haeretica, sacrae Scripturae contraria.*
ii) *Scandalosa, perniciosa.*

Matt. 25:46: "These shall go into everlasting punishment: but the just, into life everlasting."

See also: Mt. 7:22–23; Lk. 16:26; Jn. 17:12; Rev. 20:10; 16th Synod of Toledo (DH 574); Fourth Lateran Council, DH 801; Benedict XII, Constitution *Benedictus Deus*, DH 1002; Council of Florence, Decree *Laetentur Caeli*, DH 1306; John Paul II, Letter of the Congregation for the Doctrine of the Faith, *Recentiores Episcoporum*, *AAS* 71 (1979): 941; *Catechism of the Catholic Church*, 1033–37.

— 6 —

I am in agreement with the many Synod Fathers who observed that "the baptized who are divorced and civilly

> remarried need to be more fully integrated into Christian communities in the variety of ways possible, while avoiding any occasion of scandal. The logic of integration is the key to their pastoral care, a care which would allow them not only to realize that they belong to the Church as the body of Christ, but also to know that they can have a joyful and fruitful experience in it. They are baptized; they are brothers and sisters; the Holy Spirit pours into their hearts gifts and talents for the good of all.... Such persons need to feel not as excommunicated members of the Church, but instead as living members, able to live and grow in the Church and experience her as a mother who welcomes them always, who takes care of them with affection and encourages them along the path of life and the Gospel." (*AL* 299)

If understood as meaning that the divorced and civilly remarried who choose their situation with full knowledge and full consent of the will are not in a state of serious sin, and that they can receive sanctifying grace and grow in charity:

i) *Haeretica, sacrae Scripturae contraria.*
ii) *Scandalosa, prava, perversa.*

Mk. 10:11–12: "Whosoever shall put away his wife and marry another, committeth adultery against her. And if the wife shall put away her husband, and be married to another, she committeth adultery."

See also: Ex. 20:14; Mt. 5:32, 19:9; Lk. 16:18; 1 Cor. 7:10–11; Heb. 10:26–29; Council of Trent, Session 6, canons 19–21, 27 (DH 1569–71, 1577); Session 24, canons 5 and 7 (DH 1805, 1807); Innocent XI, Condemned Propositions of the "Laxists," 62–63 (DH 2162–63); Alexander VIII, Decree of the Holy Office on "Philosophical Sin," DH 2291; John Paul II, *Veritatis Splendor* 65–70, *AAS* 85 (1993): 1185–89 (DH 4964–67).

—7—

> It is [sic] can no longer simply be said that all those in any "irregular" situation are living in a state of mortal sin and are deprived of sanctifying grace. More is involved here than mere ignorance of the rule. A subject

> may know full well the rule, yet have great difficulty in understanding "its inherent values," or be in a concrete situation which does not allow him or her to act differently and decide otherwise without further sin. (*AL* 301)

Understood as meaning that a Catholic believer can have full knowledge of a divine law and voluntarily choose to break it in a serious matter, but not be in a state of mortal sin as a result of this action:

i) *Haeretica, sacrae Scripturae contraria.*
ii) *Prava, perversa.*

Council of Trent, Session 6, canon 20: "If anyone says that a justified man, however perfect he may be, is not bound to observe the commandments of God and of the Church but is bound only to believe, as if the Gospel were merely an absolute promise of eternal life without the condition that the commandments be observed, let him be anathema" (DH 1570).

See also: Mk. 8:38; Lk. 9:26; Heb. 10:26–29; 1 Jn. 5:17; Council of Trent, Session 6, canons 19 and 27; Clement XI, Constitution *Unigenitus*, on the errors of Pasquier Quesnel, 71 (DH 2471); John Paul II, Apostolic Exhortation *Reconciliatio et Paenitentia* 17, *AAS* 77 (1985): 222; *Veritatis Splendor* 65–70, *AAS* 85 (1993): 1185–89 (DH 4964–67).

— 8 —

> It is [sic] can no longer simply be said that all those in any "irregular" situation are living in a state of mortal sin and are deprived of sanctifying grace. More is involved here than mere ignorance of the rule. A subject may know full well the rule, yet have great difficulty in understanding "its inherent values," or be in a concrete situation which does not allow him or her to act differently and decide otherwise without further sin. (*AL* 301)

Understood as saying that a person with full knowledge of a divine law can sin by choosing to obey that law:

i) *Haeretica, sacrae Scripturae contraria.*
ii) *Prava, perversa.*

Ps. 18:8: "The law of the Lord is unspotted, converting souls."

See also: Ecclesiasticus 15:21; Council of Trent, Session 6, canon 20; Clement XI, Constitution *Unigenitus*, on the errors of Pasquier Quesnel, 71 (DH 2471); Leo XIII, *Libertas Praestantissimum*, *ASS* 20 (1887–88): 598 (DH 3248); John Paul II, *Veritatis Splendor* 40, *AAS* 85 (1993): 1165 (DH 4953).

— 9 —

> Conscience can do more than recognize that a given situation does not correspond objectively to the overall demands of the Gospel. It can also recognize with sincerity and honesty what for now is the most generous response which can be given to God, and come to see with a certain moral security that it is what God himself is asking amid the concrete complexity of one's limits, while yet not fully the objective ideal. (*AL* 303)

Understood as meaning that conscience can truly judge that actions condemned by the Gospel, and in particular, sexual acts between Catholics who have civilly remarried following divorce, can sometimes be morally right or requested or commanded by God:

i) *Haeretica, sacrae Scripturae contraria.*
ii) *Scandalosa, prava, perversa, perniciosa, impia, blasphema.*

Council of Trent, Session 6, canon 21: "If anyone says that Jesus Christ was given by God to men as a Redeemer in whom they are to trust but not also as a Lawgiver whom they are bound to obey, let him be anathema" (DH 1571).

Council of Trent, Session 24, canon 2: "If anyone says that it is lawful for Christians to have several wives at the same time, and that this is not forbidden by any divine law, let him be anathema" (DH 1802).

Council of Trent, Session 24, canon 5: "If anyone says that the marriage bond can be dissolved because of heresy or difficulties in cohabitation or because of the wilful absence of one of the spouses, let him be anathema" (DH 1805).

Council of Trent, Session 24, canon 7: "If anyone says that the Church is in error for having taught and for still teaching that in accordance with the evangelical and apostolic doctrine, the marriage bond cannot be dissolved because of adultery on the part of one of the spouses and that neither of the two, not even the innocent one who has given no cause for infidelity, can contract another marriage during the lifetime of the other, and that the husband who dismisses an adulterous wife and marries again and the wife who dismisses and adulterous husband and marries again are both guilty of adultery, let him be anathema" (DH 1807).

See also: Ps. 5:5; Ps. 18:8–9; Ecclesiasticus 15:21; Heb. 10:26–29; Jas. 1:13; 1 Jn. 3:7; Innocent XI, Condemned propositions of the "Laxists," 62–63 (DH 2162–63); Clement XI, Constitution *Unigenitus*, on the errors of Pasquier Quesnel, 71 (DH 2471); Leo XIII, encyclical letter *Libertas Praestantissimum*, *ASS* 20 (1887–88): 598 (DH 3248); Pius XII, Decree of the Holy Office on situation ethics, DH 3918; Second Vatican Council, Pastoral Constitution *Gaudium et Spes* 16; John Paul II, *Veritatis Splendor* 54, *AAS* 85 (1993): 1177; *Catechism of the Catholic Church*, 1786–87.

— 10 —

> I earnestly ask that we always recall a teaching of Saint Thomas Aquinas and learn to incorporate it in our pastoral discernment: "Although there is necessity in the general principles, the more we descend to matters of detail, the more frequently we encounter defects... In matters of action, truth or practical rectitude is not the same for all, as to matters of detail, but only as to the general principles; and where there is the same rectitude in matters of detail, it is not equally known to all... The principle will be found to fail, according as we descend further into detail." It is true that general rules set forth a good which can never be disregarded or neglected, but in their formulation they cannot provide absolutely for all particular situations. (*AL* 304)

Understood as meaning that moral principles and moral truths contained in divine revelation and in the natural law do not include negative prohibitions that absolutely forbid particular kinds of action under any and all circumstances:

i) *Haeretica, sacrae Scripturae contraria.*
ii) *Scandalosa, prava, perversa.*

John Paul II, *Veritatis Splendor* 115: "Each of us knows how important is the teaching which represents the central theme of this

Encyclical and which is today being restated with the authority of the Successor of Peter. Each of us can see the seriousness of what is involved, not only for individuals but also for the whole of society, with the reaffirmation of the universality and immutability of the moral commandments, particularly those which prohibit always and without exception intrinsically evil acts" (DH 4971).

See also: Rom. 3:8; 1 Cor. 6:9–10; Gal. 5:19–21; Rev. 22:15; Fourth Lateran Council, ch. 22 (DH 815); Council of Constance, Bull *Inter Cunctas* 14 (DH 1254); Paul VI, *Humanae Vitae* 14: *AAS* 60 (1968) 490–91; John Paul II, *Veritatis Splendor* 83, *AAS* 85 (1993): 1199 (DH 4970).

— II —

> I understand those who prefer a more rigorous pastoral care which leaves no room for confusion. But I sincerely believe that Jesus wants a Church attentive to the goodness which the Holy Spirit sows in the midst of human weakness, a Mother who, while clearly expressing her objective teaching, "always does what good she can, even if in the process, her shoes get soiled by the mud of the street." (*AL* 308)

If understood as meaning that Our Lord Jesus Christ wills that the Church abandon her perennial discipline of refusing the Eucharist to the divorced and remarried and of refusing absolution to the divorced and remarried who do not express contrition for their state of life and a firm purpose of amendment with regard to it:

i) *Haeretica, sacrae Scripturae contraria.*
ii) *Scandalosa, prava, perversa, impia, blasphema.*

1 Cor. 11:27: "Whosoever shall eat this bread, or drink the chalice of the Lord unworthily, shall be guilty of the body and of the blood of the Lord."

Familiaris Consortio 84: "Reconciliation in the sacrament of Penance, which would open the way to the Eucharist, can only be granted to those who, repenting of having broken the sign of the Covenant and of fidelity to Christ, are sincerely ready to undertake a way of life that is no longer in contradiction to the indissolubility of marriage. This means, in practice, that when, for serious reasons, such as for example the children's upbringing, a man and a woman cannot satisfy the obligation to separate, they 'take on themselves the duty to live in complete continence, that is, by abstinence from the acts proper to married couples.'"

Second Lateran Council, canon 20: "Because there is one thing that conspicuously causes great disturbance to holy Church, namely false penance, we warn our brothers in the episcopate, and priests, not to allow the souls of the laity to be deceived or dragged off to hell by false penances. It is certain that a penance is false when many sins are disregarded and a penance is performed for one only, or when it is done for one sin in such a way that the penitent does not renounce another" (DH 717).

See also: Mt. 7:6; Mt. 22:11–13; 1 Cor. 11:28–30; Heb. 13:8; Council of Trent, Session 14, Decree on Penance, cap. 4; Council of Trent, Session 13, Decree on the Most Holy Eucharist (DH 1646–47); Innocent XI, Condemned propositions of the "Laxists," 60–63 (DH 2160–63); *Catechism of the Catholic Church*, 1385, 1451, 1490.

B. PROPOSITIONS FALLING UNDER LESSER CENSURES

— 12 —

> Saint John Paul II proposed the so-called "law of gradualness" in the knowledge that the human being "knows, loves and accomplishes moral good by different stages of growth." This is not a "gradualness of law" but rather a gradualness in the prudential exercise of free acts on the part of subjects who are not in a position to understand, appreciate, or fully carry out the objective demands of the law. (*AL* 295)

If understood as meaning that free acts that do not fully carry out the objective demands of divine law can be morally good:

i) *Erronea in fide.*
ii) *Scandalosa, prava.*

1 Jn. 3:4: "Whosoever committeth sin, committeth also iniquity; and sin is iniquity."

See also: Leo XIII, *Libertas Praestantissimum*, *ASS* 20 (1887–88): 598 (DH 3248); John Paul II, *Veritatis Splendor* 40, *AAS* 85 (1993): 1165 (DH 4953).

— 13 —

> There are two ways of thinking which recur throughout the Church's history: casting off and reinstating. The Church's way, from the time of the Council of Jerusalem, has always been the way of Jesus, the way of mercy and reinstatement. The way of the Church is not to condemn anyone for ever. (*AL* 296)
>
> No one can be condemned for ever, because that is not the logic of the Gospel! (*AL* 297)

Understood as meaning that in circumstances where an offender does not cease to commit an offence the Church does not have the power or the right to inflict punishments or condemnations without later remitting them or lifting them, or that the Church does not have the power or the right to condemn and anathematise individuals after their death:

i) *Erronea in fide.*
ii) *Scandalosa, perniciosa, derogans praxi sive usui et disciplinae Ecclesiae.*

1983 *Code of Canon Law*, can. 1358: "The remission of a censure cannot be granted except to an offender whose contempt has been purged."

Third Council of Constantinople, Condemnation of the Monothelites and of Pope Honorius I: "As to these self-same men whose impious teachings we have rejected, we have also judged it necessary to banish their names from the holy Church of God, that is, the name of Sergius, who began to write about this impious doctrine, of Cyrus of Alexandria, of Pyrrhus, of Paul and of Peter and of those who have presided on the throne of this God-protected city, and the same for those who have been like-minded. Then also (the name) of Theodore who was bishop of Pharan. All these aforenamed persons were mentioned by Agatho, the most holy and thrice-blessed pope of elder Rome, in his letter to the . . . emperor, and rejected by him as having thought in a way contrary to our orthodox faith; and we determine that they are also subject to anathema. Along with these we have seen fit to banish from the holy Church of God and to anathematize also Honorius, the former pope of the elder Rome" (DH 550).

See also: Second Council of Constantinople, canons 11–12; Lateran Synod, canon 18 (DH 518–20); Leo II, Letter *Regi Regum*, DH 563; Fourth Council of Constantinople, canon 11; Council of Florence, *Decree for the Jacobites*, DH 1339–46; *Code of Canon Law* (1917), canons 855, 2214, 2241:1 and 2257; *Code of Canon Law* (1983), canons 915 and 1311; *Code of Canon Law for Eastern Churches*, canon 1424:1.

— 14 —

> The divorced who have entered a new union, for example, can find themselves in a variety of situations, which should not be pigeonholed or fit into overly rigid classifications leaving no room for a suitable personal and pastoral discernment. One thing is a second union consolidated over time, with new children, proven fidelity, generous self-giving, Christian commitment, a consciousness of its irregularity and of the great difficulty of going back without feeling in conscience that one would fall into new sins. (*AL* 298)

If understood as meaning that persons who are civilly married to someone other than their true spouse can show Christian virtue by being sexually faithful to their civil partner:

i) *Erronea in fide.*
ii) *Scandalosa.*

1 Cor. 7:10–11: "To them that are married, not I but the Lord commandeth, that the wife depart not from her husband; and if she depart, that she remain unmarried, or be reconciled to her husband. And let not the husband put away his wife."

See also: Gen. 2:21; Mal. 2:15–16; Mt. 5:32, 19:9; Mk. 10:11–12; Lk. 16:18; Heb. 13:4; Leo I, Letter *Quam Laudabiliter*, DH 283; Leo I, Letter *Regressus Ad Nos*, DH 311–14; Innocent III, Letter *Gaudemus in Domino*, DH 777–79; Second Council of Lyons, Profession of Faith of Emperor Michael Palaeologus (DH 860); Council of Trent, Session 24, canons 5, 7; Pius VI, *Rescript. ad Episc. Agriens.*, July 11, 1789; Leo XIII, *Arcanum*, *ASS* 12 (1879–80): 388–94; Pius XI, *Casti Connubii*, *AAS* 22 (1930): 546–50 (cf. DH 3706–10); John Paul II, Apostolic Exhortation *Familiaris Consortio* 19, 80–81, 84, *AAS* 74 (1982): 92–149; *Catechism of the Catholic Church*, 1643–49.

— 15 —

> The Church acknowledges situations "where, for serious reasons, such as the children's upbringing, a man and woman cannot satisfy the obligation to separate." [Footnote 329: In such situations, many people, knowing and accepting the possibility of living "as brothers and sisters" which the Church offers them, point out that if certain expressions of intimacy are lacking, "it often happens that faithfulness is endangered and the good of the children suffers."] (*AL* 298)[6]

Understood as endorsing claims that divorced and civilly remarried couples have an obligation of sexual faithfulness to each other rather than to their true spouses, or that their living "as brother and sister" could be either a culpable occasion of sin against that supposed obligation, or a culpable cause of harm to their children:

i) *Erronea in fide.*
ii) *Scandalosa, prava, perversa.*

Ecclesiasticus 15:21: "He hath commanded no man to do wickedly, and he hath given no man licence to sin."
See also: Rom. 3:8, 8:28; 1 Thess. 4:7; Jas. 1:13–14; John Paul II, *Veritatis Splendor* 79–83, *AAS* 85 (1993): 1197–99 (cf. DH 4969–70).

— 16 —

> Since "the degree of responsibility is not equal in all cases," the consequences or effects of a rule need not necessarily always be the same. [Footnote 336: This is also the case with regard to sacramental discipline, since discernment can recognize that in a particular situation no grave fault exists.] (*AL* 300)
>
> Because of forms of conditioning and mitigating factors, it is possible that in an objective situation of sin — which may not be subjectively culpable, or fully such — a person can be living in God's grace, can love

---

6 N. B. The last clause in double quotation marks misleadingly applies to divorced and civilly married couples a statement of Vatican Council II, *Gaudium et Spes* 51, that refers only to validly married couples.

> and can also grow in the life of grace and charity, while receiving the Church's help to this end. [Footnote 351: In certain cases, this can include the help of the sacraments. Hence, "I want to remind priests that the confessional must not be a torture chamber, but rather an encounter with the Lord's mercy." I would also point out that the Eucharist "is not a prize for the perfect, but a powerful medicine and nourishment for the weak."] (*AL* 305)

Understood as saying that absence of grave fault due to diminished responsibility can permit admission to the Eucharist in the cases of divorced and civilly remarried persons who do not separate, nor undertake to live in perfect continence, but remain in an objective state of adultery and bigamy:

i) *Erronea in fide, falsa.*
ii) *Scandalosa.*

John Paul II, *Familiaris Consortio* 84: "The Church reaffirms her practice, which is based upon Sacred Scripture, of not admitting to Eucharistic Communion divorced persons who have remarried. They are unable to be admitted thereto from the fact that their state and condition of life objectively contradict that union of love between Christ and the Church which is signified and effected by the Eucharist. Besides this, there is another special pastoral reason: if these people were admitted to the Eucharist, the faithful would be led into error and confusion regarding the Church's teaching about the indissolubility of marriage. Reconciliation in the sacrament of Penance, which would open the way to the Eucharist, can only be granted to those who, repenting of having broken the sign of the Covenant and of fidelity to Christ, are sincerely ready to undertake a way of life that is no longer in contradiction to the indissolubility of marriage. This means, in practice, that when, for serious reasons, such as for example the children's upbringing, a man and a woman cannot satisfy the obligation to separate, they 'take on themselves the duty to live in complete continence, that is, by abstinence from the acts proper to married couples.'"

1 Jn. 2:20: "You have the unction from the Holy One, and know all things."

See also Ez. 3:17; Mt. 28:20; 1 Cor. 11:27–29; Eph. 5:30–32; Second Lateran Council, DH 717; Paul V, *Rituale Romanum* 49;

Benedict XIV, Confirmation of the Synod of the Maronites; Encyclical letter *Ex Omnibus*; *Code of Canon Law* (1917), canon 855; *Code of Canon Law* (1983), canon 915; Congregation for the Doctrine of the Faith, Letter to bishops of the Catholic Church concerning the reception of Eucharistic communion by those faithful who after a divorce have entered a new marriage, *AAS* 86 (1994): 974–79; *Code of Canon Law for Eastern Churches*, canon 712; *Catechism of the Catholic Church*, 1650, 2390; Congregation for the Doctrine of the Faith, Concerning Some Objections to the Church's Teaching on the Reception of Holy Communion by Divorced and Remarried Members of the Faithful, in *Documenti e Studi—On the Pastoral Care of the Divorced and Remarried* (Vatican City, 1998), 20–29; Pontifical Council for Legislative Texts (PCLT), *Declaration Concerning the Admission to Holy Communion of Faithful Who Are Divorced and Remarried*; Benedict XVI, Apostolic Exhortation *Sacramentum Caritatis* 29, *AAS* 99 (2007), 128–29.

— 17 —

> The divorced who have entered a new union, for example, can find themselves in a variety of situations, which should not be pigeonholed or fit into overly rigid classifications leaving no room for a suitable personal and pastoral discernment. One thing is a second union consolidated over time, with new children, proven fidelity, generous self-giving, Christian commitment, a consciousness of its irregularity and of the great difficulty of going back without feeling in conscience that one would fall into new sins. (*AL* 298)

If understood as meaning that the divorced and remarried can either sin or culpably expose themselves to the occasion of sin by abstaining from sexual relations in accordance with the perennial teaching and discipline of the Church:

i) *Temeraria, falsa.*
ii) *Scandalosa, prava, derogans praxi et disciplinae Ecclesiae.*

Ecclesiasticus 15:16: "If thou wilt keep the commandments and perform acceptable fidelity for ever, they shall preserve thee."

See also: 1 Cor. 7:11, 10:13; John Paul II, *Veritatis Splendor* 102–3, *AAS* 85 (1993): 1213–14; Apostolic Exhortation, *Familiaris*

Consortio 84, *AAS* 74 (1982) 92–149; *Catechism of the Catholic Church*, 1650; Benedict XVI, Apostolic Exhortation *Sacramentum Caritatis* 99 (2007), 128–29.

— 18 —

> There are also the cases of those who made every effort to save their first marriage and were unjustly abandoned, or of "those who have entered into a second union for the sake of the children's upbringing, and are sometimes subjectively certain in conscience that their previous and irreparably broken marriage had never been valid." (*AL* 298)

If understood as meaning that subjective certainty in conscience about the invalidity of a previous marriage is sufficient on its own to excuse from guilt or legal penalty those who contract a new marriage when their previous marriage is recognised as valid by the Church:

i) *Temeraria, falsa.*
ii) *Scandalosa.*

Council of Trent, Session 24, canon 12: "If anyone says that matrimonial cases do not belong to ecclesiastical judges, let him be anathema" (DH 1812).

See also: Leo XIII, *Arcanum, ASS* 12 (1879), 393; *Code of Canon Law* (1983), canons 1059–60, 1085.

— 19 —

> The teaching of moral theology should not fail to incorporate these considerations. (*AL* 311)

Understood as meaning that the teaching of moral theology in the Catholic Church should present as probable or true any of the propositions censured above:

i) *Falsa.*
ii) *Scandalosa, prava, perversa, perniciosa.*

Matt. 5:19: "He therefore that shall break one of these least commandments, and shall so teach men, shall be called least in the kingdom of heaven."

See also: Is. 5:20; Mt. 28:20; 1 Tim. 6:20; Jas. 3:1; Pius IX, Bull *Ineffabilis Deus*, DH 2802; First Vatican Council, Constitution *Dei Filius*, cap. 4 (DH 3020); Pius X, Motu Proprio *Sacrorum Antistitum*, DH 3541; Congregation for the Doctrine of the Faith, *Iusiurandum fidelitatis in suscipiendo officio nomine Ecclesiae exercendo*, *AAS* 81 (1989): 106; Congregation for the Doctrine of the Faith, *Donum Veritatis*, On the ecclesial vocation of the theologian, *AAS* 82 (1990): 1559; John Paul II, *Veritatis Splendor* 115–16, *AAS* 85 (1993): 1223–24; Congregation for the Doctrine of the Faith, *Notification on the Works of Father Jon Sobrino, S. J.*, n. 2 (DH 5107).

The propositions censured above have been condemned in many previous magisterial documents. It is urgently necessary that their condemnation be repeated by the Supreme Pontiff in a definitive and final manner and that it be authoritatively stated that *Amoris Laetitia* does not require any of them to be believed or considered as possibly true.

B

Correctio filialis de haeresibus propagatis

FILIAL CORRECTION CONCERNING THE PROPAGATION OF HERESIES

July 16, 2017
Feast of Our Lady of Mt Carmel

Most Holy Father,
 With profound grief, but moved by fidelity to our Lord Jesus Christ, by love for the Church and for the papacy, and by filial devotion toward yourself, we are compelled to address a correction to Your Holiness on account of the propagation of heresies effected by the Apostolic Exhortation *Amoris Laetitia* and by other words, deeds, and omissions of Your Holiness.
 We are permitted to issue this correction by natural law, by the law of Christ, and by the law of the Church, which three things Your Holiness has been appointed by divine providence to guard. By natural law: for as subjects have by nature a duty to obey their superiors in all lawful things, so they have a right to be governed according to law, and therefore to insist, where need be, that their superiors so govern. By the law of Christ: for His Spirit inspired the apostle Paul to rebuke Peter in public when the latter did not act according to the truth of the gospel (Gal. 2). St. Thomas Aquinas notes that this public rebuke from a subject to a superior was licit on account of the imminent danger of scandal concerning the faith,[1] and "the gloss of St. Augustine" adds that on this occasion: "Peter gave an example to superiors, that if at any time they should happen to stray from the straight path, they should not disdain to be reproved by their subjects" (ibid.). The law of the Church also constrains us, since it states that "Christ's faithful . . . have the right, indeed at times the duty, in keeping with their knowledge, competence, and position, to manifest to the sacred pastors their views on matters which concern the good of the Church."[2]

---

1 *Summa theologiae* II-II, q. 33, a. 4, ad 2.
2 *Code of Canon Law* 212 §§ 2–3; *Code of Canons of Eastern Churches* 15 § 3.

Scandal concerning faith and morals has been given to the Church and to the world by the publication of *Amoris Laetitia* and by other acts through which Your Holiness has sufficiently made clear the scope and purpose of this document. Heresies and other errors have in consequence spread through the Church; for while some bishops and cardinals have continued to defend the divinely revealed truths about marriage, the moral law, and the reception of the sacraments, others have denied these truths, and have received from Your Holiness not rebuke but favour. Those cardinals, by contrast, who have submitted dubia to Your Holiness, in order that by this time-honoured method the truth of the gospel might be easily affirmed, have received no answer but silence.

Most Holy Father, the Petrine ministry has not been entrusted to you that you might impose strange doctrines on the faithful, but so that you may, as a faithful steward, guard the deposit against the day of the Lord's return (Lk. 12; 1 Tim. 6:20). We adhere wholeheartedly to the doctrine of papal infallibility as defined by the First Vatican Council, and therefore we adhere to the explanation which that same council gave of this charism, which includes this declaration: "The Holy Spirit was not promised to the successors of Peter that they might, by His revelation, make known some new doctrine, but that, by His assistance, they might religiously guard and faithfully expound the revelation or deposit of faith transmitted by the apostles."[3] For this reason, Your Predecessor, Blessed Pius IX, praised the collective declaration of the German bishops, who noted that "the opinion according to which the pope is 'an absolute sovereign because of his infallibility' is based on a completely false understanding of the dogma of papal infallibility."[4] Likewise, at the Second Vatican Council, the Theological Commission which oversaw the Dogmatic Constitution on the Church, *Lumen Gentium*, noted that the powers of the Roman pontiff are limited in many ways.[5]

Those Catholics, however, who do not clearly grasp the limits of papal infallibility are liable to be led by the words and actions of Your Holiness into one of two disastrous errors: either they will come to embrace the heresies which are now being propagated, or,

---

[3] *Pastor Aeternus*, cap. 4.
[4] Denzinger-Hünermann (DH) 3117, Apostolic Letter *Mirabilis Illa Constantia*, March 4, 1875.
[5] *Relatio* of the Theological Commission on n. 22 of *Lumen gentium*, in *Acta Synodalia*, III/I:247.

aware that these doctrines are contrary to the word of God, they will doubt or deny the prerogatives of the popes. Others again of the faithful are led to put in doubt the validity of the renunciation of the papacy by Pope Emeritus Benedict XVI. Thus, the Petrine office, bestowed upon the Church by our Lord Jesus Christ for the sake of unity and faith, is so used that a way is opened for heresy and for schism. Further, noting that practices now encouraged by Your Holiness's words and actions are contrary not only to the perennial faith and discipline of the Church but also to the magisterial statements of Your predecessors, the faithful reflect that Your Holiness's own statements can enjoy no greater authority than that of former popes; and thus the authentic papal magisterium suffers a wound of which it may not soon be healed.

We, however, believe that Your Holiness possesses the charism of infallibility, and the right of universal jurisdiction over Christ's faithful, in the sense defined by the Church. In our protest against *Amoris Laetitia* and against other deeds, words, and omissions related to it, we do not deny the existence of this papal charism or Your Holiness's possession of it, since neither *Amoris Laetitia* nor any of the statements which have served to propagate the heresies which this exhortation insinuates are protected by that divine guarantee of truth. Our correction is indeed required by fidelity to infallible papal teachings which are incompatible with certain of Your Holiness's statements.

As subjects, we do not have the right to issue to Your Holiness that form of correction by which a superior coerces those subject to him with the threat or administration of punishment.[6] We issue this correction, rather, to protect our fellow Catholics—and those outside the Church, from whom the key of knowledge must not be taken away (cf. Lk. 11:52)—hoping to prevent the further spread of doctrines which tend of themselves to the profaning of all the sacraments and the subversion of the Law of God.

We wish now to show how several passages of *Amoris Laetitia*, in conjunction with acts, words, and omissions of Your Holiness, serve to propagate seven heretical propositions.[7] The passages of *Amoris Laetitia* to which we refer are the following:

---

6 Cf. *Summa theologiae* II-II, q. 33, a. 4.

7 This section therefore contains the *Correctio* properly speaking, and is that to which the signatories intend principally and directly to subscribe.

Saint John Paul II proposed the so-called "law of gradualness" in the knowledge that the human being "knows, loves and accomplishes moral good by different stages of growth." This is not a "gradualness of law" but rather a gradualness in the prudential exercise of free acts on the part of subjects who are not in a position to understand, appreciate, or fully carry out the objective demands of the law. (*AL* 295)

There are two ways of thinking which recur throughout the Church's history: casting off and reinstating. The Church's way, from the time of the Council of Jerusalem, has always been the way of Jesus, the way of mercy and reinstatement. The way of the Church is not to condemn anyone for ever. (*AL* 296)

No one can be condemned for ever, because that is not the logic of the Gospel! (*AL* 297)

The divorced who have entered a new union, for example, can find themselves in a variety of situations, which should not be pigeonholed or fit into overly rigid classifications leaving no room for a suitable personal and pastoral discernment. One thing is a second union consolidated over time, with new children, proven fidelity, generous self-giving, Christian commitment, a consciousness of its irregularity and of the great difficulty of going back without feeling in conscience that one would fall into new sins. The Church acknowledges situations "where, for serious reasons, such as the children's upbringing, a man and woman cannot satisfy the obligation to separate." [Footnote 329: In such situations, many people, knowing and accepting the possibility of living "as brothers and sisters" which the Church offers them, point out that if certain expressions of intimacy are lacking, "it often happens that faithfulness is endangered and the good of the children suffers."] There are also the cases of those who made every effort to save their first marriage and were unjustly abandoned, or of "those who have entered into a second union for the sake of the children's upbringing, and are sometimes subjectively certain in conscience that their previous and irreparably broken marriage had never been valid." Another thing is a new union arising from a recent divorce, with all the suffering and confusion which this entails for children and entire families, or the case of someone who has consistently failed in his obligations to the family. It must remain clear that this is not the ideal which the Gospel proposes for marriage and the family. The Synod Fathers stated that the discernment of pastors must always take place "by adequately distinguishing," with an approach which "carefully discerns situations." We know that no "easy recipes" exist. (*AL* 298)

I am in agreement with the many Synod Fathers who observed that "the baptized who are divorced and civilly remarried need to be more fully integrated into Christian communities in the variety of ways possible, while avoiding any occasion of scandal. The logic of integration is the key to their pastoral care, a care which would allow them not only to realize that they belong to the Church as the body of Christ, but also to know that they can have a joyful and fruitful experience in it. They are baptized; they are brothers and sisters; the Holy Spirit pours into their hearts gifts and talents for the good of all.... Such persons need to feel not as excommunicated members of the Church, but instead as living members, able to live and grow in the Church and experience her as a mother who welcomes them always, who takes care of them with affection and encourages them along the path of life and the Gospel." (*AL* 299)

Since "the degree of responsibility is not equal in all cases," the consequences or effects of a rule need not necessarily always be the same. [Footnote 336: This is also the case with regard to sacramental discipline, since discernment can recognize that in a particular situation no grave fault exists.] (*AL* 300)

It is [sic] can no longer simply be said that all those in any "irregular" situation are living in a state of mortal sin and are deprived of sanctifying grace. More is involved here than mere ignorance of the rule. A subject may know full well the rule, yet have great difficulty in understanding "its inherent values, or be in a concrete situation which does not allow him or her to act differently and decide otherwise without further sin." (*AL* 301)

Conscience can do more than recognize that a given situation does not correspond objectively to the overall demands of the Gospel. It can also recognize with sincerity and honesty what for now is the most generous response which can be given to God, and come to see with a certain moral security that it is what God himself is asking amid the concrete complexity of one's limits, while yet not fully the objective ideal. (*AL* 303)

I earnestly ask that we always recall a teaching of Saint Thomas Aquinas and learn to incorporate it in our pastoral discernment: "Although there is necessity in the general principles, the more we descend to matters of detail, the more frequently we encounter defects... In matters of action, truth or practical rectitude is not the same for all, as to matters of detail, but only as to the general principles; and where there is the same rectitude in matters of detail, it is not equally known to all... The principle will be found to fail, according as we descend further into detail." It is true that general rules set forth a good which can never be disregarded or neglected, but in their formulation they cannot provide absolutely for all particular situations. (*AL* 304)

Because of forms of conditioning and mitigating factors, it is possible that in an objective situation of sin — which may not be subjectively culpable, or fully such — a person can be living in God's grace, can love and can also grow in the life of grace and charity, while receiving the Church's help to this end. [Footnote 351: In certain cases, this can include the help of the sacraments. Hence, "I want to remind priests that the confessional must not be a torture chamber, but rather an encounter with the Lord's mercy." I would also point out that the Eucharist "is not a prize for the perfect, but a powerful medicine and nourishment for the weak."] (*AL* 305)

I understand those who prefer a more rigorous pastoral care which leaves no room for confusion. But I sincerely believe that Jesus wants a Church attentive to the goodness which the Holy Spirit sows in the midst of human weakness, a Mother who, while clearly expressing her objective teaching, "always does what good she can, even if in the process, her shoes get soiled by the mud of the street." (*AL* 308)

The teaching of moral theology should not fail to incorporate these considerations. (*AL* 311)

The words, deeds, and omissions of Your Holiness to which we wish to refer, and which in conjunction with these passages of *Amoris Laetitia* are serving to propagate heresies within the Church, are the following:

— Your Holiness has refused to give a positive answer to the *dubia* submitted to you by Cardinals Burke, Caffarra, Brandmüller, and Meisner, in which you were respectfully requested to confirm that the Apostolic Exhortation *Amoris Laetitia* does not abolish five teachings of the Catholic faith.

— Your Holiness intervened in the composition of the *Relatio post disceptationem* for the Extraordinary Synod on the Family. The *Relatio* proposed allowing Communion for divorced-and-remarried Catholics on a "case-by-case basis," and said pastors should emphasize the "positive aspects" of lifestyles the Church considers gravely sinful, including civil remarriage after divorce and premarital cohabitation. These proposals were included in the *Relatio* at your personal insistence, despite the fact that they did not receive the two-thirds majority required by the Synod rules for a proposal to be included in the *Relatio*.

— In an interview in April 2016, a journalist asked Your Holiness if there are any concrete possibilities for the divorced and remarried that did not exist before the publication of *Amoris Laetitia*. You replied "Io posso dire, si. Punto"; that is, "I can say yes. Period." Your Holiness then stated that the reporter's question was answered by the presentation given by Cardinal Schönborn on *Amoris Laetitia*. In this presentation Cardinal Schönborn stated:

> My great joy as a result of this document resides in the fact that it coherently overcomes that artificial, superficial, clear division between "regular" and "irregular," and subjects everyone to the common call of the Gospel, according to the words of St. Paul: "For God has consigned all to disobedience, that He may have mercy on all" (Rom. 11:32). ... what does the Pope say in relation to access to the sacraments for people who live in "irregular" situations? Pope Benedict had already said that "easy recipes" do not exist (*AL* 298, note 333). Pope Francis reiterates the need to discern carefully the situation, in keeping with St. John Paul II's *Familiaris Consortio* (84) (*AL* 298). "Discernment must help to find possible ways of responding to God and growing

in the midst of limits. By thinking that everything is black and white, we sometimes close off the way of grace and of growth, and discourage paths of sanctification which give glory to God" (*AL* 205). He also reminds us of an important phrase from *Evangelii Gaudium* 44: "A small step, in the midst of great human limitations, can be more pleasing to God than a life which appears outwardly in order but moves through the day without confronting great difficulties" (*AL* 304). In the sense of this "via caritatis" (*AL* 306), the Pope affirms, in a humble and simple manner, in a note (351), that the help of the sacraments may also be given "in certain cases."[8]

Your Holiness amplified this statement by asserting that *Amoris Laetitia* endorses the approach to the divorced and remarried that is practised in Cardinal Schönborn's diocese, where they are permitted to receive communion.

—On September 5, 2016 the bishops of the Buenos Aires region issued a statement on the application of *Amoris Laetitia*. In it they stated:

> 6) En otras circunstancias más complejas, y cuando no se pudo obtener una declaración de nulidad, la opción mencionada puede no ser de hecho factible. No obstante, igualmente es posible un camino de discernimiento. Si se llega a reconocer que, en un caso concreto, hay limitaciones que atenúan la responsabilidad y la culpabilidad (cf. 301–302), particularmente cuando una persona considere que caería en una ulterior falta dañando a los hijos de la nueva unión, *Amoris laetitia* abre la posibilidad del acceso a los sacramentos de la Reconciliación y la Eucaristía (cf. notas 336 y 351). Estos a su vez disponen a la persona a seguir madurando y creciendo con la fuerza de la gracia....
>
> 9) Puede ser conveniente que un eventual acceso a los sacramentos se realice de manera reservada, sobre todo cuando se prevean situaciones conflictivas. Pero al mismo tiempo no hay que dejar de acompañar a la comunidad

---

8   https://press.vatican.va/content/salastampa/en/bollettino/pubblico/2016/04/08/160408a.html.

para que crezca en un espíritu de comprensión y de acogida, sin que ello implique crear confusiones en la enseñanza de la Iglesia acerca del matrimonio indisoluble. La comunidad es instrumento de la misericordia que es «inmerecida, incondicional y gratuita» (297).

10) El discernimiento no se cierra, porque «es dinámico y debe permanecer siempre abierto a nuevas etapas de crecimiento y a nuevas decisiones que permitan realizar el ideal de manera más plena» (303), según la «ley de gradualidad» (295) y confiando en la ayuda de la gracia.

In translation:

6) In other, more complex cases, and when a declaration of nullity has not been obtained, the above-mentioned option may not, in fact, be feasible. Nonetheless, a path of discernment is still possible. If it comes to be recognized that, in a specific case, there are limitations that mitigate responsibility and culpability (cf. 301–302), especially when a person believes they would incur a subsequent wrong by harming the children of the new union, *Amoris Laetitia* offers the possibility of access to the sacraments of Reconciliation and Eucharist (cf. footnotes 336 and 351). These sacraments, in turn, dispose the person to continue maturing and growing with the power of grace....

9) It may be right for eventual access to sacraments to take place privately, especially where situations of conflict might arise. But at the same time, we have to accompany our communities in their growing understanding and welcome, without this implying creating confusion about the teaching of the Church on the indissoluble marriage. The community is an instrument of mercy, which is "unmerited, unconditional and gratuitous" (297).

10) Discernment is not closed, because it "is dynamic; it must remain ever open to new stages of growth and to new decisions which can enable the ideal to be more fully realized" (303), according to the "law of gradualness" (295) and with confidence in the help of grace.

This asserts that according to *Amoris Laetitia* confusion is not to be created about the teaching of the Church on the indissolubility of marriage, that the divorced and remarried can receive the sacraments, and that persisting in this state is compatible with receiving the help of grace. Your Holiness wrote an official letter dated the same day to Bishop Sergio Alfredo Fenoy of San Miguel, a delegate of the Argentina bishops' Buenos Aires region, stating that the bishops of the Buenos Aires region had given the only possible interpretation of *Amoris Laetitia*:

> Querido hermano:
>
> Recibí el escrito de la Región Pastoral Buenos Aires «Criterios básicos para la aplicación del capítulo VIII de *Amoris laetitia*." Muchas gracias por habérmelo enviado; y los felicito por el trabajo que se han tomado: un verdadero ejemplo de acompañamiento a los sacerdotes...y todos sabemos cuánto es necesaria esta cercanía del obispo con su clero y del clero con el obispo. El prójimo «más prójimo» del obispo es el sacerdote, y el mandamiento de amar al prójimo como a sí mismo comienza para nosotros obispos precisamente con nuestros curas.
>
> El escrito es muy bueno y explícita cabalmente el sentido del capitulo VIII de *Amoris Laetitia*. No hay otras interpretaciones.

> Beloved brother,
>
> I received the document from the Buenos Aires Pastoral Region, "Basic Criteria for the Application of Chapter Eight of *Amoris Laetitia*." Thank you very much for sending it to me. I thank you for the work they have done on this: a true example of accompaniment for the priests...and we all know how necessary is this closeness of the bishop with his clergy and the clergy with the bishop. The neighbor "closest" to the bishop is the priest, and the commandment to love one's neighbor as one's self begins for us, the bishops, precisely with our priests.
>
> The document is very good and completely explains the meaning of chapter VIII of *Amoris Laetitia*. There are no other interpretations.[9]

---

9 http://en.radiovaticana.va/news/2016/09/12/pope_endorses_argentine_bishops_document_on_amoris_laetitia/1257635.

—Your Holiness appointed Archbishop Vincenzo Paglia as president of the Pontifical Academy for Life and grand chancellor of the Pontifical Pope John Paul II Institute for Studies on Marriage and Family. As head of the Pontifical Council for the Family, Archbishop Paglia was responsible for the publication of a book, *Famiglia e Chiesa, un legame indissolubile* (Libreria Editrice Vaticana, 2015), that contains the lectures given at three seminars promoted by that dicastery on the topics of "Marriage: Faith, Sacrament, Discipline"; "Family, Conjugal Love, and Generation"; and "The Wounded Family and Irregular Unions: What Pastoral Attitude." This book and the seminars it described were intended to put forward proposals for the Synod on the Family, and promoted the granting of communion to divorced and remarried Catholics.

—Guidelines for the diocese of Rome were issued under Your Holiness's authority permitting the reception of the Eucharist under certain circumstances by civilly divorced and remarried Catholics living *more uxorio* with their civil partner.

—Your Holiness appointed Bishop Kevin Farrell as prefect of the newly established Dicastery for Laity, Family, and Life, and promoted him to the rank of cardinal. Cardinal Farrell has expressed support for Cardinal Schönborn's proposal that the divorced and remarried should receive communion. He has stated that the reception of communion by the divorced and remarried is a "process of discernment and of conscience."[10]

—On January 17, 2017, the *Osservatore Romano*, the official journal of the Holy See, published the guidelines issued by the archbishop of Malta and the bishop of Gozo for the reception of the Eucharist by persons living in an adulterous relationship. These guidelines permitted the sacrilegious reception of the Eucharist by some persons in this situation, and stated that in some cases it is impossible for such persons to practise chastity and harmful for them to attempt to practise chastity. No criticism of these guidelines was made by the *Osservatore Romano*, which presented them as legitimate exercises of episcopal teaching and authority. This publication was an official act of the Holy See that went uncorrected by yourself.

---

10 https://www.ncronline.org/news/vatican/new-cardinal-farrell-amoris-laetitia-holy-spirit-speaking.

CORRECTIO[11]

His verbis, actis, et omissionibus, et in iis sententiis libri *Amoris Laetitia* quas supra diximus, Sanctitas Vestra sustentavit recte aut oblique, et in Ecclesia (quali quantaque intelligentia nescimus nec iudicare audemus) propositiones has sequentes, cum munere publico tum actu privato, propagavit, falsas profecto et haereticas:

1. Homo iustificatus iis caret viribus quibus, Dei gratia adiutus, mandata obiectiva legis divinae impleat; quasi quidvis ex Dei mandatis sit iustificatis impossibile; seu quasi Dei gratia, cum in homine iustificationem efficit, non semper et sua natura conversionem efficiat ab omni peccato gravi; seu quasi non sit sufficiens ut hominem ab omni peccato gravi convertat.[12]

2. Christifidelis qui, divortium civile a sponsa legitima consecutus, matrimonium civile (sponsa vivente) cum alia contraxit; quique cum ea more uxorio vivit; quique cum plena intelligentia naturae actus sui et voluntatis propriae pleno ad actum consensu eligit in hoc rerum statu manere: non necessarie mortaliter peccare dicendus est, et gratiam sanctificantem accipere et in caritate crescere potest.[13]

---

11 The text is followed immediately below by a translation. The supporting notes are, however, attached to the Latin propositions.

12 Council of Trent, Sess. 6, canon 18: "If anyone says that the commandments of God are impossible to observe even for a man who is justified and established in grace, let him be anathema" (DH 1568). See also: Gen. 4:7; Deut. 30:11–19; Ecclesiasticus 15: 11–22; Mk. 8:38; Lk. 9:26; Heb. 10:26–29; 1 Jn. 5:17; Zosimus, 15th (or 16th) Synod of Carthage, can. 3 on grace, DH 225; Felix III, Second Synod of Orange, DH 397; Council of Trent, Sess. 5, can. 5; Sess. 6, can. 18–20, 22, 27 and 29; Pius V, Bull *Ex Omnibus Afflictionibus*, on the errors of Michael du Bay, 54, DH 1954; Innocent X, Constitution *Cum Occasione*, on the errors of Cornelius Jansen, 1, DH 2001; Clement XI, Constitution *Unigenitus*, on the errors of Pasquier Quesnel, 71, DH 2471; John Paul II, Apostolic Exhortation *Reconciliatio et Paenitentia* 17, *AAS* 77 (1985): 222; *Veritatis Splendor* 65–70, *AAS* 85 (1993): 1185–89, DH 4964–67.

13 Mk. 10:11–12: "Whosoever shall put away his wife and marry another, committeth adultery against her. And if the wife shall put away her husband, and be married to another, she committeth adultery." See also: Ex. 20:14; Mt. 5:32, 19:9; Lk. 16:18; 1 Cor. 7:10–11; Heb. 10:26–29; Council of Trent, Sess. 6, can. 19–21, 27, DH 1569–71, 1577; Sess. 24, can. 5 and 7, DH 1805, 1807; Innocent XI, Condemned propositions of the "Laxists,"

3. Christifidelis qui alicuius mandati divini plenam scientiam possidet et deliberata voluntate in re gravi id violare eligit, non semper per talem actum graviter peccat.[14]

4. Homo potest, dum divinae prohibitioni obtemperat, contra Deum ea ipsa obtemperatione peccare.[15]

5. Conscientia recte ac vere iudicare potest actus venereos aliquando probos et honestos esse aut licite rogari posse aut etiam a Deo mandari, inter eos qui matrimonium civile contraxerunt quamquam sponsus cum alia in matrimonio sacramentali iam coniunctus est.[16]

62–63, DH 2162–63; Alexander VIII, Decree of the Holy Office on "Philosophical Sin," DH 2291; John Paul II, *Veritatis Splendor*, 65–70, *AAS* 85 (1993): 1185–89 (DH 4964–67).

14 Council of Trent, Sess. 6, can. 20: "If anyone says that a justified man, however perfect he may be, is not bound to observe the commandments of God and of the Church but is bound only to believe, as if the Gospel were merely an absolute promise of eternal life without the condition that the commandments be observed, let him be anathema" (DH 1570). See also: Mk. 8:38; Lk. 9:26; Heb. 10:26–29; 1 Jn. 5:17; Council of Trent, Sess. 6, can. 19 and 27; Clement XI, Constitution *Unigenitus*, on the errors of Pasquier Quesnel, 71, DH 2471; John Paul II, Apostolic Exhortation *Reconciliatio et Paenitentia* 17, *AAS* 77 (1985): 222; *Veritatis Splendor* 65–70, *AAS* 85 (1993): 1185–89, DH 4964–67.

15 Ps. 18:8: "The law of the Lord is unspotted, converting souls." See also: Ecclesiasticus 15:21; Council of Trent, Sess. 6, can. 20; Clement XI, Constitution *Unigenitus*, on the errors of Pasquier Quesnel, 71, DH 2471; Leo XIII, *Libertas Praestantissimum*, *ASS* 20 (1887–88): 598 (DH 3248); John Paul II, *Veritatis Splendor* 40, *AAS* 85 (1993): 1165 (DH 4953).

16 Council of Trent, Sess. 6, can. 21: "If anyone says that Jesus Christ was given by God to men as a redeemer in whom they are to trust but not also as a lawgiver whom they are bound to obey, let him be anathema," DH 1571. Council of Trent, Sess. 24, can. 2: "If anyone says that it is lawful for Christians to have several wives at the same time, and that this is not forbidden by any divine law, let him be anathema," DH 1802. Council of Trent, Sess. 24, can. 5: "If anyone says that the marriage bond can be dissolved because of heresy or difficulties in cohabitation or because of the wilful absence of one of the spouses, let him be anathema," DH 1805. Council of Trent, Sess. 24, can. 7: "If anyone says that the Church is in error for having taught and for still teaching that in accordance with the evangelical and apostolic doctrine, the marriage bond cannot be dissolved because of adultery on the part of one of the spouses and that neither of the two, not even the innocent one who has given no cause for infidelity, can contract another marriage during the lifetime of the other, and that the husband who dismisses an adulterous wife and marries again and the

6. Principia moralia et veritas moralis quae in divina revelatione et in lege naturali continentur non comprehendunt prohibitiones qualibus genera quaedam actionis absolute vetantur utpote quae propter obiectum suum semper graviter illicita sint.[17]

7. Haec est voluntas Domini nostri Iesu Christi, ut Ecclesia disciplinam suam perantiquam abiciat negandi Eucharistiam et Absolutionem iis qui, divortium civile consecuti et matrimonium civile ingressi, contritionem et propositum firmum sese emendandi ab ea in qua vivunt vitae conditione noluerunt patefacere.[18]

---

wife who dismisses an adulterous husband and marries again are both guilty of adultery, let him be anathema," DH 1807.

See also: Ps. 5:5; Ps. 18:8–9; Ecclesiasticus 15:21; Heb. 10:26–29; Jas. 1:13; 1 Jn. 3:7; Innocent XI, Condemned propositions of the "Laxists," 62–63, DH 2162–63; Clement XI, Constitution *Unigenitus*, on the errors of Pasquier Quesnel, 71, DH 2471; Leo XIII, *Libertas Praestantissimum*, *ASS* 20 (1887–88): 598, DH 3248; Pius XII, Decree of the Holy Office on situation ethics, DH 3918; Second Vatican Council, Pastoral Constitution *Gaudium et Spes* 16; John Paul II, *Veritatis Splendor* 54, *AAS* 85 (1993): 1177; *Catechism of the Catholic Church*, 1786–87.

17   John Paul II, *Veritatis Splendor* 115: "Each of us knows how important is the teaching which represents the central theme of this Encyclical and which is today being restated with the authority of the Successor of Peter. Each of us can see the seriousness of what is involved, not only for individuals but also for the whole of society, with the reaffirmation of the universality and immutability of the moral commandments, particularly those which prohibit always and without exception intrinsically evil acts," DH 4971. See also: Rom. 3:8; 1 Cor. 6:9–10; Gal. 5:19–21; Rev. 22:15; Fourth Lateran Council, chapter 22, DH 815; Council of Constance, Bull *Inter Cunctas* 14, DH 1254; Paul VI, *Humanae Vitae* 14, *AAS* 60 (1968): 490–91; John Paul II, *Veritatis Splendor* 83, *AAS* 85 (1993): 1199, DH 4970.

18   1 Cor. 11:27: "Whosoever shall eat this bread, or drink the chalice of the Lord unworthily, shall be guilty of the body and of the blood of the Lord." *Familiaris Consortio*, 84: "Reconciliation in the sacrament of Penance, which would open the way to the Eucharist, can only be granted to those who, repenting of having broken the sign of the Covenant and of fidelity to Christ, are sincerely ready to undertake a way of life that is no longer in contradiction to the indissolubility of marriage. This means, in practice, that when, for serious reasons, such as for example the children's upbringing, a man and a woman cannot satisfy the obligation to separate, they 'take on themselves the duty to live in complete continence, that is, by abstinence from the acts proper to married couples.'" Second Lateran Council, can. 20, DH 717: "Because there is one thing that conspicuously causes great disturbance to holy Church, namely false penance, we warn our brothers in the episcopate, and priests, not to allow the souls of the

TRANSLATION

By these words, deeds, and omissions, and by the above-mentioned passages of the document *Amoris Laetitia*, Your Holiness has upheld, directly or indirectly, and, with what degree of awareness we do not seek to judge, both by public office and by private act propagated in the Church the following false and heretical propositions:

1. A justified person has not the strength with God's grace to carry out the objective demands of the divine law, as though any of the commandments of God are impossible for the justified; or as meaning that God's grace, when it produces justification in an individual, does not invariably and of its nature produce conversion from all serious sin, or is not sufficient for conversion from all serious sin.

2. Christians who have obtained a civil divorce from the spouse to whom they are validly married and have contracted a civil marriage with some other person during the lifetime of their spouse, who live *more uxorio* with their civil partner, and who choose to remain in this state with full knowledge of the nature of their act and full consent of the will to that act, are not necessarily in a state of mortal sin, and can receive sanctifying grace and grow in charity.

3. A Christian believer can have full knowledge of a divine law and voluntarily choose to break it in a serious matter, but not be in a state of mortal sin as a result of this action.

4. A person is able, while he obeys a divine prohibition, to sin against God by that very act of obedience.

5. Conscience can truly and rightly judge that sexual acts between persons who have contracted a civil marriage with each other, although one or both of them is sacramentally married to another person, can sometimes be morally right or requested or even commanded by God.

---

laity to be deceived or dragged off to hell by false penances. It is certain that a penance is false when many sins are disregarded and a penance is performed for one only, or when it is done for one sin in such a way that the penitent does not renounce another."

See also: Mt. 7:6; Mt. 22:11–13; 1 Cor. 11:28–30; Heb. 13:8; Council of Trent, Sess. 14, Decree on Penance, cap. 4; Council of Trent, Sess. 13, Decree on the Most Holy Eucharist, DH 1646–47; Innocent XI, Condemned propositions of the "Laxists," 60–63, DH 2160–63; *Catechism of the Catholic Church*, 1385, 1451, 1490.

6. Moral principles and moral truths contained in divine revelation and in the natural law do not include negative prohibitions that absolutely forbid particular kinds of action, inasmuch as these are always gravely unlawful on account of their object.

7. Our Lord Jesus Christ wills that the Church abandon her perennial discipline of refusing the Eucharist to the divorced and remarried and of refusing absolution to the divorced and remarried who do not express contrition for their state of life and a firm purpose of amendment with regard to it.

These propositions all contradict truths that are divinely revealed, and that Catholics must believe with the assent of divine faith. They were identified as heresies in the petition concerning *Amoris Laetitia* that was addressed by forty-five Catholic scholars to the cardinals and Eastern patriarchs of the Church.[19] It is necessary for the good of souls that they be once more condemned by the authority of the Church. In listing these seven propositions we do not intend to give an exhaustive list of all the heresies and errors which an unbiased reader, attempting to read *Amoris Laetitia* in its natural and obvious sense, would plausibly take to be affirmed, suggested, or favoured by this document: a letter sent to all the cardinals of the Church and to the Eastern Catholic patriarchs lists nineteen such propositions. Rather, we seek to list the propositions which Your Holiness's words, deeds, and omissions, as already described, have in effect upheld and propagated, to the great and imminent danger of souls.

At this critical hour, therefore, we turn to the *cathedra veritatis*, the Roman Church, which has by divine law preeminence over all the churches, and of which we are and intend always to remain loyal children, and we respectfully insist that Your Holiness publicly reject these propositions, thus accomplishing the mandate of our Lord Jesus Christ given to St. Peter and through him to all his successors until the end of the world: "I have prayed for thee, that thy faith fail not: and thou, being once converted, confirm thy brethren."

We respectfully ask for Your Holiness's apostolic blessing, with the assurance of our filial devotion in our Lord and of our prayer for the welfare of the Church.

---

19   See the preceding document.

ORIGINAL SIGNATORIES

Dr Gerard J. M. van den Aardweg
European editor, *Empirical Journal of Same-Sex Sexual Behavior*

Fr Claude Barthe
Diocesan Priest

Philip M. Beattie
BA (Leeds), MBA (Glasgow), MSc (Warwick), Dip.Stats (Dublin) Associate Lecturer, University of Malta (Malta)

Fr Jehan de Belleville
Religious

Fr Robert Brucciani
District superior of the SSPX in Great Britain

Prof. Mario Caponnetto
University Professor, Mar de la Plata (Argentina)

Mr Robert F. Cassidy, STL

Fr Isio Cecchini
Parish priest in Tuscany

Salvatore J. Ciresi, MA
Director of the St. Jerome Biblical Guild, Lecturer at the Notre Dame Graduate School of Christendom College

Fr Linus F. Clovis, PhD, JCL, MSc, STB, DipEd
Director of the Secretariat for Family and Life

Fr Paul Cocard
Religious

Fr Thomas Crean OP, STD

Prof. Matteo D'Amico
Professor of History and Philosophy, Senior High School of Ancona

Dr Chiara Dolce, PhD
Research doctor in Moral Philosophy at the University of Cagliari

Deacon Nick Donnelly, MA

Petr Dvorak
Head of Department for the Study of Ancient and Medieval Thought at the Institute of Philosophy, Czech Academy of Sciences, Prague; Assistant Professor of Philosophy at Saints Cyril and Methodius Theological Faculty, Palacky University, Olomouc, Czech Republic

H. E. Mgr Bernard Fellay
Superior General of the SSPX

Christopher Ferrara Esq.
Founding President of the American Catholic Lawyers' Association

Prof. Michele Gaslini
Professor of Public Law at the University of Udine

Prof. Corrado Gnerre
Professor at the Istituto Superiore di Scienze Religiose of Benevento, Pontifical Theological University of Southern Italy

Dr Ettore Gotti Tedeschi
Former President of the Institute for Works of Religion (IOR), Professor of Ethics at the Catholic University of the Sacred Heart, Milan

Part II: Letters and Statements to the Pope or the Bishops

Dr Maria Guarini, STB
Pontificia Università Seraphicum, Rome; editor of the website *Chiesa e post concilio*

Prof. Robert Hickson, PhD
Retired Professor of Literature and of Strategic-Cultural Studies

Fr John Hunwicke
Former Senior Research Fellow, Pusey House, Oxford

Fr Jozef Hutta
Diocesan Priest

Prof. Isebaert Lambert
Full Professor at the Catholic University of Louvain, and at the Flemish Katholieke Universiteit Leuven

Dr John Lamont STL, DPhil (Oxon.)

Fr Serafino M. Lanzetta, STD
Lecturer in Dogmatic Theology, Theological Faculty of Lugano, Switzerland; Priest in charge of St Mary's, Gosport, in the diocese of Portsmouth

Prof. Massimo de Leonardis
Professor and Director of the Department of Political Sciences at the Catholic University of the Sacred Heart in Milan

Msgr. Prof. Antonio Livi
Academic of the Holy See; Dean emeritus of the Pontifical Lateran University; Vice-rector of the church of Sant'Andrea del Vignola, Rome

Dr Carlo Manetti
Professor in Private Universities in Italy

Prof. Pietro De Marco
Former Professor at the University of Florence

Prof. Roberto de Mattei
Former Professor of the History of Christianity, European University of Rome; former Vice President of the National Research Council (CNR)

Fr Cor Mennen
Lecturer in Canon Law at the Major Seminary of the Diocese of 's-Hertogenbosch (Netherlands). Canon of the cathedral chapter of the diocese of 's-Hertogenbosch

Prof. Stéphane Mercier
Lecturer in Philosophy at the Catholic University of Louvain

Don Alfredo Morselli, STL
Parish priest of the archdiocese of Bologna

Martin Mosebach
Writer and essayist

Dr Claude E. Newbury MB, BCh, DTM&H, DOH, MFGP, DCH, DPH, DA, MMed
Former Director of Human Life International in Africa south of the Sahara; former Member of the Human Services Commission of the Catholic Bishops of South Africa

Prof. Lukas Novak
Assistant Professor, Faculty of Arts and Philosophy, Charles University, Prague

Fr Guy Pagès
Diocesan Priest

Prof. Paolo Pasqualucci
Professor of Philosophy (retired), University of Perugia

Prof. Claudio Pierantoni
Professor of Medieval Philosophy in the Philosophy Faculty of the University of Chile; Former Professor of Church History and Patrology at the Faculty of Theology of the Pontificia Universidad Católica de Chile

Father Anthony Pillari, JCL, MCL

Prof. Enrico Maria Radaelli
Philosopher, editor of the works of Romano Amerio

Dr John Rao
Associate Professor of History, St. John's University, NYC; Chairman, Roman Forum

Dr Carlo Regazzoni
Licentiate in Philosophy at University of Freiburg

Dr Giuseppe Reguzzoni
External Researcher at the Catholic University of Milan and former editorial assistant of *Communio*, International Catholic Review (Italian edition)

Arkadiusz Robaczewski, MA (Phil.)

Fr Settimio M. Sancioni, STD
Licence in Biblical Science

Prof. Andrea Sandri
Research Associate, Catholic University of the Sacred Heart in Milan

Dr Joseph Shaw
Tutor in Moral Philosophy, St Benet's Hall, University of Oxford

Fr Paolo M. Siano, HED (Historiae Ecclesiasticae Doctor)

Dr Cristina Siccardi
Historian of the Church

Dr Anna Silvas
Adjunct research fellow, University of New England, NSW, Australia

Prof. Dr Thomas Stark
Phil.-Theol. Hochschule Benedikt XVI, Heiligenkreuz

Rev. Glen Tattersall
Parish priest, Parish of Bl. John Henry Newman, archdiocese of Melbourne; Rector, St Aloysius' Church

Prof. Giovanni Turco
Associate Professor of Philosophy of Public Law at the University of Udine; Member Correspondent of the Pontificia Accademia San Tommaso d'Aquino

Prof. Piero Vassallo
Former editor of Cardinal Siri's theological review *Renovatio*

Prof. Arnaldo Vidigal Xavier da Silveira
Former Professor at the Pontifical University of São Paulo, Brazil

Msgr. José Luiz Villac
Former Rector of the Seminary of Jacarezinho

Part II: Letters and Statements to the Pope or the Bishops

ADDED ON 24TH SEPTEMBER 2017

Leo Darroch
President, *Foederatio Internationalis Una Voce* 2007–2013

Dr Mauro Faverzani
Editor of the Magazine *Radici Cristiane* (Italy)

H. E. Mgr Rene Henry Gracida, DD
Bishop Emeritus of the Diocese of Corpus Christi, Texas

Fr Pio Idowu, BA (Phil.)
Religious

Fr Luis Eduardo Rodríguez Rodríguez
Parish priest, Parroquia del Espíritu Santo y N. S. de La Antigua, Diocese de Los Teques, Venezuela

Wolfram Schrems, MA (Phil.), MA (Theol.)
Catechist for adults, writer, pro-life advocate, Vienna (Austria)

ON 25TH SEPTEMBER 2017

Dr Antonio Aragoni, MA (Religious Science)

Dr Riccardo Calzavara
Professor

Dr Riccardo Cavalli
Professor

Gianpaolo De Vita, PhD (Phil.)
University of Salerno

Dr Andrea Martini, MA (Education Science)

Fr Michel Morille
France

Fr Cyrille Perret
France

Fr Andrew Pinsent, BA, MA, DPhil, PhB, STB, Phl, PhD
Director of the Ian Ramsey Center for Science and Religion, Oxford; Priest of the Diocese of Arundel and Brighton

Prof. Leonardo Schwinden
Professor of Philosophy, Universidad Federal de Santa Catarina, Brazil

Patrick Tomeny Jr, MD, MPH, DABA

ON 26TH SEPTEMBER 2017

Dr Salvatore Giuseppe Alessi, BA (Phil.), BA (Theol.)
Economist, Italy

Fr Enrique Eduardo Alsamora
Spain

Dr Winfried Aymans
Professor em. of Canon Law, University of Munich

Fr William Barrocas

Fr Giorgio Bellei
Italy

Dr Richard Belleville, PhD
Formerly Chairman of Philosophy Department, Anna Maria College, Paxton (MA)

Fr Alejo Benitez
Spain

Fr Felix-Maximilian-Marie Bogoridi-Liven
France

Dr Nicola Bonora
Professor

Fr Nathaniel Brazil

Dr Johannes Bronish, PhD (Phil.)

Dr Isobel Camp, PhD
Professor of Philosophy at the Pontifical University of St. Thomas Aquinas, Angelicum (Rome)

Fr José Miguel Marqués Campo
Spain

Prof. Neri Capponi
Former Professor of Canon Law at the University of Florence; Judge of the Tuscany Ecclesiastical Matrimonial Court

Dr Fabiano Caso, PhD (Phil.), PhD (Theol.), BA (Theoretic Phil.)
Psychoanalyst, Italy

Fr Jose Chamakalayil

Sister M. Blaise Chukwu
Religious

Dr Francisco Fernández de la Cigoña
Journalist and writer, Spain

Dr Angelo Elli, MA (Phil.)
Italy

Dr Manuel Fantoni, PhD
Italy

Fr Marazsi Ferenc

Fr Thomas Agustin Gazpocnetti, Lic. Phil.

Dr Rossana Giannelli, MA (Phil.)
Italy

Fr Alvaro Salvador Gutiérrez Félix
Professor of Philosophy, Diocese of Mexicali, Mexico

Dr Christian Hecht, PhD (Phil.), BA (Theol.)

Fr John Houston

Fr Czeslaw Kolasa

Michael Theodor van Laack, BA (Theol.)

Dr Moisés Gomes de Lima
Professor

Fr Eduardo Guzmán López, STL
Parish priest, Spain

Fr Andrea Mancinella
Diocese of Albano

Fr Antonio Mancini
Italy

Dr Jose Marquez, Lic. Canon Law

Fr Peter Masik, PhD
Professor of Dogmatic Theology, Bratislava

Dr Martin Mayer, PhD (Theol.)

Fr Fabiano Montanaro
Defensor Vinculi by the Rota Romana, Rome

Dr Arroyo Moreno, Lic. Phil.
Professor em. at the University Panamerica and University Anahuac, Spain

Dr Renata Negri
Professor, Italy

Prof. Hermes Rodrigues Nery
Bioethicist; journalist and writer; Director of Movimento Legislação e Vida, Brazil

Fr Bernard Pellabeuf
France

Fr Eros Pellizzari
Italy

Thomas Pfeifer, BA (Phil.)

Dr Lucrecia Rego de Planas
University Professor, Mathematician, Master in Religious Science and Humanities, Doctor in Interdisciplinary Research

Fr Vidko Podrzaj
Priest of the Chapel of Our Lady of Good Success

Dr José Arturo Quarracino
Philosopher, Spain

Dr Kevin Regan, MD, BA, MA (Theol.)

Fr Robert Repenning

Fr Jasson Rodas

Fr Darrell Roman

Fr Giovanni Romani
Italy

Fr George M. Roth
USA

Dr Alvear Sanìn
Editor, writer, columnist

Dr Mauro Scaringi, MA (Phil.)
RE Professor, Italy

Dr Nikolaus Staubach, PhD
Professor at the University of Münster

Rev. Prof. Alberto Strumia, MA (Physics), STD
Professor em. of Mathematical Physics, University of Bari (I), Italy

Fr Tam X. Tran, STL
Pastor, Archdiocese of Washington, USA

Dr Andreas Trutzel, BA (Theol.)

Fr Humberto Jordán Sánchez Vázquez
Diocesan Priest

Dr Beata Vertessy
Professor, Hungary

Fr Marcelo Villegas
Spain

Dr Hubert Windisch
Professor em.

Dr Paul Winske
Professor, Germany

Fr Ernst-Werner Wolff
Germany

Dr Giorgio Zauli
Professor, writer, Italy

ON 28TH SEPTEMBER 2017

John F. Ambs
  Senior Executive Service, US Intelligence Community

Brother André Marie MICM, BA (Humanities), MA (Theol.)
  Prior of Saint Benedict Center in Richmond, New Hampshire

Prof. Denis Crouan, PhD (Theol.)
  President of the Association Pro Liturgia, France

Fr James Duncan, SJ
  Professor em. of Theology, Maison St. Michel, Brussels

Ester Maria Ledda
  Italy

Patrick Linbeck, BA, STL
  Board Member of the Avila Foundation and Texas Right to Life

Artur Paczyna
  President (2007–2016) of Silesian Association of the Faithful of the Latin Tradition

Dr Hon. J. D. Rasnick
  Sitting judge, Superior court probate court and municipal court judge; President Una Voce Georgia

Trey Tagert, BA (Phil. University of Dallas), MTS (University of Dallas)

Prof. Giovanni Zenone, PhD
  President, Fede & Cultura (Italy)
  Director, Gondolin Institute Press (Colorado, USA)

ON 29TH SEPTEMBER 2017

Fr Daniel Becker, BS, MS, M.Div., PhD
  Parish priest, Diocese of Worcester (USA)

Fr Remus Mircea Birtz, BA, STL, STD, BA (Christian Architecture)
  Church historian, Romania

Prof. Balázs Déri
  Professor at Eötvös Loránd University, Budapest

Fr Mark Gantley, JCL, Judicial Vicar,
  Diocese of Honolulu (HI, USA)

Fr Alphonsus Maria Krutsinger CSSR
  Religious, Preacher of Parish Missions

Prof. Cesar Félix Sanchez Martínez
  Professor of Philosophy of Nature, Philosophy of History and History of Philosophy (Modern and Contemporary) at the Archdiocesan Seminary of Saint Jerome, Arequipa-Perú

Dr Peter Micallef-Eynaud, MD (UCathSCJ), MSc (PH Med), BA (Rel. St.), MA (Theol. Melit.)

Prof. Nigel John Morgan
Professor em. of History of Art, University of Cambridge

Dr Eric E. Puosi, PhD
Lecturer in Systematic Theology and History of the Reformation, Viareggio, Italy

Fr Michael Sauer, MA (Theol.)
Diocese of Eichstätt, Germany

Dr med. Christian Spaemann, MA (Phil.)
Specialist in Psychiatry and Psychotherapeutic medicine, Germany

ON 30TH SEPTEMBER 2017

James Bogle Esq, TD, MA, Dip. Law
Barrister of the Middle Temple, London; Chairman of the Catholic Union of Great Britain 2000–2011, Vice-Chairman 2011–2014; President International *Una Voce* Federation 2013–2015; former Chairman of the Order of Christian Unity; Knight of Malta

Fr Carlo Brivio
Diocesan priest, Lombardia (Italy)

Pablo Esteban Camacho, PHB & MSc, BA (Phil.)

Fr Walter Covens
Diocesan priest, Martinica

David Percival C. Flores
Human Resources Professional Diocese of Malolos, Philippines

Dr med. Francisco Arturo Cuenca Flórez
Bogotá, Colombia

Dr Lee Fratantuono, AB Holy Cross; AM Boston College; PhD Fordham
Professor and Chair of Classics, Ohio Wesleyan University, Delaware, Ohio (USA)

Deacon Franco Gerevini
Diocese of Bergamo (Italy)

Dr Michael Kakooza, PhD (Wales) in Communication & Ideology
Consultant, Uganda Technology & Management University; Former Deputy Vice Chancellor, Research, Innovation & Development, KIM University, Rwanda

Dr Robert Lazu, PhD (Phil.)
Writer and lecturer, Romania

Philip James Maguire
Former Senior Journalist for the *Melbourne Catholic Advocate*, Sunday *Herald Sun* newspaper and Australian Broadcasting Commission; Former Senior Adviser to the Victorian State National Party Leader Neerim East, Victoria (Australia)

Dr Paul A. Scott, MA, PhD (Dunelm), FRHistS
Associate Professor of French, Co-Director of Undergraduate Studies in French, General Editor of *The Year's Work in Modern Language Studies* (Brill); Department of French, Francophone and Italian Studies, School of Languages, Literatures & Cultures, University of Kansas (USA)

Fr Denis Tolardo
Parochial Vicar, Veneto (Italy)

Fr Christian Viña, BA (Theol.)
Parish priest, Archidiocese de La Plata, Argentina

John-Henry Westen, MA
LifeSiteNews Co-Founder and Editor-in-Chief

Elizabeth Yore, JD
Attorney and International Child Advocate; Former General Counsel at the Illinois Department of Children and Family Services; General Counsel at the National Center for Missing and Exploited Children

ON 2ND OCTOBER 2017

Fr Paul Aulagnier
Institut du Bon Pasteur, France

Noel R. Bagwell, III, Esq, BA (Phil.)
Attorney, Tennessee (USA)

Dr Jaspreet Singh Boparai, MA (Oxon.), MA (Courtauld Institute), MA (Warburg Institute), PhD (Cantab.)
Former fellow, Harvard University Institute for Italian Renaissance Studies (Villa I Tatti)

Dr Joseph Burke, PhD
Former Chair of Economics at Ave Maria University (USA)

Rev. A. B. Carter, BSc (Hons.) ARCS DipPFS
Leader Marriage & Family Life Commission, Diocese of Portsmouth, England

Dr Michael Cawley, PhD
Psychologist, Former University Instructor
Pennsylvania, USA

Fr Gregory Charnock
Diocesan Priest, St Bartholomew Catholic Parish, Western Cape, South Africa

Gina Connolly, BA (Theol.), MTh, P. G. C. E
Ireland

John Connolly, BA, BA (Theol.), BSc, MA
Ireland

Tonny-Leonard Farauanu, STM, STL
Cluj-Napoca, Romania

Fr Ian Farrell
Parish priest, St Joseph's, Salford, UK

Richard Fitzgibbons, MD
Psychiatrist, served as a consultant to the Congregation for Clergy at the Vatican and as adjunct professor at the Pontifical John Paul II Institute for Studies on Marriage and Family at Catholic University of America

Dr Marie I. George, PhD
Professor of Philosophy at St. John's University, New York (USA)

Dr Luca Gili, PhD (Leuven)
Assistant Professor of Philosophy, Université du Québec à Montréal, Canada

Philip Gudgeon, MA Cantab. Modern & Medieval Languages, BA (London Philosophy and Theology), BA (Theol., Gregorian University, Rome)

Dr Colin Harte, PhD (Theol.)
England

Sarah Henderson, DCHS, BA, MA (Maryvale)

Dr Thomas Klibengajtis, PhD
Former Assistant Professor at the Chair of Systematic Theology, Institute of Catholic Theology at the Technical University of Dresden (Germany)

Leo Kronberger, MD, MSc
Graz, Austria

Dr Joseph F. McCabe, PhD
University of Ottawa (Canada)

Brian M. McCall, BA (Yale University), MA (University of London), JD (University of Pennsylvania)
Associate Dean for Academic Affairs; Orpha and Maurice Merrill Professor in Law, University of Oklahoma (USA)

Marilyn Meyer, MA Economics, George Washington University; MA Semitics, The Catholic University of America
Assisi, Italy

Fr Nicholas Milich
Watsonville, CA, Diocese of Monterey, California (USA)

Michael More, OCDS, MA (Theol.)

Dr Jacopo Parravicini, PhD
Physicist at University of Milano-Bicocca, Milano (Italy)

Deacon Joe Pasquella
Diocese of Buffalo, NY

Dr Robert L. Phillips, DPhil (Oxon.)
Professor em. of Philosophy, University of Connecticut (USA)

Dr Thomas Pink
Professor of Philosophy at King's College, London

Fr Paolo O. Pirlo
Manila, Philippines

Kim David Poletto, JD, MTS (Madonna University)
Civil Attorney and Advocate for the Archdiocese of Denver (USA)

Lance L. Ravella, AB (Phil. University of California), MA (Phil. San Francisco State University)

John Reid, BCL, DipEurL, KCHS

Fr Michael E. Rodríguez, BA (Phil.), STB (Theol.)
Priest of the Diocese of El Paso, Texas (USA)

John Schmude, JD
Presiding Judge, 247th Texas State District Court, Harris County Civil Justice Center

Dr Carl Winsløw, PhD in Mathematical Sciences, 1994 (U. of Tokyo, Japan)
Full professor at the Faculty of Science, University of Copenhagen, Copenhagen, Denmark

ON 5TH OCTOBER 2017

Dr Peter Adamic, PhD, P. Stat.
Associate Professor, Department of Mathematics & Computer Science, Laurentian University, Ontario (Canada)

Fr Kenneth Allen
Pastor at St. Jane de Chantal Parish, Archdiocese of New Orleans, Abita Springs, Louisiana (USA)

Martin Blackshaw
Catholic writer and former *Remnant* columnist

Henry von Blumenthal, MA (Theol.) Oxon.
Knight of Honour and Devotion, Order of Malta

Prof. Mario Bombaci
Professor of Philosophy and Bioethics

Fr J. Alejandro Díaz
Parish priest of Santa Ana, La Plata, Argentina; Auditor of the Platense Ecclesistical Tribunal; Exorcist of the Archidiocese

Fr Francisco José Suárez Fernández
Diocesan Priest, Valencia (Spain)

Dr med. Leonardo Lopes, MA, PhD
University of São Paulo, Brazil

Peter R. Mackin, BEd (Hons), PGCPS
United Kingdom

Patricia McKeever, BEd, MTh
Editor, *Catholic Truth* (Scotland)

Prof. Dominique Millet
University Professor, Sorbonne-Paris

Prof. Giorgio Nicolini
Professor, writer, Director of Tele Maria

Dr Patrick M. Owens, PhD
Professor of Patristic literature, Church History, and Classics at Accademia Vivarium Novum, Calvin College, Frascati (Rome); former professor at Wyoming Catholic College (WY, USA)

Giovanni Radhitio Putra Sadewo, MEd
Department of Psychology and Counselling
School of Psychology and Public Health, PhD Candidate in Cross-Cultural Psychology, La Trobe University Victoria, Australia

Dr Matt Salyer, PhD
Assistant Professor of English, Department of English and Philosophy, USA

Eric Sammons, MA (Theol.)

Dr Brody Smith, PhD (U. of California), OCDS

Dr Scott M. Sullivan, PhD
President of The Aquinas School of Theology and Philosophy (Texas, USA)

Suor Maria Veronica della Passione
Hermit of Saint Francis, Italy

Part II: Letters and Statements to the Pope or the Bishops

ON 9TH OCTOBER 2017

Prof. Emiliano Cuccia
Professor of Medieval Philosophy at Universidad Nacional de Cuyo, Mendoza, Argentina and Postdoctoral Fellow at CONICET (Argentina)

Fr Daniele Nicosia
Priest, hermit of the diocese of Agrigento (Italy)

ON 15TH OCTOBER 2017

Fr Paul Acton
Military Ordinariate of Canada Barrie, ON (Canada)

Fr Maksym Adam Kopiec, STD
Franciscan Priest, Professor of theology at Pontifical University Antonianum, Rome

Prof. Barbara R. Nicolosi Harrington, PhD
Associate Professor, Honors College, Azusa Pacific University, California (USA)

Fr Andrew Plishka, BA (Phil.) MA (Theol.)
Illinois (USA)

Edgardo Juan Cruz Ramos, CPMO
President *Una Voce*, Puerto Rico

Fr John Saward
Diocesan Priest, England

Robert Siscoe
Contributor to *The Remnant* and *Catholic Family News*, Texas (USA)

Fr William J Slattery, PhD, STL
Ireland

Prof. Anthony M. Wachs, PhD
Assistant Professor of Rhetoric, Communication Ethics, and the Catholic Intellectual Tradition, Department of Communication & Rhetorical Studies, Duquesne University of the Holy Spirit, Pittsburgh, PA (USA)

David Wachs, MD (Theol.), MA
Aberdeen in the Diocese of Sioux Falls SD (USA)

ON 23RD OCTOBER 2017

Prof. Christophe Buffin de Chosal
Historian and writer, Belgium

Prof. Juan F. Franck, PhD (Phil.) (IAP, Liechtenstein)
Buenos Aires, Argentina

Frà Ugo Ginex
Saint Mary's Hermitage

Fr John Rice
Parish priest, Shaftesbury UK

Fr Scott Settimo
Diocese of Juneau, Alaska (USA)

Fr Ritchie Vincent
Diocese of Madras-Mylapore, Chennai, India

Christopher Wendt, MA (Theol.)
Cadiz, Ohio (USA)

ELUCIDATION

In order to elucidate our *Correctio*, and to put forward a firmer defence against the spread of errors, we wish to draw attention to two general sources of error which appear to us to be fostering the heresies that we have listed. We speak, firstly, of that false understanding of divine revelation which generally receives the name of Modernism, and secondly, of the teachings of Martin Luther.

A. THE PROBLEM OF MODERNISM

The Catholic understanding of divine revelation is frequently denied by contemporary theologians, and this denial has led to widespread confusion among Catholics on the nature of divine revelation and faith. In order to prevent any misunderstanding that might arise from this confusion, and to justify our claim about the current propagation of heresies within the Church, we will describe the Catholic understanding of divine revelation and faith, which is presumed in this document.

This description is also necessary in order to respond to the passages in *Amoris Laetitia* where it is asserted that the teachings of Christ and of the magisterium of the Church should be followed. These passages include the following: "Unity of teaching and practice is certainly necessary in the Church" (*AL* 3). "Faithful to Christ's teaching we look to the reality of the family today in all its complexity" (*AL* 32). "The teaching of the encyclical *Humanae Vitae* and the Apostolic Exhortation *Familiaris Consortio* ought to be taken up anew" (*AL* 222). "The teaching of the Master (cf. Mt 22:30) and Saint Paul (cf. 1 Cor 7:29–31) on marriage is set—and not by chance—in the context of the ultimate and definitive dimension of our human existence. We urgently need to rediscover the richness of this teaching" (*AL* 325). These passages might be seen as ensuring that nothing in *Amoris Laetitia* serves to propagate errors contrary to Catholic teaching. A description of the true nature of adherence to Catholic teaching will clarify our assertion that *Amoris Laetitia* does indeed serve to propagate such errors.

We therefore ask Your Holiness to permit us to recall the following truths, which are taught by Holy Scripture, Sacred Tradition, the universal consensus of the Fathers, and the magisterium of the

Church, and which summarise Catholic teaching on faith, divine revelation, infallible magisterial teaching, and heresy:

1. The gospels of Matthew, Mark, Luke, and John, whose historical character the Church unhesitatingly asserts, faithfully hand on what Jesus Christ, while living among men, really did and taught for their eternal salvation until the day He was taken up into heaven.[1]

2. Jesus Christ is true God and true man. In consequence, all his teachings are the teachings of God Himself.[2]

3. All the propositions that are contained in the Catholic faith are truths communicated by God.[3]

---

1   Clement VI, *Super Quibusdam*, to the Catholicos of the Armenians, qu. 14, DH 1065: "We ask whether you have believed and do believe that the New and Old Testament, in all their books, which the authority of the Roman Church has handed down to us, contain undoubted truth in all things." Second Vatican Council, *Dei Verbum* 18–19: "What the Apostles preached in fulfilment of the commission of Christ, afterwards they themselves and apostolic men, under the inspiration of the divine Spirit, handed on to us in writing: the foundation of faith, namely, the fourfold Gospel, according to Matthew, Mark, Luke and John. Holy Mother Church has firmly and with absolute constancy held, and continues to hold, that the four Gospels just named, whose historical character the Church unhesitatingly asserts, faithfully hand on what Jesus Christ, while living among men, really did and taught for their eternal salvation until the day He was taken up into heaven."

See also: Lk. 1:1–4; Jn. 19:35; 2 Pet. 1:16; Pius IX, *Syllabus of Errors* 7; Leo XIII, *Providentissimus Deus, ASS* 26 (1893–94): 276–77; Pius X, *Lamentabili Sane* 13–17; *Praestantia Scripturae, ASS* 40 (1907): 724ff.

2   1 Jn. 5:10: "He that believeth in the Son of God has the testimony of God in himself. He that believeth not the Son, maketh him a liar." Council of Chalcedon, Definition, DH 301: "Following the holy fathers, we all with one voice teach the confession of one and the same Son, our Lord Jesus Christ: the same perfect in divinity and perfect in humanity, the same truly God and truly man, of a rational soul and a body; consubstantial with the Father as regards his divinity, and the same consubstantial with us as regards his humanity." Second Vatican Council, *Dei Verbum* 4: "After speaking in many and varied ways through the prophets, 'now at last in these days God has spoken to us in His Son.' For He sent His Son, the eternal Word, who enlightens all men, so that He might dwell among men and tell them of the innermost being of God. Jesus Christ, therefore, the Word made flesh, was sent as 'a man to men.' He 'speaks the words of God.'" See also: Mt. 7:29; Mt. 11:25–27; Mk. 1:22; Lk. 4:32; Jn. 1:1–14; Pius X, *Lamentabili Sane* 27.

3   First Vatican Council, *Dei Filius*, cap. 3: "Faith, which is the beginning of human salvation, the Catholic Church professes to be a supernatural

4. In believing these truths with an assent that is an act of the theological virtue of faith, we are believing the testimony of a speaker. The act of divine faith is a particular form of the general intellectual activity of believing a proposition because a speaker asserts it, and because the speaker is held to be honest and knowledgeable with respect to the assertion he is making. In an act of divine faith, God is believed when he says something, and he is believed because he is God and hence is knowledgeable and truthful.[4]

5. Belief in divine testimony differs from belief in the testimony of human beings who are not divine, because God is all-knowing

---

virtue, by means of which, with the grace of God inspiring and assisting us, we believe to be true what He has revealed." Pius X, *Lamentabili Sane* 22 (condemned proposition): "The dogmas that the Church holds out as revealed are not truths which have fallen from heaven." See also: 1 Thess. 2:13; Pius X, *Lamentabili Sane* 23–26; *Pascendi Dominici Gregis*, *ASS* 40 (1907): 611; Congregation for the Doctrine of the Faith, Declaration *Mysterium Ecclesiae*, DH 4538.

4 Jn. 3:11: "Amen, Amen, I say to thee, that we speak what we know and we testify what we have seen, and you receive not our testimony." Jn. 14:6: "I am the way, the truth, and the life." 1 Jn. 5:9–10: "If we receive the testimony of men, the testimony of God is greater. For this is the testimony of God, which is greater, because he hath testified of his Son. He that believeth in the Son of God hath the testimony of God in himself. He that believeth not the Son, maketh him a liar." First Vatican Council, *Dei Filius*, cap. 3, can. 2: "If anyone says that divine faith is not distinct from the natural knowledge of God and of moral truths; that, therefore, for divine faith it is not necessary that the revealed truth be believed on the authority of God who reveals it, let him be anathema." Pius X, *Lamentabili Sane*, 26 (condemned proposition): "The dogmas of the faith are to be held only according to their practical sense; that is to say, as preceptive norms of conduct and not as norms of believing." Piux X, *Oath Against the Errors of Modernism*, DH 3542: "I hold with certainty and I sincerely confess that faith is not a blind inclination of religion welling up from the depth of the subconscious under the impulse of the heart and the inclination of a morally conditioned will, but is the genuine assent of the intellect to a truth that is received from outside by hearing. In this assent, given on the authority of the all-truthful God, we hold to be true what has been said, attested to, and revealed, by the personal God, our creator and Lord."

See also: Jn. 8:46, 10:16; Rom. 11:33; Heb. 3:7, 5:12; Pius IX, *Qui Pluribus*, in *Acta* (Rome, 1854) 1/1, 6–13; *Syllabus of Errors* 4–5; Pius X, *Lamentabili Sane* 20; *Pascendi Dominici Gregis*, *ASS* 40 (1907): 604ff.; Congregation for the Doctrine of the Faith, Declaration *Dominus Iesus* on the Unicity and Salvific Universality of Jesus Christ and the Church, 7.

and perfectly good. In consequence, he can neither lie nor be deceived. It is thus impossible for divine testimony to be mistaken. Because the truths of the Catholic faith are communicated to us by God, the assent of faith that is given to them is most certain. A Catholic believer cannot have rational grounds for doubting or disbelieving any of these truths.[5]

6. Human reason by itself can establish the truth of the Catholic faith based on the publicly available evidence for the divine origin of the Catholic Church, but such reasoning cannot produce an act of faith. The theological virtue of faith and the act of faith can only be produced by divine grace. A person who has this virtue but then freely and knowingly chooses to disbelieve a truth of the Catholic faith sins mortally and loses eternal life.[6]

---

5 Num. 23:19: "God is not a man that he should lie." Pius IX, *Qui Pluribus*, DH 2778: "Who is or can be ignorant that all faith is to be given to God who speaks and that nothing is more suitable to reason itself than to acquiesce and firmly adhere to what it has determined to be revealed by God, who can neither deceive nor be deceived?" First Vatican Council, *Dei Filius*, cap. 3: "Faith, which is the beginning of human salvation, the Catholic Church professes to be a supernatural virtue, by means of which, with the grace of God inspiring and assisting us, we believe to be true what He has revealed, not because we perceive its intrinsic truth by the natural light of reason, but because of the authority of God himself, who makes the revelation and can neither deceive nor be deceived." First Vatican Council, *Dei Filius*, cap. 3, can. 6: "If anyone says that the condition of the faithful and those who have not yet attained to the only true faith is alike, so that Catholics may have a just cause for calling in doubt, by suspending their assent, the faith which they have already received from the teaching of the Church, until they have completed a scientific demonstration of the credibility and truth of their faith: let him be anathema." Second Vatican Council, *Lumen Gentium*, 12: "The entire body of the faithful, anointed as they are by the Holy One, cannot err in matters of belief." Congregation for the Doctrine of the Faith, Declaration *Mysterium Ecclesiae*, DH 4538: "All dogmas, since they are divinely revealed, must be believed with the same divine faith."

See also: Rev. 3:14; Innocent XI, Condemned propositions of the "Laxists," 20–21, DH 2120–21; Pius IX, *Syllabus of Errors* 15–18; Pius X, *Lamentabili Sane* 25.

6 Mk. 16:20: "They going forth preached everywhere, the Lord working withal, and confirming the word with signs that followed." 2 Cor. 3:5: "Not that we are sufficient to think anything of ourselves, as of ourselves: but our sufficiency is from God." 1 Pet. 3:15: "Sanctify the Lord, Christ, in your hearts, being ready always to satisfy everyone that asketh you a reason of that hope which is in you." Tit. 3:10–11: "A man that is a heretic, after

7. The truth of a proposition consists in its saying of what is, that it is; scholastically expressed, it consists in *adaequatio rei et intellectus*. Every truth is as such true, no matter by whom or when or in what circumstances it is considered. No truth can contradict any other truth.⁷

---

the first and second admonition, avoid: knowing that he, that is such an one, is subverted, and sinneth, being condemned by his own judgement." Rev. 22:19: "If any man shall take away from the words of the book of this prophecy, God shall take away his part out of the book of life and out of the holy city." First Vatican Council, *Dei Filius*, cap. 3: "In order that the submission of our faith should be in harmony with reason, it was God's will that there should be linked to the internal assistance of the Holy Spirit external indications of his revelation, that is to say divine acts, and first and foremost miracles and prophecies, which clearly demonstrating as they do the omnipotence and infinite knowledge of God, are most certain signs of revelation and are suited to the understanding of all people. Hence Moses and the prophets, and especially Christ our Lord himself, worked many manifest miracles and delivered prophecies. . . . So that we could fulfil our duty of embracing the true faith and of persevering unwaveringly in it, God, through his only-begotten Son, founded the Church, and endowed her with clear notes of his institution to the end that she might be recognised by all as the guardian and teacher of the revealed word. To the Catholic Church alone belong all those things, so many and so marvellous, which have been divinely ordained to make for the manifest credibility of the Christian faith." First Vatican Council, *Dei Filius*, cap. 3: "Although the assent of faith is by no means a blind movement of the mind, yet no one can accept the gospel preaching in the way that is necessary for achieving salvation without the inspiration and illumination of the Holy Spirit, who gives to all facility in accepting and believing the truth. And so faith in itself, even if it does not work through charity, is a gift of God, and its operation is a work belonging to the order of salvation."

See also: Second Council of Orange, can. 7; Innocent XI, Condemned propositions of the "Laxists," 20–21; Gregory XVI, Theses subscribed to by Louis-Eugène Bautain, 6, DH 2756; Pius IX, *Syllabus of Errors* 15–18; Pius X, *Pascendi Dominici Gregis*, ASS 40 (1907): 596–97; *Oath Against the Errors of Modernism*, DH 3539; Pius XII, *Humani Generis*, AAS 42 (1950): 571.

7   Second Vatican Council, *Gaudium et Spes* 15: "Man judges rightly that by his intellect he surpasses the material universe, for he shares in the light of the divine mind. . . . His intelligence is not confined to observable data alone, but can with genuine certitude attain to reality itself as knowable." John Paul II, *Fides et Ratio* 27: "Every truth, if it is authentic, presents itself as universal and absolute, even if it is not the whole truth. If something is true, then it must be true for all people and at all times."

8. The Catholic faith does not exhaust all the truth about God, because only the divine intellect can fully comprehend the divine being. Nonetheless every truth of the Catholic faith is entirely and completely true, in that the features of reality that such a truth describes are exactly as these truths present them to be. There is no difference between the content of the teachings of the faith and how things are.⁸

9. The divine speech that communicates the truths of the Catholic faith is expressed in human languages. The inspired Hebrew and Greek text of the Holy Scriptures is itself uttered by God in

---

John Paul II, *Fides et Ratio* 82: "This prompts a second requirement: that philosophy verify the human capacity to know the truth, to come to a knowledge which can reach objective truth by means of that *adaequatio rei et intellectus* to which the Scholastic doctors referred."

See also: Pius XII, *Humani Generis*, *AAS* 42 (1950): 562–63, 571–72, 574–75; John XXIII, *Ad Petri Cathedram*, *AAS* 1959 (51): 501–2; John Paul II, *Fides et Ratio* 4–10, 12–14, 49, 54, 83–85, 95–98.

8 1 Cor. 2:9–10: "As it is written: 'That eye hath not seen, nor ear heard, neither hath it entered into the heart of man, what things God hath prepared for them that love him.' But to us God hath revealed them, by his Spirit." 1 Cor. 2:12–13: "We have received not the spirit of this world, but the Spirit that is of God; that we may know the things that are given us from God: which things also we speak." Pius XII, *Humani Generis*, DH 3882–83: "Some hold that the mysteries of faith are never expressed by truly adequate concepts but only by approximate and ever changeable notions, in which the truth is to some extent expressed, but is necessarily distorted. Wherefore they do not consider it absurd, but altogether necessary, that theology should substitute new concepts in place of the old ones in keeping with the various philosophies which in the course of time it uses as its instruments, so that it should give human expression to divine truths in various ways which are even somewhat opposed, but still equivalent, as they say.... I t is evident from what We have already said, that such efforts not only lead to what they call dogmatic relativism, but that they actually contain it." Congregation for the Doctrine of the Faith, Declaration *Mysterium Ecclesiae* 5, DH 4540: "As for the meaning of dogmatic formulas, this remains ever true and constant in the Church, even when it comes to be expressed with greater clarity and to be more fully understood. The faithful therefore must shun the opinion, first, that dogmatic formulations, or some category of them, cannot signify the truth in a determinate way, but can only offer changeable approximations to it, which to a certain extent distort or alter it; and secondly, that these formulations only express the truth in an indeterminate way, and that one must continue to seek this truth by further approximations of this kind." See also: Pius X, *Lamentabili Sane*, 4.

all of its parts. It is not a purely human report or interpretation of divine revelation, and no part of its meaning is due solely to human causes. In believing the teaching of the Holy Scriptures we are believing God directly. We are not believing the statements made by God on the basis of believing the testimony of some other, non-divine person or persons.[9]

10. When the Catholic Church infallibly teaches that a proposition is a divinely revealed part of the Catholic faith and is to be believed with the assent of faith, Catholics who assent to this teaching are believing what God has communicated, and are believing it on account of His having said it.[10]

---

9   1 Thess. 2:13: "We give thanks to God without ceasing: because, that when you had received of us the word of the hearing of God, you received it not as the word of men, but (as it is indeed) the word of God." 1 Tim. 3:16: "All scripture, inspired of God, is profitable to teach." 2 Pet. 1:20–21: "No prophecy of scripture is made by private interpretation. For prophecy came not by the will of man at any time; but the holy men spoke, inspired by the Holy Ghost." Pius XII, *Divino Afflante Spiritu*, *AAS* 35 (1943): 299–300: "It is absolutely wrong and forbidden 'either to narrow inspiration to certain passages of Holy Scripture, or to admit that the sacred writer has erred,' since divine inspiration 'not only is essentially incompatible with error but excludes and rejects it as absolutely and necessarily as it is impossible that God Himself, the supreme Truth, can utter that which is not true. This is the ancient and constant faith of the Church.' This teaching, which Our Predecessor Leo XIII set forth with such solemnity, We also proclaim with Our authority." Second Vatican Council, *Dei Verbum* 11: "Holy Mother Church, relying on the belief of the Apostles, holds that the books of both the Old and New Testaments in their entirety, with all their parts, are sacred and canonical because, written under the inspiration of the Holy Spirit, they have God as their author and have been handed on as such to the Church herself. In composing the sacred books, God chose men, and while employed by Him they made use of their powers and abilities, so that with Him acting in them and through them, they, as true authors, consigned to writing all and only those things which He wanted."

See also: Jn. 10:16, 35; Heb. 3:7, 5:12; Leo XIII, *Providentissimus Deus*, DH 3291–92; Pius X, *Lamentabili Sane* 9–11; Pascendi Dominici Gregis, *ASS* 40 (1907): 612–13; Benedict XV, *Spiritus Paraclitus*, *AAS* 12 (1920), 393; Pius XII, *Humani Generis*, DH 3887.

10   1 Thess. 2:13: "We give thanks to God without ceasing: because, that when you had received of us the word of the hearing of God, you received it not as the word of men, but (as it is indeed) the word of God." First Vatican Council, *Dei Filius*, cap. 3: "Faith, which is the beginning of human salvation, the Catholic Church professes to be a supernatural

11. The languages in which divine revelation is expressed, and the cultures and histories that shaped these languages, do not constrain, distort, or add to the divine revelation that is expressed in them. No part or aspect of the Holy Scriptures or of the infallible teaching of the Church concerning the content of divine revelation is produced only by the languages and historical conditions in which they are expressed, but not by God's action in communicating truths. Hence, no part of the content of the teaching of the Church can be revised or rejected on the grounds that it is produced by historical circumstances rather than by divine revelation.[11]

---

virtue, by means of which, with the grace of God inspiring and assisting us, we believe to be true what He has revealed, not because we perceive its intrinsic truth by the natural light of reason, but because of the authority of God himself, who makes the revelation and can neither deceive nor be deceived.... Further, by divine and Catholic faith all those things are to be believed which are contained in the word of God as found in scripture and tradition, and which are proposed by the Church as to be believed as divinely revealed, whether by her solemn judgment or in her ordinary and universal magisterium." See also: Jn. 10:16; Heb. 3:7, 5:12; Pius XII, *Mystici Corporis Christi*, *AAS* 35 (1943): 216.

11   Pius XII, *Humani Generis*, DH 3883: "The Church cannot be tied to any and every passing philosophical system. Nevertheless, those notions and terms which have been developed though common effort by Catholic teachers over the course of the centuries to bring about some understanding of dogma are certainly not based on any such weak foundation. They are based on principles and notions deduced from a true knowledge of created things. In the process of deduction, this knowledge, like a star, gave enlightenment to the human mind through the Church. Hence it is not surprising that some of these notions have not only been employed by the Ecumenical Councils, but even sanctioned by them, so that it is wicked to depart from them." Congregation for the Doctrine of the Faith, Declaration *Mysterium Ecclesiae* 5, DH 4540: "As for the meaning of dogmatic formulas, this remains ever true and constant in the Church, even when it comes to be expressed with greater clarity and to be more fully understood. The faithful therefore must shun the opinion, first, that dogmatic formulations, or some category of them, cannot signify the truth in a determinate way, but can only offer changeable approximations to it, which to a certain extent distort or alter it; and secondly, that these formulations only express the truth in an indeterminate way, and that one must continue to seek this truth by further approximations of this kind." John Paul II, *Fides et Ratio* 87: "One must remember that even if the statement of a truth is limited to some extent by times and by forms of culture, the truth or the error with which it deals can nevertheless be recognised and evaluated as such, however great the distance of space or

12. The magisterial teaching of the Church after the death of the last apostle must be understood and believed as a single whole. It is not divided into a past magisterium and a contemporary or living magisterium that can ignore earlier magisterial teaching or revise it at will.[12]

13. The pope, who has the supreme authority in the Church, is not himself exempt from the authority of the Church, in accordance with divine and ecclesiastical law. He is bound to accept and uphold the definitive teaching of his predecessors in the papal office.[13]

---

time." John Paul II, *Fides et Ratio* 95: "The word of God is not addressed to any one people or to any one period of history. Similarly, dogmatic statements, while reflecting at times the culture of the period in which they were defined, formulate an unchanging and ultimate truth." Congregation for the Doctrine of the Faith, Declaration *Dominus Iesus* 6: "The truth about God is not abolished or reduced because it is spoken in human language; rather, it is unique, full, and complete, because he who speaks and acts is the Incarnate Son of God."

See also: Jn. 10:35; 2 Tim. 3:16; 2 Pet. 1:20–21; Rev. 22:18–19; Leo XIII, *Providentissimus Deus*, DH 3288; Pius X, *Lamentabili Sane* 4; John Paul II, *Fides et Ratio* 84.

12 Gal. 1:9: "If anyone preach to you a gospel, besides that which you have received, let him be anathema." First Vatican Council, *Dei Filius*, cap. 4, can. 3: "If anyone says that it is possible that at some time, with the progress of knowledge, a sense should be assigned to the dogmas propounded by the Church which is different from that which the Church has understood and does understand: let him be anathema." Pius X, *Oath Against the Errors of Modernism*, DH 3541: "I sincerely hold that the doctrine of faith was handed down to us from the apostles through the orthodox Fathers with the same sense and always with the same meaning. Therefore, I entirely reject the heretical fiction that dogmas evolve and change from one meaning to another, different from the meaning which the Church held previously. I also condemn every error that substitutes for the divine deposit which has been given to the spouse of Christ to be carefully guarded by her, some philosophical invention or product of human reflection, gradually formed by human effort and due to be perfected in the future by unlimited progress."

See also: 1 Tim. 6:20; 2 Tim. 1:13–14; Heb. 13:7–9; Jude 3; Pius IX, *Ineffabilis Deus*, DH 2802; Pius X, *Lamentabili Sane* 21, 54, 50, 60, 62; *Pascendi Dominici Gregis*, ASS 40 (1907): 616ff.; Pius XII, *Humani Generis*, DH 3886; Congregation for the Doctrine of the Faith, Declaration *Mysterium Ecclesiae*, DH 4540.

13 First Vatican Council, *Pastor Aeternus*, cap. 4: "The Holy Spirit was promised to the successors of Peter not so that they might, by his revelation, make known some new doctrine, but that, by his assistance, they

14. A heretical proposition is a proposition that contradicts a divinely revealed truth that is included in the Catholic faith.[14]

15. The sin of heresy is committed by a person who possesses the theological virtue of faith, but then freely and knowingly chooses to disbelieve or doubt a truth of the Catholic faith. Such a person sins mortally and loses eternal life. The judgement of the Church upon the personal sin of heresy is exercised only by a priest in the sacrament of penance.[15]

16. The canonical crime of heresy is committed when a Catholic a) publicly doubts or denies one or more truths of the Catholic faith, or publicly refuses to give assent to one or more truths of the Catholic faith, but does not doubt or deny all these truths or deny the existence of Christian revelation, and b) is pertinacious in this denial. Pertinacity consists in the person in question continuing to publicly doubt or deny one or more truths of the Catholic faith after having been warned by competent ecclesiastical authority that his doubt or denial is a rejection of a truth of the faith, and that this doubt or denial must be renounced and the

---

might religiously guard and faithfully expound the revelation or deposit of faith transmitted by the apostles.... This gift of truth and never-failing faith was therefore divinely conferred on Peter and his successors in this see so that they might discharge their exalted office for the salvation of all, and so that the whole flock of Christ might be kept away by them from the poisonous food of error and be nourished with the sustenance of heavenly doctrine." Second Vatican Council, *Dei Verbum* 10: "The task of authentically interpreting the word of God, whether written or handed on, has been entrusted exclusively to the living magisterium of the Church, whose authority is exercised in the name of Jesus Christ. This magisterium is not above the word of God, but serves it. It teaches only what has been handed on, listening to it devoutly, guarding it scrupulously and explaining it faithfully in accord with a divine commission and with the help of the Holy Spirit. It draws from this one deposit of faith everything which it presents for belief as divinely revealed."

See also: Mt. 16:23; Gratian, *Decretum*, Pt. 1, dist. 40, ch. 6; Innocent III, second sermon "On the consecration of the supreme pontiff," ML, 656; fourth sermon "On the consecration of the supreme pontiff," ML 670; Pius IX, Letter *Mirabilis Illa Constantia* to the bishops of Germany, DH 3117 (cf. DH 3114).

14 Cf. 1983 *Code of Canon Law*, 751; *Code of Canons of Oriental Churches*, 1436.

15 Cf. Mk. 16:16; Jn. 3:18; Jn. 20:23; Rom. 14:4; Gal. 1:9; 1 Tim. 1:18–20; Jude 3–6; Council of Florence, *Cantate Domino*, DH 1351; Council of Trent, Sess. 14, can. 9.

truth in question must be publicly affirmed as divinely revealed by the person being warned.[16]

(The above descriptions of the personal sin of heresy and of the canonical crime of heresy are given solely in order to be able to exclude them from the subject of our protest. We are only concerned with heretical propositions propagated by the words, deeds, and omissions of Your Holiness. We do not have the competence or the intention to address the canonical issue of heresy.)

B. THE INFLUENCE OF MARTIN LUTHER

In the second place, we feel compelled by conscience to advert to Your Holiness's unprecedented sympathy for Martin Luther, and to the affinity between Luther's ideas on law, justification,

---

16 Cf. Mt. 18:17; Tit. 3:10–11; Pius X, *Lamentabili Sane* 7; *Code of Canon Law*, 751, 1364; *Code of Canons of Oriental Churches*, 1436. [Editors' note: some theologians and canonists assert that pertinacity can be judged to exist in the absence of a formal ecclesiastical warning, when it is clear from publicly available evidence that the person persistently doubting or denying a truth of the faith must know that the truth he is denying is taught by the Church as being divinely revealed and requiring the assent of faith. See, e.g., De Lugo, *De virtute fidei divina* (Lyon, 1546), disp. XX, sect. 5, 157, p. 569: "Si enim aliunde constare posset ex ipsa doctrinae notorietate et qualitate personae, aliisque circumstantia, non potuisse reum ignorare oppositione illius doctrinae cum Ecclesia, eo ipso iudicabitur haereticus.... Ratio enim est clara, quia monitio externa solum deservire potest, ut errans advertat ad oppositionem sui erroris cum doctrina Ecclesiae. Si ergo id totum ipse multo melius scit ex libris, et definitionibus conciliorum, quam ex monitoris verbuis scire possit, non est cur necessaria sit alia monitio, ut pertinax sit contra Ecclesiam" (If it can be ascertained from the notoriety of the doctrine denied, the characteristics of the person denying it, and other circumstances, that he could not be unaware that the thesis he is advancing is contrary to the doctrine of the Church, then from these facts alone he will be considered a heretic.... The reason for this is clear; an external admonition can only serve to make the person who is admonished aware of the opposition between his view and that of the Church. If he knows much better about this opposition through books and the definitions of councils than he could through the words of his admoniser, there is no reason to require another admonition for him to be pertinacious in his opposition to the Church). De Lugo asserts that this is the common opinion of theologians, and that the requirement for such an admonition is not always accepted by the Holy Office. Later canonists such as Vermeersch and Noldin agree with him on this point. The assertion of the *correctio* thus seems to be too restrictive here.]

and marriage, and those taught or favoured by Your Holiness in *Amoris Laetitia* and elsewhere.[17] This is necessary in order that our protest against the seven heretical propositions listed in this document may be complete; we wish to show, albeit in summary form, that these are not unrelated errors, but rather form part of a heretical system. Catholics need to be warned not only against these seven errors, but also against this heretical system as such, not least by reason of Your Holiness's praise of the man who originated it.

Thus, in a press conference on June 26, 2016, Your Holiness stated:

> I think that the intentions of Martin Luther were not mistaken. He was a reformer. Perhaps some methods were not correct. But in that time, if we read the story of the pastor, a German Lutheran who then converted when he saw reality—he became Catholic—in that time, the Church was not exactly a model to imitate. There was corruption in the Church, there was worldliness, attachment to money, to power... and this he protested. Then he was intelligent and took some steps forward justifying, and because he did this [sic]. And today Lutherans and Catholics, Protestants, all of us agree on the doctrine of justification. On this point, which is very important, he did not err.[18]

In a homily in the Lutheran Cathedral in Lund, Sweden, on October 31, 2016, Your Holiness stated:

> As Catholics and Lutherans, we have undertaken a common journey of reconciliation. Now, in the context of the commemoration of the Reformation of 1517, we have a new opportunity to accept a common path, one that has taken shape over the past fifty years in the ecumenical dialogue between the Lutheran World Federation and the Catholic Church. Nor can we be resigned to the division and distance that our separation has created

---

17 The signatories do not intend in this section principally to describe the thought of Martin Luther, a subject concerning which all of them do not have the same expertise, but rather to describe certain false notions of marriage, justification, and law which appear to them to have inspired *Amoris Laetitia*.

18 http://www.catholicnewsagency.com/news/full-text-pope-francis-inflight-press-conference-from-armenia-45222/.

between us. We have the opportunity to mend a critical moment of our history by moving beyond the controversies and disagreements that have often prevented us from understanding one another.

Jesus tells us that the Father is the "vinedresser" (cf. [Jn 15] v. 1) who tends and prunes the vine in order to make it bear more fruit (cf. v. 2). The Father is constantly concerned for our relationship with Jesus, to see if we are truly one with him (cf. v. 4). He watches over us, and his gaze of love inspires us to purify our past and to work in the present to bring about the future of unity that he so greatly desires.

We too must look with love and honesty at our past, recognizing error and seeking forgiveness, for God alone is our judge. We ought to recognize with the same honesty and love that our division distanced us from the primordial intuition of God's people, who naturally yearn to be one, and that it was perpetuated historically by the powerful of this world rather than the faithful people, which always and everywhere needs to be guided surely and lovingly by its Good Shepherd. Certainly, there was a sincere will on the part of both sides to profess and uphold the true faith, but at the same time we realize that we closed in on ourselves out of fear or bias with regard to the faith which others profess with a different accent and language. [...]

The spiritual experience of Martin Luther challenges us to remember that apart from God we can do nothing. "How can I get a propitious God?" This is the question that haunted Luther. In effect, the question of a just relationship with God is the decisive question for our lives. As we know, Luther encountered that propitious God in the Good News of Jesus, incarnate, dead and risen. With the concept "by grace alone," he reminds us that God always takes the initiative, prior to any human response, even as he seeks to awaken that response. The doctrine of justification thus expresses the essence of human existence before God.[19]

---

19   http://w2.vatican.va/content/francesco/en/homilies/2016/documents/papa-francesco_20161031_omelia-svezia-lund.pdf.

In addition to stating that Martin Luther was correct about justification, and in close accordance with this view, Your Holiness has declared more than once that our sins are the place where we encounter Christ (as in your homilies of September 4 and September 18, 2014), justifying this view with St. Paul, who in fact glories in his own "infirmities" (*astheneìais*, cf. 2 Cor. 12:5, 9) and not in his sins, so that the power of Christ may dwell in him.[20] In an address to members of Communion and Liberation on March 7, 2015, Your Holiness said:

> The privileged place of encounter is the caress of Jesus' mercy regarding my sin. This is why you may have heard me say, several times, that the place for this, the privileged place of the encounter with Jesus Christ is my sin.[21]

Furthermore, in addition to other propositions of *Amoris Laetitia* which have been listed in the letter sent to all the cardinals and Eastern Catholic patriarchs, and which have been therein qualified as heretical, erroneous, or ambiguous, we read also this:

> We should not however confuse different levels: there is no need to lay upon two limited persons the tremendous burden of having to reproduce perfectly the union existing between Christ and his Church, for marriage as a sign entails "a dynamic process..., one which advances gradually with the progressive integration of the gifts of God." (*AL* 122)

While it is true that the sacramental sign of matrimony entails a dynamic process toward holiness, it is beyond doubt that by the sacramental sign the union of Christ with his Church is perfectly reproduced by grace in the married couple. It is not a question of imposing a tremendous burden on two limited persons, but rather of acknowledging the work of the sacrament and of grace (*res et sacramentum*).

Surprisingly we notice here, as in several other parts of this Apostolic Exhortation, a close relationship with Luther's disparagement of

---

[20] http://en.radiovaticana.va/news/2014/09/04/pope_recognize_your _sins_and_be_transformed_by_christ/1105890; http://en.radiovaticana.va /news/2014/09/18/pope_at_santa_marta_the_courage_to_admit_we_are _sinners/1106766.

[21] http://www.vatican.va/content/francesco/en/speeches/2015/march/ documents/papa-francesco_20150307_comunione-liberazione.html.

marriage. For the German revolutionary, the Catholic conception of a sacrament as effective *ex opere operato*, in an allegedly "mechanical" way, is unacceptable. Although he maintains the distinction of *signum et res*, after 1520, with *The Babylonian Captivity of the Church*, he no longer applies it to marriage. Luther denies that marriage has any reference to sacramentality, on the grounds that we nowhere read in the Bible that the man who marries a woman receives a grace of God, and that neither do we read anywhere that marriage was instituted by God to be a sign of anything. He claimed that marriage is a mere symbol, adding that although it can represent the union of Christ with the Church, such figures and allegories are not sacraments in the sense we use the term (cf. *Luther's Works* [LW] 36:92). For this reason, marriage — whose fundamental aim is to conceive children and to raise them up in the ways of God (cf. LW 44:11–12) — according to Luther belongs to the order of creation and not to that of salvation (cf. LW 45:18); it is given only in order to quench the fire of concupiscence, and as a bulwark against sin (cf. LW 3, Gen. 16:4).

Moreover, beginning with his personal vision about how human nature is corrupted by sin, Luther is conscious that man is not always anxious to respect God's law. Therefore, he is convinced that there is a double manner by which God rules over mankind, to which corresponds a double moral vision about marriage and divorce. Thus divorce is generally admitted by Luther in the case of adultery, but only for non-spiritual people.

His reasoning is that there are two forms of divine government in this world: the spiritual and the temporal. By his spiritual government, the Holy Spirit leads Christians and righteous people under the Gospel of Christ; by his temporal government, God restrains non-Christians and the wicked in order to maintain an outward peace (cf. LW 45:91). Two also are the laws regulating moral life: one is spiritual, for those living under the influence of the Holy Spirit, the other is temporal or worldly, for those who cannot comply with the spiritual one (cf. LW 45:88–93). This double moral vision is applied by Luther to adultery in reference to Mt 5:32: hence, Christians must not divorce even in the case of adultery (the spiritual law); but divorce exists and was granted by Moses because of sin (the worldly law). The permission to divorce is thus seen as a limit put by God upon carnal people to restrain their misbehaviour and prevent them from doing worse on account of their wickedness (cf. LW 45:31).

How can we not see here a close similarity with what has been suggested by Your Holiness in *Amoris Laetitia*? On the one hand marriage is supposedly safeguarded as a sacrament, while on the other hand divorce and remarriage are regarded "mercifully" as a status quo to be—although only "pastorally"—integrated into the life of the Church, thus openly contradicting the word of our Lord. Luther was led to an acceptance of remarriage by his identification of concupiscence with sin; for he recognized marriage as a remedy for concupiscence. In reality, concupiscence is not as such sinful, just as remarriage when one has a living spouse is not a status, but a privation of truth.

However, Luther's self-contradiction, generated by his twofold view of marriage—itself seen as something that pertains properly to the Law and not to the Gospel—is then supposedly overcome by the precedence of faith: a "cordial trust" in order to adhere subjectively to God. He claims that faith justifies man insofar as the punishing justice withdraws into mercy and is changed permanently into forgiving love. This is made possible out of a "joyful bargain" (*fröhlicher Wechseln*) by which the sinner can say to Christ: "You are my righteousness just as I am your sin" (LW 48:12; cf. also 31:351; 25:188). By this "happy exchange," Christ becomes the only sinner and we are justified through the acceptance of the Word in faith.

In Your pilgrimage to Fatima for the beginning of this providential centenary, Your Holiness clearly alluded to this Lutheran view about faith and justification, stating on May 12, 2017:

> Great injustice is done to God's grace whenever we say that sins are punished by his judgment, without first saying—as the Gospel clearly does—that they are forgiven by his mercy! Mercy has to be put before judgment and, in any case, God's judgment will always be rendered in the light of his mercy. Obviously, God's mercy does not deny justice, for Jesus took upon himself the consequences of our sin, together with its due punishment. He did not deny sin, but redeemed it on the cross. Hence, in the faith that unites us to the cross of Christ, we are freed of our sins; we put aside all fear and dread, as unbefitting those who are loved (cf. 1 Jn. 4:18).[22]

---

22 http://www.vatican.va/content/francesco/en/speeches/2017/may/documents/papa-francesco_20170512_benedizione-candele-fatima.html.

The gospel does not teach that all sins will in fact be forgiven, nor that Christ alone experienced the "judgement" or justice of God, leaving only mercy for the rest of mankind. While there is a "vicarious suffering" of our Lord in order to expiate our sins, there is not a "vicarious punishment," for Christ was "made sin for us" (cf. 2 Cor. 5:21) and not a sinner. Out of divine love, and not as the object of God's wrath, Christ offered the supreme sacrifice of salvation to reconcile us with God, taking upon himself only the consequences of our sins (cf. Gal. 3:13). Hence, so that we may be justified and saved, it is not sufficient to have faith that our sins have been removed by a supposed vicarious punishment; our justification lies in a conformity to our Saviour achieved by that faith which works through charity (cf. Gal. 5:6).

Most Holy Father, permit us also to express our wonderment and sorrow at two events occurring in the heart of the Church, which likewise suggest the favour in which the German heresiarch is held under Your pontificate. On January 15, 2016, a group of Finnish Lutherans were granted Holy Communion in the course of a celebration of Holy Mass that took place at St. Peter's basilica. On October 13, 2016, Your Holiness presided over a meeting of Catholics and Lutherans in the Vatican, addressing them from a stage on which a statue of Martin Luther was erected.

SUMMARY OF THE *CORRECTIO FILIALIS*

A twenty-five-page letter signed by forty Catholic clergy and lay scholars was delivered to Pope Francis on August 11. Since no answer was received from the Holy Father, it is being made public today, September 24, the Feast of Our Lady of Ransom and of Our Lady of Walsingham. The letter, which is open to new signatories, now[23] has the names of sixty-two clergy and lay scholars from twenty countries, who also represent others lacking the necessary freedom of speech. It has a Latin title: *Correctio filialis de haeresibus propagatis* ("A filial correction concerning the propagation of heresies"). It states that the pope has, by his Apostolic Exhortation

---

23 The original letter of July 16 was signed by forty-five. By the time it was released to the public on September 24, it had gained an additional seventeen. It would eventually garner two hundred and fifty signatures.

Amoris Laetitia, and by other related words, deeds, and omissions, effectively upheld seven heretical positions about marriage, the moral life, and the reception of the sacraments, and has caused these heretical opinions to spread in the Catholic Church. These seven heresies are expressed by the signatories in Latin, the official language of the Church.

This letter of correction has three main parts. In the first part, the signatories explain why, as believing and practising Catholics, they have the right and duty to issue such a correction to the supreme pontiff. Church law itself requires that competent persons not remain silent when the pastors of the Church are misleading the flock. This involves no conflict with the Catholic dogma of papal infallibility, since the Church teaches that a pope must meet strict criteria before his utterances can be considered infallible. Pope Francis has not met these criteria. He has not declared these heretical positions to be definitive teachings of the Church, or stated that Catholics must believe them with the assent of faith. The Church teaches no pope can claim that God has revealed some new truth to him, which it would be obligatory for Catholics to believe.

The second part of the letter is the essential one, since it contains the "Correction" properly speaking. It lists the passages of *Amoris Laetitia* in which heretical positions are insinuated or encouraged, and then it lists words, deeds, and omissions of Pope Francis which make it clear beyond reasonable doubt that he wishes Catholics to interpret these passages in a way that is, in fact, heretical. In particular, the pope has directly or indirectly countenanced the beliefs that obedience to God's Law can be impossible or undesirable, and that the Church should sometimes accept adultery as compatible with being a practising Catholic.

The final part, called "Elucidation," discusses two causes of this unique crisis. One cause is Modernism. Theologically speaking, Modernism is the belief that God has not delivered definite truths to the Church, which she must continue to teach in exactly the same sense until the end of time. Modernists hold that God communicates to mankind only experiences, which human beings can reflect on, so as to make various statements about God, life, and religion; but such statements are only provisional, never fixed dogmas. Modernism was condemned by Pope St. Pius X at the start of the twentieth century, but it revived in the middle of the century. The great and continuing confusion caused in the Catholic Church by Modernism obliges the signatories to describe the true meaning of "faith," "heresy," "revelation," and "magisterium."

A second cause of the crisis is the apparent influence of the ideas of Martin Luther on Pope Francis. The letter shows how Luther, the founder of Protestantism, had ideas on marriage, divorce, forgiveness, and divine law which correspond to those which the pope has promoted by word, deed, and omission. It also notes the explicit and unprecedented praise given by Pope Francis to the German heresiarch.

The signatories do not venture to judge the degree of awareness with which Pope Francis has propagated the seven heresies which they list. But they respectfully insist that he condemn these heresies, which he has directly or indirectly upheld.

The signatories profess their loyalty to the holy Roman Church, assure the pope of their prayers, and ask for his apostolic blessing.

PRESS RELEASE AND HISTORICAL PRECEDENT

In an epoch-making act, Catholic clergy and lay scholars from around the world have issued what they are calling a "Filial Correction" to Pope Francis. No similar action has been taken since the Middle Ages. Then, Pope John XXII was admonished in 1333 for errors which he later recanted on his deathbed. In the present case, the spiritual sons and daughters of Pope Francis accuse him of propagating heresies contrary to the Catholic faith. Their letter, delivered to the Roman Pontiff at his Santa Marta residence on August 11, 2017, and now made fully public, states that the Roman Pontiff has supported heretical positions about marriage, the moral life, and the Eucharist.

The letter of correction has three main parts, as follows:

In the first part, the sixty-two signatories explain why, as believing and practicing Catholics, they have the right and duty to issue such a correction to the pope. This does not contradict the Catholic doctrine of papal infallibility, because Pope Francis has not promulgated heretical opinions as dogmatic teachings of the Church. While professing their obedience to his legitimate commands and teachings, they maintain that Francis has upheld and propagated heretical opinions by various direct or indirect means.

The second part of the letter is the essential one. It contains the "Correction" properly speaking, written in Latin, the official language of the Church. It lists the passages of *Amoris Laetitia*, Pope Francis's document on marriage and family life, in which he insinuates or encourages heretical positions. Because some commentators have argued that these texts can be interpreted in an orthodox way, the Correction goes on to list Pope Francis's other words, deeds, and omissions which make it clear beyond reasonable doubt that he wishes Catholics to interpret these passages in a way that is, in fact, heretical. In particular, the pope has advocated the beliefs that obedience to God's moral law can be impossible or undesirable, and that Catholics should sometimes accept adultery as compatible with being a follower of Christ.

The final part, called "Elucidation," discusses two causes of this unique crisis. One cause is Modernism. Theologically speaking, Modernism is the belief that God has not delivered definite truths to the Church, which she must continue to teach in exactly the same sense until the end of time. Modernism therefore focuses on experiences and holds that doctrines about God, faith, and morals are always provisional and subject to revision. Significantly, Pope St. Pius X condemned Modernism at the start of the twentieth century. A second cause of the crisis is the influence of the ideas of Martin Luther on Pope Francis. The letter shows how Luther had ideas on marriage, divorce, forgiveness, and divine law which correspond to those which the pope has promoted. It also notes the explicit and unprecedented praise given by Pope Francis to the German heresiarch.

The signatories make no judgment about Pope Francis's culpability in propagating the seven heresies that they list, since it is not their task to judge whether the sin of heresy has been committed (the sin of heresy, that is, formal heresy, is committed when a person departs from the faith by doubting or denying some revealed truth with a full choice of the will). It should however be noted that others who have spoken up in defense of the Catholic faith have been subject to reprisals. Thus, the signatories speak for a large number of clergy and lay faithful who lack freedom of speech.

It will be noticed that Bishop Bernard Fellay has signed the correction. His signature came after the document was delivered to the pope, but he now expresses the agreement of the Society of St. Pius X with its contents. Pope Francis has recently extended a welcoming hand to the SSPX in order to integrate them legally into the Catholic Church.

The signatories respectfully insist that Pope Francis condemn the heresies that he has directly or indirectly upheld, and that he teach the truth of the Catholic faith in its integrity.

C

Open Letter to the Bishops of the Catholic Church

SUMMARY

The *Open Letter to the Bishops of the Catholic Church* is the third stage in a process that began in the summer of 2016. At that time, an ad hoc group of Catholic clergy and scholars wrote a private letter to all the cardinals and Eastern Catholic patriarchs, pointing out heresies and other serious errors that appeared to be contained in or favoured by Pope Francis's Apostolic Exhortation *Amoris Laetitia*. The following year, after Pope Francis had continued by word, deed, and omission to propagate many of these same heresies, a "Filial Correction" was addressed to the pope by many of the same people, as well as by other clergy and scholars. This second letter was made public in September 2017, and a petition in support of it was signed by some 14,000 people. The authors of that letter stated however that they did not seek to judge whether Pope Francis was aware that he was causing heresy to spread.

The present *Open Letter to the Bishops of the Catholic Church* goes a stage further in claiming that Pope Francis is guilty of the crime of heresy. This crime is committed when a Catholic knowingly and persistently denies something which he knows that the Church teaches to be revealed by God. Taken together, the words and actions of Pope Francis amount to a comprehensive rejection of Catholic teaching on marriage and sexual activity, on the moral law, and on grace and the forgiveness of sins.

The Open Letter also indicates the link between this rejection of Catholic teaching and the favour shown by Pope Francis to bishops and other clergy who have either been guilty of sexual sins and crimes, such as former Cardinal Theodore McCarrick, or who have protected clergy guilty of sexual sins and crimes, such as the late Cardinal Godfried Danneels. This protection and promotion of clerics who reject Catholic teaching on marriage, sexual activity, and on the moral law in general, even when these clerics personally violate the moral and civil law in horrendous ways, is consistent enough to be considered a policy on the part of Pope Francis. At the least it is evidence of disbelief in the truth of Catholic teaching on these subjects. It also indicates a strategy to impose rejection of these teachings on the Church, by naming to influential posts individuals whose personal lives are based on violation of these truths.

The authors consider that a heretical papacy may not be tolerated or dissimulated to avoid a worse evil. It strikes at the basic good of the Church and must be corrected. For this reason, the study concludes by describing the traditional theological and legal principles that apply to the present situation. The authors respectfully request the bishops of the Church to investigate the accusations contained in the letter, so that if they judge them to be well founded, they may free the Church from her present distress, in accordance with the hallowed adage, "Salus animarum suprema lex" ("the salvation of souls is the highest law"). They can do this by admonishing Pope Francis to reject these heresies, and if he should persistently refuse, by declaring that he has freely deprived himself of the papacy.

While this Open Letter is an unusual, even historic, document, the Church's own laws say that "Christ's faithful have the right, and, indeed, sometimes the duty, according to their knowledge, competence, and dignity, to manifest to the sacred pastors their judgement about those things which pertain to the good of the Church."[1] While Catholics hold that a pope speaks infallibly in certain strictly defined conditions, the Church does not say that he cannot fall into heresy outside these conditions.

The signatories to the Open Letter include not only specialists in theology and philosophy, but also academics and scholars from other fields. This fits well with the central claim of the Open Letter, that Pope Francis's rejection of revealed truths is evident to any well-instructed Catholic who is willing to examine the evidence. The signatures of Fr Aidan Nichols, O. P., and of Professor John Rist will be noted. Fr Nichols is one of the best-known theologians in the English-speaking world, and the author of many books on a wide range of theological topics, including the work of Hans Urs von Balthasar and Joseph Ratzinger. Professor Rist, who is known for his work in classical philosophy and the history of theology, has held chairs and professorships at the University of Toronto, the Augustinianum in Rome, the Catholic University of America, the University of Aberdeen, and the Hebrew University of Jerusalem.

---

1   *Code of Canon Law*, 212 §3.

The Open Letter is released just after the celebration of Holy Week and Easter Week, in the hopes that the present "passion" of the Church will soon give way to a full resurrection of God's saving truth. A select bibliography to support the case made in the Open Letter concerning the heresies of Pope Francis has also been made available by the organizers.

OPEN LETTER TO THE BISHOPS OF THE CATHOLIC CHURCH

Easter Week, 2019

Your Eminence, Your Beatitude, Your Excellency,

We are addressing this letter to you for two reasons: first, to accuse Pope Francis of the canonical delict of heresy, and second, to request that you take the steps necessary to deal with the grave situation of a heretical pope.

We take this measure as a last resort to respond to the accumulating harm caused by Pope Francis's words and actions over several years, which have given rise to one of the worst crises in the history of the Catholic Church.

We are accusing Pope Francis of the canonical delict of heresy. For the canonical delict of heresy to be committed, two things must occur: the person in question must doubt or deny, by public words and/or actions, some divinely revealed truth of the Catholic faith that must be believed with the assent of divine and Catholic faith; and this doubt or denial must be pertinacious, that is, it must be made with the knowledge that the truth being doubted or denied has been taught by the Catholic Church as a divinely revealed truth which must be believed with the assent of faith, and the doubt or denial must be persistent.

While accusing a pope of heresy is, of course, an extraordinary step that must be based on solid evidence, both these conditions have been demonstrably fulfilled by Pope Francis. We do not accuse him of having committed the delict of heresy on every occasion upon which he has seemed to publicly contradict a truth of the faith. We limit ourselves to accusing him of heresy on occasions where he has publicly denied truths of the faith, and then consistently acted in a way that demonstrates that he disbelieves these truths that he has publicly denied. We do not claim that he has denied truths of the faith in pronouncements that satisfy the conditions for an infallible papal teaching. We assert that this would be impossible, since it would be incompatible with the guidance given to the Church by the Holy Spirit. We deny that this could even appear to be the case to any reasonable person, since Pope Francis has never made a pronouncement that satisfies the conditions for infallibility.

We accuse Pope Francis of having, through his words and actions, publicly and pertinaciously demonstrated his belief in the following propositions that contradict divinely revealed truth (for each proposition we provide a selection of scriptural and magisterial teachings that condemn them as contrary to divine revelation; these references are conclusive but are not intended to be exhaustive.)

— I —

> A justified person has not the strength with God's grace to carry out the objective demands of the divine law, as though any of the commandments of God are impossible for the justified; or as meaning that God's grace, when it produces justification in an individual, does not invariably and of its nature produce conversion from all serious sin, or is not sufficient for conversion from all serious sin.

Council of Trent, Session 6, canon 18: "If anyone says that the commandments of God are impossible to observe even for a man who is justified and established in grace, let him be anathema" (DH 1568).

See also: Gen. 4:7; Deut. 30:11–19; Ecclesiasticus 15:11–22; Mk. 8:38; Lk. 9:26; Heb. 10:26–29; 1 Jn. 5:17; Zosimus, 15th (or 16th) Synod of Carthage, canon 3 on grace, DH 225; Felix III, Second Synod of Orange, DH 397; Council of Trent, Session 5, canon 5; Session 6, canons 18–20, 22, 27 and 29; Pius V, Bull *Ex Omnibus Afflictionibus*, on the errors of Michael du Bay, 54, DH 1954; Innocent X, Constitution *Cum Occasione*, on the errors of Cornelius Jansen, 1, DH 2001; Clement XI, Constitution *Unigenitus*, on the errors of Pasquier Quesnel, 71, DH 2471; John Paul II, Apostolic Exhortation *Reconciliatio et Paenitentia* 17, *AAS* 77 (1985): 222; *Veritatis Splendor* 65–70, *AAS* 85 (1993): 1185–89, DH 4964–67.

— II —

> A Christian believer can have full knowledge of a divine law and voluntarily choose to break it in a serious matter, but not be in a state of mortal sin as a result of this action.

Council of Trent, Session 6, canon 20: "If anyone says that a justified man, however perfect he may be, is not bound to observe the commandments of God and of the Church but is bound only to believe, as if the Gospel were merely an absolute promise of eternal life without the condition that the commandments be observed, let him be anathema" (DH 1570).

See also: Mk. 8:38; Lk. 9:26; Heb. 10:26–29; 1 Jn. 5:17; Council of Trent, Session 6, canons 19 and 27; Clement XI, Constitution *Unigenitus*, on the errors of Pasquier Quesnel, 71, DH 2471; John Paul II, Apostolic Exhortation *Reconciliatio et Paenitentia* 17, *AAS* 77 (1985): 222; *Veritatis Splendor* 65–70, *AAS* 85 (1993): 1185–89, DH 4964–67.

— III —

> A person is able, while he obeys a divine prohibition, to sin against God by that very act of obedience.

Ps. 18:8: "The law of the Lord is unspotted, converting souls." See also: Ecclesiasticus 15:21; Council of Trent, Session 6, canon 20; Clement XI, Constitution *Unigenitus*, on the errors of Pasquier Quesnel, 71, DH 2471; Leo XIII, *Libertas Praestantissimum*, *ASS* 20 (1887–88): 598 (DH 3248); John Paul II, *Veritatis Splendor* 40, *AAS* 85 (1993): 1165 (DH 4953).

— IV —

> Conscience can truly and rightly judge that sexual acts between persons who have contracted a civil marriage with each other, although one or both of them is sacramentally married to another person, can sometimes be morally right, or requested or even commanded by God.

Council of Trent, Session 6, canon 21: "If anyone says that Jesus Christ was given by God to men as a redeemer in whom they are to trust but not also as a lawgiver whom they are bound to obey, let him be anathema," DH 1571.

Council of Trent, Session 24, canon 2: "If anyone says that it is lawful for Christians to have several wives at the same time, and that this is not forbidden by any divine law, let him be anathema," DH 1802.

Council of Trent, Session 24, canon 5: "If anyone says that the marriage bond can be dissolved because of heresy or difficulties in cohabitation or because of the wilful absence of one of the spouses, let him be anathema," DH 1805.

Council of Trent, Session 24, canon 7: "If anyone says that the Church is in error for having taught and for still teaching that in accordance with the evangelical and apostolic doctrine, the marriage bond cannot be dissolved because of adultery on the part of one of the spouses and that neither of the two, not even the innocent one who has given no cause for infidelity, can contract another marriage during the lifetime of the other, and that the husband who dismisses an adulterous wife and marries again and the wife who dismisses an adulterous husband and marries again are both guilty of adultery, let him be anathema," DH 1807.

See also: Ps. 5:5; Ps. 18:8–9; Ecclesiasticus 15:21; Heb. 10:26–29; Jas. 1:13; 1 Jn. 3:7; Innocent XI, Condemned propositions of the "Laxists," 62–63, DH 2162–63; Clement XI, Constitution *Unigenitus*, on the errors of Pasquier Quesnel, 71, DH 2471; Leo XIII, *Libertas Praestantissimum, ASS* 20 (1887–88): 598, DH 3248; Pius XII, Decree of the Holy Office on situation ethics, DH 3918; Second Vatican Council, Pastoral Constitution *Gaudium et Spes* 16; John Paul II, *Veritatis Splendor* 54, *AAS* 85 (1993): 1177; *Catechism of the Catholic Church*, 1786–87.

—v—

> It is false that the only sexual acts that are good of their kind and morally licit are acts between husband and wife.

1 Cor. 6:9–10: "Do not err: neither fornicators, nor idolaters, nor adulterers, nor the effeminate, nor liers with mankind [male homosexuals], nor thieves, nor covetous, nor drunkards, nor railers, nor extortioners, shall possess the kingdom of God."

Jude 7: "As Sodom and Gomorrah, and the neighbouring cities, in like manner, having given themselves to fornication, and going after other flesh, were made an example, suffering the punishment of eternal fire."

See also: Rom. 1:26–32; Eph. 5:3–5; Gal. 5:19–21; Pius IX, *Casti Connubii* 10, 19–21, 73; Paul VI, *Humanae Vitae* 11–14; John Paul II, *Evangelium Vitae* 13–14.

—VI—

> Moral principles and moral truths contained in divine revelation and in the natural law do not include negative prohibitions that absolutely forbid particular kinds of action, inasmuch as these are always gravely unlawful on account of their object.

John Paul II, *Veritatis Splendor* 115: "Each of us knows how important is the teaching which represents the central theme of this Encyclical and which is today being restated with the authority of the Successor of Peter. Each of us can see the seriousness of what is involved, not only for individuals but also for the whole of society, with the reaffirmation of the universality and immutability of the moral commandments, particularly those which prohibit always and without exception intrinsically evil acts," DH 4971.

See also: Rom. 3:8; 1 Cor. 6:9–10; Gal. 5:19–21; Rev. 22:15; Fourth Lateran Council, chapter 22, DH 815; Council of Constance, Bull *Inter Cunctas* 14, DH 1254; Paul VI, *Humanae Vitae* 14, *AAS* 60 (1968) 490–91; John Paul II, *Veritatis Splendor* 83, *AAS* 85 (1993): 1199, DH 4970.

—VII—

> God not only permits, but positively wills, the pluralism and diversity of religions, both Christian and non-Christian.

John 14:6: "I am the way, and the truth, and the life. No man cometh to the Father, but by me."

Acts 4:11–12: "This is the stone which was rejected by you the builders, which is become the head of the corner. Neither is there salvation in any other. For there is no other name under heaven given to men, whereby we must be saved."

See also Ex. 22:20; Ex. 23:24; 2 Chron. 34:25; Ps. 95:5; Jer. 10:11; 1 Cor. 8:5–6; Gregory XVI, *Mirari Vos* 13–14; Pius IX,

Qui Pluribus 15; *Singulari Quidem* 3–5; First Vatican Council, *Profession of Faith*; Leo XIII, *Immortale Dei* 31; *Satis Cognitum* 3–9; Pius XI, *Mortalium Animos* 1–2, 6.

These heresies are interconnected. The basis of Catholic sexual morality consists in the claim that sexual activity exists for the sake of procreation within marriage and is morally wrong if knowingly engaged in outside of this sphere. The claim that forms part of (IV) above, that persons who are civilly divorced from their spouse can licitly engage in sexual activity with another who is not their spouse, repudiates this basis. Consequently, to assert (IV) is to permit the legitimation of many kinds of sexual activity outside of marriage, not just sexual intercourse between the civilly married. Pope Francis has protected and promoted homosexually active clerics and clerical apologists for homosexual activity. This indicates that he believes that homosexual activity is not gravely sinful. These beliefs fall under the broader claim made in (V), to the effect that not all sexual acts between persons who are not married are morally wrong. The claim that a Christian believer can have full knowledge of a divine law and voluntarily choose to break it in a serious matter, and not be in a state of mortal sin as a result of this action, depends on Pope Francis's endorsement of Luther's claim that justification does not demand observance of the divine law. Taken together, all these positions amount to a comprehensive rejection of Catholic teaching on marriage and sexual activity, Catholic teaching on the nature of the moral law, and Catholic teaching on grace and justification.

EVIDENCE FOR POPE FRANCIS'S BEING GUILTY OF THE DELICT OF HERESY

This evidence is twofold: Pope Francis's public statements, and his public actions (the statements quoted below from *Amoris Laetitia* should not be read as isolated utterances, but in their true meaning in the context of the whole of chapter VIII of that document). These two forms of evidence are related. His public actions serve to establish that the public statements listed below were meant by him to be understood in a heretical sense.[2]

---

[2] We indicate the heresy or heresies supported by each statement or act, by providing in brackets the Roman numeral of the heresy in the list above.

A. POPE FRANCIS'S PUBLIC STATEMENTS CONTRADICTING TRUTHS OF THE FAITH

1. *Amoris Laetitia* 295: "Saint John Paul II proposed the so-called 'law of gradualness' in the knowledge that the human being 'knows, loves and accomplishes moral good by different stages of growth.' This is not a 'gradualness of law' but rather a gradualness in the prudential exercise of free acts on the part of subjects who are not in a position to understand, appreciate, or fully carry out the objective demands of the law." (I, II, IV)

2. *Amoris Laetitia* 298: "The divorced who have entered a new union, for example, can find themselves in a variety of situations, which should not be pigeonholed or fit into overly rigid classifications leaving no room for a suitable personal and pastoral discernment. One thing is a second union consolidated over time, with new children, proven fidelity, generous self-giving, Christian commitment, a consciousness of its irregularity and of the great difficulty of going back without feeling in conscience that one would fall into new sins. The Church acknowledges situations 'where, for serious reasons, such as the children's upbringing, a man and woman cannot satisfy the obligation to separate.' [Footnote 329: In such situations, many people, knowing and accepting the possibility of living 'as brothers and sisters' which the Church offers them, point out that if certain expressions of intimacy are lacking, 'it often happens that faithfulness is endangered and the good of the children suffers.'] There are also the cases of those who made every effort to save their first marriage and were unjustly abandoned, or of 'those who have entered into a second union for the sake of the children's upbringing, and are sometimes subjectively certain in conscience that their previous and irreparably broken marriage had never been valid.' Another thing is a new union arising from a recent divorce, with all the suffering and confusion which this entails for children and entire families, or the case of someone who has consistently failed in his obligations to the family. It must remain clear that this is not the ideal which the Gospel proposes for marriage and the family. The Synod Fathers stated that the discernment of pastors must always take place 'by adequately distinguishing,' with an approach which 'carefully discerns situations.' We know that no 'easy recipes' exist." (III, IV)

3. *Amoris Laetitia* 299: "I am in agreement with the many Synod Fathers who observed that 'the baptized who are divorced and

civilly remarried need to be more fully integrated into Christian communities in the variety of ways possible, while avoiding any occasion of scandal. The logic of integration is the key to their pastoral care, a care which would allow them not only to realize that they belong to the Church as the body of Christ, but also to know that they can have a joyful and fruitful experience in it. They are baptized; they are brothers and sisters; the Holy Spirit pours into their hearts gifts and talents for the good of all.... Such persons need to feel not as excommunicated members of the Church, but instead as living members, able to live and grow in the Church and experience her as a mother who welcomes them always, who takes care of them with affection and encourages them along the path of life and the Gospel.'" (II, IV)

4. *Amoris Laetitia* 301: "It is [sic] can no longer simply be said that all those in any 'irregular' situation are living in a state of mortal sin and are deprived of sanctifying grace. More is involved here than mere ignorance of the rule. A subject may know full well the rule, yet have great difficulty in understanding 'its inherent values, or be in a concrete situation which does not allow him or her to act differently and decide otherwise without further sin.'" (II, III, IV)

5. *Amoris Laetitia* 303: "Conscience can do more than recognize that a given situation does not correspond objectively to the overall demands of the Gospel. It can also recognize with sincerity and honesty what for now is the most generous response which can be given to God, and come to see with a certain moral security that it is what God himself is asking amid the concrete complexity of one's limits, while yet not fully the objective ideal." (II, IV, V)

6. *Amoris Laetitia* 304: "I earnestly ask that we always recall a teaching of Saint Thomas Aquinas and learn to incorporate it in our pastoral discernment: 'Although there is necessity in the general principles, the more we descend to matters of detail, the more frequently we encounter defects.... In matters of action, truth or practical rectitude is not the same for all, as to matters of detail, but only as to the general principles; and where there is the same rectitude in matters of detail, it is not equally known to all.... The principle will be found to fail, according as we descend further into detail.' It is true that general rules set forth a good which can never be disregarded or neglected, but in their formulation they cannot provide absolutely for all particular situations." (VI)

7. On September 5, 2016, the bishops of the Buenos Aires region issued a statement on the application of *Amoris Laetitia*, in which they stated:

> 6) In other, more complex cases, and when a declaration of nullity has not been obtained, the above-mentioned option may not, in fact, be feasible. Nonetheless, a path of discernment is still possible. If it comes to be recognized that, in a specific case, there are limitations that mitigate responsibility and culpability (cf. 301–302), especially when a person believes they would incur a subsequent wrong by harming the children of the new union, *Amoris Laetitia* offers the possibility of access to the sacraments of Reconciliation and Eucharist (cf. footnotes 336 and 351). These sacraments, in turn, dispose the person to continue maturing and growing with the power of grace....
>
> 9) It may be right for eventual access to sacraments to take place privately, especially where situations of conflict might arise. But at the same time, we have to accompany our communities in their growing understanding and welcome, without this implying creating confusion about the teaching of the Church on the indissoluble marriage. The community is an instrument of mercy, which is "unmerited, unconditional and gratuitous" (297).
>
> 10) Discernment is not closed, because it "is dynamic; it must remain ever open to new stages of growth and to new decisions which can enable the ideal to be more fully realized" (303), according to the "law of gradualness" (295) and with confidence in the help of grace.[3]

This asserts that according to *Amoris Laetitia*, although the indissolubility of marriage is not denied, the divorced and remarried can receive the sacraments, and that persisting in this state is compatible with receiving the help of grace. Pope Francis wrote an official letter dated the same day to Bishop Sergio Alfredo Fenoy of San Miguel, a delegate of the Argentina bishops' Buenos Aires region, stating that the bishops of the Buenos Aires region had given the only possible interpretation of *Amoris Laetitia*:

---

3 For the Spanish original, see above, pp. 82–83.

Beloved brother,

I received the document from the Buenos Aires Pastoral Region, "Basic Criteria for the Application of Chapter Eight of *Amoris Laetitia*." Thank you very much for sending it to me. I thank you for the work they have done on this: a true example of accompaniment for the priests ... and we all know how necessary is this closeness of the bishop with his clergy and the clergy with the bishop. The neighbor "closest" to the bishop is the priest, and the commandment to love one's neighbor as one's self begins for us, the bishops, precisely with our priests. The document is very good and completely explains the meaning of chapter VIII of *Amoris Laetitia*. There are no other interpretations.[4]

This letter to the Bishops of Buenos Aires was then published in the *Acta Apostolicae Sedis* of October 2016, with a note saying that Pope Francis had ordered its publication as an act of the authentic magisterium. This note does not assert that the statements of *Amoris Laetitia* or of the Buenos Aires bishops themselves constitute part of the authentic magisterium; it states with magisterial authority that the Buenos Aires bishops' understanding of what Pope Francis meant to say in *Amoris Laetitia* is correct.

It must be noted that the denial of Communion to divorced and invalidly remarried or cohabiting couples is, in itself, a doctrine based on Sacred Scripture and founded upon the divine law.[5] To assert the possibility of giving Holy Communion to divorced and invalidly remarried couples implies, by a necessary inference, the belief in heresies II, IV, and V, or else a denial of the dogma of the indissolubility of marriage.[6]

---

4 For the Spanish original, see above, p. 84.
5 Cf. *Familiaris Consortio* 84. See also: *Dichiarazione del Pontificio Consiglio per i Testi Legislativi: Circa l'ammissibilità alla Santa Comunione dei divorziati risposati* (*L'Osservatore Romano*, July 7, 2000, p. 1; *Communicationes* 32 [2000]).
6 Cf. Cardinal G. Müller, in: Riccardo Cascioli, "Vogliono far tacere Benedetto perché dice la verità," *La Nuova Bussola quotidiana*, http://www.lanuovabq.it/it/vogliono-far-tacere-benedetto-xvi-perche-dice-la-verita: "An emeritus bishop, when he celebrates Mass, shouldn't he tell the truth in the homily? Should he not talk about the indissolubility of marriage just because other active bishops have introduced new rules that are not in harmony

8. On June 16, 2016, at a Pastoral Congress for the diocese of Rome, Pope Francis stated that many "cohabiting" couples have the grace of matrimony. (II, IV, V)

9. In a press conference on June 26, 2016, Pope Francis stated: "I think that the intentions of Martin Luther were not mistaken. He was a reformer. Perhaps some methods were not correct.... And today Lutherans and Catholics, Protestants, all of us agree on the doctrine of justification. On this point, which is very important, he did not err." (I)

10. In a homily in the Lutheran Cathedral in Lund, Sweden, on October 31, 2016, Pope Francis stated:

> The spiritual experience of Martin Luther challenges us to remember that apart from God we can do nothing. "How can I get a propitious God?" This is the question that haunted Luther. In effect, the question of a just relationship with God is the decisive question for our lives. As we know, Luther encountered that propitious God in the Good News of Jesus, incarnate, dead and risen. With the concept "by grace alone," he reminds us that God always takes the initiative, prior to any human response, even as he seeks to awaken that response. The doctrine of justification thus expresses the essence of human existence before God. (I)

11. On October 31, 2016, Pope Francis signed the Joint Statement on the occasion of the Joint Catholic-Lutheran Commemoration of the Reformation, which included the assertion: "We are profoundly thankful for the spiritual and theological gifts received through the Reformation." (I)

12. On February 4, 2019, Pope Francis and Ahmad Al-Tayyeb, the Grand Imam of Al-Azhar Mosque, publicly signed and issued a statement entitled *Document on Human Fraternity*. In it, they made the following assertions:

---

with divine law? Rather, it is the active bishops who do not have the power to change divine law in the Church. They have no right to tell a priest that he must give communion to a person who is not in full communion with the Catholic Church. No one can change this divine law; if anyone does so, he is a heretic, a schismatic." Cf. http://magister.blogautore.espresso.repubblica.it/2019/04/17/between-the-two-popes-there-is-%E2%80%9Cfracture-%E2%80%9D-the-silence-of-francis-against-benedict/.

Freedom is a right of every person: each individual enjoys the freedom of belief, thought, expression and action. The pluralism and the diversity of religions, colour, sex, race and language are willed by God in His wisdom, through which He created human beings. This divine wisdom is the source from which the right to freedom of belief and the freedom to be different derives.[7] (VII)

B. POPE FRANCIS'S PUBLIC ACTIONS THAT INDICATE A REJECTION OF TRUTHS OF THE FAITH

Understood in their most obvious sense, the statements listed above are heretical. This was pointed out, in regard to many of them, in the Filial Correction sent to Pope Francis and in the theological censures of *Amoris Laetitia* that were sent to the College of Cardinals by forty-five Catholic scholars. They have been understood in a heretical sense by a large part of the church, which has taken them to legitimize belief and actions that conform to them. Pope Francis has not corrected anyone who has publicly interpreted these statements in a heretical sense, even when the persons upholding these heretical understandings have been bishops or cardinals.

These statements are not however the only evidence for Pope Francis's public adherence to heresy. It is possible to demonstrate belief in a proposition by actions as well as by words. Canon law has always admitted non-verbal actions as evidence for heresy; for example, refusing to kneel before the Blessed Sacrament has been considered to furnish evidence for disbelief in the doctrine of the Real Presence. Non-verbal actions on their own can indicate belief in a heresy, or they can do so in conjunction with verbal and written statements. In the latter case, they provide a context that makes

---

[7] Pope Francis has offered some informal explanations of this statement, but none of these explanations offers an unambiguous interpretation that is compatible with the Catholic faith. Any such interpretation would have to specify that God positively wills the existence only of the Christian religion. Since the statement is a joint statement with the Grand Imam, it cannot be interpreted in a sense that the Grand Imam would reject. Since the Grand Imam rejects the position that God positively wills only the existence of the Christian religion, it is not possible to give an orthodox interpretation to the statement. We therefore understand this statement in its natural sense as a denial of a truth of the Catholic faith.

clear that the verbal and written statements in question are to be understood in a heretical sense. A large number of Pope Francis's public actions have manifested his belief in the heresies listed above, in one or the other of these two ways. We provide a summary list of such actions below. This list is not meant to be exhaustive. Nor does it need to be exhaustive; when taken in conjunction with the statements of Pope Francis given above, the number and gravity of the actions listed below are sufficient to establish beyond a reasonable doubt that Pope Francis has publicly manifested his belief in the heresies we accuse him of holding.

Pope Francis's actions manifest his belief in the heresies listed above in several ways. Such actions include protecting, promoting, and praising clerics and laymen who have manifested their beliefs in these heresies, or who have consistently acted in ways that defy the truths which these heresies contradict. Canon law has traditionally considered that protecting, promoting, and helping heretics can itself be evidence of heresy. By praising clerics and laity who advance these heresies, or by naming them to influential posts, or by protecting clerics of this kind from punishment or demotion when they have committed gravely immoral and criminal acts, he assists them to spread their heretical beliefs. By choosing heretical prelates for the most important posts in the Roman Curia, he manifests an intention to impose these heresies upon the whole Church. By protecting clerics who are guilty of immoral and criminal sexual acts even when this protection causes grave scandal to the Church and threatens to lead to calamitous action by the civil authorities, he manifests disbelief in Catholic teaching on sexual morality, and shows that support of heretical and criminal clerics is more important to him than the well-being of the Church. By publicly praising individuals who have dedicated their careers to opposing the teaching of the Church and the Catholic faith, and to promoting and committing crimes condemned by divine revelation and natural law, he communicates the message that the beliefs and actions of these individuals are legitimate and praiseworthy.

It is noteworthy that his public approval and endorsement are not indiscriminate; he does not often extend his praise to Catholics who are known for being entirely faithful to the teaching of the faith, or hold up the behaviour of individual Catholics of this kind as examples to follow. And it is also to be observed how he has demoted or sidelined those of faithful and orthodox stamp.

The following is a list of actions that indicate belief in the heresies above.

CARDINAL DOMENICO CALCAGNO. Cardinal Calcagno was known to have protected Nello Giraudo, a priest who had abused a same-sex minor, before Pope Francis's election. Pope Francis retained him in office as president of the Administration of the Patrimony of the Holy See until he reached retirement age in 2017. (II, V)

CARDINAL FRANCESCO COCCOPALMERIO. Cardinal Coccopalmerio publicly stated in 2014 that Catholic leaders must emphasise the positive elements in homosexual relationships, and that in certain circumstances it would be wrong to deny communion to persons living in adulterous relationships or to require them to dissolve their relationship. He has shown other indications of approval of homosexual activity. Pope Francis has appointed him to a number of important posts including a working group tasked with speeding up the process for assessing the nullity of marriage, and to the board of review within the Congregation of the Doctrine of the Faith that reviews appeals from clergy found guilty of sexual abuse of minors. (II, IV, V)

CARDINAL BLASE CUPICH. At the 2015 Synod on the Family Cardinal Cupich supported the proposals that persons living in adulterous relationships and sexually active homosexuals could receive the Eucharist in good conscience under certain circumstances. Pope Francis appointed him as Archbishop of Chicago in 2014, named him a Cardinal in 2016, and named him a member of the Congregation for Bishops and the Congregation for Catholic Education. (II, IV, V)

CARDINAL GODFRIED DANNEELS. Cardinal Danneels was requested in 1997 and 1998 to take action on the catechism textbook *Roeach*, which was used in Belgium under his authority. This textbook corrupted minors with a sexual education contrary to Catholic principles, teaching them to seek whatever sexual lust they like, solitary, heterosexual, or homosexual. It presented standard propaganda claims used for legitimizing the sexual abuse of prepubescent children. He defended the textbook and refused to have it altered or removed, even when Belgian parents objected that it encouraged pedophilia. He acted to protect the pedophile Bishop Roger Vangheluwe after it became known that Vangheluwe sexually abused his own nephew, beginning when the nephew was five years old. When the nephew, then an adult, asked Danneels to take some action against Vangheluwe, Danneels refused, told the nephew to keep quiet about the abuse, and told the nephew that he should acknowledge his own guilt. All these actions were public knowledge in 2010. Cardinal Danneels stood at the side of Pope Francis on the balcony of St. Peter's when the pope made his first public appearance after his election. Pope Francis named him as a special delegate to the 2015 Synod on the Family. At his death in 2019, Pope Francis praised him as a "zealous pastor" who "served the Church with dedication." (II, IV, V)

CARDINAL JOHN DEW. Cardinal Dew argued for the admission of adulterous couples to the Eucharist at the synod on the Eucharist in 2005. Pope Francis named him a cardinal in 2015 and named him as a special delegate to the 2015 Synod on the Family. (II, IV, V)

CARDINAL KEVIN FARRELL. Cardinal Farrell has expressed support for the proposal that the divorced and remarried should receive communion. Pope Francis has named him prefect of the newly established Dicastery for Laity, Family, and Life, promoted him to the rank of cardinal, and made him cardinal camerlengo. (II, IV, V)

CARDINAL OSWALD GRACIAS. Cardinal Gracias has publicly expressed the opinion that homosexuality may be an orientation given to people by God. Pope Francis appointed him as one of the organisers of the Vatican summit on sexual abuse in February 2019. (II, IV, V)

CARDINAL JOZEF DE KESEL. In 2014 Cardinal de Kesel, then bishop of Bruges, appointed Father Tom Flamez as a pastor after he had been convicted of sexual abuse. He did not remove Fr Antoon Stragier from ministry until 2015, although Stragier's crimes were known to the diocese in 2004. Pope Francis chose Bishop de Kesel as Archbishop of Mechelen-Brussels in November 2015 and named him a cardinal in November 2016. (II, IV, V)

CARDINAL RODRIGUEZ MARADIAGA. In an address to the University of Dallas in 2013, Cardinal Maradiaga stated that the Second Vatican Council "meant an end to the hostilities between the Church and modernism, which was condemned in the First Vatican Council," and claimed that "modernism was, most of the time, a reaction against injustices and abuses that disparaged the dignity and the rights of the person." He stated that "within the people, there is not a dual classification of Christians—laity and clergy, essentially different," and that "to speak correctly, we should not speak of clergy and laity, but instead of community and ministry."

He asserted: "Christ himself did not proclaim or preach Himself, but the Kingdom. The Church, as His disciple and His servant, ought to do the same."

Cardinal Maradiaga failed to act on accusations of sexual misbehaviour with seminarians and peculation by José Juan Pineda Fasquelle, auxiliary bishop of Tegucigalpa. These accusations were the subject of an apostolic visit carried out by Bishop Alcides Jorge Pedro Casaretto, who presented a report to Pope Francis in May 2017. Bishop Fasquelle resigned his office in July 2018 at the age of 57. Maradiaga refused to investigate complaints made by 48 out of 180 seminarians about homosexual misbehaviour at the Honduras seminary, and attacked the complainants. Pope Francis named Maradiaga as a member and coordinator of the council of nine cardinals that he set up in 2013 to advise him in the government of the universal church. (II, IV, V)

FORMER CARDINAL THEODORE MCCARRICK. According to numerous credible accusers, former Cardinal McCarrick pressured seminarians to engage in homosexual relations with him. These charges were known to the Holy See as early as 2002. Between 2005 and 2007, the Diocese of Metuchen and the Archdiocese of Newark paid financial settlements to two priests who had accused McCarrick of abuse. Pope Francis was personally informed of this behaviour in 2013, and was told that Pope Benedict had placed restrictions upon him. Pope Francis brought McCarrick out of retirement and used him for many important tasks, including trips as a representative of the Holy See to Israel, Armenia, China, Iran and Cuba. He accompanied Pope Francis on his trips to Israel and Cuba. When Archbishop Carlos Maria Viganò asserted in August 2018 that Pope Francis had known from 2013 that McCarrick was a serial predator, the pope refused to answer this claim. In February 2019, the former cardinal was returned to the lay state. Despite the example of the former cardinal's behavior, the subject of the homosexual abuse of adults, and in particular of seminarians, was excluded from discussion at the summit on sexual abuse that took place in Rome in the same month. (II, IV, V)

CARDINAL DONALD WUERL. Cardinal Wuerl allowed Fr George Zirwas to continue in ministry after learning that he had committed numerous crimes of sexual abuse. Wuerl resigned as Archbishop of Washington after his actions in this and other cases of sexual abuse were criticised by a Pennsylvania grand jury report. When Wuerl resigned as a result of these failures, Pope Francis praised him for his nobility, kept him in charge of the Archdiocese of Washington as apostolic administrator, and retained him as a member of the Congregation for Bishops. (II, IV, V)

ARCHBISHOP MARIO ENRICO DELPINI. As vicar general of the archdiocese of Milan, Delpini moved Fr Mauro Galli to a new parish after being informed that Galli had sexually abused a young man. Delpini admitted this in a court deposition in 2014. The Holy See was made aware of this. Pope Francis named him as archbishop of Milan in 2017. (II, IV, V)

BISHOP JUAN BARROS MADRID. Barros covered up the grave sexual crimes of Fr Fernando Karadima, who was convicted of sexual abuse by a Church tribunal in 2011. Pope Francis appointed Barros bishop of Osorno in 2015 despite strong protests from the faithful and described his critics as calumniators. Bishop Barros accepted responsibility and resigned in 2018 after Pope Francis admitted he had made "serious mistakes" in dealing with his case. (II, IV, V)

BISHOP JUAN CARLOS MACCARONE. Maccarone was bishop of Santiago de Estero in Argentina and dean of the Faculty of Theology of the Pontifical University of Buenos Aires. In 2005, a video of Maccarone being sodomized by a taxi driver was made public. He subsequently retired as bishop. After this incident, Archbishop Bergoglio signed a declaration of solidarity with Maccarone issued by the Argentine Bishops' conference, of which he was then the head. (II, IV, V)

BISHOP JOSÉ TOLENTINO MENDONÇA. In 2013 Mendonça praised the theology of Sr. Teresa Forcades, who defends the morality of homosexual acts and claims that abortion is a right, and who stated that "Jesus of Nazareth did not codify, nor did he establish rules." Pope Francis made him an archbishop and head of the Vatican Secret Archives in 2018. He also chose him to preach the Lenten retreat to the pope and high curial officials in 2018. (II, IV, V, VI)

BISHOP GUSTAVO ÓSCAR ZANCHETTA. Zanchetta had been named by Pope Francis as bishop of Oran in Argentina in 2013. Zanchetta engaged in homosexual misconduct, including the sexual harassment of seminarians. Photographic evidence of this was submitted to the Holy See in 2015. In December 2017 Pope Francis named Zanchetta as assessor of the Administration of the Patrimony of the Apostolic See. (II, IV, V)

MGR. BATTISTA MARIO SALVATORE RICCA. Battista Ricca was engaged in grave homosexual misbehaviour while employed in the papal nunciature in Uruguay. This included getting trapped in an elevator with a male prostitute and having to be rescued by the fire department. After these scandals had become public, Pope Francis put him in charge of his residence, the Casa Santa Marta, and named him as prelate of the Istituto delle Opere di Religione. (II, IV, V)

FR JULIO GRASSI. Grassi was convicted in 2009 of sexually abusing a teenage boy. The Argentine Bishops' Conference under the chairmanship of Cardinal Bergoglio made great efforts to prevent Grassi's conviction. The Bishops' Conference commissioned a four-volume work for this purpose that slandered Grassi's victims. Grassi stated that all through his legal process, Archbishop Bergoglio had "held his hand." (II, IV, V)

FR MAURO INZOLI. Fr Inzoli was condemned for sexual abuse of minors to reduction to the lay state by the CDF in 2012 in the first instance, but the enforcement of that sentence was suspended after he appealed, and in 2014 Pope Francis changed it into the much milder prescription to lead a retired life. In 2016 he was arrested and condemned by an Italian court. Only after he fell under the civil judgement did Pope Francis finally reduce him to the lay state. (II, IV, V)

FR JAMES MARTIN, S.J. Martin is a well-known advocate for the legitimising of homosexual relationships and homosexual activity. In 2017 Pope Francis appointed him as a consultant to the Secretariat of Communications of the Holy See. (II, IV, V)

FATHER TIMOTHY RADCLIFFE, O.P. In 2013 Radcliffe stated that homosexual activity can be expressive of Christ's self-gift. Pope Francis appointed him as a consultor to the Pontifical Council for Justice and Peace in May 2015. (II, IV, V)

EMMA BONINO. Emma Bonino is the foremost political activist on behalf of abortion and euthanasia in Italy, and has boasted of personally performing many abortions. In 2015 Pope Francis received her at the Vatican, and in 2016 he praised her as one of Italy's "forgotten greats." (II, IV, V, VI)

PONTIFICAL ACADEMY FOR LIFE. In 2016, Pope Francis dismissed all 132 members of the Pontifical Academy for Life. He removed the requirement that members of the Academy swear to uphold Catholic teachings on human life and to not perform destructive research on the embryo or fetus, elective abortion, or euthanasia. The forty-five new members of the Academy whom he appointed include several persons who reject Catholic moral teaching. Fr Maurizio Chiodi has argued for euthanasia through denial of food and water, and has rejected Catholic teaching on the morality of contraception. Fr Alain Thomasset has rejected the idea of intrinsically evil actions and has stated that some homosexual relationships can be paths of holiness. Fr Humberto Miguel Yanez holds that artificial contraception can be licit under some circumstances. Professor Marie-Jo Thiel rejects the Church's teaching that homosexual acts are intrinsically evil and her teaching that contraception is morally wrong. Prof. Nigel Biggar holds that abortion up to eighteen weeks of pregnancy can be licit, and accepts that euthanasia can in some cases be justified. (II, IV, V, VI)

Promoting reception of the Eucharist by divorced and remarried persons

Pope Francis has persistently promoted the reception of the Eucharist under certain circumstances by persons who have civilly divorced their spouse and are living in a sexual relationship with someone else. His letter to the bishops of Buenos Aires cited above explicitly endorsed this practice. He intervened in the composition of the *Relatio post disceptationem* for the 2014 Synod on the Family. His addition to the *Relatio* proposed allowing Communion for divorced-and-remarried Catholics on a "case-by-case basis," and said pastors should emphasize the "positive aspects" of lifestyles the Church considers gravely sinful, including civil remarriage after divorce and premarital cohabitation. These proposals were included in the *Relatio* at his personal insistence, despite the fact that they did not receive the two-thirds majority required by the Synod rules for a proposal to be included in the *Relatio*. He issued guidelines for the diocese of Rome permitting the reception of the Eucharist under certain circumstances by civilly divorced-and-remarried Catholics living *more uxorio* with their civil partner. These teachings and actions are themselves an offence against the faith, since the teaching that Catholics with a living spouse who are openly cohabiting with someone else may not receive the Eucharist is at least a truth belonging to the secondary object of the infallibility of the Church. It is at least a truth whose acceptance is necessary in order that the deposit of faith can be effectively defended or proposed with sufficient authority. We do not deny that it is part of divinely revealed Sacred Tradition. Its denial has not been listed as a heresy espoused by Pope Francis because some Catholic theologians worthy of respect have maintained that it does not form part of the divinely revealed deposit of faith. Denial of this truth gives support to heresies (IV) and (V) listed above.

Other indications

On June 9, 2014, Pope Francis received the leaders of the militantly pro-homosexual Tupac Amaru organisation from Argentina at the Vatican, and blessed their coca leaves for use in their pagan religious rituals, which involve recognition of the coca plant as sacred. (II, IV, V, VII)

Pope Francis has failed to speak a word in support of popular campaigns to preserve Catholic countries from abortion and homosexuality—for example, before the referendum to introduce abortion into Ireland in May 2018. (II, IV, V, VI)

At the opening mass of the Synod on Youth in 2018, Pope Francis carried a staff in the form of a "stang," an object used in satanic rituals. (VI, VII)

During the Synod on Youth in 2018, Pope Francis wore a distorted rainbow-coloured cross, the rainbow being a popularly promoted symbol of the homosexual movement. (II, IV, V)

Pope Francis has concluded an agreement with China that permits the Chinese government to choose Catholic bishops in that country, and has ordered a number of faithful Catholic bishops to yield their dioceses to bishops appointed by the state. China is an atheist state that persecutes Christians, and enforces an immoral population policy that includes promotion of contraception, and coerced abortion on a massive scale. This population policy is a high priority for the Chinese government and has caused incalculable harm. Control of the Church by the Chinese government will ensure that the Church in China can offer no resistance to this policy. (II, VI)

Pope Francis has refused to deny that *Amoris Laetitia* teaches heresies (IV), (V) and (VI) listed above, when requested to do so in the *dubia* submitted to him by Cardinals Brandmüller, Burke, Caffarra, and Meisner in September 2016. These *dubia* specifically mentioned grave disorientation and great confusion of many faithful concerning matters of faith and morals resulting from *Amoris*

Laetitia. The submission of *dubia* by bishops and the provision of an answer to them is an entirely traditional and normal procedure, so the refusal to answer these *dubia* is a deliberate choice on the part of Pope Francis.

C. POPE FRANCIS'S PERTINACITY IN ADHERING TO HERETICAL PROPOSITIONS

Pope Francis completed the theological studies necessary for ordination, obtained a licentiate in philosophy and a licentiate in theology, and became a university professor in theology at the Facultades de Filosofía y Teología de San Miguel, a Jesuit university and seminary in Argentina. He subsequently became the Rector of these faculties. The Apostolic Exhortation *Familiaris Consortio* and the encyclical *Veritatis Splendor*, which condemn many of the heresies listed above, were issued while he was a priest and a bishop respectively. He has cited *Familiaris Consortio* in his writings, and took part in a theological conference on *Veritatis Splendor* in 2004 in which he made a contribution to the conference asserting the doctrine denied in heresy (VI) given above. The *dubia* mentioned above, which were sent to Pope Francis privately in September 2016 and made public in November of the same year, recall the passages in *Veritatis Splendor* and *Familiaris Consortio*. He can therefore be presumed to be well informed enough on Catholic doctrine to know that the heresies he is professing are contrary to Catholic doctrine. Their heretical nature was also documented and pointed out to him in a filial correction addressed to him by a number of Catholic scholars in August 2017, and made public in September of the same year.[8]

THE REQUEST WE MAKE TO YOU AS BISHOPS

We therefore request that your Lordships urgently address the situation of Pope Francis's public adherence to heresy. We recognise with gratitude that some among you have reaffirmed the truths contrary to the heresies which we have listed, or else have warned of serious dangers threatening the Church in this pontificate. We recall, for example, that His Eminence Cardinal Burke already stated in October 2014 that the Church appears like a rudderless ship, and along with His Eminence Cardinal Pujats, the late

---

8 See the preceding document in this book. On the question of pertinacity in heresy, see the editors' note 16 on p. 113.

Cardinal Caffarra, and several other bishops, signed a Declaration of Fidelity to the Church's unchangeable teaching on marriage in September 2016. We recall also the statement of His Eminence Cardinal Eijk in May last year that the present failure to transmit doctrine faithfully, on the part of the bishops in union with the successor of St. Peter, evokes the great deception foretold for the last days; and somewhat similar remarks made more recently by His Eminence Cardinal Gerhard Müller in his Manifesto of Faith. For these and other such interventions by cardinals and bishops, which have gone some way to reassure the faithful, we give thanks to God.

Yet in so grave and unprecedented an emergency we believe that it will no longer suffice to teach the truth as it were abstractly, or even to deprecate "confusion" in the Church in rather general terms. For Catholics will hardly believe that the pope is attacking the faith unless this be said expressly; and hence, merely abstract denunciations risk providing a cover for Pope Francis to advance and to achieve his goal.

Despite the evidence that we have put forward in this letter, we recognise that it does not belong to us to declare the pope guilty of the delict of heresy in a way that would have canonical consequences for Catholics. We therefore appeal to you as our spiritual fathers, vicars of Christ within your own jurisdictions and not vicars of the Roman pontiff, publicly to admonish Pope Francis to abjure the heresies that he has professed. Even prescinding from the question of his personal adherence to these heretical beliefs, the pope's behaviour in regard to the seven propositions contradicting divinely revealed truth, mentioned at the beginning of this Letter, justifies the accusation of the delict of heresy. It is beyond a doubt that he promotes and spreads heretical views on these points. Promoting and spreading heresy provides sufficient grounds in itself for an accusation of the delict of heresy. There is, therefore, superabundant reason for the bishops to take the accusation of heresy seriously and to try to remedy the situation.

Since Pope Francis has manifested heresy by his actions as well as by his words, any abjuration must involve repudiating and reversing these actions, including his nomination of bishops and cardinals who have supported these heresies by their words or actions. Such an admonition is a duty of fraternal charity to the pope, as well as a duty to the Church. If—which God forbid!—Pope Francis does not bear the fruit of true repentance in response to these admonitions, we request that you carry out your duty of office to declare that he has committed the canonical delict of heresy and that he must suffer the canonical consequences of this crime.

These actions do not need to be taken by all the bishops of the Catholic Church, or even by a majority of them. A substantial and representative part of the faithful bishops of the Church would have the power to take these actions. Given the open, comprehensive, and devastating nature of the heresy of Pope Francis, willingness publicly to admonish Pope Francis for heresy appears now to be a necessary condition for being a faithful bishop of the Catholic Church.

This course of action is supported and required by canon law and the tradition of the Church. We provide below a brief account of the canonical and theological basis for it.

We ask the Holy Trinity to enlighten Pope Francis to reject every heresy opposed to sound doctrine, and we pray that the Blessed Virgin Mary, Mother of the Church, may gain for your Lordships the light and strength to defend the faith of Christ. Permit us to say with all boldness that in acting thus, you will not have to face that reproach of the Lord: "You have not gone up to face the enemy, nor have you set up a wall for the house of Israel, to stand in battle in the day of the Lord" (Ezekiel 13:5).

We humbly request your blessing, and assure you of our prayers for your ministry and for the Church.

Yours faithfully in Christ,

ORIGINAL SIGNATORIES

Georges Buscemi
President of Campagne Québec-Vie, member of the John Paul II Academy for Human Life and Family

Robert Cassidy, STL

Fr Thomas Crean, OP, STD

Matteo d'Amico
Professor of History and Philosophy, Senior High School of Ancona

Deacon Nick Donnelly, MA

Maria Guarini, STB, Pontificia Università Seraphicum, Rome
Editor of the website *Chiesa e postconcilio*

Prof. Robert Hickson, PhD
Retired Professor of Literature and of Strategic-Cultural Studies

Fr John Hunwicke
Former Senior Research Fellow, Pusey House, Oxford

Peter Kwasniewski, PhD

John Lamont, DPhil (Oxon.)

Brian M. McCall
Orpha and Maurice Merrill Professor in Law; Editor in Chief of *Catholic Family News*

Fr Cor Mennen, JCL
Diocese of 's-Hertogenbosch (Netherlands), canon of the cathedral Chapter; lecturer at the diocesan Seminary of 's-Hertogenbosch

Stéphane Mercier, STB, PhD
Former Lecturer at the Catholic University of Louvain

Fr Aidan Nichols, OP

Paolo Pasqualucci
Professor of Philosophy (retired), University of Perugia

Dr Claudio Pierantoni
Professor of Medieval Philosophy, University of Chile; former Professor of Church History and Patrology at the Pontifical Catholic University of Chile

Prof. John Rist

Dr Anna Silvas
Adjunct Senior Research Fellow, Faculty of Humanities, Arts, Social Sciences and Education, University of New England

Prof. Dr W. J. Witteman
Physicist, emeritus professor, University of Twente

ADDED ON MAY 1, 2019

Fr William Barrocas

Pedro Erik Carneiro, PhD

Michael J. Cawley III, PhD
Psychologist

Fr Gregory Charnock, BA LLB
Diocesan Priest, St Bartholomew Catholic Parish, Western Cape, South Africa

Ernesto Echavarria, KSG

Sarah Henderson, DCHS, BA, MA

Edward T. Kryn, MD

Alan Moy, MD
Scientific Director and Founder, John Paul II Medical Research Institute

Jack P. Oostveen
Emeritus Assistant Professor Geomechanics, Delft University of Technology, The Netherlands; Acting President of the International Federation *Una Voce*, 2006–2007

Harriet Sporn
Hermit

Dr Zlatko Šram
Croatian Center for Applied Social Research

Dr Hubert Windisch
Pastoral theologian, Graz/Freiburg/Regensburg

ON MAY 2, 2019

Fr Daniel J. Becker, PhD

Deacon Andrew Carter, BSc (Hons.) ARCS DipPFS

Dr Lee Fratantuono
 Professor and Chair of Classics, Ohio Wesleyan University

Fr Paul John Kalchik, STB, MD

Thomas Klibengajtis, PhD
 Theologian

Patrick Linbeck, BA, STL
 Board Member of Texas Right to Life

Nancy E. Martin, MA Theology

Fr Boguslaw Nowak, SVD

Abbé Guy Pagès

Quintilio Palozzi, PhD in Philosophy
 Retired Professor

Dr M. Elizabeth Phillips, MD

Dr Brian Charles Phillips, MD, FRSCS

Dr Robert L. Phillips, DPhil (Oxon.)
 Professor em. of Philosophy, University of Connecticut (USA)

Fr Luis Eduardo Rodríguez Rodríguez
 Parish priest, Diocese of Los Teques, Venezuela

Fr Darrell Roman

Robert Siscoe
 Author

Prof. Dr Peter Stephan

Dr Patrick Toner
 Associate Professor of Philosophy, Wake Forest University, Winston Salem

Elizabeth D. Wickham, PhD
 Executive Director, LifeTree

ON MAY 3, 2019

Prof. Mario Bombaci
 Professor of Philosophy and Bioethics

Erick Chastain, PhD
 Postdoctoral Research Associate, Department of Psychiatry, University of Wisconsin-Madison

Lynn M. Colgan Cohen, OFS, MA

Fr Ian Farrell, STL

James Fennessy, MA, MSW, JD, LCSW

Patricia McKeever, BEd, MTh
 Head of Religious Education (ret.)

Prof. Dr Juan Carlos Valdes Ossandón
 Former Professor of History of Medieval Philosophy, Pontifical Catholic University of Chile

Harold A. Reyes, MRE

Padre Gabriele Rossi, FAM, JCD

Daniel Younan, BA Phil, MA Th

Part II: Letters and Statements to the Pope or the Bishops

ON MAY 4, 2019

Fr Jeremy Davies, MA, MBBS

Dr Jochem Hauser
 Professor em., Ostfalia University

Dr Rudolf Hilfer, Dr.rer.nat. Dr.rer.pol.

Mark McMenamin
 Professor of Geology

Renacito R. Ramos, MD, DFM

Fr Andreas Wanka

ON MAY 6, 2019

Dr Robert Adams & Mrs Sonia Adams

Biagio Buonomo, PhD
 Former writer for *L'Osservatore Romano*

Fr Thomas Edward Dorn

Marie I. George, PhD

Prof. Maksym Adam Kopiec, OFM

Fr Wilhelm Meir
 Ziemetshausen, Diözese Augsburg

Dominique Millet-Gérard
 Professor of French and Comparative Literature, Sorbonne Université, Paris

Fr Giovanni P. Ortiz Berrios

Fr Tullio Rotondo, STD

Fr Tam X. Tran, STL
 Pastor, Archdiocese of Washington, USA

ON MAY 7, 2019

Carlo Foresti
 Lawyer

Adrie A. M. van der Hoeven, MSc
 Physicist

Prof. Cesar Félix Sanchez Martínez
 Professor of Philosophy of Nature, Philosophy of History and History of Philosophy (Modern and Contemporary) at the Archdiocesan Seminary of Saint Jerome, Arequipa, Perú

Mark Vatuone, JD, LLM

ON MAY 10, 2019

Fr Edward B. Connolly

Fr Paul Driscoll, MA

Michael Lofton, MTS

Rafael M. Reynante, MA, MSM

Fr Michael Yelavich

ON MAY 13, 2019

Martin Mosebach
   Author

ON MAY 21, 2019

Ivan M. Rodriguez, PhD	Dr Mauro Scaringi, MA (Phil.)
Fr Timothy J. Sauppé, STL	

ON MAY 31, 2019

Mary McMenamin, MA Biblical Theology	Fr Michael Menner

ON JUNE 26, 2019

Lynn M. Colgan Cohen, OFS, MA	Antonio Marcantonio, MA

CANON LAW AND CATHOLIC THEOLOGY CONCERNING THE SITUATION OF A HERETICAL POPE

The situation of a pope falling into heresy has long been a subject of discussion by Catholic theologians. This situation was brought into prominence after the ecumenical Third Council of Constantinople anathematized the Monothelite heresy in 681, and posthumously anathematized Pope Honorius for his support of this heresy; this condemnation of Honorius as a heretic was repeated by Pope St. Leo II when he ratified the acts of that Council. Since that time, Catholic theologians and canonists have reached a consensus on several essential points concerning the implications of a pope falling into public heresy. We will briefly present these points here.

It is agreed that no pope can uphold heresy when teaching in a way that satisfies the conditions for an infallible magisterial statement. This restriction does not mean that a pope cannot be guilty of heresy, since popes can and do make many public statements that are not infallible; many popes indeed never issue an infallible definition.

It is agreed that the Church does not have jurisdiction over the pope, and hence that the Church cannot remove a pope from office by an exercise of superior authority, even for the crime of heresy.

It is agreed that the evil of a heretical pope is so great that it should not be tolerated for the sake of some allegedly greater good. Suárez expresses this consensus as follows: "It would be extremely harmful to the Church to have such a pastor and not be able to defend herself from such a grave danger; furthermore it would go against the dignity of the Church to oblige her to remain subject to a heretic Pontiff without being able to expel him from herself; for such as are the prince and the priest, so the people are accustomed to be." St. Robert Bellarmine states: "Wretched would be the Church's condition if she were forced to take as her pastor one who manifestly conducts himself as a wolf."[9]

It is agreed that ecclesiastical authorities have a responsibility to act to remedy the evil of a heretical pope. Most theologians hold that the bishops of the Church are the authorities that have an absolute duty to act in concert to remedy this evil.

It is agreed that a pope who is guilty of heresy and remains obstinate in his heretical views cannot continue as pope.[10] Theologians and canonists discuss this question as part of the subject of the loss of papal office. The causes of the loss of papal office that they list always include death, resignation, and heresy. This consensus corresponds to the position of untutored common sense, which says that in order to be pope one must be a Catholic. This position is based on patristic tradition and on fundamental theological principles concerning ecclesiastical office, heresy, and membership

---

9   *Controversies*, Third Controversy, Bk. 2, ch. 30.
10 See, e.g., Thomas de Vio Cajetan, *De Comparatione auctoritatis papae et concilii cum Apologia eiusdem tractatus* (Rome: Angelicum, 1936); Melchior Cano, *De Locis theologicis*, Bk. 6, ch. 8; Bañez, *In IIaIIae*, q. 1, a. 10; John of St. Thomas, *Cursus theologici* II-II, "De auctoritate Summi Pontificis," d. 8, ad 3, De depositione papae; Suárez, *De fide*, disp. 10; St. Robert Bellarmine, *De Romano Pontifice*, bk. 2; Billuart, *Cursus theologiae*, Pars II-II; St. Alphonsus Liguori, *Vindiciae pro suprema Pontificis potestate adversus Iustinum Febronium*; Cardinal Charles Journet, *L'Église du Verbe Incarné*, vol. 1: *L'hiérarchie apostolique* (Éditions Saint-Augustin, 1998), 980–83.

of the Church.[11] The Fathers of the Church denied that a heretic could possess ecclesiastical jurisdiction of any kind. Later doctors of the Church understood this teaching as referring to public heresy that is subject to ecclesiastical sanctions, and held that it was based on divine law rather than ecclesiastical positive law. They asserted that a heretic of this kind could not exercise jurisdiction because their heresy separated them from the Church, and no one expelled from the Church could exercise authority in it.[12]

The canon law of the Church supports this theological consensus. The first canon to give explicit consideration to the possibility of papal heresy is found in the *Decretum* of Gratian. Distinction XL, canon 6 of the *Decretum* states that the pope can be judged by no one, unless he is found to have deviated from the faith: "Cunctos ipse iudicaturus a nemine est iudicandus, nisi deprehendatur a fide devius."[13]

The wording of this statement seems to have been influenced by Cardinal Humbert's *De sancta Romana ecclesia* (1053), which stated that the pope is immune from judgment by anyone except in questions of faith: "a nemine est iudicandus nisi forte deprehendatur a fide devius." The claim made in the canon is a development of Pope Gregory the Great's statement that evil prelates must be tolerated by their subjects if this can be done while saving the faith.[14]

The canonical assertion that the pope can be judged for heresy came into being as an explication of the canonical principle that the pope is judged by no one. The statement in this canon is an enunciation of a privilege; its object is to assert that the pope has the widest possible exemption from judgement by others.

---

11 See, e.g., St. Augustine, *Sermon* 181; Pope Pius IX, Bull *Ineffabilis Deus* defining the doctrine of the Immaculate Conception.
12 This principle is applied to the loss of the papal office for heresy by St. Robert Bellarmine, *De Romano Pontifice*, Bk. 2, ch. 30. Later authors have qualified this assertion by accepting that heretical clerics can exercise jurisdiction in certain extraordinary circumstances, because it is supplied to them by the Church. None of these authors has however accepted that a pope whose heresy is manifest and established can possess or exercise papal jurisdiction. The Church cannot grant papal jurisdiction, and a heretical pope cannot grant this jurisdiction to himself.
13 He, the one who is to judge all, is to be judged by none, unless he be found straying from the faith.
14 *Moralia in Iob* XXV, c. 16: "Subditi praelatos etiam malos tolerant, si salva fide possint..."

This canon was included, along with the rest of the *Decretum* of Gratian, in the *Corpus iuris canonici,* which formed the basis of canon law in the Latin Church until 1917. Its authority is supported by papal authority itself, since the canon law of the Church is upheld by papal authority. It was taught by Pope Innocent III, who asserted in his sermon on the consecration of the Supreme Pontiff that "God was his sole judge for other sins, and that he could be judged by the Church only for sins committed against the faith."[15] Rejection of the canon in the *Decretum* would undermine the canonical foundation for papal primacy itself, since this canon forms part of the legal basis for the principle that the pope is judged by no one.

The canon was universally accepted by the Church after the compilation and publication of the *Decretum*. The heresy referred to in this canon is understood by virtually all authors to mean externally manifested heresy (the thesis that a pope loses his office for purely internal heresy was advanced by Juan de Torquemada, O. P., but it has been conclusively refuted and has been rejected by all canonists and theologians ever since). Neither the 1917 *Code of Canon Law* nor the 1983 *Code of Canon Law* abrogates the principle that a heretical pope loses the papal office. This is agreed by all commentators on these codes, who state that this principle is correct.[16]

The early canonical tradition generally requires that in the specific case of papal heresy, the pope must be admonished several times before being treated as a heretic. The *Summa* of Rufinus, the *Summa antiquitate et tempore* (after 1170), and the *Summa* of Johannes Faventius (after 1171) all assert that the pope must be warned a second and third time to desist from heresy before he can be judged to be a heretic. The *Summa* of Huguccio states that before the pope can be judged a heretic, he must be admonished

---

15 "In tantum enim fides mihi necessaria est, ut cum de caeteris peccatis solum Deum iudicium habeam, propter solum peccatum quod in fide committitur possem ab Ecclesia judicari."

16 See, e.g., *Jus Canonicum ad Codicis Normam Exactum*, Franciscus Wernz and Petrus Vidal (Gregorianum, 1924–1949), II (1928), n. 453; *Introductio in Codicem*, 3rd ed., Udalricus Beste (Collegeville: St. John's Abbey Press, 1946), can. 221; *New Commentary on the Code of Canon Law*, John P. Beal, James A. Coriden, and Thomas J. Green, eds. (New York: Paulist, 2000), p. 1618.

to abandon heresy and must contumaciously defend his error in response to such admonition.

Sedevacantist authors have argued that a pope automatically loses the papal office as the result of public heresy, with no intervention by the Church being required or permissible. This opinion is not compatible with Catholic tradition and theology, and is to be rejected. Its acceptance would throw the Church into chaos in the event of a pope embracing heresy, as many theologians have observed. It would leave each individual Catholic to decide whether and when the pope could be said to be a heretic and to have lost his office. It should instead be accepted that the pope cannot fall from office without action by the bishops of the Church.[17] Such action must include adjuring the pope more than once to reject any heresies that he has embraced, and declaring to the faithful that he has become guilty of heresy if he refuses to renounce these heresies. The incompatibility between heresy and membership of the Church is what leads to the loss of the papal office by a heretical pope. The Church's determining that a pope is a heretic, and the announcement of his heresy by the bishops of the Church, is what makes the pope's heresy a juridical fact, a fact from which his loss of office ensues.

There are some lesser differences of opinion between Catholic theologians concerning the measures that the Church must take in dealing with a heretical pope. The school of Cajetan and John of St. Thomas asserts that in order for the papal office to be lost, the Church, after ascertaining and pronouncing that the pope is a heretic, must also command the faithful to avoid him for his heresy. The school of St. Robert Bellarmine does not reject the step of commanding the faithful to avoid the pope as a heretic, but it does not consider it a necessary precondition for the pope's losing office for heresy. Both these schools have adherents, up to and including the present day. We do not take a position on these disputed questions, whose resolution is a matter for the bishops of the Church.

---

[17] We do not reject the possibility that a pope who publicly rejected the Catholic faith and publicly converted to a non-Catholic religion could thereby lose the papal office; but this hypothetical case does not resemble the current situation.

SELECT BIBLIOGRAPHY TO SUPPORT THE CASE MADE IN THE OPEN LETTER

Fr Robert Dodaro, O. S. A., *Remaining in the Truth of Christ. Marriage and Communion in the Catholic Church*. Contributions by Paul Mankowski, S. J.; Dr John M. Rist; Archbishop Cyril Vasil', S. J.; Walter Cardinal Brandmüller; Gerhard Ludwig Cardinal Müller; Carlo Cardinal Caffarra; Velasio Cardinal De Paolis; Raymond Leo Cardinal Burke. Ignatius Press, San Francisco, 2014.

John Finnis and Germain Grisez, "An Open Letter to Pope Francis." https://www.firstthings.com/web-exclusives/2016/12/an-open-letter-to-pope-francis.

Fr Thomas Weinandy, O. F. M. Cap., "Letter to Pope Francis." http://www.ncregister.com/blog/edward-pentin/full-text-of-father-weinandys-letter-to-pope-francis.

Fr Aidan Nichols, O. P., "Leading theologian: change canon law to correct papal errors." https://catholicherald.co.uk/leading-theologian-change-canon-law-to-correct-papal-errors.

Fr Brian Harrison, O. S., "Analysis of *Amoris Laetitia*." https://www.lifesitenews.com/opinion/priest-pope-francis-pastoral-revolution-goes-against-2000-years-of-tradition.

Fr Thomas Crean, O. P., "*Amoris Laetitia* Is Not a Thomistic Document." https://thewandererpress.com/catholic/news/our-catholic-faith/fr-thomas-crean-op-amoris-laetitia-is-not-a-thomistic-document.

Athanasius Schneider, "*Amoris Laetitia*: a need for clarification in order to avoid a general confusion." http://www.ncregister.com/blog/edward-pentin/bishop-schneider-amoris-laetitia-demands-clarification.

Dr Christian Brugger, "Five serious problems with chapter 8 of *Amoris Laetitia*." *Catholic World Report*, April 22, 2016, http://www.catholicworldreport.com/2016/04/22/five-serious-problems-with-chapter-8-of-amoris-laetitia.

Dr Josef Seifert, "*Amoris Laetitia*, Joy, Sadness and Hopes." *AEMAET: Wissenschaftliche Zeitschrift für Philosophie und Theologie* 5.2 (2016): 160–249, http://aemaet.de, ISSN 2195-173X.

Dr Claudio Pierantoni, "The Arian crisis and the current controversy about *Amoris Laetitia*: a parallel." *AEMAET: Wissenschaftliche Zeitschrift für Philosophie und Theologie*, 5.2 (2016): 250–78, https://aemaet.de/index.php/aemaet/article/view/40.

Dr Robert A. Gahl Jr., "Healing through Repentance." *First Things*, July 26, 2016.

Fr Brian Harrison, O. S., "Divorced and Invalidly Remarried Catholics. The Magisterial Tradition—Part II." *Latin Mass* (Fall 2017): 14–19.

Benito Amado (pseudonym), "Elenchus rationum sophisticarum Rocci Buttiglionis." *Adelante la fe*, May 18, 2017, https://adelantelafe.com/elenchum-rationum-sophisticarum-rocci-buttiglionis.

Dr Josef Seifert, "Does pure Logic threaten to destroy the entire moral Doctrine of the Catholic Church?" *AEMAET: Wissenschaftliche Zeitschrift für Philosophie und Theologie*, 6.2 (2017): 2–9.

Dr Christian Brugger, "Yes, *Amoris Laetitia* 303 really undermines Catholic moral teaching: scholar." https://www.lifesitenews.com/news/yes-amoris-laetitia-303-really-undermines-catholic-moral-teaching-scholar.

Dr John R. T. Lamont, "The meaning of *Amoris Laetitia* according to Pope Francis." https://rorate-caeli.blogspot.com/2018/02/important-guest-essay-meaning-of-amoris.html. [Included in the present volume as chapter 5 in Part III.]

Dr Claudio Pierantoni, "Le fallacie di Rocco Buttiglione in materia di Teologia morale e Teologia sacramentaria." In Antonio Livi, ed., *La legge eterna di Dio e l'insegnamento morale della Chiesa di oggi. Discussioni teologiche sulla riforma della prassi pastorale voluta dall'Amoris Laetitia*. With contributions by Luca Gili, Ivo Kerze, Claudio Pierantoni. Rome: Casa Editrice Leonardo Da Vinci.

Dr John Lamont, "Francis and the Joint Declaration on Human Fraternity: A Public Repudiation of the Catholic Faith." https://rorate-caeli.blogspot.com/2019/02/guest-article-francis-and-joint.html.

Dr Josef Seifert, "Grave Concerns About Pope Francis's Abu Dhabi Document." https://gloria.tv/article/FL9X8LzsDd8v4yYN39TCeEsrM.

Benedict XVI, Pope Emeritus, "The Church and the scandal of sexual abuse." *Corriere della Sera*, https://www.corriere.it/english/19_aprile_11/benedict-xvi-the-church-and-the-scandal-of-sexual-abuse-8e40d438-5b9c-11e9-ba57-a3df5eacbd16.shtml.

Gerhard Cardinal Müller: Interview with Riccardo Cascioli, *La Nuova Bussola Quotidiana*, http://www.lanuovabq.it/it/vogliono-far-tacere-benedetto-xvi-perche-dice-la-verita; see also Sandro Magister, "Between the Two Popes There Is 'Fracture.' The Silence of Francis Against Benedict," http://magister.blogautore.espresso.repubblica.it/2019/04/17/between-the-two-popes-there-is-%E2%80%9Cfracture-%E2%80%9D-the-silence-of-francis-against-benedict.

An Appeal to the Cardinals of the Catholic Church

POPE FRANCIS HAS REVISED THE *CATECHISM of the Catholic Church* to read, "the death penalty is inadmissible because it is an attack on the inviolability and dignity of the person." This statement has been understood by many, both inside and outside the Church, to teach that capital punishment is intrinsically immoral and thus is always illicit, even in principle.

Though no Catholic is obliged to support the use of the death penalty in practice (and not all of the undersigned do support its use), to teach that capital punishment is always and intrinsically evil would contradict Scripture. That the death penalty can be a legitimate means of securing retributive justice is affirmed in Genesis 9:6 and many other biblical texts, and the Church holds that Scripture cannot teach moral error. The legitimacy in principle of capital punishment is also the consistent teaching of the magisterium for two millennia. To contradict Scripture and tradition on this point would cast doubt on the credibility of the magisterium in general.

Concerned by this gravely scandalous situation, we wish to exercise the right affirmed by the Church's *Code of Canon Law*, which at Canon 212 states:

> The Christian faithful are free to make known to the pastors of the Church their needs, especially spiritual ones, and their desires. According to the knowledge, competence, and prestige which they possess, they have the right and even at times the duty to manifest to the sacred pastors their opinion on matters which pertain to the good of the Church and to make their opinion known to the rest of the Christian faithful, without prejudice to the integrity of faith and morals, with reverence toward their pastors, and attentive to common advantage and the dignity of persons.

We are guided also by the teaching of St. Thomas Aquinas, who states:

---

1   Published online at *First Things* on August 15, 2018.

If the faith were endangered, a subject ought to rebuke his prelate even publicly. Hence Paul, who was Peter's subject, rebuked him in public, on account of the imminent danger of scandal concerning faith, and, as the gloss of Augustine says on Galatians 2:11, "Peter gave an example to superiors, that if at any time they should happen to stray from the straight path, they should not disdain to be reproved by their subjects." (*Summa Theologiae*, Part II-II, Question 33, Article 4, ad 2)

Hence we, the undersigned, issue the following appeal:

To their Most Reverend Eminences, the Cardinals of the Holy Roman Church,

Since it is a truth contained in the Word of God, and taught by the ordinary and universal magisterium of the Catholic Church, that criminals may lawfully be put to death by the civil power when this is necessary to preserve just order in civil society, and since the present Roman pontiff has now more than once publicly manifested his refusal to teach this doctrine, and has rather brought great confusion upon the Church by seeming to contradict it, and by inserting into the *Catechism of the Catholic Church* a paragraph which will cause and is already causing many people, both believers and non-believers, to suppose that the Church considers, contrary to the Word of God, that capital punishment is intrinsically evil, we call upon Your Eminences to advise His Holiness that it is his duty to put an end to this scandal, to withdraw this paragraph from the *Catechism*, and to teach the Word of God unadulterated; and we state our conviction that this is a duty seriously binding upon yourselves, before God and before the Church.

Sincerely,

Hadley Arkes
Edward N. Ney Professor in American Institutions Emeritus, Amherst College

Joseph Bessette
Alice Tweed Tuohy Professor of Government and Ethics, Claremont McKenna College

Patrick Brennan
John F. Scarpa Chair in Catholic Legal Studies, Villanova University

J. Budziszewski
Professor of Government and Philosophy, University of Texas at Austin

Isobel Camp
Professor of Philosophy, Pontifical University of St. Thomas Aquinas

Richard Cipolla
Priest, Diocese of Bridgeport

Eric Claeys
Professor of Law, Antonin Scalia Law School, George Mason University

Travis Cook
Associate Professor of Government, Belmont Abbey College

S. A. Cortright
Professor of Philosophy, Saint Mary's College

Cyrille Dounot
Professor of Legal History, Université Clermont Auvergne

Patrick Downey
Professor of Philosophy, Saint Mary's College

Eduardo Echeverria
Professor of Philosophy and Theology, Sacred Heart Major Seminary

Edward Feser
Associate Professor of Philosophy, Pasadena City College

Alan Fimister
Assistant Professor of Theology, St. John Vianney Theological Seminary

Luca Gili
Assistant Professor of Philosophy, Université du Québec à Montréal

Brian Harrison
Scholar in Residence, Oblates of Wisdom Study Center

L. Joseph Hebert
Professor of Political Science, St. Ambrose University

Rafael Hüntelmann
Lecturer in Philosophy, International Seminary of St. Peter

John Hunwicke
Priest, Personal Ordinariate of Our Lady of Walsingham

Robert C. Koons
Professor of Philosophy, University of Texas at Austin

Peter Koritansky
Associate Professor of Philosophy, University of Prince Edward Island

Peter Kwasniewski
Independent Scholar, Wausau, Wisconsin

John Lamont
Author, *Divine Faith*

Roberto de Mattei
Author, *The Second Vatican Council: An Unwritten Story*

Robert T. Miller
Professor of Law, University of Iowa

Gerald Murray
Priest, Archdiocese of New York

Lukas Novak
Lecturer in Philosophy, University of South Bohemia

Thomas Osborne
Professor of Philosophy, University of St. Thomas

Michael Pakaluk
Professor of Ethics, Catholic University of America

Claudio Pierantoni
Professor of Medieval Philosophy, University of Chile

Thomas Pink
Professor of Philosophy, King's College London

Part II: Letters and Statements to the Pope or the Bishops

Andrew Pinsent
Research Director of the Ian Ramsey Centre, University of Oxford

Alyssa Pitstick
Independent Scholar, Spokane, Washington

Donald S. Prudlo
Professor of Ancient and Medieval History, Jacksonville State University

Anselm Ramelow
Chair of the Department of Philosophy, Dominican School of Philosophy and Theology

George W. Rutler
Priest, Archdiocese of New York

Matthew Schmitz
Senior Editor, *First Things*

Josef Seifert
Founding Rector, International Academy of Philosophy

Joseph Shaw
Fellow of St Benet's Hall, University of Oxford

Anna Silvas
Adjunct Senior Research Fellow, University of New England

Michael Sirilla
Professor of Dogmatic and Systematic Theology, Franciscan University of Steubenville

Joseph G. Trabbic
Associate Professor of Philosophy, Ave Maria University

Giovanni Turco
Associate Professor of Philosophy, University of Udine

Michael Uhlmann
Professor of Government, Claremont Graduate University

John Zuhlsdorf
Priest, Diocese of Velletri-Segni

The foregoing names were selected by First Things *for publication. However, the document was signed by a larger number, some of whose names were omitted (for unexplained reasons). Here are the additional signatories of the original appeal:*

Fr Claude Barthe
Diocesan Priest

Dame Colleen Bayer
Founder, Family Life International NZ

James Bogle Esq.
Barrister (trial attorney), former President FIUV, former Chairman of the Catholic Union of Great Britain

Fr John Boyle

Judie Brown
President, American Life League

Fr Michael Gilmary Cermak

Fr Richard Cipolla

Fr Linus F. Clovis

Hon. Donald J. Devine
Senior Scholar, The Fund for American Studies

Dr Maria Guarini
Editor of the website *Chiesa e postconcilio*

John D. Hartigan
: Retired attorney and past member, Public Policy Committee of the New York State Catholic Conference

Dr Maike Hickson
: Journalist

Dr Robert Hickson
: Retired Professor of Literature and Strategic-Cultural Studies

Fr Albert Kallio
: Professor of Philosophy at Our Lady of Guadalupe Monastery, New Mexico

Fr Serafino M. Lanzetta

Dr Robert Lazu
: Independent Scholar and Writer

Dr James P. Lucier
: Former Staff Director, U. S. Senate Committee on Foreign Relations

Dr Pietro De Marco
: Former professor of Sociology of Religion, University of Florence

Dr Joseph Martin
: Associate Professor of Communication, Montreat College

Dr Brian McCall
: Associate Dean for Academic Affairs and Associate Director of the Law Center, Orpha and Maurice Merrill Professor in Law, University of Oklahoma

Fr Paul McDonald
: Parish priest of Chippawa, Ontario

Dr Stéphane Mercier
: Former lecturer in Philosophy at the Catholic University of Louvain (Belgium)

Fr Alfredo Morselli
: Parish priest in the diocese of Bologna

Maureen Mullarkey
: Senior Contributor, *The Federalist*

Fr Reto Nay

Dr Claude E. Newbury
: Former Director of Human Life International in Africa south of the Sahara

Giorgio Nicolini
: Writer, Director of *Tele Maria*

Dr Paolo Pasqualucci
: Retired Professor of Philosophy, University of Perugia, Italy

Prof. Enrico Maria Radaelli
: Philosopher

Richard M. Reinsch II
: Editor, *Law and Liberty*

R. J. Stove
: Writer and editor

Fr Alberto Strumia
: Retired professor of Mathematical Physics, University of Bari, Italy

Fr Glen Tattersall
: Parish Priest, Parish of St. John Henry Newman, archdiocese of Melbourne; Rector, St Aloysius' Church

Dr Thomas Ward
: Founder of the National Association of Catholic Families and former Corresponding Member of the Pontifical Academy for Life

E

Contra recentia sacrilegia

PROTEST AGAINST POPE FRANCIS'S SACRILEGIOUS ACTS

WE THE UNDERSIGNED CATHOLIC CLERGY AND lay scholars protest against and condemn the sacrilegious and superstitious acts committed by Pope Francis, the Successor of Peter, in connection with the recent Amazon Synod held in Rome.

These sacrilegious acts are the following:

— On October 4, Pope Francis attended an act of idolatrous worship of the pagan goddess Pachamama.

— He allowed this worship to take place in the Vatican Gardens, thus desecrating the vicinity of the graves of the martyrs and of the church of the Apostle Peter.

— He participated in this act of idolatrous worship by blessing a wooden image of Pachamama.

— On October 7, the idol of Pachamama was placed in front of the main altar at St. Peter's and then carried in procession to the Synod Hall. Pope Francis said prayers in a ceremony involving this image and then joined in this procession.

— When wooden images of this pagan deity were removed from the church of Santa Maria in Traspontina, where they had been sacrilegiously placed, and thrown into the Tiber by Catholics outraged by this profanation of the church, Pope Francis, on October 25, apologized for their removal and another wooden image of Pachamama was returned to the church. Thus, a new profanation was initiated.

— On October 27, in the closing Mass for the synod, he accepted a bowl used in the idolatrous worship of Pachamama and placed it on the altar.

— Pope Francis himself confirmed that these wooden images were pagan idols. In his apology for the removal of these idols from a Catholic church, he specifically called them Pachamama, a name for a false goddess of mother earth according to pagan religious belief in South America.

Different features of these proceedings have been condemned as idolatrous or sacrilegious by Cardinal Walter Brandmüller, Cardinal

Gerhard Müller, Cardinal Jorge Urosa Savino, Archbishop Carlo Maria Viganò, Bishop Athanasius Schneider, Bishop José Luis Azcona Hermoso, Bishop Rudolf Voderholzer, and Bishop Marian Eleganti. Lastly, Cardinal Raymond Burke has given the same assessment of this cult in an interview.

This participation in idolatry was anticipated by the statement entitled *Document on Human Fraternity*, signed by Pope Francis and Ahmad Al-Tayyeb, the Grand Imam of Al-Azhar Mosque, on February 4, 2019. This statement asserted that: "The pluralism and the diversity of religions, colour, sex, race and language are willed by God in His wisdom, through which He created human beings. This divine wisdom is the source from which the right to freedom of belief and the freedom to be different derives."

Pope Francis's involvement in idolatrous ceremonies is an indication that he meant this statement in a heterodox sense, which allows pagan worship of idols to be considered a good positively willed by God.

Moreover, despite privately advising Bishop Athanasius Schneider that "You [the Bishop] can say that the phrase in question on the diversity of religions means the permissive will of God...", Francis has never corrected the Abu Dhabi statement accordingly. In his subsequent audience address of April 3, 2019 Francis, answering the question "Why does God permit that there are so many religions?," referred in passing to the "permissive will of God" as explained by Scholastic theology, but gave the concept a positive meaning, declaring that "God *wanted* to permit this" because while "there are so many religions" they "*always* look to heaven, they *look to God*" (emphasis added). There is not the slightest suggestion that God permits the existence of false religions in the same way He permits the existence of evil generally. Rather, the clear implication is that God permits the existence of "so many religions" because they are *good*, in that they "*always* look to heaven, they look to God."

Worse, Pope Francis has since confirmed the uncorrected Abu Dhabi statement by establishing an "interfaith committee," which later received the official name of "Higher Committee," located in the United Arab Emirates, to promote the "goals" of the document; and promoting a directive issued by the Pontifical Council for Interreligious Dialogue addressed to the heads of all the Roman Catholic institutes of higher studies, and indirectly to Catholic university professors, asking that they give the "widest possible dissemination to the document," including its uncorrected assertion that God wills the "diversity of religions" just as He wills the diversity of colour, sex, race and language.

The rendering of worship to anyone or anything other than the one true God, the Blessed Trinity, is a violation of the First Commandment. Absolutely all participation in any form of the veneration of idols is condemned by this Commandment and is an objectively grave sin, independently of the subjective culpability that only God can judge.

St. Paul taught the early Church that the sacrifice offered to pagan idols was not offered to God but rather to the demons when he said in his First Letter to the Corinthians:

> What then? Do I say, that what is offered in sacrifice to idols, is any thing? Or, that the idol is any thing? But the things which the heathens sacrifice, they sacrifice to demons, and not to God. And I would not that you should be made partakers with demons. You cannot drink the chalice of the Lord, and the chalice of demons: you cannot be partakers of the table of the Lord, and of the table of demons. (1 Cor. 10:19–21)

By these actions Pope Francis has incurred the reproach uttered by the Second Council of Nicaea:

> Many pastors have destroyed my vine, they have defiled my portion. For they followed unholy men and trusting to their own frenzies they calumniated the holy Church, which Christ our God has espoused to himself, and they failed to distinguish the holy from the profane, asserting that the icons of our Lord and of his saints were no different from the wooden images of satanic idols.

With immense sorrow and deep love for the Chair of Peter, we beg Almighty God to spare the guilty members of His Church on earth the punishment that they deserve for these terrible sins.

We respectfully ask Pope Francis to repent publicly and unambiguously of these objectively grave sins and of all the public offences that he has committed against God and the true religion, and to make reparation for these offences.

We respectfully ask all the bishops of the Catholic Church to offer fraternal correction to Pope Francis for these scandals, and to warn their flocks that according to the divinely revealed teaching of the Catholic faith, they will risk eternal damnation if they follow his example of offending against the First Commandment.

November 9, 2019
In Festo dedicationis Basilicae Lateranensis
Terribilis est locus iste: hic domus Dei est et porta cæli; et vocabitur aula Dei

Dr Gerard J. M. van den Aardweg
The Netherlands

Dr Robert Adams
Physician in Emergency & Family Medicine

Donna F. Bethell, JD

Tom Bethell
Senior editor of *The American Spectator*

François Billot de Lochner
President of Liberté politique, France

Dr Biagio Buonomo, PhD
Former culture columnist (1990–2013) for *L'Osservatore Romano*

Rev. Deacon Andrew Carter, BSc (Hons), ARCS, DipPFS
Leader, Marriage & Family Life Commission, Diocese of Portsmouth, England

Mr Robert Cassidy, STL

Dr Michael Cawley, PhD
Psychologist; former University Instructor, Pennsylvania, USA

Dr Erick Chastain, PhD
Postdoctoral Research Associate, Department of Psychiatry, University of Wisconsin-Madison

Fr Linus F. Clovis

Lynn Colgan Cohen, OFS, MA

Rev Edward B. Connolly
Pastor Emeritus, St. Joseph Parish, St. Vincent de Paul Parish, Girardville PA

Fr Paolo D'Angona
Diocese of Roermond, Netherlands

Prof. Roberto de Mattei
Former Professor of the History of Christianity, European University of Rome; former Vice President of the National Research Council (CNR)

José Florencio Domínguez
Philologist and translator

Deacon Nick Donnelly, MA
Catholic Pastoral & Educational Studies (Spiritual Formation), England

Fr Thomas Edward Dorn
Pastor of Holy Redeemer Parish in New Bremen OH in the Archdiocese of Cincinnati

Michael B. Ewbank, PhD
Loras College (ret.), USA

Fr Jerome Fasano
Pastor, St John the Baptist Church, Front Royal, Virginia, USA

Dr James Fennessy, MA, MSW, JD, LCSW
Matawan, New Jersey, USA

Christopher A. Ferrara, JD
Founding President of the American Catholic Lawyers' Association

Fr Jay Finelli
Tiverton, RI, USA

Fr Nicholas Fleming, STL

Dr Lee Fratantuono, AB, AM, PhD

Prof. Michele Gaslini
Professor of Public Law, University of Udine, Italy

Dr Linda M. Gourash, MD

Dr Maria Guarini, STB
Editor of *Chiesa e postconcilio*

Prof. Growuo Guys, PhD

Fr Brian W. Harrison, OS, STD
Associate professor of theology of the Pontifical Catholic University of Puerto Rico (ret.); Scholar in Residence, Oblates of Wisdom Study Center, St. Louis, Missouri, USA

Sarah Henderson, DCHS, MA (RE & Catechetics), BA (Mus)

Prof. Robert Hickson, PhD
Professor of Literature and of Strategic-Cultural Studies (ret.)

Dr Maike Hickson, PhD
Writer and journalist

Prof. Rudolf Hilfer, Dr.rer.pol., Dr.rer.nat.
Professor of Theoretical Physics at Universität Stuttgart

Fr John Hunwicke
Former Senior Research Fellow, Pusey House, Oxford

Dr Colin H. Jory, MA, PhD
Historian, Canberra, Australia

Fr Edward J. Kelty, OS, JCD
Defensor Vinculi, SRNC Rota Romana 2001–2019; Former Judicial Vicar, Archdiocese of Ferrara; Judge, Archdiocese of Ferrara

Dr Ivo Kerže
Professor of Philosophy

Dr Thomas Klibengajtis
Former Assistant Professor of Catholic Systematic Theology, Institute of Catholic Theology, Technical University Dresden, Germany

Dr Peter A. Kwasniewski, PhD

Dr John Lamont, DPhil (Oxon.)

Dr Dorotea Lancellotti
Catechist, cofounder of *Cooperatores Veritatis*

Dr Ester Ledda
Consecrated laywoman, co-founder of *Cooperatores Veritatis*

Fr Patrick Magee, FLHF
Franciscan of Our Lady of the Holy Family; canonical hermit in the Diocese of Fall River, Massachusetts

Dr Carlo Manetti
Jurist and lecturer, Italy

Dr Christopher Manion, PhD, KM
Humanae Vitae Coalition, Front Royal, Virginia, USA

Antonio Marcantonio, MA

Michael J. Matt
Editor, *The Remnant*, USA

Jean-Pierre Maugendre
General delegate, Renaissance catholique, France

Prof. Brian M. McCall
Orpha and Maurice Merrill Professor in Law; Editor-in-Chief, *Catholic Family News*

Msgr John F. McCarthy, JCD, STD
Professor of moral theology, Pontifical Lateran University (ret.)

Deacon Eugene G. McGuirk, BA, MA, MBA

Patricia McKeever, BEd, MTh
Editor, *Catholic Truth*, Scotland

Mary Angela McMenamin, MA in Biblical Theology

Fr Cor Mennen
Lecturer in canon law at the diocesan Seminary of 's-Hertogenbosch and member of the cathedral chapter

Rev Michael Menner
Pastor

Dr Stéphane Mercier, PhD, STB
Former research fellow and lecturer at the University of Louvain

Fr Alfredo Maria Morselli

Dr Claude E. Newbury, MB, BCh, DTM & H, DPH, DOH, MFGP, DCH, DA, MPrax Med

Prof. Giorgio Nicolini
Writer, Director of *Tele Maria*

Fr John O'Neill, STB, Dip TST
Priest of the Diocese of Parramatta, member of Australian Society of Authors

Marco Paganelli
Journalist and writer

Fr Guy Pagès
Archdiocese of Paris, France

Prof. Paolo Pasqualucci
Professor of Philosophy (ret.), University of Perugia, Italy

Fr Dean P. Perri
Diocese of Providence, Our Lady of Loreto Church

Dr Brian Charles Phillips, MD

Dr Mary Elizabeth Phillips, MD

Dr Robert Phillips
Professor (emeritus) Philosophy: Oxford University, Wesleyan University, University of Connecticut

Prof. Claudio Pierantoni
Professor of Medieval Philosophy, University of Chile; former Professor of Church History and Patrology at the Pontifical Catholic University of Chile

Fr Felice Prosperi

Prof. Enrico Maria Radaelli
Professor of Aesthetic Philosophy and Director of the Department of Aesthetic Philosophy of the International Science and Commonsense Association (ISCA), Rome, Italy

Edgardo J. Cruz Ramos
President, *Una Voce* Puerto Rico

Dr Carlo Regazzoni
Philosopher of Culture, Therwill, Switzerland

Prof. John Rist
Professor em. of Classics and Philosophy, University of Toronto

Dr Ivan M. Rodriguez, PhD

Fr Luis Eduardo Rodríguez
Pastor, Diocesan Catholic Priest, Caracas, Venezuela

John F. Salza, Esq.

Fr Timothy Sauppé, STL
Pastor of St. Mary's, Westville, IL, and St. Isaac Jogues, Georgetown, IL

Fr John Saward
Priest of the Archdiocese of Birmingham, England

Prof. Dr Josef Seifert
Director of the Dietrich von Hildebrand Institute of Philosophy, at the Gustav Siewerth Akademie, Bierbronnen, Germany

Mary Shivanandan
Author and consultant

Dr Cristina Siccardi
Church historian and author

Dr Anna M. Silvas
Senior research adjunct, University of New England NSW Australia

Henry Sire
Church historian and author, England

Robert J. Siscoe
Author

Jeanne Smits
Journalist, writer, France

Dr Stephen Sniegoski, PhD
Historian and author

Prof. Dr Heinz Sproll
University of Augsburg

Dr Zlatko Šram, PhD
Croatian Center for Applied Social Research

Abbé Guillaume de Tanoüarn
Doctor of Literature

Rev Glen Tattersall
Parish priest, Parish of St. John Henry Newman, Australia

Prof. Giovanni Turco
Associate professor of Philosophy of Public Law, University of Udine, Italy

Fr Frank Unterhalt
Pastor, Archdiocese of Paderborn, Germany

José Antonio Ureta
Author

Adrie A. M. van der Hoeven, MSc
Physicist

Dr Norbert van der Sluis
Pastoorparochie Maria, Moeder van de Kerk, Bisdom 's-Hertogenbosch

Archbishop Carlo Maria Viganò

Dr Gerd J. Weisensee, MSC
Switzerland

John-Henry Westen, MA
LifeSiteNews Co-Founder and Editor-in chief

Dr Elizabeth C. Wilhelmsen, PhD
 University of Nebraska-Lincoln (ret.)

Willy Wimmer
 Secretary of State, Ministry of Defense (ret.), Germany

Prof. em. Dr Hubert Windisch
 Priest and theologian, Germany

Mo Woltering, MTS
 Headmaster, Holy Family Academy, Manassas, Virginia, USA

Miguel Ángel Yáñez
 Editor, *Adelante la Fe*

ADDED ON 12TH NOVEMBER 2019

Fr Fabian Adindu

Fr Pablo Ormazabal Albistur

Fr Alex Anderson

Fr Daniel Becker

Dr Christian Behrendt

Fr Andrew Benton

Fr Kenneth Bolin

Fr John Boughton

Fr Edmund Castronovo

Fr Jason Charron

Fr David M. Chiantella

Don Michiele Chimienti

Fr Pat Scanlan Cloyne

Dr John Jay Conlon

Fr Peter John Dang

Fr Matthew DeGance, SDB

Fr Mark Desser

Maristela Neves de Mesquita Rodrigues dos Santos

Fr Patrick Fenton

Fr Vincenzo Fiore

Fr John Fongemie, FSSP

Prof. Dr Felix Fulders

Matt Gaspers
 Managing Editor, *Catholic Family News*

Fr Brian Geary

Dr Stefano Gizzi
 Comm. S. Gregorio Magno

Fr James Gordon

Fr Iouis Guardiola

Fr Vince Huber

Fr David Kemna

Paul King, Esq.

Fr Peter Klos

Grzegorz Korwin-Szymanowski
 Journalist

Leo Kronberger, MD, MSC

Tammy Layton, ASA, BA, MA

Fr Scott Lemaster, MA, MDiv

Fr Michael Magiera

Fr Albert P. Marcello III, JCL
 Defensor vinculi, Diocese of Providence

Dr Taylor R. Marshall

Mag. César Félix Sánchez Martínez
    Professor of Philosophy of Nature and History of Modern and Contemporary Philosophy

Fr James Mawdsley

Fr Richard McNally ss.cc

Fr Fidelis Moscinski

David Moss

Bishop Robert Mutsaerts
    Auxiliary bishop of 's-Hertogenbosch, Netherlands

Fr Terence Mary Naughtin, OFM Conv.

Fr John Osman, MA, STL

Dr Quintilio Paolozzi, PhD

Enza Pasquali

Fr Roberto J. Perez, O. Carm.

Fr Steven Scherrer, MM, ThD

José Narciso Barbosa Soares

Mag. Wolfram Schrems

Dr Michael Sirilla

Fr Grzegorz Śniadoch, IBP

Fr Arnis Suleimanovs

Fr Andrew Szymakowski, JCL

Marco Tosatti
    Stilum Curiae

Sac. Bernardo M. Trelle

Fr Bernward Van der Linden, FSSP

João Luiz da Costa Carvalho Vidigal

Fr Jason Vidrine

Christine de Marcellus Vollmer

Fr Edwin Wagner, FSO

Fr Frank Watts

Prof. Mag. Manfred Weindl

Dr Piotr Wolochowicz, PhD

13TH NOVEMBER 2019

Philippe Pichot Bravard
    Maître de conférences HDR, writer

Br Johannes Elisa of the Cross, OCDS

Dr James P. Lucier, PhD
    Former Staff Director, U. S. Senate Foreign Relations Committee

Fr Tim Meares

Fr Tullio Rotondo
    Doctor of Sacred Theology and Jurisprudence

Fr Aleksandrs Stepanovs

Fr Vaughn Treco

14TH NOVEMBER 2019

Sonja J. H. Hissink, MA
   Haarlem, Netherlands

Fr Luis Marja de la SS. Trinidad y de la Santa Cruz

Fr Peter Masik

William Melichar, OCDS, JD, MA

Philippe Pichot Bravard

Mirella Sacilotto Sharkey, PhD

Fr Kazimierz Stefek

15TH NOVEMBER 2019

Gillian Barry, MA Ed

Catherine Young

18TH NOVEMBER 2019

James Bogle, Esq.
   Barrister (trial attorney); President International *Una Voce* Federation 2013–2015

Prof. Pedro Luis Llera Vázquez

19TH NOVEMBER 2019

Rev. Joseph D. Santos Jr.
   Priest of the Archdiocese of Braga; Parochial Administrator in Providence, R. I.

John P. Zmirak, PhD

PART III
Articles and Interviews

I

Some Concerns about Amoris Laetitia[1]

DR ANNA M. SILVAS

IN THIS TALK I WOULD LIKE TO OUTLINE SOME of the more pressing concerns I have with *Amoris Laetitia*. These reflections are organised into three sections. Part One will outline general concerns about *AL*; Part Two will focus on the now-infamous Chapter Eight; and Part Three will suggest some of the implications of *AL* for priests and Catholicism.

I am aware that *Amoris Laetitia*, as an apostolic exhortation, does not come under any rubric of infallibility. Still it is a document of the papal ordinary Magisterium, and thus it makes the idea of critiquing it, especially doctrinally, mighty difficult. It seems to me an unprecedented situation. I wish there were a great saint, like St. Paul, or St. Athanasius or St. Bernard or St. Catherine of Siena, who could have the courage and the spiritual credentials, i.e., prophecy of the truest kind, to speak the truth to the successor of Peter and recall him to a better frame of mind. At this hour, hierarchical authority in the Church seems to have entered a strange paralysis. Perhaps this is the hour for prophets—but true prophets. Where are the saints, of *nooi* (intellects) long purified by contact with the living God in prayer and *ascesis*, gifted with the anointed word, capable of such a task? Where are these people?

GENERAL CONCERNS ABOUT *AL*

Graven upon tablets of stone by the finger of the living God (Ex 31:18, 32:15), the "ten words" proclaimed to mankind for all ages: "You shall not commit adultery" (Ex 20:14) and: "You shall not covet your neighbour's wife" (Ex 20:17). Our Lord himself declared: "Whoever divorces his wife and marries another, commits

---

[1] Given at the Annual Conference of the Australian Confraternity of Catholic Clergy, Armidale, NSW Australia, on May 6, 2016. Published by Sandro Magister at *Chiesa*, June 7, 2016.

adultery against her" (Mk 10:11). And the Apostle Paul repeated the language: "She will be called an adulteress if she lives with another man while her husband is alive" (Rom 7:3).

Like a deafening absence, the term "adultery" is entirely absent from the lexicon of *Amoris Laetitia*. Instead we have something called "'irregular' unions" or "'irregular' situations," with "irregular" in quotation marks as if to distance the author even from this usage.

"If you love me keep my commandments," says our Lord (Jn 14:15), and the Gospel and Letters of John repeat this admonition of our Lord in various ways. It means, not that our conduct is justified by our subjective feelings, but rather, our subjective disposition is verified in our conduct, i.e., in the obediential act. Alas, as we look into *AL*, we find that "commandments," too, are entirely absent from its lexicon, as is also obedience. Instead we have something called "ideals," appearing repeatedly throughout the document.

Other key words I miss too from the language of this document: the fear of the Lord. You know, that awe of the sovereign reality of God that is the beginning of wisdom, one of the gifts of the Holy Spirit in Confirmation. But indeed this holy fear has long vanished from a vast sweep of modern Catholic discourse. It is a semitic idiom for *eulabeia* and *eusebia* in Greek, or in Latin, *pietas* and *religio*, the core of a Godward disposition, the very spirit of religion.

Another register of language also missing in *AL* is that of eternal salvation. There are no immortal souls in need of eternal salvation to be found in this document! True, we do have "eternal life" and "eternity" named in 166 and 168 as the seemingly inevitable "fulfillment" of a child's destiny, but with no hint that any of the imperatives of grace and struggle—in short, of eternal *salvation*—are involved in getting there.

It is as if one's faith-filled intellectual culture is formed to certain echoes of words that one listens for, and their absence is dinning in my ears. Let us look then into what we have in the document itself.

Why the sheer wordiness of it, all 260 pages of it, more than three times the length of *Familiaris Consortio*? This is surely a great pastoral discourtesy. Yet Pope Francis wants "each part" to be "read patiently and carefully" (7). Well, some of us have had to do so. And so much of it is of a tedious, lightweight character. In general I find Pope Francis's discourse, not only here, but everywhere else, flat and one-dimensional. "Shallow" might capture it, and "facile" too: no sense of depth upon depth lying beneath words holy and true, inviting us to launch into the deep.

One of the least pleasant features of *Amoris Laetitia* are Pope Francis's many impatient "throw-away" comments, cheap-shots that so lower the tone of the discourse. One is often left puzzling as to the ground of these comments. For example, in the infamous footnote 351, he lectures priests that "the confessional must not be a torture chamber." A torture chamber? In another example, in 36, he says: "we often present marriage in such a way that its unitive meaning, its call to grow in love and its ideal of mutual assistance, are overshadowed by an almost exclusive insistence on the duty of procreation." Anyone slightly acquainted with the development of doctrine on marriage knows that the unitive good has received a great deal of renewed focus since at least *Gaudium et Spes* 49, with a back history of some decades. To me, these impulsive, unfounded caricatures are unworthy of what should be the dignity and seriousness of an Apostolic Exhortation.[2]

In 121 and 122, we have a perfect example of the erratic quality of Pope Francis's discourse. At first describing marriage as "a precious sign" and as "the icon of God's love for us," within a few lines this imaging of Christ and his Church becomes a "tremendous burden" to have to impose on spouses. He used the phrase earlier in 37. But who has ever expected sudden perfection of the married; who has not conceived of marriage as a lifelong project of growth in the living-out of the sacrament?

Pope Francis's language of emotion and passion (125, 242, 143, 145) owes nothing to the Fathers of the Church or the expositors of the spiritual life in the great Tradition, but rather to the mentality of the popular media. His simple conflation of *eros* and sexual

---

2 Other examples: the "throwaway populism" of: "families are not a problem. They are first and foremost an opportunity" (7). In 37, again, a throwaway caricature bearing no relation to reality: "We have long thought that simply by stressing doctrinal, bioethical and moral issues, without encouraging openness to grace, we were providing sufficient support to families." What world is he referring to? John Paul II's entire pontificate was an extraordinary invitation to grace to the married. Another cheap shot in 38, vague and unsubstantiated opinionizing. In 49, another cheap shot, whose background is similarly obscure. Similarly, another caricature in 134. Number 314 begins with two populist broadsides: "stones to throw at people's lives" and "one used to hiding behind the Church's teachings."

desire in 151 succumbs to the secularist view of it, and ignores Pope Benedict's *Deus Caritas Est,* steeped in a thoughtful exposition of the mystery of *eros* and *agape* and the Cross.

One balks at the ambiguous language of 243 and 246, implying that somehow it is the Church's fault, or something the Church has to be anxiously apologetic about, when her members enter upon an objectively adulterous union, and thereby exclude themselves from Holy Communion. This is a governing idea that pervades the entire document.

Several times in the course of reading this document I have paused and wondered: "I haven't heard of Christ for pages."[3] All too often we are subjected to long tracts of homespun avuncular advice that could be given by any secular journalist without the faith—the sort of thing to be found in the pages of *Reader's Digest,* or one of those "Lifestyle" inserts in weekend newspapers.

It is true, some doctrines of the Church are robustly upheld, e.g., against same-sex unions (52) and polygamy (53), gender ideology (56) and abortion (84); there are affirmations of the indissolubility of marriage (63), and its procreative end, and an upholding of *Humanae Vitae* (68, 83), the sovereign rights of parents in the education of their children (84), the right of every child to a mother and a father (172, 175), the importance of fathers (176, 177). You can even occasionally find a poetic thought, such as "the gaze" of contemplative love between spouses (127–28), or the maturing of good wine as an image of the maturing of spouses (135).

But all this laudable doctrine is undermined, I submit, by the overall rhetoric of the Exhortation, and by that of Pope Francis's entire papacy. These affirmations of Catholic doctrine are welcome, but, it needs to be asked, do they have any more weight than that of the passing and erratic enthusiasm of the current incumbent

---

[3] For example, 37 and preceding (ch. 2), as mere socio-political analysis, or at worse, as in the later part of ch. 4 (after a series of homilies threaded along Paul's hymn to charity), homespun psychological advice that could be found in any popular secular venue, specially with "Dialogue," at 136 et seq., and with the friendly advice to pregnant mothers, and other aspects of the family (180 et seq.), the pages of advice to the married, which any secular person without faith might give (ch. 6). Similarly, in ch. 7, on pedagogy, pages and pages go by where a relationship with Christ never enters in, or prayer, or the Liturgy. Christ makes a late appearance at 287.

of St. Peter's Chair? I am serious here. My instinct is that the next position threatening to crumble will be the issue of same-sex "marriage." If it is possible to construct a justification of states of objective adultery on the basis of recognizing "the constructive elements in those situations not yet corresponding to the Church's teaching on marriage" (292), "when such unions attain a particular stability, legally recognized, are characterized by deep affection and responsibility for their offspring" (293), etc., how long can you defer applying exactly the same line of reasoning to same-sex partnerships? And yes, children may be involved, as we know very well from the gay agenda. Already, the former editor of the *Catechism*,[4] to whose hermeneutic of *AL* as a "development of doctrine" Pope Francis has referred us, appears to be "evolving" on the potential for "good" same-sex "unions."

READING CHAPTER EIGHT

And all that was before I came to reading Chapter Eight. I have wondered if the extraordinary prolixity of the first seven chapters was meant to wear us down before we came to this crucial chapter, and catch us off-guard. To me, the entire tenor of Chapter Eight is problematic, not just 304 and footnote 351. As soon as I finished it, I thought to myself: Clear as a bell: Pope Francis wanted some form of the Kasper Proposal from the beginning. Here it is. Kasper has won. It explains Pope Francis's terse comments at the end of the 2015 Synod, when he censured narrow-minded "pharisees"—evidently those who had frustrated a better outcome, according to his agenda. "Pharisees"? The sloppiness of his language! They were the modernists, in a way, of Judaism, the masters of ten-thousand nuances—and most pertinently, those who tenaciously upheld the practice of divorce and remarriage. The real analogues of the Pharisees in this whole affair are Kasper and his allies.

To press on. The words of 295 on St. John Paul's comments on the "law of gradualness" in *FC* 34 seem to me subtly treacherous and corruptive. For they try to co-opt and corrupt John Paul in support precisely of a situational ethics that the holy pope bent all his loving pastoral intelligence and energy to oppose. Let us hear then what St. John Paul really says about the law of gradualness:

---

4   Namely, Cardinal Christoph Schönborn.

> Married people ... cannot however look on the law as merely an ideal to be achieved in the future: they must consider it as a command of Christ the Lord to overcome difficulties through constancy. And so what is known as "the law of gradualness" or step-by-step advance cannot be identified with a "gradualness of the law," as if there were differing degrees or forms of precept in God's law for different individuals and situations. In God's plan, all husbands and wives are called in marriage to holiness...

Footnote 329 of *AL* also presents another surreptitious corruption. It cites a passage of *Gaudium et Spes* 51, concerning the intimacy of married life. But by an undetected sleight of hand it is placed in the mouth of the divorced and remarried instead. Such corruptions surely indicate that references and footnotes, which in this document are made to do some heavy lifting, need to be properly verified.

Already in 297, we see the responsibility for "irregular situations" being shifted to the discernment of pastors. Step by subtle step the arguments advance a definite agenda. Number 299 queries how "current forms of exclusion currently practiced" can be surmounted, and 301 introduces the idea of "conversation with the priest in the internal forum." Can you not already detect where the argument is going?

So we arrive at 301, which drops the guarded manner as we descend into the maelstrom of "mitigating factors." Here it seems the "mean old Church" has finally been superseded by the "nice new Church." In the past we may have thought that those living in "irregular situations" without repentance were in a state of mortal sin. Now, however, they may not be in a state of mortal sin, after all; indeed, sanctifying grace may be at work in them. It is then explained, in an excess of pure subjectivism, that "a subject may know full well the rule, yet have great difficulty in understanding its 'inherent value.'" Here is a mitigating factor to beat all mitigating factors. On this argument, then, do we now exculpate the original envy of Lucifer, because he had "great difficulty in understanding" the "inherent value," to him, of the transcendent Majesty of God? At which point, I feel, reverend gentlemen, that we have lost all foothold, and fallen like Alice into a parallel universe, where nothing is quite what it seems to be.

A series of quotations from St. Thomas Aquinas are brought to bear, on which I am not qualified to comment, except to say that, obviously, proper verification and contextualization are strongly indicated. Number 304 is a highly technical apologia for moral casuistry, argued in exclusively philosophical terms without a hint of Christ or of faith. One cannot but think that this was supplied by another hand. It is not Francis's style, even if it is his belief.

Finally, we come to the crucial 305. It commences with two of the sort of throwaway caricatures that recur throughout the document. The new doctrine that Pope Francis had flagged a little earlier he now repeats and reasserts: a person can be in an objective situation of mortal sin—for that is what he is speaking about—and still be living and growing in God's grace, all the "while receiving the help of the Church," which, the infamous footnote 351 declares, can include, "in certain cases," both Confession and Holy Communion. I am sure that there are by now many busily attempting to "interpret" all this according to a "hermeneutic of continuity," to show its harmony, I presume, with Tradition. I might add, that in this 305, Pope Francis quotes himself four times. In fact, it appears that Pope Francis's most frequently cited reference through *AL* is himself, and that in itself is interesting.

In the rest of the chapter Pope Francis changes tack. He makes an inverted admission that his approach may leave "room for confusion" (308). To this he responds with a discussion of "mercy." At the very beginning, in 7, he declared that "everyone should feel challenged by Chapter Eight." Yes we do, but not quite in the blithe heuristic sense he meant it. Pope Francis has freely admitted in time past that he is the sort of person who loves to "make messes." Well, I think we can concede that he has certainly achieved that here.

Let me tell you of a rather taciturn and cautious friend, a married man, who expressed to me, before the Apostolic Exhortation was published: "I do hope he avoids ambiguity." Well, reverend gentlemen, I think even the most pious reading of *AL* cannot say that it has avoided ambiguity. To use Pope Francis's own words, "widespread uncertainty and ambiguity" (33) can certainly be applied to this document, and I venture to say, to his whole papacy. If we are put into the impossible situation of critiquing a document of the ordinary Magisterium, consider whether in *Amoris Laetitia* Pope Francis himself is relativizing the authority of the Magisterium by eliding the magisterium of Pope John Paul, specially in *Familiaris*

Consortio and *Veritatis Splendor*. I challenge any of you to soberly reread the encyclical *Veritatis Splendor*, say 95–105, and not conclude that there is a deep dissonance between that Encyclical and this Apostolic Exhortation. In my younger years, I anguished over the conundrum: how can you be obedient to the disobedient? For a pope, too, is called to obedience — indeed, preeminently so.

THE WIDER IMPLICATIONS OF *AL*

The serious difficulties I foresee, for priests in particular, arise from clashing interpretations of the loopholes discreetly planted throughout *AL*. What will a young new priest do, who, well-informed, wishes to maintain that the divorced and remarried can in no wise by admitted to Holy Communion, while his parish priest has a policy of "accompaniment," which on the contrary envisages that they can? What will a parish priest with a similar sense of fidelity do, if his bishop and diocese decide for a more liberal policy? What will one region of bishops do in relation to another region of bishops, as each set of bishops decides how to cut and divide the "nuances" of this new doctrine, so that in the worst case, what is held to be mortal sin on one side of the border, is "accompanied away" and condoned on the other side of the border? We know it is already happening, officially, in certain German dioceses, and unofficially in Argentina — and even here [Australia], for years, as I can vouch from my own family.[5]

---

[5] Surely a guide to estimating Pope Francis's mind in this document and his purpose throughout the Synod process is his own known past practice. There is the famous case, after he became Pope, of his cold-calling an Argentinian woman who had written to him, Jacquelina Sabetta, in an "irregular situation." "Father Bergoglio," as he called himself, endorsed her reception of Holy Communion there and then. Such was his "accompaniment." See www.christiantoday.com/article/pope.francis.tells.divorced.woman.she.should.be.allowed.to.receive.communion/36987.htm. It appears there may have been other cases since he became Pope, e.g. www.dailymail.co.uk/news/article-2972258/Pope-wants-scrap-centuries-old-ban-priests-marrying-told-divorced-woman-living-sin-receive-Holy-Communion-claims-confidante.html. While he was Archbishop of Buenos Aires, it is clear that Bergoglio readily overlooked the admission of the divorced and remarried to Holy Communion. "In the 2013 book, *Pope Francis, Untying the Knot*, author Paul Vallely, an admirer of Francis, explains that in Argentina, Communion for divorced and remarried Catholics is considered as no big deal. 'In Buenos Aires he [Bergoglio] came across more concrete problems,' said Father Augusto Zampini, a diocesan priest

Such an outcome is so appalling that it may mark (as another friend, also a married man, suggested) the collapse of the Catholic Christian narrative. But of course other aspects of ecclesial and social deterioration have also brought us to this point: the havoc of pseudo-renewal in the Church in the past few decades, the numbingly stupid policy of inculturation applied to a deracinated Western culture of militant secularism, the relentless, progressive erosion of marriage and the family in society, the greater attack on the Church from within than from without that Pope Benedict so lamented, the long defection of certain theologians and laity in the matter of contraception, the frightful sexual scandals, the countless casual sacrileges, the loss of the spirit of the Liturgy, the *de facto* internal schisms on a whole range of serious issues and approaches, thinly papered-over with a semblance of *de jure* Church unity, the patterns of profound spiritual and moral dissonance that seethe beneath the tattered title of "Catholic" these days. And we wonder that the Church is in a weakened state and fading away?

We might also trace the long diachronic antecedents of *AL*. Being something of an ancient soul, I see this document as the bad fruit of certain second-millennium developments in the Western Church. I briefly point to two in particular: the sharply rationalist and dualist form of Thomism fostered among the Jesuits in the sixteenth century, and in that context, their elaboration of the casuistic understanding of mortal sin in the seventeenth century. The art of casuistry was pursued in a new category of sacred science called "Moral Theology," in which, it seems to me, the slide-rule of calculation is skilfully plied to estimate the minimum culpability necessary to avoid the imputation of mortal sin — technically,

---

of the city. 'When you're working in a shanty town, 90 percent of your congregation are single or divorced. You have to learn that Communion for the divorced and remarried is not an issue there. Everyone takes Communion.' Vallely goes on to comment, 'Bergoglio never altered his doctrinal orthodoxy on such matters but he did not allow dogma to overrule the priority of pastoral concern.' Vallely then quotes Buenos Aires 'slum' priest Father Juan Isasmendi, who said: 'He [Bergoglio] was never rigid about the small and stupid stuff, because he was interested in something deeper.' Thus Bergoglio comes from a background where Communion for divorced and remarried is considered a minor issue (the 'small and stupid stuff') as compared to larger concerns of preferential option for the poor." Text from mcjeffentrailsofthecoming.blogspot.com/2015/02/the-coming-burke-bergoglio-conflict.html, accessed November 16, 2020.

at any rate. What a spiritual goal! What a spiritual vision! Today, reverend fathers, casuistry rears its ugly head in the new form of situational ethics, and *AL*, quite frankly, is full of it—even though it was expressly condemned by St. John Paul II in the encyclical *Veritatis Splendor*.

PERORATION

Can I exhort you in any way that can help? St. Basil has a great homily on the text: "Only take heed to yourself and guard your soul diligently" (Deut 4:9). We must attend to our own dispositions first. The Desert Fathers have several stories in which a young monk secures his eternal salvation through the heroic meekness of his obedience to a seriously flawed abba. And he ends by bringing about the repentance and salvation of his abba too. We must not let ourselves be tempted into any reaction of hostility to Pope Francis, lest we become part of the devil's game. This deeply flawed Holy Father, too, we must honour, and carry in charity, and pray for. With God nothing shall be impossible. Who knows whether God has got Jorge Bergoglio into this position in order to find a sufficient number to pray efficaciously for the salvation of his soul?

I notice that Cardinals Müller and Sarah and Pell are silent. What wisdom there may be in that—for the time being.

Meanwhile, you who have responsibilities in the governance of the Church will have to make practical dispositions in regard to the thorny issues of *AL*. First of all, in our own minds, we should have no doubt what the real teaching of the Gospel is and ever will be. Obviously, whatever strategy of pressing for an official clarification of projected pastoral practice that can be devised must be tried. I particularly urge this on bishops. Remember how they compromised themselves with their statements about "conscience" in the 1970s? Some of you may find yourselves in very difficult situations in regard to your peers, almost calling for the virtues of a Confessor of the Faith. Are you ready for the whipping, figuratively speaking, that you may incur? You could, of course, choose the illusory safety of conventional shallowness and superficial good cheer, a great temptation of ecclesiastics as company men. I don't advise it. The times are serious, perhaps much more serious than we suspect. We are being put to the test. The Lord is here. He is calling you.

A FEW THOUGHTS ON THE APPROPRIATE EUCHARISTIC DISPOSITION OF THE DIVORCED AND REMARRIED

I lately had some email correspondence in which a friend made some points on the worthy Eucharistic dispositions of those in "irregular situations." In my reply I expressed my own thoughts on what I think is the spiritually and sacramentally advisable conduct of a Catholic who is in an "irregular situation."

There is a lovely woman who usually comes to Mass in our Cathedral and sits at the back. I had a conversation with her, and learned she was in one of these "irregular situations." She is still very diligent in coming to Mass, but does not partake of Holy Communion. She does not rail against the Church, or say "It's the Church's fault," or "How unjust the Church is!," which sentiments indeed I have heard from others, whom I have gently called to order. I find this woman's conduct admirable in the circumstances.

The best stance in prayer for those who are in these situations and cannot as yet bring themselves to the measure of repentance required (and so to Confession), but who do not want to let go of looking Godward, is to present themselves to the Lord at Mass precisely in their state of privation and need, not going forward to "grasp" the Eucharist, but endeavoring to lay themselves open to the intervention of grace and a change of circumstances, if and when it be possible. My sense of their plight is: it is better that they hold themselves honestly, if painfully, in the tension of their situation before God, without subterfuge. I think this is to position themselves best for the triumph of grace. Who of us cannot identify with this unequal situation in the spiritual contest of our own life, i.e., of battling hard with some seemingly intractable passion, and scarcely finding our way out of it, or perhaps being bogged down a long time in some sin before our moral life emerges into a place of greater freedom? Remember Augustine's famous prayer to God in the lead-up to his definitive conversion: "Domine, da mihi castitatem, sed noli modo" — "O Lord, give me chastity, but not yet." I think that when such people attend Mass and refrain from taking Communion, it is potentially a great witness to all of us. And yes, it does cry out to us to consider our own dispositions in going forward to partake of our Lord's most holy, deifying Body and Blood.

Apropos of which, it occurs to me to report a saying of the actor Richard Harris, a "hell-raiser" of a lapsed Catholic for many a year: "I'm divorced twice, but I would prefer to die a bad Catholic than have the Church change to suit me."⁶ I find more truthfulness in that than in...well, I had better not say it.

EPILOGUE

Generally inhabiting an older sort of Christian world as I do, let me leave you with a word from a much-loved Master, St. Basil the Great, who knows nothing of these things, least of all that insidious germ of subjectivism that crept in with Nominalism, the Protestant Reformation, and the century of early Modernity, the sixteenth century, and now entirely floods our society and so many in our Church. Hear then the following appeal of St. Basil to the married, coming down to us across the centuries:

> Then do you think the Gospels apply to those with a wife? Look, it has been made clear to you that we shall all have to give an account of our obedience to the Gospel, both monks and those who are married. The only concession (συγγνώμη) to one who has entered into marriage will be the lack of self-control (ἀκρασία) in his desire for and intercourse with the female (τῆς πρὸς τὸ θῆλυ ἐπιθυμιάς τε καὶ συνουσίας). But the other commands have been laid down for all alike and are fraught with peril for any who transgress them. For when Christ proclaimed the Gospel of the Father's commands, He was addressing those in the world. He clearly testified to this by his answer when he was privately questioned by His disciples: "And what I say to you I say to all" (Mk 13:27). Do not slacken, then, you who have chosen communion with a wife (κοινωνίαν γυναικὸς), as if you had some kind of right to embrace the world. Rather, you have need of greater labors and vigilance in gaining your salvation, inasmuch as you have chosen to dwell in the midst of the toils and in the very stronghold of the rebellious powers, and night and day all your senses are impelled toward desire of the allurements to sin which are before your eyes. Be sure of this, that you will neither escape doing battle with the Evil One nor gain the victory over him without a great struggle to

---

6 *London Observer*, October 25, 1987, reported by Karl Schmude in *Catholic Weekly*, April 27, 1988.

observe the Gospel teachings. How shall you, stationed in the very thick of the battle, be able to win the contest against the Enemy, who wanders over all the earth under heaven, and rages about like a mad dog, seeking whom he may devour, as we learn from the history of Job? If you refuse battle with your antagonist, take to yourself another world where he is not; there you shall be able to avoid conflict with him and take your ease without peril to Gospel teachings.[7]

Thank you!

---

[7] *On Renunciation*, PG 31, 629A.

2

"Chaos was raised to a principle by the stroke of a pen"[1]

INTERVIEW WITH DR ROBERT SPAEMANN

GREATLY VALUED AS AN ADVISOR BY SAINT John Paul II, a friend of Benedict XVI, and widely held to be the most important German Catholic philosopher of recent decades, Robert Spaemann, emeritus professor of philosophy at the University of Munich, expressed a distinctly critical interpretation of *Amoris Laetitia* in this interview with Anian Christoph Wimmer, editor of CNA's German-language edition.

CNA: Professor Spaemann, you have accompanied the papacies of John Paul II and Benedict XVI with your philosophy. Many believers are now asking, whether and how Pope Francis's post-synodal apostolic exhortation Amoris Laetitia *should be read in continuity with the teachings of the Church and these previous Popes. How do you see this?*

Prof. Dr Spaemann: For the most part, it is possible, although the direction allows for consequences which cannot be made compatible with the teaching of the Church. Article 305 together with footnote 351—in which it is stated that believers can be allowed to the sacraments "in an objective situation of sin," "because of mitigating factors"—directly contradicts article 84 of Pope John Paul II's exhortation *Familiaris Consortio*.

What then is Pope John Paul II's exhortation about?

John Paul II explains human sexuality as a "real symbol for the giving of the whole person," and namely, "without any temporal or other limitation." He thus formulates very clearly in article 84 that remarried divorcees must refrain from sex if they want to go to communion. A change in the practice of the administration

---

1 Published by Anian Christoph Wimmer, "Full text: Interview with Robert Spaemann on *Amoris Laetitia*," *Catholic News Agency*, April 29, 2016. Translation by Richard Andrew Krema.

of the sacraments would therefore be no "further development of *Familiaris Consortio*," as Cardinal Kasper said, but rather a breach in her [the Church's] essential anthropological and theological teaching on marriage and human sexuality. The Church has no authority, without prior conversion [of the divorcees], to approve disordered sexual relationships through the administration of the sacraments, thereby anticipating God's mercy—regardless of how these situations are to be judged on a human and moral level. The door here—as with the ordination of women to the priesthood—is closed.

Couldn't someone object that the anthropological and theological reflections you mentioned are indeed correct—yet God's mercy is not bound to such limits, but it is linked to the concrete situation of the individual person?

God's mercy concerns the heart of the Christian faith in the Incarnation and Redemption. Of course, God has each individual person in his or her own situation in view. He knows each person better than they know themselves. The Christian life, however, is not a pedagogical event in which marriage is aimed for as an "ideal," as *Amoris Laetitia* appears to suggest in many places. The whole realm of relationships, especially sexual relationships, concerns the dignity of the human person, his or her personhood and freedom. It has to do with the body as a "Temple of God" (1 Cor 6:19). Every violation to this realm, even if it were to occur often, is, therefore, also a violation of one's relationship with God, to which Christians know they are called—a sin against God's holiness, and always in need of purification and conversion.

God's mercy consists in always allowing this conversion anew. Of course, it is not bound to definite limits, but the Church on her part requires a proclamation of conversion and does not have the authority to overstep established boundaries by administering the sacraments [when conversion is not in evidence], and to abuse God's mercy. That would be imprudent. Therefore clergy who comply with the existing order judge no one; rather, they take into consideration and announce these boundaries of God's holiness—a salvific promulgation. I don't want to comment any further to insinuate that they would "hide behind the Church's teachings" and "sit on the chair of Moses" so as to throw "stones...at people's lives" (*AL* 305). It may be noted that the respective verses in the Gospel are alluded to mistakenly. Jesus indeed says that the Pharisees and scribes sit on the chair of Moses, but he expressly emphasizes that the disciples should adhere to what they say. They should not, however, live like them (Matt 23:2).

Pope Francis has stressed that we should not focus on only single sentences of his teachings; rather the whole should be kept in mind.
Concentrating on the stated passages is fully justified in my eyes. It cannot be expected in a papal exhortation that people will rejoice in a pleasant text and ignore decisive sentences that change the teachings of the Church. There is actually only a clear yes or no decision: to give Communion or not. There is no intermediary between them.

The Holy Father emphasizes in his exhortation that nobody may be allowed to be condemned forever.
I find it difficult to understand what he means there. That the Church is not allowed to condemn anyone personally—of course not forever, which she cannot do, thank God—is clear. When it concerns sexual relationships that objectively contradict the Christian way of life, I would like to know from the Pope, after what time and under what circumstances objectively sinful conduct is changed into conduct pleasing to God.

Is it, in your perspective, actually an issue of a breach with the teaching tradition of the Church?
That it is an issue of a breach emerges doubtlessly for every thinking person who knows the respective texts.

Regardless whether or not one agrees with this assessment, the question arises as to how it came to this.
It was already apparent that Francis views his predecessor Pope John Paul II from a critical distance when he canonized him together with John XXIII, although the second required miracle was not attributed to the latter. Many felt this to be manipulative: it seemed as if the Pope wanted to relativize the importance of John Paul II.
The actual problem is an influential movement in moral theology, which holds a purely situational ethics, and which can be found as early as the 17th century among the Jesuits. The quotations

from Thomas Aquinas that the Pope furnishes in *Amoris Laetitia* appear to support this direction. Here [in *AL*] it will be overlooked, however, that Thomas knows objectively sinful actions for which there are no exceptions. Among them is all sexually disordered conduct. John Paul II rejected situational ethics and condemned it in his encyclical *Veritatis Splendor*—as did Karl Rahner before him, in an essay in the 1950s that contained all of these essential and presently valid arguments. *Amoris Laetitia* also challenges *Veritatis Splendor*. With all of this, we cannot forget that it was John Paul II who centered his pontificate on the subject of divine mercy: his second encyclical was devoted to it. The diary of Sister Faustina was discovered in Krakow, and he later named her a saint. He is her authentic interpreter.

What consequences do you see for the Church?

The consequences are already foreseeable: uncertainty and confusion, from the bishops' conferences to the small parishes in the middle of nowhere. A few days ago, a priest from the Congo expressed to me his perplexity in light of this new papal document and the lack of clear precedents. According to the respective passages from *Amoris Laetitia*, not only remarried divorcees but also everyone living in some "irregular situation" could, by further nondescript "mitigating circumstances," be allowed to confess other sins and receive Communion even without trying to abandon their sexual conduct—that means without confession and conversion. Each priest who adheres to the until-now valid discipline of the sacraments could be mobbed by the faithful and be put under pressure from his bishop. Rome can now make the stipulation that only "merciful" bishops will be named, who are ready to soften the existing discipline. Chaos was raised to a principle by the stroke of a pen. The Pope must have known that he would split the Church with such a step and lead toward a schism—a schism that would not be settled on the peripheries, but rather in the heart of the Church. May God forbid that from happening.

One thing, however, seems clear to me: the concern of this Pope that the Church should overcome her own self-referentiality in order to be able to approach persons more free-handedly has been destroyed by this papal document for an unforeseeable amount of time. A secularizing push and the further decrease in the number of priests in many parts of the world are also to be expected. It has been able to be observed for quite some time that bishops and dioceses with a clear stance on faith and morality have the greatest increase in priests. We must remember the words of St. Paul in the Letter to the Corinthians: "If the bugle gives an indistinct sound, who will get ready for battle?" (1 Cor 14:8).

In your opinion, where do we go from here?
Every single cardinal, but also every bishop and priest, is called upon to preserve uprightly the Catholic discipline of the sacraments within his realm of responsibility and to confess it publicly. In case the Pope is not ready to make corrections, it remains reserved for a later pope to officially make things right.

3

The Holy Spirit Guides the Pope?[1]

FR JOHN HUNWICKE

I THINK ONE OF THE MOST STRIKING LITTLE videos I have seen for a long time shows a "Song for Pope Francis composed and performed by Emily Clarke ahead of the 2018 Papal Visit to Ireland." We see a large picture of the Holy Father mystically framed by a multitude of candles; we hear the chanteuse invoking the pontiff as if he were a *praesens numen*: "You were chosen by God above.... O come and teach us to let God's glory shine.... O papa Francis.... Lead us back to the precious Son." Is this merely the old rhetorical convention of "apostrophising" someone who is not thought of as really present? I invite you to watch YouTube and to judge for yourself.

Last summer, pictures were circulating of the altar of repose at Acireale in Sicily. Above the vessel containing the Most Holy, a large picture grinned down: Pope Francis. You will tell me that such things are abuses not, of course, willed by the Holy Father. I will ask you why it is that the cult of the bishop of Rome has reached such unprecedented heights during this pontificate.

There is, of course, nothing new about a cult of a current occupant of the Roman bishopric. Cardinal Wiseman certainly urged his people to imagine themselves "full in the panting heart of Rome" and to ask divine blessing on "our Pope, the Great, the Good." But I think the twentieth-century global village laid the foundations of an exponential leap in the papal cult—a leap harnessed closely to the developing twentieth-century concept of the International Celebrity. I suggest that we find the roots of this in the 1930s. Pius XI may still have been the Prisoner of the Vatican, but his Secretary of State, Cardinal Pacelli, who was to succeed him as Pius XII, was not imprisoned. The newsreel clips of his travels look uncannily like previews of the culture set in place by St. John Paul II, of a travelling papal circus going from country to country, doing big things at big services in a

---

[1] Given at the Gardone Conference, Italy, in June of 2017. Published here for the first time, and expanded with a reference to the priest in Jalisco, Mexico.

thoroughly big way. At a time when air travel was less of an everyday event than it is now, Pacelli was called the Cardinale Volante or the Vice-Papa. I intend to draw no equivalence between the two figures when I observe that one can even find parallels between Pius XII and that other enthusiast for choreographed mass events: Adolf Hitler. Each of them had studio photographs taken of himself in histrionic postures, so that he could study them carefully and decide which of the postures were the more effective.

I would have to concede that a papal visit might be a very strengthening experience for a besieged and insecure local Church (and in such circumstances might be even more powerful if the phenomenon were rarer). But the whole present-day business does rather suggest that the pope is a super-bishop... which he is not. He is the bishop of that Church with which all Christians are supposed to be in communion; of the Church where Peter's voice lives and speaks—so that under specified conditions he articulates the infallibility of the whole Church and has a primacy, where it is needed, of ensuring that the universal *norma fidei* is everywhere the local norm. In a healthy particular Church, surely the local successor of the apostles, the diocesan bishop, should be capable, in normal circumstances, of fulfilling the *munera apostolica* without needing the headmaster to come into his classroom and restore order. The endless and vulgar showcasing of Pope Francis demonstrates how inherently dangerous this cult of personality really is. Turning the *servus servorum Dei* into a cosmopolitan celeb obscures rather than expresses his true place in the Church Militant. Even Pio Nono did not consider that his newly-defined primacy and infallibility required him to gad around the world showing them off like a girl with a new engagement ring.

But is the personality cult of Papa Bergoglio merely vulgar? I think it is worse. I think it is dangerous and comes very close to blasphemy. Early in 2017, an image circulated on the internet of a devotional object in the form of a cross. In the middle, a round medallion showing Pope Francis. Above his head, the words "Pope Francis"; underneath, the invitation "Pray for us." And above that, a dove, with a halo demonstrating it to be the Holy Spirit—a dove diving straight down upon the pontiff.

Should we take this seriously? Is it not simply a result of what happens if you invite an illiterate "designer" to mix up a few religious motifs (the *Agnus Dei* and the open Bible feature on each side of Bergoglio) and produce something which will sell well among the tourists? Perhaps so; but the question is: how many swallows make a summer? I suggest that merely by browsing on the internet we can disturb quite a richesse of swallows—such as this over-the-top "Creed on behalf of Pope Francis" that a priest led his congregation in reciting at the end of Mass on Sunday, October 25, 2020 at St. Augustine's Church in Jalisco, Mexico. It was captured on video, transcribed, and translated. The text is as follows:

> I believe in Pope Francis as the legitimate Successor of the Apostle Peter. I believe that the Holy Ghost speaks to the Church through him. I believe that he guides the Catholic Church as a true Pastor. I believe that he is diligently concerned with all of humanity, because we are all brothers and sons of God. I believe in his magisterium, which is in perfect harmony with the faith and morals of the Church. I believe that his personal opinions reflect the evangelical attitude of the believers in Christ. I reject all offenses, aspersions, and insults towards his person. As for those who reject his authority, I affirm that they are in ecclesiastical error as much as in error of communion.[2]

Though this may be an extravagant example, it expresses a trend that can be found even among Bergoglio's closest associates. What they actually say and write about him is not merely in very poor taste, but is, as I shall demonstrate, most disturbing at the level of doctrine.

THE TEACHING OF THE POPE'S ASSOCIATES

After the publication of the Apostolic Exhortation *Amoris Laetitia*, a newly-minted Cardinal Farrell, formerly bishop of Dallas but destined to become the head of a new Dicastery for the Family, said he understood that the U. S. bishops' conference would be discussing *Amoris Laetitia* later in the year. He could hardly criticise them for doing this; indeed, *a fortiori* he had to applaud their intention. But he was clearly not entirely confident that the bishops were all reliably on-message. His unease shone through what he said (the uncertain syntax is all his Eminence's own):

---

[2] See "A new 'creed to [sic] Pope Francis' prayed at Mass in Mexico," *LifeSiteNews*, November 12, 2020.

> I think that's very important that they have discussion... But at the same time I think it's very important that we all understand that this is the Holy Spirit speaking... basically this is the Holy Spirit speaking to us. Do we believe that the Holy Spirit wasn't there in the first synod? Do we believe he wasn't in the second synod? Do we believe that he didn't inspire our Holy Father Pope Francis in writing this document?

And this conviction, that the words and actions of Bergoglio are directly and reliably guaranteed by the Holy Spirit, is by now a cliché among his admirers. Consider the words of Cardinal Maradiaga:

> I think the car of the Church has no gear to go in reverse. It pulls itself forward because the Holy Spirit is not accustomed to go backwards. He always brings us forward. I am not afraid because I know it is not Francis, it is the Holy Spirit who guides the Church, and that, if he has allowed this Pontiff to come it is for some reason, and we certainly ought to look to the future with hope...[3]

Another and even closer associate of the pope, from their time together in Argentina, is Archbishop Víctor Manuel Fernández, Rector of the Catholic University of Argentina, rumoured to have been the drafter of *Amoris Laetitia*. He deserves extensive citation. "While these people [critics of Pope Francis] seem to appear conservative as regards doctrine, fundamentally they seem not to have faith in the special assistance of the Holy Spirit, which Jesus promised the pope." And, on another occasion, very revealingly:

> The pope goes slow because he wants to be sure that the changes have a deep impact. The slow pace is necessary to ensure the effectiveness of the changes. He knows there are those hoping that the next pope will turn everything back around. If you go slowly it's more difficult to turn things back.... The pope must have his reasons, because he knows very well what he's doing. He must have an objective that we don't understand yet. You have to realise that he is aiming at reform which is irreversible. If

---

3 "Top Papal Adviser Insults the Four Dubia Cardinals," *OnePeterFive*, April 20, 2017.

one day he should sense that he's running out of time and doesn't have enough time to do what the Spirit is asking him, you can be sure he will speed up.[4]

Another witness to this *topos*, common among the Bergoglian circle, is Archbishop Vincent Nichols of Westminster. In a letter marking the fourth anniversary of Bergoglio's election, he wrote "on behalf of the Catholic Community of England and Wales" to assure the Roman bishop that "we thank God that the Holy Spirit guided the Church in the process of your election and that the same Holy Spirit guides and supports you day by day." These words are categorical enough, but it is not clear whether Nichols asserts these propositions as being true of every Roman Pontiff *ex officio* or uniquely of Bergoglio. If the former, then Nichols clearly knows better than Cardinal Ratzinger did when interviewed in 1997 about whether the Holy Spirit intervenes in the election of a pope. "I would say, not in the sense that the Holy Spirit chooses any particular pope, because there is plenty of evidence to the contrary—there have been many whom the Holy Spirit quite obviously would not have chosen." Indeed. Are we really to believe that the Holy Spirit was responsible for (to use Nichols's term) "the processes" by which Leo V, Christopher, Sergius III, Anastasius III, Lando, John X, Leo VI, Stephen VIII, and not a few others secured the papal throne? Is the direct intervention of the Holy Spirit to be discerned in the process of murdering one pope so as to seize his place? What theological account does Cardinal Nichols want us to give of the role of the Holy Spirit in the conception of John XI in the womb of Marozia and his adolescent elevation to the papacy only two decades later?

And does the Holy Spirit really guide every pope "day by day"? ("Day by day" must surely mean "daily" rather than "sometimes.") So, when Urban VI supervised daily the torture (culminating in their executions) of those cardinals who had sent him a Letter of Correction, was the Holy Spirit "day by day" his "guide"? (It was only the intervention of King Richard II which secured the life of our own learned and saintly English Cardinal Adam Easton, who once taught Greek and Hebrew at Oxford.)

But if Nichols's assertions are not advanced as being true of every pope, how do we know which *particular* popes are the Spirit-filled

---

4 *Corriere della Sera*, May 10, 2015, quoted in "On Exhortation, Müller Resists and Fernández Reveals," *OnePeterFive*, May 11, 2016.

pontiffs? Even if we can trust Nichols as a reliable discerner of spirits, he will not always be at hand to guide us.

Perhaps the weirdest expression of the idea that Bergoglio was specially chosen by the Spirit is that given early in the pontificate by Cardinal Schönborn. I can only say that if Schönborn is truly one of the intellectual giants of the College of Cardinals, that body hardly merits our admiration. "Only divine intervention could explain the speed with which the Argentine cardinal, who did not feature on any of the main lists of likely candidates compiled by Vatican experts, was elected," Schönborn informed us.

> "It was a tremendous experience of the Holy Spirit... we were driven by the Holy Spirit to this man — he was sitting in the last corner of the Sistine Chapel. This man is the chosen one. I received at least two strong signs; one I can tell, the other was in the Conclave, I can't speak about — but real signs of the Lord giving me the indication 'He is the one'..." Schönborn says that, before the Conclave, he bumped into a Latin American couple who were his friends; he asked them: "You have the Holy Spirit, can you give me advice for the Conclave that will start in a few hours?" The woman whispered into his ear "Bergoglio." "And it really hit me: if these people say Bergoglio, that's an indication of the Holy Spirit."[5]

As the Year of Mercy drew near, the Dean of the Roman Rota, Pio Vito Pinto, assured his hearers:

> What is important is that the spirit of collegiality and communion among bishops under obedience to the Pontiff begins to permeate the hearts and minds of the shepherds. The faithful are waiting with eagerness and love for such a *metanoia* and will nonetheless be patient in the Lord when faced with the good faith of their shepherds. The Jubilee Year of Mercy expects this sign of humble obedience (on the part of the Churches' shepherds) to the Spirit who speaks to them through Francis.[6]

---

5 *Vatican Insider*, May 15, 2013.
6 Cited in "Master, Doth It Not Concern Thee That We Perish?," *OnePeterFive*, September 21, 2015.

That "collegiality" is equivalent to "humble obedience" on the part of the episcopal college is perhaps a new understanding of the teaching of Vatican II.

Unsurprisingly, we can find *La Civiltà Cattolica*, under the editorship of Antonio Spadaro, S.J., informing us that

> one cannot always resort to the past, as if only in the past are there indications of the Spirit. Today as well the Spirit is guiding the Church and suggesting the courageous assumption of new perspectives... [Francis is the first] not to limit himself to what is already known, but wants to delve into a complex and relevant field, so that it may be the Spirit who guides the Church.[7]

The significance of this is that it sets the Spirit in opposition to the Tradition to which conciliar documents from Nicaea to Vatican I refer. Brazenly, the teaching of *Pastor Aeternus*—that the Holy Spirit was promised to the Successors of St Peter, *not* so that they might proclaim new doctrines but so that they might faithfully hand down the Deposit of Faith transmitted through the Apostles—is precisely and disastrously reversed. We have here the spirit of Walter Kasper, who is "always open to and ready for innovation. If you look at what has happened in the past, it would lead you to say No. But anything is possible."[8] We come near to blasphemy when this Bergoglianity is concisely expressed by the Archbishop of Malta: "Whoever wishes to discover what Jesus wants from him, he must ask the pope, *this* pope, not the one who came before him, or the one who came before that. This present pope."[9]

It is not surprising that Cardinal Gerhard Müller was, in the summer of 2017, thus summarised in *Die Tagespost*: "To rely solely upon inspiration by the Holy Spirit in theological questions? A frightening idea for [Müller]." Enquiry has elicited from a listener that the cardinal did *"wörtlich"* (literally) make this reference to the Spirit. Perhaps Müller's preference for the teaching of *Pastor Aeternus* over the novel sources of doctrine preferred by the Bergoglians contributed to his removal from the CDF.

---

7 Reported by Sandro Magister, February 7, 2017.
8 Speaking of the ordination of women: see "Female Deacons and The Hermeneutic of Perpetual Innovation," *OnePeterFive*, May 13, 2016.
9 "Archbishop Scicluna: We Are Following the Pope's Directives," *National Catholic Register*, January 30, 2017.

THE POPE'S OWN TEACHING

But what is Papa Bergoglio's own teaching? Do the Bergoglians accurately reproduce the views of their master?

It appears that they do. Here is the template which Pope Francis offered to the Synods which preceded *Amoris Laetitia*. It suggests that those synodal Fathers (and only those) who advocate the New and the Surprising speak with the certain assurance of the Holy Spirit:

> The Synod is a protected space where the Church experiences the action of the Holy Spirit. The Spirit speaks in the Synod through the language of all persons that allow themselves to be guided by the God that always surprises, by the God that reveals to little ones what he hides from the wise and intelligent, by the God that created the Law and the Sabbath for man and not vice versa, by the God that leaves the ninety-nine sheep to seek the sheep that was lost, by the God that is always greater than our logic and our calculations.

At Medellin on September 9, 2017, the current pope spoke thus: "As Jesus 'shook' the doctors of the Law to break them free of their rigidity, now also the Church is shaken by the Spirit in order to lay aside comforts and attachments." It is important to analyse what is going on here.

Our Lord Jesus Christ brought to an end the old dispensation. As the Incarnate Second Person of the Holy and Undivided Trinity, he spoke authoritatively and fulfilled the old precepts by his own "But I say unto you." This was the turning point of the Ages. Joseph Ratzinger explained it all in chapter four of his *Jesus of Nazareth: From the Baptism in the Jordan to the Transfiguration*:

> Jesus' 'I' is accorded a status that no teacher of the law can legitimately allow himself... [he makes] the open claim that he himself is on the same exalted level as the lawgiver—as God. The people's "alarm"... is precisely over the fact that a human being dares to speak with the authority of God. Either he is misappropriating God's majesty—which would be terrible—or else, and this seems almost inconceivable, he really does stand on the same exalted level as God.

A few pages later, Ratzinger quotes with approval Rabbi Jacob Neusner: "Jesus' claim to authority is at issue... Christ now stands on the mountain, he takes the place of the Torah." Ratzinger adds: "The issue that is really at the heart of the debate is thus finally laid bare. Jesus understands himself as the Torah—as the word of God in person."

In Christian teaching, that moment was unique. In Catholic doctrine, there is to be no new revelation after this; no new prophet, no new Messiah to bring yet another authoritative message. The Canon of given dogma is closed. The message and teaching of the Church is none other than that of Jesus. The Old Testament gave place to the New; but the New is to give way to no Third Testament.

Bergoglio expressed himself more fully in a passage at the 2017 Easter Vigil. We shall analyse his words.

> When the High Priest and the religious leaders, in collusion with the Romans, believed that they could calculate everything, that the final word had been spoken and that it was up to them to apply it, * God suddenly breaks in, upsets all the rules and offers new possibilities. God once more comes to meet us, to create and consolidate a new age, the age of mercy. This is the promise present from the beginning. This is God's surprise for his faithful people.

Francis begins with narrative past tenses. What he describes is what happened in the year of the Lord's resurrection (although we shall see that his description of the Jewish religious establishment is crafted to point to recalcitrant elements during the Bergoglian pontificate). At the point I have marked *, the past tenses give way to present tenses. We hardly notice this; after all, the "vivid" or "historic" present is a common enough literary convention. But, as we read on, we discover that we are clearly in the second decade of the Third Millennium. Under this pope, God breaks in, upsets all the rules, and creates a new age, the Age of Mercy. We are not surprised when the paragraph ends with a marker-concept of this pontificate: the God of Surprises.

So the parallels are precise. Just as Jesus created a new age, so does Bergoglio. Just as Jesus did this by setting aside those who "believed that the final word had been spoken and that it was up to them to apply it," so Bergoglio will set aside those in his day who do precisely the same. Just as Jesus "upset all the rules," Bergoglio is doing the same.

But this is false teaching. Bergoglio is not Jesus. There is to be no Third Age with new teaching. Moses's version of the Law was superseded, "fulfilled," by that of Jesus, but Bergoglio is not a third lawgiver sent to supersede Jesus. And the people Bergoglio so bitterly attacks, who "believe that the final word has been spoken and that it is up to them to apply it," are those people who are commissioned to serve the word of Jesus. And "all the rules" which Bergoglio sets himself to "upset" are the "rules" of Christ our Lord and Redeemer.

We have reached the very heart of the disastrous illogic wherewith Jorge Bergoglio has deceived himself. Various groups have, during the last few years, set themselves the task of itemizing and analyzing the individual and particular "heresies" of which they believe he is guilty. But there are deeper things than mere heresies, mere contradictions of what the Magisterium has defined. There are the things which, whether or not they have been defined, are part of the fundamental "grammar" of the Catholic Faith; assumptions indelibly inscribed in everything we believe and practise as Christians. The Person and the Teaching of Jesus Christ, as final and definitive and irreformable, is one of them.

CONCLUSION

Before Bergoglianity, the Roman Church was marked by what the Anglican historian of the papacy, Trevor Jalland, called "its strange, almost mystical faithfulness to type, its marked degree of changelessness, its steadfast clinging to tradition and precedent." St. John Henry Newman wrote about "the main purpose of its extraordinary gift" being its role as "a sort of *remora* or break in the development of doctrine." St. Vincent of Lérins, whom Pope Francis has recently (October 2017) begun to adduce as an advocate of innovatory "development," cited Pope St. Sixtus III as writing: "Nothing further should be permitted to novelty (*novitati*), because it is not fitting for anything to be added to what is old; the clear faith and belief of our forbears should be disturbed by no mixing in of filth (*caeni permixtione*)"; and Pope St. Celestine as writing "Let novelty cease to assault what is old" (*Commonitorium* XXXII).

Before Bergoglianity, decisions about doctrinal matters were never settled by councils and popes with an *ad hoc* declaration to the effect that "the Holy Spirit has just guided me/us to this." They were settled by a conscientious examination of what earlier conciliar and papal decisions had taught; what was self-evidently taught and believed by previous generations. This is because Christianity is incarnational, rooted in a real community of real people in a real world. The Bergoglian cult of what the Holy Spirit daily teaches us through the pope, and the cult of the God of Surprises, remind one of nothing so much as the religions of the Gnostics and Manichees — Spiritual People with their own spiritual sources of teaching which were not open to common ordinary Christians. What is most distressing about it is the endless and unscrupulous employment of the Holy Spirit as a piece of cheap machinery to evade obstacles in the pursuit of innovation.

Is this what Holy Scripture means by blasphemy against the Holy Spirit?

The Catholic Church should have the last word.

"The Holy Spirit was promised to the successors of Peter, not so that by his revelation they might publish new teaching, but so that by his assistance they might devoutly guard and faithfully expound the revelation handed down through the Apostles: the Deposit of Faith."[10]

---

10 First Vatican Council, *Pastor Aeternus*, ch. 4, n. 6.

4

Forty-five Catholic Academics Urge Cardinals to Ask Pope Francis to Fix Exhortation's Errors[1]

CLAIRE CHRETIEN

FORTY-FIVE CATHOLIC PRELATES, ACADEMICS, and clergy have submitted an appeal to the Dean of the College of Cardinals in Rome requesting that the cardinals and Eastern Catholic Patriarchs petition Pope Francis to repudiate a list of erroneous propositions that can be drawn from *Amoris Laetitia*. The appeal will be sent in various languages to the 218 living Catholic Cardinals and Patriarchs over the coming weeks.

The unnamed signatories contend that the exhortation contains "a number of statements that can be understood in a sense that is contrary to Catholic faith and morals." According to the group's press release, the signatories submitted along with their appeal a documented list of applicable theological censures specifying "the nature and degree of the errors that could be attributed to *Amoris Laetitia*."

The group's appeal asks the cardinals, in their capacities as the Pope's official advisers, to approach Pope Francis with a request that he reject "the errors listed in the document in a definitive and final manner, and to authoritatively state that *Amoris Laetitia* does not require any of them to be believed or considered as possibly true."

"We are not accusing the pope of heresy," said Dr Joseph Shaw, a signatory and a spokesman for the group of scholars and pastors, "but we consider that numerous propositions in *Amoris Laetitia* can be construed as heretical upon a natural reading of the text. Additional statements would fall under other established theological censures, such as scandalous, erroneous in faith, and ambiguous, among others."

"It is our hope that by seeking from our Holy Father a definitive repudiation of these errors we can help to allay the confusion

---

[1] Published at *LifeSiteNews*, July 14, 2016.

already brought about by *Amoris Laetitia* among pastors and the lay faithful," continued Shaw. "For that confusion can be dispelled effectively only by an unambiguous affirmation of authentic Catholic teaching by the Successor of Peter."

The group takes issue with nineteen passages in *Amoris Laetitia* that seem to contradict Catholic doctrine and maintains that the exhortation undermines the Church's teaching that divorced and civilly remarried Catholics who are not living abstinently may not receive the Sacraments. Some of the portions of the exhortation that appear to contradict the Church's teaching are related to the seeming suggestion that some would be incapable of obeying the Commandments, the objective sinfulness of certain acts, the headship of the husband, the superiority of consecrated virginity over the married life, and the legitimacy of capital punishment under certain circumstances.

According to the group's press release, Catholic prelates, scholars, professors, authors, and clergy from various pontifical universities, seminaries, colleges, theological institutes, religious orders, and dioceses around the world are among the signatories. "The signatories come from all over the world and include pastors, academics in philosophy, and some bishops, as well as theologians," Shaw told *LifeSiteNews*. He said the group has received no responses yet.

In a statement, Shaw explained why the letter has not yet been made public. "The appeal and cover letter are directed to the cardinals for action in the first place, and we have taken the view that the Sacred College should be allowed to consider the substance of the document and the action to be taken in response to it before its contents are made public," he said. "The censures are a detailed and technical theological document whose contents are not readily accessible to a non-specialist audience, and are easily misrepresented or misunderstood. Making the document public would impede the cardinals in their task by the media coverage and frequently uninformed debate and polemics it would raise."

Shaw continued, "At the same time it is important that Catholics who are troubled by some of the statements in *Amoris Laetitia* be aware that steps are being taken to address the problems it raises; hence the announcement of the document's existence. By the same token we aren't releasing the names of the signatories, though some have agreed to be named," such as Shaw himself and Father Brian Harrison, Shaw told *LifeSiteNews*. The signatories join numerous other Catholic theologians and philosophers in expressing concern that the exhortation endorses practices that are contrary to Church teaching.

Pope Francis's ambiguity means "what was certain before has become problematic," Dr Jude P. Dougherty, the dean emeritus of the School of Philosophy at The Catholic University of America, wrote after the exhortation's release.

Dr Anna M. Silvas, a professor at the University of New England (Australia) and one of the world's experts on the Church Fathers, delivered a particularly blunt criticism of *Amoris Laetitia* in which she noted the document failed to mention the term "adultery" and that even "the most pious reading of *Amoris Laetitia* cannot say that it has avoided ambiguity." The document seems to embrace situation ethics and the Kasper proposal to admit to the Sacraments those living unrepentantly in objectively sinful situations, Silvas said. "I feel that we have lost all foothold, and fallen like Alice into a parallel universe, where nothing is quite what it seems to be," she wrote.

Professor Robert Spaemann, a prominent Catholic philosopher and close personal friend of Pope Benedict XVI, said that *Amoris Laetitia* presents a "breach" with Catholic Tradition and contradicts Pope St. John Paul II's exhortation *Familiaris Consortio*.

5

The Meaning of Amoris Laetitia *According to Pope Francis*[1]

DR JOHN R.T. LAMONT

THE TEACHING OF THE APOSTOLIC EXHORTAtion *Amoris Laetitia* has been the subject of a great deal of debate since the promulgation of that document. Various interpretations of this teaching have been presented, and the differing interpretations have been used both to denounce the document as heretical and to defend it as in harmony with the teaching of the Church. Pope Francis has recently acted to clarify the meaning of the most contentious section of *Amoris Laetitia* through a statement in the October 2017 issue of the *Acta Apostolicae Sedis*, the journal that publishes the official acts of the Holy See (the title of the journal is generally abbreviated as *AAS*). The meaning and consequences of this clarification are of the first importance, and need to be carefully and accurately examined.

THE MEANING AND AUTHORITY OF THE *AAS* STATEMENT

The statement in the *AAS* has three components: i) a letter from Pope Francis to the bishops of the Buenos Aires region concerning their pastoral decree on the application of Chapter 8 of *Amoris Laetitia*, ii) the pastoral decree itself, and iii) a statement by Cardinal Parolin, the Secretary of State, asserting that the Supreme Pontiff has ordered the publication of the two preceding components in the *AAS* as statements of the authentic magisterium. The letter from Pope Francis is given the title of "Apostolic Letter" in the *AAS* statement, a title it did not bear when originally issued.

The statement in the *AAS* has a high degree of authority. The term "authentic magisterium" is explained in par. 25 of the dogmatic constitution *Lumen Gentium*, and in canon 752 of the Latin *Code of Canon Law*. The exercise of the authentic magisterium is not infallible, and hence does not require the assent of faith from Catholics, but it does require the religious submission of mind and

---

[1] Published at *Rorate Caeli*, February 23, 2018.

will, a submission that includes sincere adherence to the assertions being taught. The covering statement by Cardinal Parolin, the publication of the above documents in the *AAS* at the command of the Pope, and the new title of "Apostolic Letter" given to Pope Francis's original letter to the Buenos Aires bishops confirm that the relevant contents of the documents are teachings of the authentic magisterium of the Catholic Church. This is a rather roundabout way of conveying an official teaching of the Church, since this teaching is given in a letter about a letter about an Apostolic Exhortation, but this form of expression is not entirely without precedent or unsuitable in itself. There are precedents for a pope issuing a teaching by endorsing a statement previously made by bishops. It does however mean that the statement needs to be carefully analyzed in order to identify the content of the teaching it conveys.

The essential starting point for such an analysis is the realization that the *AAS* statement is not making a claim about Catholic faith and morals as such. It is making an assertion about the meaning of another document, the Apostolic Exhortation *Amoris Laetitia*. This assertion does not in itself endorse the meaning of the relevant section of *Amoris Laetitia* as being a teaching of Catholic faith or morals, or as being a legitimate exercise of papal authority concerning discipline or canon law. It simply describes what chapter 8 of *Amoris Laetitia* is in fact saying. A magisterial teaching concerning the meaning of a given text is not as such an endorsement of the truth of that text. Such teachings can in fact be statements that the meaning of a given text or texts is not compatible with the Catholic faith. An example of such a teaching is the bull *Ad Sanctam Beati Petri Sedem* issued by Pope Alexander VII in 1656, in which he reiterated the teachings of his predecessor Innocent X to the effect that five heretical Jansenist propositions were in fact to be found in the works of Jansenius. It is true that Pope Francis's statement in the *AAS* does not qualify the meaning it attributes to *Amoris Laetitia* as heretical. But it does not assert that this meaning is orthodox either. It is silent on this topic. *Amoris Laetitia* itself is a document that makes assertions about faith, morals, and Church discipline. The statement in the *AAS* does not add to any degree of teaching authority that is possessed by *Amoris Laetitia*. It simply clarifies what chapter 8 of *Amoris Laetitia* is itself teaching. The level of authority of the statements of *Amoris Laetitia* has been a subject of considerable debate among theologians. This debate will not be recapitulated or continued here; suffice it to say that although *Amoris Laetitia* is probably not a mere statement of personal opinion on the part of the Pope that lacks any teaching authority at all, it is not clearly presented as a teaching of the authentic magisterium in the way that the *AAS* statement is.

This method of clarification on the part of Pope Francis could be criticized as disingenuous, since many Catholics will be inclined to assume that the religious submission of mind and will that is required by the *AAS* statement is also due to the teachings of chapter 8 of *Amoris Laetitia*. However, the *AAS* statement does in itself give a determinate answer to requests for clarification of the teaching of *Amoris Laetitia* that have been made to the Pope. The answer itself is not a novel one; the meaning it assigns to *Amoris Laetitia* corresponds to the meaning that has been discerned in the document by a number of commentators, such as the signatories to the *Correctio filialis* that was sent to the Pope. In fairness to Pope Francis, it could be said that his explaining *Amoris Laetitia* by citing his previous statements is a reference to the fact that his intention and meaning have been clear all along to objective observers, and that anyone who looked at his actions during the Synod on the Family and his many statements on the subjects raised in chapter 8 of *Amoris Laetitia* should have been able to tell that he meant what the *AAS* statement says he meant in that chapter.

What exactly does the *AAS* statement give as the meaning of chapter 8 of *Amoris Laetitia*? Pope Francis's letter to the Buenos Aires bishops states that their pastoral latter gives the *only* correct interpretation of that chapter. It is the pastoral letter itself, therefore, that provides the explanation of *Amoris Laetitia* that is being endorsed as correct by the authentic magisterium of the Church. This letter does not address everything contained in chapter 8. It deals with the possible access to the sacraments of Catholics who have civilly divorced their living spouse and are living in a new union with another person. A number of rather general statements are made about the pastoral care of such persons. The passages of the pastoral letter that make clear recommendations about access to the sacraments for these persons are found in its paragraphs 6 and 7. Paragraph 6 states that under some circumstances, when a couple of this kind are unable to practice continence and live together as brother and sister, *Amoris Laetitia* permits them to receive absolution and to receive the Eucharist, despite the fact of engaging in a sexual relationship with someone who is not their spouse, and without imposing the preconditions of intending to abandon or actually abandoning this sexual relationship. This statement is expressed in the following words: "If it comes to be recognized that, in a specific case, there are limitations that mitigate responsibility and culpability (cf. [*AL*] 301–302), especially when a person believes they would incur a subsequent wrong by harming the children of the new union, *Amoris Laetitia* offers the possibility of access to the sacraments of Reconciliation and Eucharist (cf. footnotes 336 and 351)."

Paragraph 7 simply states that this permission is not to be understood as a universal entitlement to receive the sacraments regardless of the circumstances of the couples in question. The character of the restrictions suggested is important. Both the statement of the Buenos Aires bishops and *Amoris Laetitia* itself describe the conditions for admitting civilly divorced and remarried Catholics in very general terms that cannot serve as criteria for identifying which persons should and which should not be admitted to the sacraments. In practice, therefore, the decision about admitting such persons to the sacraments depends entirely on the decision of the individual priest. The proposal of *Amoris Laetitia* is to replace a discipline governed by law with the lawless, and hence tyrannical, authority of the priest. The practical result of abandoning the current law will of course be the unrestricted access to the sacraments that *Amoris Laetitia* forbids, but its intent of imposing clerical rule untrammelled by any law casts light on the goals and mentality of its author.

The *AAS* statement thus establishes as correct an understanding of *Amoris Laetitia* that has been presented by many people in the Church as the obvious meaning of that document, whether they support or oppose this understanding. It agrees with the statements of Cardinal Kasper on *Amoris Laetitia*; it also agrees with the authors and signatories of the *Correctio filialis*, who condemn this understanding as the second of the heresies they accuse Pope Francis of upholding.

THE MEANING OF *AMORIS LAETITIA* IN THE LIGHT OF THE *AAS* STATEMENT

What are we to make of this assertion of *Amoris Laetitia*, now that its meaning has been settled by the *AAS* statement? One position is that of Cardinal Kasper, according to which the assertion is a legitimate exercise of papal teaching and disciplinary power that must be accepted and followed by all Catholics. Another position is that of the *Correctio filialis*, according to which the assertion denies a divinely revealed truth and must be rejected as a heresy.

In order to answer this question, it is best to begin with two undoubted facts about the passages in *Amoris Laetitia* that are addressed by the *AAS* statement.

1. While it would be rash to deny any magisterial authority at all to *Amoris Laetitia*, it is certain that no part of that Apostolic Exhortation is infallibly taught. The possibility of its claims being false therefore cannot be excluded.

2. It is also certain that the positions of *Amoris Laetitia* referred to by the *AAS* statement are in flat contradiction with the teaching of another papal document, the Apostolic Exhortation *Familiaris Consortio* of Pope John Paul II issued in 1981, as a sequel to the 1980 Synod of Bishops. The text of *Familiaris Consortio* on this topic is so important and pertinent that it should be cited at length.

> 84. Daily experience unfortunately shows that people who have obtained a divorce usually intend to enter into a new union, obviously not with a Catholic religious ceremony. Since this is an evil that, like the others, is affecting more and more Catholics as well, the problem must be faced with resolution and without delay. The Synod Fathers studied it expressly. The Church, which was set up to lead to salvation all people and especially the baptized, cannot abandon to their own devices those who have been previously bound by sacramental marriage and who have attempted a second marriage. The Church will therefore make untiring efforts to put at their disposal her means of salvation.
>
> Pastors must know that, for the sake of truth, they are obliged to exercise careful discernment of situations. There is in fact a difference between those who have sincerely tried to save their first marriage and have been unjustly abandoned, and those who through their own grave fault have destroyed a canonically valid marriage. Finally, there are those who have entered into a second union for the sake of the children's upbringing, and who are sometimes subjectively certain in conscience

that their previous and irreparably destroyed marriage had never been valid.

Together with the Synod, I earnestly call upon pastors and the whole community of the faithful to help the divorced, and with solicitous care to make sure that they do not consider themselves as separated from the Church, for as baptized persons they can, and indeed must, share in her life. They should be encouraged to listen to the word of God, to attend the Sacrifice of the Mass, to persevere in prayer, to contribute to works of charity and to community efforts in favor of justice, to bring up their children in the Christian faith, to cultivate the spirit and practice of penance and thus implore, day by day, God's grace. Let the Church pray for them, encourage them and show herself a merciful mother, and thus sustain them in faith and hope.

However, the Church reaffirms her practice, which is based upon Sacred Scripture, of not admitting to Eucharistic Communion divorced persons who have remarried. They are unable to be admitted thereto from the fact that their state and condition of life objectively contradict that union of love between Christ and the Church which is signified and effected by the Eucharist. Besides this, there is another special pastoral reason: if these people were admitted to the Eucharist, the faithful would be led into error and confusion regarding the Church's teaching about the indissolubility of marriage.

Reconciliation in the sacrament of Penance, which would open the way to the Eucharist, can only be granted to those who, repenting of having broken the sign of the Covenant and of fidelity to Christ, are sincerely ready to undertake a way of life that is no longer in contradiction to the indissolubility of marriage. This means, in practice, that when, for serious reasons, such as for example the children's upbringing, a man and a woman cannot satisfy the obligation to separate, they "take on themselves the duty to live in complete continence, that is, by abstinence from the acts proper to married couples." [John Paul II, Homily at the Close of the Sixth Synod of Bishops, n. 7 (Oct. 25, 1980)]

Similarly, the respect due to the sacrament of Matrimony, to the couples themselves and their families, and also to the community of the faithful, forbids any pastor, for whatever reason or pretext even of a pastoral nature, to perform ceremonies of any kind for divorced people who remarry. Such ceremonies would give the impression of the celebration of a new sacramentally valid marriage, and would thus lead people into error concerning the indissolubility of a validly contracted marriage.

By acting in this way, the Church professes her own fidelity to Christ and to His truth. At the same time she shows motherly concern for these children of hers, especially those who, through no fault of their own, have been abandoned by their legitimate partner. With firm confidence she believes that those who have rejected the Lord's command and are still living in this state will be able to obtain from God the grace of conversion and salvation, provided that they have persevered in prayer, penance and charity.

Familiaris Consortio here clearly states what *Amoris Laetitia* denies: the divorced and remarried who do not undertake to live as brother and sister cannot be granted absolution, and cannot be admitted to eucharistic communion. This is not the full extent of the contradiction between the two documents. *Familiaris Consortio* explicitly considers those "hard cases" that *Amoris Laetitia* raises, such as persons who are subjectively convinced that their previous marriages were not valid, those who have been unjustly abandoned by their spouses, and those who enter into or remain in civil partnerships for the sake of their children's upbringing. It teaches that these "hard cases" cannot be a basis for changing the Church's discipline concerning absolution and reception of the Eucharist. It agrees with *Amoris Laetitia* in saying that the Church cannot abandon to their own devices those Catholics who have entered into second unions. However, its understanding of what it means for the Church to not abandon these people is the opposite of the one proposed by *Amoris Laetitia*. *Familiaris Consortio* describes the pastoral help of the Church in these cases as having the object of enabling such persons to cease their adulterous and bigamous relations. *Amoris*

Laetitia does not propose this as the object of their pastoral care; instead it proposes that in some cases they should be assisted to live their adulterous and bigamous relations in a good way.

The teaching of *Amoris Laetitia* on divorce and the sacraments is thus virtually a negative image of the teaching of *Familiaris Consortio*. This is not a coincidence. The passage of *Familiaris Consortio* cited above was composed to reject a progressive position on these subjects that was widely held in the Church, and that was put into practice by many priests and bishops. Pope Francis and his supporters hold this progressive position, and did not agree with *Familiaris Consortio* when it was issued. Now that he holds the supreme power in the Church, Pope Francis has issued *Amoris Laetitia* in order to do away with the traditional teaching enunciated in *Familiaris Consortio* and present the progressive view held by himself and his supporters as the teaching of the Church.

The complete opposition between *Familiaris Consortio* and *Amoris Laetitia* on these topics effectively disposes of Cardinal Kasper's claim that the teaching of *Amoris Laetitia* must be accepted by Catholics. One cannot appeal to papal authority to show that the teaching of one apostolic exhortation must be accepted over the completely contradictory teaching of another apostolic exhortation, since both exhortations are papal teachings of the same sort. This cancelling out of papal authority claims leaves us with the question of which of these contradictory teachings should be believed by Catholics. What has to be done to answer this question is to determine which of the contradictory positions is actually true. To decide between them, we must consider their respective positions in the light of divinely revealed truth.

THE ASSERTIONS OF *AMORIS LAETITIA* AND CHRIST'S TEACHING ON MARRIAGE

The position of *Amoris Laetitia* is not entirely clear on one subject, even after the *AAS* statement. We know that *Amoris Laetitia* recognizes "limitations that mitigate responsibility and culpability" for the situations of the civilly divorced and remarried living *more uxorio* with one another, and that in consequence permit them to be absolved and to receive the Eucharist. But the character of these limitations is not plainly specified. There are two possible ways in which such a specification could be made. The limitations in question could be understood as circumstances that make the actions and lives of such persons objectively good, and hence not in need of forgiveness. This is certainly what is suggested by the text of *Amoris Laetitia*. However, these limitations could instead be understood as circumstances that do not make the actions and lives of such persons objectively good, but do make them subjectively guiltless for their cohabitation and sexual relationship. Both these understandings have been presented by defenders of *Amoris Laetitia*; hence both of them need to be examined in the light of the teachings of the faith, even though the former one seems much more likely to be the actual meaning of the document.

With *Familiaris Consortio*, on the other hand, there is no doubt about its position about whether the civilly divorced and remarried can be admitted to reception of the Eucharist; such admission is forbidden under all circumstances. Unfortunately, the reason that it gives for this position is not equally clear. It states that this law is based on the Sacred Scriptures, but it does not specify how it is based on the Scriptures. This is the crucial issue in the debate. Is this absolute refusal actually commanded in the Scriptures, or does it follow with logical necessity from what is stated or commanded in the Scriptures? To judge how the teaching of *Familiaris Consortio* is related to the Scriptures, we need to consider the chief scriptural passages that are relevant to this teaching. These are the following:

> Thou shalt not commit adultery. (Exodus 20:14)
>
> Every one that putteth away his wife, and marrieth another, committeth adultery: and he that marrieth her that is put away from her husband, committeth adultery. (Luke 16:18)
>
> And the Pharisees coming to him asked him: Is it lawful for a man to put away his wife? tempting him. But he answering, saith to them: What did Moses command you? Who said: Moses permitted to write a bill of divorce, and to put her away. To whom Jesus answering, said: Because of the hardness of your heart he wrote you that precept. But from the beginning of the creation, God made them male and female. For this cause a man shall leave his father and mother; and shall cleave to his wife. And they two shall be in one flesh. Therefore now they are not two, but one flesh. What therefore God hath joined together, let not man put asunder. And in

the house again his disciples asked him concerning the same thing. And he saith to them: Whosoever shall put away his wife and marry another, committeth adultery against her. And if the wife shall put away her husband, and be married to another, she committeth adultery. (Mark 10:2–12)

And there came to him the Pharisees tempting him, and saying: Is it lawful for a man to put away his wife for every cause? Who answering, said to them: Have ye not read, that he who made man from the beginning, made them male and female? And he said: For this cause shall a man leave father and mother, and shall cleave to his wife, and they two shall be in one flesh. Therefore now they are not two, but one flesh. What therefore God hath joined together, let no man put asunder. They say to him: Why then did Moses command to give a bill of divorce, and to put away? He saith to them: Because Moses by reason of the hardness of your heart permitted you to put away your wives: but from the beginning it was not so. And I say to you, that whosoever shall put away his wife, except it be for fornication, and shall marry another, committeth adultery: and he that shall marry her that is put away, committeth adultery. His disciples say unto him: If the case of a man with his wife be so, it is not expedient to marry. Who said to them: All men take not this word, but they to whom it is given. For there are eunuchs, who were born so from their mother's womb: and there are eunuchs, who were made so by men: and there are eunuchs, who have made themselves eunuchs for the kingdom of heaven. He that can take, let him take it. (Matthew 19:3–12)

I wrote to you in an epistle, not to keep company with fornicators. I mean not with the fornicators of this world, or with the covetous, or the extortioners, or the servers of idols; otherwise you must needs go out of this world. But now I have written to you, not to keep company, if any man that is named a brother, be a fornicator, or covetous, or a server of idols, or a railer, or a drunkard, or an extortioner: with such a one, not so much as to eat. (1 Corinthians 5:9–11)

> Know you not that the unjust shall not possess the kingdom of God? Do not err: neither fornicators, nor idolaters, nor adulterers, nor the effeminate, nor liers with mankind [male homosexuals], nor thieves, nor covetous, nor drunkards, nor railers, nor extortioners, shall possess the kingdom of God. (1 Corinthians 6:9–10)
>
> But to them that are married, not I but the Lord commandeth, that the wife depart not from her husband. And if she depart, that she remain unmarried, or be reconciled to her husband. And let not the husband put away his wife. (1 Corinthians 7:10–11)
>
> For as often as you shall eat this bread, and drink the chalice, you shall shew the death of the Lord, until he come. Therefore whosoever shall eat this bread, or drink the chalice of the Lord unworthily, shall be guilty of the body and of the blood of the Lord. But let a man prove himself: and so let him eat of that bread, and drink of the chalice. For he that eateth and drinketh unworthily, eateth and drinketh judgment to himself, not discerning the body of the Lord. (1 Corinthians 11:26–29)

The qualification of the ban on divorce in Matthew 19:9 ("except it be for fornication") has been the subject of much debate, but it is not significant for our topic. The term "fornication" translates the Greek word *porneia*, which is a general term for sexual immorality. Catholics have understood the passage as either giving permission for separation but not divorce, or as referring to marriages that are null because contracted within the prohibited degrees of affinity (these marriages are referred to by the term *porneia* in 1 Corinthians 5:1 and Acts 15:20, 29). Protestants have understood the passage as providing a real exception to the ban on divorce, one that permits divorce and remarriage under certain circumstances. None of these understandings has any bearing on the teaching of *Amoris Laetitia*. Catholic teaching on the indissolubility of marriage is repeated by *Amoris Laetitia*, and the possibility of admission to the sacraments that is the subject of the *AAS* statement is one that applies precisely to those whose marriage has not been dissolved, but who are living *more uxorio* with someone else.

How, then, can we say that the teaching of *Familiaris Consortio* is based on the above Scriptural passages? We should first note that these passages do not limit themselves to condemnation of adulterous relations with a person with whom one has contracted a form of marriage. They also condemn the act of divorce itself, and the act of contracting a form of marriage with someone other than one's spouse independently of the adulterous relations that may be involved in the relationship contracted. These actions are thus themselves grave sins. There has not even been any discussion of how the civilly divorced and remarried can be permitted to receive the Eucharist despite having committed these sins; the discussion has largely been restricted to considering the compatibility of receiving the Eucharist with the sin of engaging in adulterous relations with one's civil partner. This restriction will be followed here, as it is only on this subject that a case for this compatibility has been made.

With respect to Eucharistic discipline, the possibility of the civilly divorced and remarried receiving the Eucharist can be excluded in two ways. The first way is through a divine commandment addressed to the civilly divorced and remarried that absolutely forbids them to receive the Eucharist. The second way is through a divine commandment addressed to priests and bishops absolutely forbidding them to dispense the Eucharist to persons who are civilly divorced and remarried.

The above passages undoubtedly express an absolute prohibition upon persons who are civilly married to someone who is not their spouse choosing to receive the Eucharist. They state that those guilty of grave sins may not receive the Eucharist, that adultery is a grave sin, and that those who divorce their spouse and marry someone else commit adultery. The Scriptural texts are much clearer on this subject that they are on many doctrines that have been solemnly defined as divinely revealed. Many supporters of *Amoris Laetitia* would deny this, because they deny that there are any exceptionless moral prohibitions, and claim that the Scriptures do not contain prohibitions of this sort. This claim repeats a thesis of proportionalism, a moral theory that was hotly debated during the pontificate of John Paul II and was condemned by him in the encyclical *Veritatis Splendor*. The debate over proportionalism will not be recapitulated here. It is not of great moment for the examination of Scriptural teaching, because there is no reputable case to be made for the Scriptures adhering to the proportionalist understanding of moral norms. This understanding came into existence many centuries after the completion of the New Testament, and is entirely alien to all of the varied historical and intellectual circumstances in which the Scriptural books were composed. The Scriptural commandment forbidding adultery is meant precisely as an absolute prohibition.

Some defenders of *Amoris Laetitia* have recognized the existence of this absolute prohibition, but have argued that it can be reconciled with the reception of the Eucharist by divorced and remarried persons when these persons are not fully culpable for their situation. The argument is that reception of the Eucharist is forbidden for those in a state of mortal sin, but not for those in a state of venial sin; but it is possible for persons who are committing a seriously sinful act to not be fully responsible for the act they are doing, and hence to be sinning venially rather than mortally; so reception of the Eucharist cannot be absolutely ruled out for such persons.

In order for this situation to obtain, the civilly divorced and remarried would have to either not give full consent of the will to their situation, or else not be fully knowledgeable about its being a sinful one; and this lack of consent and/or of knowledge would have to be blameless on their part. Their lack of knowledge would have to be a lack of knowledge of law, or lack of knowledge of fact.

It is difficult to conceive how a person in his right mind could have sexual relations with someone to whom he is not married, but not be aware of this fact. People who are not in their right mind would not be sinning by living in an adulterous relationship and receiving the Eucharist, because they are not responsible for their actions. But their lack of sin would not mean that what they are doing is permissible.

Many people do lack knowledge of Catholic teaching on marriage and divorce, but the difficulty here is how such a lack of knowledge could be blameless, since we are responsible for knowing the basic moral rules that apply to our state of life. It is also difficult to see how persons lacking knowledge of the sinfulness of adultery and the permanent nature of marriage could validly contract marriage in the first place, since their ignorance bears upon two things that are essential to the nature of marriage. Conditions under which one could divorce one's spouse, marry someone else, and engage in adulterous relations with that person, but not fully consent to do these things, are also difficult to conceive of.

However, we may concede for the sake of the argument that such persons could exist. The question that then arises is whether or not the Scriptural prohibition on the reception of the Eucharist by serious sinners applies to them. This depends on whether the prohibition bears solely upon the state of being in mortal sin that results from the culpable commission of grave sins, or whether it bears upon the commission of a grave sin as such.

It is certainly true that Catholics are forbidden to choose to receive the Eucharist when they are in a state of mortal sin. But it does not follow from this that it is the defiled state of the soul in mortal sin that furnishes the sole reason for the prohibition on grave sinners receiving the Eucharist, so that the absence of this defiled state of soul removes the basis for this prohibition. The Scriptural passages that express this prohibition do not qualify it by saying that those who commit grave sins with full knowledge and consent of the will must not choose to receive the Eucharist. What the Scriptural texts say is that committing grave sin is a bar to reception of the Eucharist. It is not hard to see why this commandment is not qualified by adding that the grave sin in question is one that is done with full knowledge and consent of the will. The Eucharist is the holiest thing in the universe, and nothing evil can be permitted to approach it. In the hypothetical case of a person blamelessly living in an adulterous relationship, the evil of mortal sin in the person's soul is lacking, but the objectively evil act, with its violation of the order of justice and its evil consequences, remains. Reception of the Eucharist by a person committing this evil would be a profanation of the sacrament, and hence is contrary to divine law. As the *Dictionnaire de théologie catholique* states, receiving communion in a state of merely material sin is in itself a very grave sacrilege, because objectively speaking it involves a profanation of the body and blood of Jesus Christ.[2]

This does not mean that the hypothetical persons who blamelessly engage in an adulterous relationship are necessarily committing a sin if they receive the Eucharist. They may be committing a sin in doing so, if they realize that they are violating a divine commandment to not receive it. But their extraordinary condition

---

2 "La communion, faite en état de faute matérielle, est par elle-même un très grave sacrilège, puisque, objectivement parlant, il y a profanation du corps et du sang de Jésus-Christ": *DTC* III, "Communion eucharistique," col. 505.

might also include a blameless ignorance and/or lack of consent of the will about this commandment to not receive the Eucharist, as well as about the commandment not to commit adultery. In such a case their choosing to receive the Eucharist would not be sinful. But this would not be due to the prohibition against adulterers receiving the Eucharist admitting of any exceptions; it would be due to the deficiencies in knowledge and will that alleviate or remove their guilt for violating this further commandment.

It is thus certain that the Scriptures forbid the civilly divorced and remarried to choose to receive the Eucharist. Does it also state that priests are absolutely required to refuse the Eucharist to such persons?

There are two reasons why such a prohibition might exist. One reason is that such reception of the Eucharist is itself a grave sin. A priest would refuse to permit the reception of the Eucharist under such circumstances in order to prevent this sin, the desecration of the Eucharist that it involves, and the public scandal that would result. This reason is clearly a cogent one.

It could be argued that it would not apply to the private distribution of the Eucharist to persons of the kind described above, who for some extraordinary reason are not culpable for their adulterous relations and their decision to receive the Eucharist without abandoning these relations. But the reception of the Eucharist by such persons is a profanation of the sacrament, even if they are guiltless for committing adultery and choosing to receive it. Distributing the Eucharist to them would thus be cooperation in the profanation of the sacrament. Moreover, it could not benefit the persons receiving the Eucharist in any way, because the benefit that is sought in receiving the Eucharist is grace and union with Christ. This benefit will not be granted by a communion that profanes the Eucharist, even if the persons receiving it are guiltless of the profanation that occurs.

The other reason for the priest refusing the Eucharist under these circumstances is the existence of a divine command that forbids giving the Eucharist to public grave sinners. Such a command is to be found in a number of places in the Scriptures. There are several Scriptural texts that command the expulsion of public grave sinners from the Christian community. We may take it that such expulsion includes refusal of the Eucharist. 1 Corinthians 5:1–6 refers to the expulsion of a man for an irregular marriage (to his father's wife). The chapter then generalizes this measure in verses 10 to 11 (quoted above), commanding the expulsion of a number of categories of public sinners, and concludes "Put away the evil one from among yourselves" (v. 13). 1 Timothy 1:20 refers to another such expulsion. 2 Thessalonians 3:6 states: "And we charge you, brethren, in the name of our Lord Jesus Christ, that you withdraw yourselves from every brother walking disorderly, and not according to the tradition which they have received of us." These passages together constitute a clear Scriptural mandate, and indeed a clear command, to refuse the Eucharist to public sinners. This includes public adulterers such as the civilly divorced and remarried. Some obvious reasons can be suggested for this Scriptural command: respect for the meaning and function of the Eucharist as the bond of union in Christ, the avoidance of the desecration of the Eucharist by a sacrilegious communion, and the prevention of the spiritual harm caused to those who make sacrilegious communions. To them may be added the grounds that *Familiaris Consortio* provides for the specific prohibition on giving the Eucharist to the civilly divorced and remarried.

POPE FRANCIS AND HERESY

The *AAS* statement thus settles an important and much-debated question. It establishes that Pope Francis in *Amoris Laetitia* has affirmed propositions that are heretical in the strict sense; that is, propositions that contradict truths that are divinely revealed and that must be believed with the assent of faith. It has not only established this; it has made it a religious duty for Catholics to believe that this is the case. Pope Francis is the pope, and as such he has the power to exercise the papal teaching authority within the limits set to that authority by divine law. In the *AAS* statement, he has required Catholics to give religious assent of mind and will to the assertion that *Amoris Laetitia* contains propositions that are heretical.

The heresy in question is distinctive, as it goes farther than previous denials of Catholic teaching on marriage. *Amoris Laetitia* does not uphold the Mosaic permission on divorce, or the Protestant teaching on divorce, against Christ's teaching on the indissolubility of marriage. If it did, it would be less extreme. The Mosaic law permits divorcing one person and then marrying another. It does not permit cohabiting with one person while being married to a different one, as *Amoris Laetitia* does. The latter permission in practice dissolves the notion of marriage altogether.

The profession of heresy in the *AAS* statement together with *Amoris Laetitia* is unambiguous, but indirect. The *AAS* statement endorses a further statement that attributes a heretical meaning to the statements of *Amoris Laetitia*. This indirect form of expression forms part of a strategy for promoting the heresy that is being professed. A natural understanding of *Amoris Laetitia* would discern this heresy in it, but the words of that Apostolic Exhortation did not completely exclude an orthodox understanding of it. By initially permitting this latitude of understanding, Pope Francis ensured that Catholics who rejected the heresy in question would nonetheless rally to the defence of the document, out of blind loyalty to the papacy, timidity, careerism, or a simple feeling of obligation to give the Roman Pontiff every benefit of the doubt. These defenders of *Amoris Laetitia* were very effective in confusing the issue and leading Catholics to think that the document was acceptable and was being unjustly attacked. The indirect character of the *AAS* statement avoids embarrassing these defenders, and indeed enables many of them to continue their defence. The meaning of the statement does not have to be confronted unless one follows a chain of reasoning about it, which many conservative Catholic apologists are happy to refrain from doing.

Its indirect character also weakens the opposition of those conservatives who realize that it is promoting heresy. Pope Francis has found that such conservatives are weak, vacillating, and afraid to oppose him personally. Cardinal Raymond Burke, the most high-profile conservative of this sort, has gone from saying that *Amoris Laetitia* is not an act of the papal magisterium to saying that it is impossible to understand *Amoris Laetitia* in a heterodox sense because it is a magisterial document. A direct statement of heresy might back such persons against the wall and embarrass them into contradicting it. The *AAS* statement also serves to mock and humiliate conservatives, because it constrains them to reject a legitimate magisterial teaching in order to preserve their silence about *Amoris Laetitia*.

The heresy that the *AAS* statement establishes as present in *Amoris Laetitia* does not make Pope Francis guilty of the canonical crime of heresy. This is an important point, because the crime of heresy is the only offence for which a pope can and should be removed from office. In order to commit the canonical crime of heresy, it is not sufficient to publicly state that a heretical proposition is true. One must also refuse to retract this proposition when warned by ecclesiastical authority that it is heretical and cannot be held by Catholics. The pope does not have an ecclesiastical superior, so the authority in his case would have to consist in the authority to teach rather than the authority to command. This authority is possessed by Catholic bishops, who have the right and the duty to warn the pope when he upholds heresy. In the case of Pope Francis this has not been done.

The fact that Pope Francis has not been authoritatively told that he is upholding heresy does not mean that he is simply in error about marriage, divorce, and the Eucharist. One does not have to commit the canonical crime of heresy in order to knowingly reject the teaching of the Catholic Church. Most deliberate heretics do not commit this crime, because they are not told by ecclesiastical authority to abjure their heresies. Pope Francis knows that he is contradicting Catholic teaching on this subject; he has composed *Amoris Laetitia* precisely to reject the exposition of this teaching that is to be found in *Familiaris Consortio*. He may think that adhering to the Catholic faith does not require assenting to the past teachings of the magisterium. It is likely in fact that he does think this, for this modernist position is generally held by progressive clerics of his school of thought, and he has shown signs of agreement with it in a number of statements. But acceptance of modernism is itself a more profound and universal form of heresy than rejection of specific divinely revealed truths, since it does away with the whole notion of divine revelation and faith in its teachings. There is no parallel to this betrayal in the entire history of the papacy. St. Peter denied Christ out of fear, and later repudiated his action. Pope Francis is attacking Christ's teaching in a planned and systematic fashion because he is opposed to it.

It would be wrong however to think that Pope Francis is the worst scourge afflicting the Church. The election of a bad man as pope can never be entirely ruled out. In a healthy Church, the problem of a heretical pope can and will be dealt with by the Catholic bishops, just as the immune system of a healthy body will react to disease and eradicate it. The immune system of the Church at the present is not operating. The bishops of the Catholic Church have remained silent about the heresy in *Amoris Laetitia*, and have thereby abandoned the faithful. The heretical statements of *Amoris Laetitia* have not been presented to the faithful as something that they can take or leave. Pope Francis has stated in official magisterial documents that they are papal teachings that they must accept. He has been supported in this by a large number of bishops. Pope Francis has thereby put pressure on all the Catholic faithful to reject divinely revealed truth. The faithful are not protected against this pressure by the bishops of Kazakhstan, or elsewhere, issuing a statement upholding the truths that Francis is denying. When encountering a difference of opinion between a papal document and a letter from a handful of Kazakh bishops, the faithful will naturally take the papal statement to be of higher authority. In order to protect the faithful from the attack on their belief and salvation that is being made through *Amoris Laetitia*, it is necessary to address the falsehoods in that document itself, and to condemn them by appealing to an authority that justifies the rejection of a non-infallible papal letter: the authority of divine revelation expressed in the Scriptures and repeated by the magisterium of the Church. This appeal does not have to be a canonical warning to Pope Francis that could serve as the first step in his deposition. Such a canonical warning would have to be addressed to the pope himself, and warn him of the nature of his crime and the consequences of persisting in it. It would be sufficient to take the lesser step of simply addressing the faithful to condemn *Amoris Laetitia* as heretical. Aside from Bishops Bernard Fellay and Henry Gracida, no Catholic bishops have done this.

This almost unanimous betrayal of their office by Catholic bishops, and the episcopal infidelity that this betrayal reveals, is the fundamental problem in the Church. Without this massive infidelity there would have been no constituency to elect Pope Francis in the first place, and if he had nonetheless managed to be elected he would not have been able to mount an overt assault on the faith. If this fundamental problem is not solved, the repudiation of the heresies in *Amoris Laetitia* or even the deposition of Pope Francis will not produce any lasting benefit. Other evils of a similar kind will recur, since the causes of Pope Francis's career and actions will remain. A basic reform of the Church that addresses and eradicates these causes is what is needed.

6

The Need for Consistency between Magisterium and Tradition: Examples from History[1]

DR CLAUDIO PIERANTONI

IN THIS INTERVENTION, WE WILL BRIEFLY examine the history of two popes of antiquity, Liberius and Honorius, who, for different reasons, were accused of deviating from the Tradition of the Church, during the long Trinitarian and Christological controversy, which consumed the Church from the fourth to the seventh century. In the light of the reactions of the ecclesial body to these doctrinal deviations, we will then examine the current debate that has developed around the proposals of Pope Francis in the Apostolic Exhortation *Amoris Laetitia* and the five *dubia* raised by the four cardinals.

THE CASE OF HONORIUS

We will begin with the case of Honorius I, although chronologically the second one, since it is technically clearer. In fact, he is, to this day, the only pope who has been formally condemned for heresy. We are in the early decades of the seventh century, in the context of the controversy over the two wills of Christ. The Council of Chalcedon, in 451, had affirmed that in the one Person of Christ are united two complete natures, divine and human; this solution, however, had left discontented an important part of the Eastern Churches, who were affirming that, at least after the union, just one nature ended up subsisting in Christ (Monophysitism). In order to meet the unitive needs of the Monophysite faction, Sergius, the patriarch of Constantinople, had therefore proposed a formula which, while accepting the doctrine of the two natures, counterbalanced it with the affirmation of the one operational energy of

---

1 Given at the conference "Seeking Clarity: One Year after *Amoris Laetitia*," Rome, April 22, 2017. Published at *Rorate Caeli*, April 23, 2017.

Christ (Monoenergism). We must keep in mind that the empire's political situation was, at that time, very delicate. The emperor Heraclius, having ascended the throne in 610, had to confront the massive attack of the Persians, who had invaded large areas of the Eastern Roman Empire, coming to desecrate the Holy Sepulcher in Jerusalem and going even so far as to threaten Constantinople. The emperor, however, managed to reorganize the Roman forces and lead an epic rescue, which took on the traits of a true and proper crusade, until finally defeating the Persians in 628. It was natural that, after the war, Heraclius felt the need for a religious unification of the Empire and then sought a formula of conciliation with the Monophysites, who represented the majority of the population in the newly recaptured provinces. His supporter in this policy was precisely Patriarch Sergius. Sergius, then, made himself the promoter of the doctrine that admitted the *two natures* in Christ but preached His one *operating energy*. For this doctrine, Sergius also sought the support of the bishop of Rome Honorius, who, however (considering perhaps the Greek term *enérgeia* unclear or too abstract) preferred to state that in Christ there is only one will (*una voluntas*). Pope Honorius expounded this doctrine in a letter of 634 (*Scripta Fraternitatis*) in response to the Patriarch of Constantinople,[2] and this letter was precisely the cause of his later condemnation along with Sergius. In 638, with both patriarchs dead, the Emperor Heraclius promulgated a solemn document of religious union, the *Exposition* (*Ékthesis*), in which he precisely sanctioned the formula of *una voluntas*. But in the decades that followed, after another hard struggle, this formula was definitively declared heretical. In fact, the doctrine of one will in Christ, or Monothelitism, came into conflict with the logical consequences of the dogma of the two natures, divine and human, a doctrine solidly based on biblical revelation, admirably expounded by Pope Leo the Great and solemnly sanctioned by the Council of Chalcedon. In harmony with the Chalcedonian doctrine, finally, in 681, the Third Council of Constantinople (the Sixth Ecumenical Council), condemned Patriarch Sergius and with him Pope Honorius. Here is the text:

> After having investigated the dogmatic letters written by Sergius, the former patriarch of the God-protected and imperial city, to Cyrus, who was at the time the bishop

---

2 Denzinger 487.

of Phasis, and to Honorius, then pope of elder Rome, and in like manner also the letter written in reply by that one, that is, Honorius, to the same Sergius, and after having discovered that these are entirely alien to the apostolic teachings and to the decisions of the holy councils and to all the eminent holy Fathers but instead follow the false teachings of the heretics, these we entirely reject and loathe as soul-destroying.[3]

Following the anathema against Sergius and the other bishops, then the Council concludes:

> We have seen fit to banish from the holy Church of God and to anathematize also Honorius the former pope of the elder Rome, because we have discovered in the letters written by him to Sergius that he followed in everything the opinion of that one and confirmed his impious dogma.[4]

The Council was then ratified by the reigning pope, Leo II, who also reiterated the anathema against his predecessor with the following words:

> We, in like manner, anathematize the inventors of the new error: namely, Theodore, Bishop of Pharan, Cyrus of Alexandria, Sergius, Pyrrhus, Paul, and Peter, betrayers rather than leaders of the Church of Constantinople, and also Honorius, who did not purify this Apostolic Church by the doctrine of the apostolic tradition, but rather attempted to subvert the immaculate faith by profane treason.[5]

Pope Leo II also mentions this condemnation in two letters: one to the Spanish bishops, stating concerning Honorius: "Along with Honorius, who did not immediately extinguish the flame of heretical teaching, as would befit the apostolic authority, but supported it by his negligence." The other letter is addressed to the Visigoth king of Spain, Ervigius, where it is said: "Along with these, Honorius of Rome, who allowed the immaculate rule of the apostolic

---

3   13th Session (Denzinger 550).
4   Denzinger 552.
5   Letter *Regi Regum* to the Emperor Constantine IV (Denzinger 563).

tradition that he had received from his predecessors to be stained."

Now, from the declarations of the Sixth Ecumenical Council we gather a very precise concept of the unity and coherence that must exist between: (1) the Tradition received from the Apostles, (2) the definitions of Councils, which reiterate particular points of the Tradition to clarify them in a solemn manner, and finally (3) the testimony of the Fathers who, through the centuries, although without enjoying infallibility if taken individually, confirm by their consensus the continuity of a particular teaching. It thus remains clearly stated, and then explicitly reaffirmed by the same Pope Leo II, that this body of tradition, formed by the Apostles, Councils, and Fathers, provides the measuring stick whereby Pope Honorius's dogmatic statement is evaluated, who, therefore, although deceased, is condemned in no uncertain terms by the Constantinopolitan assembly.

Then, the same Pope Leo II ratifies the Council and confirms the anathema against his predecessor, who strayed from the rule of the Apostolic tradition; not only this, but he also emphasizes the grave responsibility of Honorius for the negligence with which he favored the spread of the Monothelite heresy. It is particularly remarkable that the incumbent of the same Roman See, which for more than two centuries (at least since the time of Damasus) explicitly insisted on its superiority and prerogative in having the final word, above all in matters of doctrine, here decisively highlights the fundamental principle that the pope is subject to the rule of the Apostolic Tradition, which he has received from his predecessors. It is, as the Apostle says, a consignment (*traditio*) or a deposit, which must first of all be faithfully preserved, to be handed down in turn and taught to the brethren. Honorius is therefore condemned for having permitted the "immaculate rule of the apostolic tradition to be stained."

Therefore, at the center of Pope Leo's condemnation of his predecessor stands not his adherence to the wrong formula, which is at the center of the condemnation of Honorius on the part of the Council, but also, and I would say above all, the negligence of "permitting the rule of the apostolic tradition to be stained." In fact, taken in itself, the Honorian formula of *"una voluntas"* could also be defended, if it is not intended as referring to the natural faculty of willing, which must necessarily follow the respective nature, but as referring to the concrete decision taken by the one Person of Christ, in which evidently the wills, despite being two, human and divine, converge into a single action, because Jesus could never disobey the divine will. It is also probable that this was how Honorius precisely intended it, albeit perhaps with a certain mental reservation, conscious, how could he not be, that the formula even so left the field open to the Monothelite interpretation. What is decisive in assessing the heretical classification of Honorius is therefore precisely his negligence in not impeding, or even encouraging, the free diffusion of the Monothelite heresy.

THE CASE OF LIBERIUS

Liberius, "*natione Romanus*," was elected pope on May 17, 352, in one of the most delicate moments of the Arian controversy. His predecessor, Julius I, had tenaciously defended the faith established by the Council of Nicaea in 325, which declared the Son consubstantial with the Father. Julius had had, in this, the decisive support of the emperor of the West, Constans. But with Constans dead, Pope Julius found himself, along with all the bishops of the West, at the mercy of the pressures of his brother Constantius, emperor of the East, who instead supported the majority position of the Eastern episcopate, contrary to Nicaea. According to the Eastern bishops, in fact, the formula of Nicaea left no room for the personal difference between the Father and the Son. Left the only emperor, Constantius was anxious to restore the unity of the Church, precisely according to the Eastern perspective, contrary to Nicaea. To this end, he called a council at Arles in 353, in Gaul, which passed over in silence the faith of Nicaea and, in addition, condemned Athanasius, bishop of Alexandria, the only Eastern bishop who tenaciously defended the formula of "consubstantial." Even the legates of the pope, present at the Council, signed the condemnation of Athanasius. But Liberius disavowed their work, and asked Constantius to convene a new council, which would confirm the faith of Nicaea. This Council took place in 355 in Milan. But here again, the bishops loyal to the pope failed in their attempt to sign the Nicene Creed, and the condemnation of Athanasius was confirmed. The three bishops who refused to sign were deposed and exiled in the East.

At this point, the storm was gathering now around Pope Liberius's head: in fact, the pope had not directly participated in the Council, but the emperor was also determined to extort his signature. To this end he sent an emissary with a large sum of money to offer to the pope, but he decidedly refused it; then the minister deposited it at St. Peter's tomb as an offering for the Church: but Liberius had the money thrown out from the church, as a sacrilegious offering. At this point, the emperor passed directly to violent action: he had Liberius kidnapped at night, to avoid the resistance of the people, and had him transferred to Milan, the residence of the emperor of the West at that time. After a dramatic meeting, in which Liberius did not yield to the pressures of Constantius, the pope was deposed and sent into exile in Thrace. We are at the beginning of 356. Meanwhile, in those years, the doctrinal situation was further complicated: in particular, the anti-Nicene front split itself into three parties: (1) those closest to Nicaea, who considered the Son, though not equal, at least "similar to the Father *in substance*": the *homoiousiani*; (2) those farthest from Nicaea, who denied any similarity of the Son to the Father: the *anhómoioi*; (3) a middle path claimed by the party of *homoion*, the *homoioi*, who affirmed a general similarity of the Son to the Father (without mentioning his "substance"). This last party was the one closest to the wishes of the emperor, because of its generality, which, apparently, promised to satisfy everyone in a possible union, albeit a rather superficial one.

This uncertain doctrinal situation, combined with the cold and the pain of exile in Thrace, unfortunately began to bend the pope's resistance, who, after about a year, ended up yielding. Liberius's concession is attested to by four letters handed down by St. Hilary.[6] It is also attested to by St. Athanasius[7] and St. Jerome.[8] We know from these documents that Liberius signed a formula of faith published in a Council of Sirmium: we do not know if it was the first formula of Sirmium, dating back to 351, which allowed the faith of Nicaea to fall apart, but at least trying to affirm the closeness of the Son to the Father, or the second formula of Sirmium, of 357, which instead decisively affirmed the dissimilarity of the Son from the Father, and additionally forbade the use of "consubstantial" (*homousios*) and also of "similar according to substance" (*homoiousios*). But regardless, it is clear that Liberius thus repudiated the faith of Nicaea and went so far as to excommunicate Athanasius, who was

---

6   In *Collectanea Antiariana Parisina*.
7   Ibid.
8   *De viris illustribus* 97.

its most important defender. Liberius's dramatic about-face made a great impression and was severely stigmatized, especially by St. Hilary. By now docile to the emperor, Liberius after some time received permission to return to Rome, where he was reinstated as bishop. Here he was benevolently received by the people, but, now weakened and wounded in his prestige and in his role of leading the episcopate, he had neither the strength nor the will to oppose the ultimate realization of Constantius' plans, who, in the next double Council of Rimini and Seleucia (359), finally obtained the triumph of the generic formula of "the Son similar to the Father" by holding the Western bishops hostage at Rimini until they had signed; this formula was later confirmed in a further council at Constantinople the following year (360). This formula, with its generality, gave a card of citizenship to the moderate Arian factions, and, excluding the use of the term *ousía* (substance), proscribed both the *homoiousiani* and the *homousiani*, that is, the orthodox bishops faithful to Nicaea. In the months that followed, all the Arian prelates, as adept in dialectic as in political dealings, who had made careers thanks to the favor of Constantius, consolidated their power in the principal episcopal sees. This is the moment when, according to the famous phrase of St. Jerome, "the world groaned to find itself Arian." The success of the ecclesiastical policy tenaciously pursued by Constantius seemed definitive and the situation appeared stable, for an indeterminate time, in favor of the Arians: to human eyes, the formula of faith defined at Nicaea 35 years before now seemed completely outdated. Of the more than a thousand bishops who accounted for Christianity, only three remained unshakeable to resist in exile (Athanasius of Alexandria, Hilary of Poitiers, and Lucifer of Cagliari), apparently now cut off from the course of events.

However, just when all seemed peaceful, the military situation on the Persian front suddenly deteriorated, which forced Constantius to take up arms and go to the East. In Gaul, soon after, the army proclaimed the Caesar Julian as emperor. So, suddenly, the Empire was threatened by external enemies and at the same time was on the verge of a civil war. This, however, was providentially avoided, thanks to the sudden death of Constantius by a fever, November 361: the emperor was just 44 years old.

Having just ascended the imperial throne, Julian, later called the Apostate, declared war on the Christian faith and the return of the Roman state to traditional paganism. This allowed the exiled bishops to return home, and wiped out with a clean slate, one can say, all the ecclesiastical policy of Constantius. At this point, since the nightmare of the threats of Constantinus had ceased, Pope Liberius sent out an encyclical that considered the formula approved at Rimini and Constantinople invalid, and demanded that the bishops of Italy accept the Nicene Creed. In 366, at a synod held in Rome shortly before his death, he even had the joy of obtaining the signature of the Nicene creed from a delegation of the Eastern bishops. Upon his death, he was revered as a confessor of the faith, but soon his cult was interrupted, certainly for the memory of his concession, and his name does not appear in Roman liturgical memory.

Unlike Honorius, Liberius received no formal condemnation, certainly due to the fact that, on the one hand, his defection was due not to a spontaneous willingness but to a strong physical pressure, and, on the other hand, when the pressure stopped, the pope solemnly reaffirmed the orthodox faith of Nicaea. For this reason, even though his moral fault of concession was objectively grave, the doctrinal consequences were not so grave because, beyond the statements extorted out of him, the pope's mind had remained orthodox; and in any case, a little later the doctrinal situation was untangled, paradoxically, by Julian's apostasy.

However, despite their differences, taken in a general way, the two cases of Liberius and Honorius have an important point in common: both of their interventions took place while the process of formulating the respective dogmas was still in progress, the Trinitarian dogma in the case of Liberius and the Christological in the case of Honorius. In fact, although at Nicaea the consubstantiality of the Father and the Son had been established dogmatically, a formula was still lacking to define the Trinity of Persons with a technical term; so too, while at Chalcedon the dual nature of Christ was affirmed, the specification was still lacking that would come only two centuries later with the formal affirmation of the two wills.

THE CASE OF FRANCIS

Now, this point that unites the doctrinal deviation of the two popes of antiquity is undoubtedly their extenuating circumstances; but unfortunately this very thing is what contrasts them to the doctrinal deviation that is occurring during the current pontificate, which, instead, has a strong aggravating factor in the pope's setting himself, not against doctrines that are as yet unclear or in the process of being formulated, but against doctrines that, in addition to being firmly anchored in tradition, have already been exhaustively debated in recent decades and clarified in detail by the recent Magisterium. So this is not only a deviation of the Magisterium from Tradition taken in general, but also a direct contradiction of the pronouncements of the very recent Magisterium. Therefore, in the case of Pope Francis, the panorama gets considerably more complicated. Naturally, I hardly need to recall the historical events, which are very recent and well known to the informed public from the reports that bombard us daily. So I will confine myself to strictly indispensable points, trying to give an overview of this most serious crisis, which now looms as the most serious among those faced by the Church throughout its history.

The conflict starts from a seemingly confined point, which the insufficiently attentive observer tends to perceive as a more pastoral and disciplinary interest than a strictly dogmatic one—that is, the possibility of granting sacramental communion, at least in certain special cases, to people who cohabitate with a person other than their legitimate spouse. It is therefore surprising for many that a deviation from doctrine on this seemingly confined point is such a deadly Trojan horse, capable of triggering, from inside the very edifice of the Church, a strategic dynamiting of all its defenses and of its very foundations.

I start by stating my conviction that this attack, on a spiritual level, far surpasses the intentions and subjective consciousness of the supporters of the so-called progressive line, or more precisely, the modernist one; our struggle, it is good to keep in mind, is not against persons, "against flesh and blood, but against principalities and power, against the rulers of the world of this darkness" (Eph 6:12). But still, on a historical level, there is an obligation to report and not to obscure the fact that this is supported and encouraged by a series of concrete persons among whom, unfortunately, the person of the pope stands out.

Our aim will be, therefore, to show how, from the particular point of communion for the divorced and remarried, the discourse extends to the entire edifice of Catholic doctrine by inevitable logical consequence. Naturally, at the practical level, the doctrinal deviation in question was already present in previous decades and with it, therefore, even the underground schism that it signifies. Yet when one goes from an abuse at the practical level to its justification at the doctrinal level through a text of the papal magisterium and through positive statements and actions of the same pope to support it, the situation changes radically. Also, because the effort to theoretically justify this position necessarily comes to touch other points of doctrine. And it happens that the more a theologian, who denies a point of Tradition, struggles to find arguments to support his thesis, the more he ends up sinking in the quicksand of contradiction and absurdity. This is because the Deposit of Faith, preserved by the Tradition, is not a system of merely human fallible thought, where an incoherent or erroneous element could be introduced, which could then be corrected without harm, even to the benefit of the truth. In the Deposit of Faith, each element is connected to all of the others with infallible consequentiality. Hence, by struggling to defend the first error, appealing to other elements, one ends up twisting and distorting them all.

We see, in four points, the progress of this destruction.

First point. If marriage is indissoluble, and yet in some cases communion can be given to the divorced and remarried, it seems evident that this indissolubility is no longer considered absolute, but only a general rule that can admit exceptions. Now this, as Cardinal Caffarra has explained well, contradicts the nature of the sacrament of marriage, which is not a simple promise, as solemn as it may be, made before God, but an action of grace that works at the properly *ontological* level. The action that makes the two become one flesh has, in fact, a definitive character and it cannot be erased. In addition, this action of grace, founded on the very order of creation and directed towards people's well-being, as sacrament assumes the function of signifying the indissoluble union between Christ the Bridegroom and His Church. If the sacrament of the Eucharist makes present in our midst the sacrifice of Christ, by which the Redeemer is inseparably united to the mystical body of His bride the Church, for its part the sacrament of marriage is not only a symbol but also concretely realizes a visible and real representation of this mystery: it is, at the same time, *sign* and *reality*.

Therefore, when it is said that marriage is indissoluble, it is not simply a general rule that is being stated; rather, what is said is that marriage *ontologically* cannot be dissolved, because in it is contained the sign and the reality of the indissoluble marriage between God and his People; and this mystical marriage, it will be useful to remember, is precisely the end of the whole divine plan of Creation and Redemption.

Second point. We can observe that the author of *Amoris Laetitia*, albeit in a manner not entirely clear, is aware that his proposal is vulnerable in this aspect. In fact, numerous attempts to put the tradition of indissolubility into doubt have also recently been refuted both on the biblical and patristic levels and on the dogmatic one.[9] Therefore, the author has instead chosen to insist, in his argumentation, on the subjective side of moral action. The subject, he says, may not be able to be in mortal sin because, for various reasons, he is not fully aware that his situation constitutes adultery. Now this, which in general terms can certainly happen, in the use that our text makes of it instead involves an evident contradiction. In fact, here all the discourse is centered on the need for discernment of individual situations and on offering people "accompaniment." Yet it is clear that precisely the discernment and accompaniment of individual situations directly contrast with the supposition that the subject remains, for an indefinite time, unaware of his situation. And the author, far from perceiving this contradiction, pushes it to the further absurdity of affirming that a profound discernment can lead the subject to have the certainty that his situation, objectively contrary to the divine law, is precisely what God wants from him. That is, the subjective element of ignorance, which can certainly diminish responsibility in many cases, here paradoxically is transformed into an element of knowledge, on the basis of which the subject can come to establish with certainty that God wants him to behave objectively contrary to His own law, that law which emanates from His eternal and infallible Wisdom.

Third point. Recourse to the previous argument, in its turn, betrays a dangerous confusion that, in addition to the doctrine of the sacraments, goes so far as to undermine the very notion of the Divine Law. On this point, we must above all point out that here a merely positive divine disposition is not at stake, as can be the laws governing incidental aspects of the cult, which, as such, are adapted to different historical circumstances: for example, the

---

9   Cf. R. Dodaro, ed., *Remaining in the Truth of Christ* (San Francisco: Ignatius Press, 2014).

dietary laws of the Jews, laws on blood sacrifices, or circumcision. At stake here is the law of God understood as the source of the natural law, reflected in the Ten Commandments. This is given to man because it is suited to governing his fundamental behaviors, not limited to particular historical circumstances, but founded on his very nature, whose author is precisely God. To serve as a simple comparison for us: the positive law that governs the movement of a car in a certain country is one thing; the instruction booklet written by the vehicle manufacturer is another thing. If I exceed a speed limit for a vital emergency, let us suppose, I can also be morally justified, because the rule, while just in itself, is not absolute, for it is not intrinsically linked to the essence of the vehicle. If I contravene the directive of the manufacturer, who tells me that the car was designed to run on gasoline, no emergency or exception, certainly no discernment, will serve to ensure that the car could run with diesel. To use diesel is not therefore a bad thing because it is "forbidden" by some external law, but it is intrinsically irrational, because it contradicts the very nature of the vehicle. Therefore, to suppose that the natural law may admit exceptions is a true and proper contradiction, it is a supposition that does not understand its true essence and therefore confuses it with positive law. The presence of this grave confusion is confirmed by the repeated attack, present in *Amoris Laetitia*, against the petty legalists, the presumed "Pharisees" who are hypocrites and hard of heart. This attack, in fact, betrays a complete misunderstanding of the position of Jesus toward the Law. His criticism of pharisaic behavior is based precisely on a clear distinction between positive law (the "precepts of men") to which the Pharisees are so attached, and the fundamental Commandments, which are instead the first requirement, indispensable, that he himself asks of the aspiring disciple. On the basis of this equivocation, one understands the real reason why, after having so greatly insulted the Pharisees, the pope ends up, *de facto*, aligning himself with their own position in favor of divorce, against that of Jesus.

Fourth point. But, even more deeply, it is important to observe that this confusion profoundly distorts the very essence of the Gospel and its necessary grounding in the person of Christ. According to the Gospel, Christ is not simply a good man who came into the world to preach a message of peace and justice. He is, first of all, the *Logos*, the Word who was in the beginning and who, in the fullness of time, becomes incarnate. It is significant that the insistence of Pope John Paul II on the objectivity of the moral law, affirmed in *Veritatis Splendor* (1993), is then completed with its necessary foundation in rational truth, which, in turn, is referred to as the presupposition of faith (*Fides et Ratio*, 1998). And it is also very significant that his successor, Benedict XVI, right from his homily *Pro eligendo romano pontifice*, made precisely the *Logos* the linchpin of his teaching, showing clearly that the origin of the modern attack on the faith is carried out precisely on philosophical presuppositions—precisely, therefore, on the doctrine of the *Logos*, a doctrine not by coincidence fought to the death with the subjectivism of modern theories of knowledge.

It is clear that ethical subjectivism can find space only within a subjectivist or immanentist epistemology. If the object of the human mind, in fact, is not based in the final analysis on the transcendent Truth that illuminates it, which is the same Truth by which things come into existence, then the mind cannot truly know things, and its concepts are empty formalities that cannot reflect reality.

Now, one of the postulates most dear to Pope Francis, according to which "realities are more important than ideas," finds justification in the realm of this subjectivist philosophy. A maxim like this, in fact, makes sense only in a vision in which there cannot exist *true* ideas that faithfully reflect reality and can even judge and direct it. If instead we accept, with the Christian tradition, that the Word of God is the eternal Wisdom which, on the one hand, creates the world and, on the other hand, illuminates the human mind, then we must accept that in this eternal Wisdom there is precisely an Idea, a Model, which is superior to historical reality, an Idea that governs the created reality in its intimate structure and gives it the law in its deepest sense; and that this Wisdom, if it is such, is also able to effectively communicate that knowledge to the intelligent creature which has been formed like unto God, in order that it can know and love Him. The Gospel, then, taken as a whole, presupposes this metaphysical and epistemological structure, where the Truth is in the first place the conforming of things to the intellect, and the Intellect is in the first place the divine one: indeed, the divine Word.

So it is on the same divine Word that the importance, in the Christian message, of "right doctrine" is based, since doctrine, expressed in concepts, far from being a mere formality emanated by the human intellect, is instead precisely a reflection of the Word both in its philosophical aspect, as a theory of knowledge and rational theology, and in its historical aspect, as the Tradition that comes to us from the coming of Christ on earth. That is why, in the heretical tendency that *Amoris Laetitia* demonstrates — above all, if read in light of many other statements of the pope and of his closest collaborators — the attack on reason and the natural law is accompanied by the attack carried out on the historical tradition of Jesus. In his divine nature, Christ is the Truth; indeed, the Truth became man in Christ. Therefore, the attack carried out on the Truth destroys at the same time the historical truth of Christ, which is also the principal truth of all history; with that, therefore, it destroys the ontological truth as well as the truth and historical visibility of the Church, of its Tradition and of its Sacraments, which constitute the purpose and the effect of the coming of Christ.

Hence, the error of this attitude consists not only and not so much in denying one or even several specific points of Catholic doctrine, but precisely in discrediting the very nature of "doctrine" itself and its necessary link with reason. In fact, if "realities are more important than ideas," it is not only *a* doctrine, but *doctrine itself* that loses relevance. In the beginning is not the *Logos*, but the *Praxis*. "Im Anfang war die Tat," "In the beginning was the Action," as Dr Faust said, retranslating the Gospel. In this atmosphere, it can be understood how it is possible that the editor of *La Civiltà Cattolica* could state that it is pastoral practice that must guide doctrine, and not vice versa, and that in theology "two plus two can equal five."[10] It explains why a Lutheran lady can receive communion together with her Catholic husband: the practice, in fact, the action, is that of the Lord's Supper, which they have in common, while where they differ is only "the interpretations, the explanations," mere concepts after all. But it also explains how, according to the superior general of the Society of Jesus (Fr Arturo Sosa), the incarnate Word is not capable of coming into contact with his creatures through the means that he himself chose, the apostolic Tradition: in fact, it would be necessary to know what Jesus truly said, but we cannot, he says, "since at the time there was

---

10 See George Weigel, "Theology Isn't Math; But It *Is* Theology," *First Things*, January 25, 2017.

no tape recorder." The superior general is not in the least touched by the reflection that, if Eternal Wisdom had thought that a tape recorder was the most suitable means to make us know His words, he would have certainly chosen it. And, with the conceit of *homo technologicus,* he comes to tell us that a machine, an inanimate being, would be a more efficacious means than the living tradition of human beings, which passes through the heart and faith of the Apostles and their successors, who were personally chosen by Him for this very purpose.

Even more deeply, in this atmosphere, it is finally explained why the pope cannot answer "yes" or "no" to the *dubia.* If, in fact, "realities are more important than ideas," then man does not even need to think with the principle of non-contradiction, he has no need of principles that say "this yes and this no" and need not even obey a transcendent natural law, which is not identified with reality itself. In short, man does not need doctrine, because the historical reality suffices for itself. It is the *Weltgeist,* the Spirit of the World.

CONCLUSION

To conclude, from the comparison of the current situation with that of previous "heretical popes," a similarity emerges, but also a clear difference. The similarity lies in the fact that in all three cases, at the end, what is being sought is a compromise formula, a political solution that can collect the greater number of consensus votes, but without deepening its truth content and its consistency with Tradition. History shows that these attempts are doomed to failure, because the subsequent development of reflection inevitably brings to the surface the contradictions that some tried to conceal.

The essential difference which we note between the ancient and the modern situation is instead the following. Without taking anything away from the severity of the ancient Trinitarian and Christological controversies or the drama of the events that involved Liberius and Honorius (and without downplaying their responsibilities), in comparison with the current situation their doctrinal deviations appear limited to particular points, albeit very important ones, and were derived, in large part, less from the heretical minds of the Pontiffs than from the political pressures and from a theological terminology still on the path of formulation. What instead leaps to the attention in the current situation is precisely the underlying doctrinal deformation that, as skillful as it may be in evading directly heterodox formulations, still maneuvers in a coherent way to carry forward an attack not only against particular dogmas like the indissolubility of marriage and the objectivity of the moral law, but even against the very concept of right doctrine, and with it, of the very Person of Christ as *Logos*. The first victim of this doctrinal deformation is precisely the pope, who (I hazard to conjecture) is hardly aware of this, being the victim of a generalized epochal alienation from Tradition in large segments of theological teaching; after him, there are innumerable victims who fall into deception.

In this situation, the *dubia*, these five questions submitted by the four cardinals, were certainly a fundamental turning point, a powerful light of truth that has been cast on this chaos, and for this we must thank them deeply. Though they are few and apparently isolated, their questions are still courageous statements of truth. In fact, they are not the only ones who speak; there speaks the *Logos* "from whose mouth comes a sharp sword" (Rev 19:15). Now, these five questions have put the pope in a stalemate. If he were to answer them by denying the Tradition and the Magisterium of his predecessors, he would pass to being formally heretical, so he cannot do it. If instead he were to answer them in harmony with the previous Magisterium, he would contradict a great part of the doctrinally relevant actions taken during his pontificate, so it would be a very difficult choice. He, therefore, has chosen silence because, humanly speaking, the situation appears to have no way out. But in the meantime, the confusion and the *de facto* schism extend throughout the Church.

In the light of all this, it therefore becomes more necessary than ever, as initially provided for at least by Cardinal Burke, to make a further act of courage, truth, and charity, on the part of the cardinals, but also of the bishops and then of all the qualified laity who would like to adhere to it. In such a serious situation of danger for the faith and of generalized scandal, it is not only licit, but even obligatory for an inferior to fraternally correct his superior, always doing so in charity; not even hierarchical or religious obedience can be used, in this case of general danger, as an excuse to silence the truth. In short, a fraternal correction frankly addressed to Peter is necessary, for his good and the good of the whole Church.

Some, with regard to this proposed fraternal correction to the pope, have expressed the fear that it could lead to a formal schism.

But on reflection, this fear proves to be entirely unfounded. In fact, all the conditions are lacking for formal schism. There is no record, to begin with, that any of the cardinals would want to hold that Francis is not the pope, and even less, that someone wants to get himself elected antipope. The true schism, which is increasing every day, is rather a *de facto* one, which only a correction may restrain. A fraternal correction, in the end, is not an act of hostility, lack of respect, or disobedience. It is nothing other than a declaration of truth: *caritas in veritate*. The pope, even before being pope, is our brother, and this is therefore a primordial duty of charity towards him. We will be called to account for his destiny, as well as that of all those who rely on his guidance. The wicked man, God says through the prophet Ezekiel, "will die for his sin," but if you, watchman, do not warn him, "I will require an account from you of his death" (Ezek 33:8).

Christian brothers: cardinals, bishops, priests, professors, friends all. Christ came into the world "to bear witness to the Truth" (Jn 18:37). We just have to follow him, bearing witness to the truth; not tomorrow, but today, "while the day lasts" (Jn 11:9). The time is short; "it has lowered the sails" (1 Cor 7:29).[11]

---

11 The original text says: ὁ καιρὸς συνεσταλμένος ἐστίν. In ancient Greek, the verb συστέλλω is used as a nautical term, having as its first meaning: to draw together, to shorten sail, e.g. συστείλας ἄκροισι χρώμενος τοῖς ἱστίοις (Ar.Ra.999): see Liddell and Scott, *Greek-English Lexicon*, 1507. The Apostle is here referring to eschatological times with the metaphor of a ship lowering its sails and entering the harbour.

7

A Year After Amoris Laetitia: *A Timely Word*[1]

DR ANNA M. SILVAS

"I SAW THE SNARES THAT THE ENEMY SPREADS out all over the world, and I said, groaning: 'What can get through so many snares?' Then I heard a voice saying to me: 'Humility.'" So said Abba Antony the Great, Father of Monks. And so also it seems to me, in accepting to speak to you now, a year after *Amoris Laetitia*. Please forgive me, for it seems to me any number of more qualified lay faithful should be speaking ahead of me. The current field of the Church is so strewn with canonical, theological, and ecclesiological snares, one would hardly dare say anything, so strange is this hour in the Church.

If I were to point to one issue in the present crisis in the Church, it would be "modernity," and that mood in the Church that so greatly prizes "modernity" and follows it at all costs. Theologian Tracey Rowland points out that "the modern" to which we were urged to update was never defined in the documents of Vatican II — a truly extraordinary lacuna. She says: "The absence of a theological examination of this cultural phenomenon called 'modernity' or 'the modern world' by Conciliar fathers in the years 1962–65 is perhaps one of the most striking features of the documents of the Second Vatican Council."[2] The Latin word *moderna* means the just now, the latest, the most recent. The cult of modernity happens when we make this an overriding object of desire, so as to gain the approval of the elite classes, the captains of the media and arbiters of culture. If I were to place the finger of diagnosis, it would be precisely on this emulous desire.

Two years ago or so, a young friend of mine, Elyse Beck, who is

---

[1] Given at the conference "Seeking Clarity: One Year after *Amoris Laetitia*," Rome, April 22, 2017. Published at Sandro Magister's *Settimo Cielo*, April 21, 2017.

[2] Tracey Rowland, *Culture and the Thomist Tradition* (London: Routledge, 2003), 13.

a teacher and passionately committed in her Catholic faith, took a new job in a new Catholic school. One day, some of her Year 8 students did a class exercise in "politics." Her students were in the second year of high school, so they had been through eight years of Catholic schooling, and through the whole sacramental "program"—horrible word that; what does its use signify? She asked: if her students were candidates for an upcoming election, what would be their policies? To her surprise, every one of them, except for one boy, nominated same-sex marriage and the LGBT agenda. So she began to engage them in remedial conversation. That brought home to me how far the values of a purely secular modernity have more ascendency among "Catholics" today than do the values of the life in Christ and the teachings of the Church. Immersion in the practices of modernity has led to a *de facto* situation in which the *mythos* of modernity has seeped into the very bone marrow and veins of Catholics. It permeates their way of thinking and acting implicitly. I look around, and I begin to wonder, with horror, how much this is now true of the leadership of the Church, perhaps even among the best of them. How many are deeply, deeply, more tributary to the modern world's "program" than obedient to Christ's summons to our deepest mind and heart?

Under St. John Paul II, we seemed to have something of a "push-back" for a while, at least in some areas, especially his intense explication of the nuptial mystery of our first creation, in support of *Humanae Vitae*. This continued under Benedict XVI, with some attempt to address liturgical decay and the moral "filth" of clerical sexual abuse. We had hoped that some remediation at least was in train. Now, in the few short years of Pope Francis's pontificate, the stale and musty spirit of the seventies has resurged, bringing with it seven other demons. And if we were in any doubt about this before, *Amoris Laetitia* and its aftermath in the past year make it perfectly clear that this is our crisis. That this alien spirit appears to have finally swallowed up the See of Peter, dragging ever-widening cohorts of compliant higher church leadership into its net, is its most dismaying and indeed shocking aspect to many of us, the Catholic lay faithful. I look up at any number of higher prelates, bishops, and theologians, and I cannot detect in them, by all that is holy, the least level of the *sensus fidelium*—and these are bearers of the Church's teaching office? Who would risk his immortal soul by trusting to their moral judgment in Confession?

In preparation for this paper, I thoughtfully re-read *Amoris Laetitia* after nearly a year. As I waded into the murky waters of chapter eight, I was overwhelmingly confirmed in my reading of it last year. In fact, it seemed to me a worse document than I had thought it was, and I had thought it very bad.

There is no need here to offer further detailed analyses, carried out by so many thoughtful commentators in the intervening year, such as the early heroes Robert Spaemann and Roberto de Mattei, Bishop Schneider, the "Forty-five Theologians," Finnis and Grisez, and many others, all of whom should appear on a roll-call of honour when the history of these times comes to be written.

There is one group, however, whose approach I find very strange: the intentionally orthodox among higher prelates and theologians who treat the turmoil arising from *Amoris Laetitia* as a matter of "misinterpretations." They will focus on the text alone, abstracted from any of the known antecedents in the words and acts of Pope Francis himself or its wider historical context. It is as if they interpose a chasm that cannot be crossed between the person of the pope on the one hand, over whose signature this document was published, and the "text" of the document on the other hand. With the Holy Father safely quarantined out of all consideration, they are free to address the problem, which they identify as a "misuse" of the text. They then express the pious plea that the Holy Father will "correct" these errors of interpretation.

No doubt the perceived constraints of piety to the successor of Peter account for these contorted manoeuvres. I know, I know! We have been facing down that conundrum for a year or longer. But to any sane and thoughtful reader, who, in the words of the Forty-five Theologians' censures, is "not trying to twist the words of the document in any direction, but ... take the natural or the immediate impression of the meaning of the words to be correct," this smacks of a highly-wrought artificiality. Pope Francis's "intent" in this text is perfectly recoverable from the text itself, reading normally and naturally and without filters. Let us try some examples.

The first of the cardinals' five *Dubia* concludes: "Can the expression 'in certain cases' found in Note 351 of the exhortation *Amoris Laetitia* be applied to divorced persons who are in a new union and who continue to live *more uxorio*?" Without doubt, a papal clarification of the intent in this footnote is of urgent importance to the Church. Nevertheless, what the pope intended is clear from the beginning of this very section 301. His topic is "those living in 'irregular situations.'" All that is said a few lines later about those in situations of objective sin growing in grace and charity and sanctification — maybe with the help of the sacraments, Holy Communion in particular — is posted under this heading of "irregular situations." That those in supposedly "sanctifying" "irregular situations" who are admitted to the Eucharist include the divorced and civilly remarried who do not intend to abrogate their sexual relationship is flagged in 298, where, in footnote 329, a passage in *Gaudium et Spes* 51 that discusses the question of temporary continence within marriage, as taught by St. Paul, is outrageously transposed to those who are not in a Christian marriage, i.e., in "irregular situations," becoming an argument that they should not have to live as brother and sister. The intention, prefaced by a misrepresentation of St. John Paul II and a bare-faced lie about the meaning of *GS* 51, is clear. So where is the difficulty in understanding what the pope intends?

In 299, Pope Francis asks us to discern "which of the various forms of exclusion currently practised in the liturgical, pastoral, educational and institutional framework, can be surmounted." This indicates his aim clearly: how are we going to overcome those "exclusions," liturgical first of all, practised till now? Where is the difficulty in grasping Pope Francis's intent? And there are many other instances like this. As early as the preface he alerts us that "everyone should feel challenged by chapter eight," and then late in that chapter (308) admits obliquely that his approach may "leave room for confusion." Let us believe him: this is his intent, which is not at all that difficult to grasp.

We have noted the abstract focus on the text alone that punctiliously excludes the acts and the person of Pope Francis from all consideration of the document's intent. Also strictly excluded as a means of ascertaining the pope's mind are the wider historical antecedents. To pick off a few in a galaxy of incidents, these include Archbishop Bergoglio's known practice in his archdiocese of tacitly admitting to Holy Communion all comers: the cohabiting, as well as the divorced and civilly remarried;[3] his personal choice of

---

3 "Above all he encouraged his priests not to deny communion to anyone, whether they be married, or cohabiting, or divorced and remarried. With no fuss and without making this decision public, the then-archbishop of

Cardinal Kasper to deliver the opening address of the 2014 Synod, as if we are to politely turn a blind eye to the entire back-history of Kasper's activities on these issues; the various ways in which these two synods were massaged, such as the papal order that a proposition on communion for the divorced and remarried, voted down by the bishops in the 2014 synod, be included in the final Relation;[4] his scathing condemnations of the "Pharisees" and other rigid persons in his concluding address at the conclusion of the 2015 Synod; and more recently, his warm praise of Bernard Häring, the doyen of dissenting moral theologians throughout the 1970s and '80s, whose 1989 book on admitting the divorced and civilly remarried to the Eucharist in imitation of the Eastern Orthodox *oikonomia* was ammunition in Kasper's saddle bag. Then of course there was Pope Francis's endorsement of the Argentinian bishops' "interpretation" of *AL*, precisely in the way that he intended: "No hay otras interpretaciones."[5] You know all these incidents, and many, many more, almost on a daily basis, in which it is not at all difficult to grasp Francis's intent.

Pope Francis, I am sure, is very well aware of the doctrine of papal infallibility, knows how high are its provisos—and is astute enough never to trigger its mechanism. The unique prestige of the papacy in the Catholic Church, together with the practical affective papalism of many Catholics, are however useful assets, and these he will exploit to the full. For to Francis—and we have to grasp this—infallibility doesn't matter, it doesn't matter at all, if he can succeed in being the sort of change-agent in the Church he wants to be. That this is his spirit we learn in *AL* 3 where he says:

> Since "time is greater than space," I would make it clear that not all discussions of doctrinal, moral or pastoral issues need to be settled by interventions of the magisterium. Unity of teaching and practice is certainly necessary in the Church, but this does not preclude various

---

Buenos Aires was already doing what the popes at the time prohibited, but he would later permit once he became pope." Sandro Magister, "The Man Who Had To Be Elected Pope," *OnePeterFive*, April 2, 2017.

4 *Relatio Synodi* 2014, §52.

5 "Pope: 'No other interpretation' of *Amoris Laetitia* than allowing communion for divorced/remarried in some cases," *LifeSiteNews*, September 9, 2016. For text and commentary, see above, 82–84, 135–36, and 215–33.

ways of interpreting some aspects of that teaching or drawing certain consequences from it. This will always be the case as the Spirit guides us towards the entire truth (cf. Jn 16:13), until he leads us fully into the mystery of Christ and enables us to see all things as he does.[6]

But I think "the spirit" to which Francis so soothingly alludes has more to do with the *Geist* of Herr Hegel than with the Holy Spirit of whom our blessed Lord speaks, the Spirit of Truth whom the world cannot receive, because it neither sees him nor knows him (Jn 14:17). The Hegelian *Geist*, on the other hand, manifests itself in the midst of contradictions and oppositions, surmounting them in a new synthesis, without eliminating the polarities or reducing one to the other. This is the gnostic spirit of the cult of modernity.

So Francis will pursue his agenda without papal infallibility, and without fussing about magisterial pronouncements. We are in a world of dynamic fluidity here, of starting open-ended processes, of sowing seeds of desired change that will triumph over time. Other theorists—you have here in Italy Gramsci and his manifesto of cultural Marxism—teach how to achieve revolution by stealth. So within the Church, Francis and his collaborators deal with the matter of doctrine not by confronting theory head on (because if they did so they would be defeated), but by an incremental change of praxis, played to the siren song of plausible persuasions, until the praxis is sufficiently built up over time to a point of no return. Such underhand tactics are clearly playing to the tune of Hegelian dialectic. That this is Pope Francis's *modus operandi* may be inferred from a certain "behind the scenes incident" in the 2015 Synod:

> "If we speak explicitly about communion for the divorced and remarried," said Archbishop Forte, reporting a joke of Pope Francis, "you do not know what a terrible mess we will make. So we won't speak plainly, (but) do it in a way that the premises are there, then I will draw out the conclusions." "Typical of a Jesuit," Abp Forte joked.[7]

---

6   See Deacon Jim Russell, "Pope Francis's 'Time is Greater than Space': What Does It Mean?," *Aleteia*, May 24, 2016.
7   "Forte: Pope Did Not Want to Speak 'Plainly' of Communion for Remarried," *OnePeterFive*, May 7, 2016.

Then slowly, region by region, bishops around the world begin to "interpret" *AL* to mean that the Church has now "developed" her pastoral praxis to admit the divorced and civilly remarried to the Eucharist, setting aside the gravest of sacramental provisos that obtained up till now—provided of course that a sonorous note of "accompaniment" is struck. And when Pope Francis sees this happening, what is his response? He rejoices to find that they have accurately picked up his cues in *AL*. I have already mentioned his famous "No hay otras interpretaciones" to the Argentinian bishops; the latest is his letter of thanks to the bishops of Malta for their interpretations.

I think it an injustice to blame these bishops for "misuse" of *AL*. On the contrary, they have drawn the conclusions patent to any thoughtful, unblinkered reader of this papal document. The blame, however, and the tragedy for the Church lies in the intent embedded and articulated well enough in *Amoris Laetitia* itself, and in the naïve papalism on the part of bishops, which has so poor a purchase on the Church's imperishable obedience of faith that it cannot perceive when it is under most dangerous attack, even from that most lofty quarter.

In this game of subterfuge and incremental intent, the elaborate talk of painstaking "discernment" and "accompaniment" of difficult moral situations has a definite function—as a temporary blind for the ultimate goal. Have we not seen how the dark arts of the "hard case" work in secular politicking, used to pivot the next tranche of social reengineering? So it is now in the politics of the Church. The final result will be precisely in accord with Archbishop Bergoglio's tacit practice for years in Buenos Aires. Make no mistake: the end game is a more or less indifferent permission for any who present themselves for Holy Communion. And so we attain the longed-for haven of all-inclusiveness and "mercy": the terminal trivialization of the Eucharist, of sin and repentance, of the sacrament of Matrimony, of any belief in objective and transcendent truth, the evisceration of language, and of any stance of compunction before the living God, the God of Holiness and Truth. If I may adapt here a saying of St. Thomas Aquinas: "mercy without truth is the mother of dissolution."[8]

---

8 *Super Matthaeum*, cap. V, lec. 2. The original statement is: "Mercy without justice is the mother of dissolution."

Pope Francis has absolutely no intention of playing by anyone's "rules"—least of all yours or mine or anyone else's "rules" for the papacy. You know well what he thinks of "rules." He tell us constantly. It is one of the milder disparagements in his familiar stock of insults. When I hear those who lecture us that Pope Francis is the voice of the Holy Spirit in the Church today, I do not know whether to laugh at the naivety of it, or weep at the damage being done to immortal souls. I would say that yes, Francis is the agent of a spirit, namely the Hegelian *Geist* of "modernity" very much at work in the Church. It is, as I said earlier, a stale and musty spirit, an old spirit that has no life in it, a privative force that only knows how to feed parasitically on what already is. I am not sure that Newman's *Essay on the Development of Christian Doctrine* does not give us all we need to face the present crisis. In his seven "notes" or criteria for discerning genuine development of doctrine from its corruption, he provides the needed response to the Hegelian praxis dialectically overwhelming *theoria*. The seventh note is "chronic vigour." Over time, a corruption shows itself to be exceedingly vigorous—but only at the beginning of the "infection," since it does not possess the life to sustain itself in the long term. It will run its course and die out. The Life of Grace, however, possesses in itself the Divine Life, and will therefore throw off in the course of time all that militates against it. Truth perdures. There will be moments of high drama, but, eventually, it must necessarily prevail. It is the way in which grace acts in the organic development of nature, the very reverse of the gnostic "time is greater than space."

My dear fellow believers in Christ Jesus our Lord, this false spirit shall not, cannot ultimately prevail. In the sixteenth century, the Protestant revolt demoted marriage from the standing of a sacrament, and set in train the secularisation of marriage in the West. Constantinople began to lose its purchase on the accuracy of the Gospel of marriage with the Emperor Justinian and his Roman civil law of divorce. As the scandalous example of adulterous emperors and empresses remarried in the lifetime of their true spouses filtered down into the Church and became the custom, so a fair-seeming theology of *oikonomia* grew up to cloak this grave breach with holy Tradition. This is what Häring, Kasper, and Co., in their ignorant folly, have been invoking as an example for us to follow. Until now the Catholic Church in communion with Rome held fast the dominical and apostolic teaching on the sacramentality and indissolubility of Christian marriage. I qualify that: you should study the recent history of the Coptic Church on this issue: it is most inspiring and encouraging. Let us take the Copts for our allies, in this and in other ways too.

Is it still a possibility, the cardinals' proposed fraternal correction of the pope? We heard of this last November, and it surely lifted our beleaguered spirits. But now it is the end of April, and nothing has come of it. I cannot help but think of that passage from Shakespeare: "There is a tide in the affairs of men...," and wonder if the tide has come and gone, and we the lay faithful are left stranded again.

Yet Cardinal Burke has recently said: "Until these questions are answered, there continues to spread a very harmful confusion in the Church, and one of the fundamental questions is in regards to the truth that there are some acts that are always and everywhere wrong, what we call intrinsically evil acts, and so, we cardinals will continue to insist that we get a response to these honest questions."[9]

Well, I hope so, dear cardinals, I hope so. We, the faithful, beg you: forget about calculating prudent outcomes. Real prudence should tell you when it is the right time for courageous witness, whose other name is martyrdom. Pope Francis will not heed a fraternal correction as John XXII once did. But you know what? It would not matter much even if he did publish some statement along those lines. Let one twenty-four-hour news-cycle go by, and we had better not count on it that further utterances will not subtly undercut or openly contradict what was said the day before. If we have not learnt that about his manner by now, then we truly are the stupidest of sheep — or shepherds, as the case may be. Pardon me if I venture to say this, but, however we account for it, the papacy is not working right now in the Church. Peter has become a *skandalon* again, the "rock" a stumbling block (cf. Mt 16:16–24). Until we face this reality, unbelievable as it may seem, we are bound in intimidation and illusion, and the way out (1 Cor 10:13) that the Lord offers us will be deferred. What kind of prophet do you want to show you the times? Hananiah or Jeremiah (cf. Jer 28)? Choose.

What, then, is the plight of us, the lay faithful, in these days of severe trial in the Church? I could hardly better the following

---

9 See Charles Collins, "Burke again says Pope must answer 'Amoris' questions," *Crux*, March 27, 2017.

remarks by Roderick Halvorsen from Santa, Idaho, commenting on an article by Steve Skojec at OnePeterFive. Halvorsen came into the Catholic Church from Protestantism some years ago, and has no intention of leaving, but sees the follies of liberal Protestantism metastasizing in the Catholic Church. He speaks here of us, the lay faithful:

> But in reality, God is testing us. He is asking us to be in relationship with HIM, yes, personally and intimately and truly. He has taken all the "crutches" of Catholicism away; the power, the glory, the world's respect, trustworthy leaders and models, in short, all the stuff that can be of assistance to the faith, but is unnecessary to the faith, and like wealth and worldly success, can be the source of a weakening of our faith, when we begin to shift our trust to the "culture" of the faith, instead of to the person of our faith: Jesus Christ.

"Jesus answered, and said to him: If anyone loves me, he will keep my word, and my Father will love him, and we will come to him, and make our abode with him" (Jn 14:23). To this abode, this abiding, this being "hidden with Christ in God" (Col 3:3), therefore, we must go.

It is a wonderful thing that, in the midst of social, cultural, and ecclesial collapse, I see signs of a common cause between monasticism and the lay faithful who are seeking this interior abiding with Christ. Rod Dreher's *The Benedict Option* that appeared a few weeks ago attests this movement. For not in efficient political programs, but "below the radar," so to speak, in the humble life of community ordered in Christ, monastic communities quietly established advance outposts of a new liturgical universe in the rubble of the western Roman empire. In other ways too, the lay faithful—and I have in mind especially the domestic churches of families—sense the worsening crises of these times, and intuit that for them the way of spiritual contest is in the local community, in the small, the hidden, the unimportant in this world's eyes. They have little or no role in the ecclesiastical world, or perhaps in worldly success either. Such seekers hunger for an alternative liturgy of life and community, prayer and work, and some of them are sensing that deep monasticism has a word for them. A dear friend in the John Paul II Institute in Melbourne, sadly soon to close,

Conor Sweeney, likes to use the hobbits in Tolkien's mythology as an analogy for this hidden alternative Christian lifestyle. For it was the hobbits, an insignificant folk, who had no part in the counsels of the mighty, who against all odds had the decisive role in overturning the powerful forces of the dark Lord threatening to engulf the whole of Middle Earth in a reign of savagery.

I have another friend, Michael Ryan, a married man and father, whose shining light of inspiration among the saints is St. Bruno. Imagine it: the witness of the most intentionally contemplative monastic life in the Western Church, the Carthusians, a beacon of hope to the lay faithful? For deep monasticism is all about *moné*, "abode" or "abiding" in Christ, about waiting and watching with hope-filled faith, as "useful" as the Prophet Habbakuk standing upon his watch and stationing himself on the watchtower, as "useful" as Simeon and Anna haunting the temple and waiting their life long for the dawning light of salvation and knowing him when he came, as "useful" as the women who sat at a distance and watched at our Lord's tomb on the eve of the first Good Friday, as "useful" as our all-holy Lady, Mary, taking her stand beside the Cross. Perhaps prayer, prayer of this sort, is the most radically political act of all, and the very core of Christianity? Where, O where, have we Catholics been?

Our Lord himself used to rise long before dawn and watch in the night hours, even in the days of his busiest ministry. The disciples, awed one day by the mystery of his prayer, felt a deep wistful attraction: "Lord, teach us to pray." This is the one emulous desire that we do need: Jesus, the one model to whose imitation we can give ourselves completely, and we will not be betrayed. Can we, is it at all possible to learn something of the sentiments that filled his human mind and heart in those solitary hours of intimacy with his Father? Yes, we can, for in his great compassion he shared them with us in a form of words: sacred words, holy words of complete trustworthy power and truth:

Abba! Abbuna de b'ashmayo, yithqaddash shm'okh...

Our Father, who are in heaven, hallowed be Thy Name...

8

"By far the worst document that has ever come out with a papal signature"[1]

INTERVIEW WITH DR CLAUDIO PIERANTONI ON THE *FILIAL CORRECTION*

THE RECENT "FILIAL CORRECTION" CHARGING Pope Francis with permitting the spread of seven heresies, at least by omission, has provoked admiration and consternation among Catholics and drawn considerable attention in the secular media. But what led those who authored or contributed to the Correction to take such a rare and serious step? We travelled to Santiago, Chile, where we had the opportunity for an in-depth interview with Professor Claudio Pierantoni, who is one of the lay scholars who helped shape the "filial correction." Prof. Pierantoni, who was born in Rome, is currently a professor of Medieval Philosophy in the Philosophy Faculty of the University of Chile (Santiago). He has two PhDs: in the History of Christianity and in Philosophy. In this extensive interview, we discuss the immediate trigger for the correction, namely the chaos following the Apostolic Exhortation *Amoris Laetitia*, the philosophical roots of the crisis, and why Professor Pierantoni describes the present situation as "apocalyptic."

Professor Pierantoni, what personally led you to be part of the Filial Correction *initiative?*

Dr Pierantoni: I started thinking about this [matter] as soon as the document *Amoris Laetitia* came out. Immediately it attracted my attention, when I read the article of Professor de Mattei,[2] and

---

[1] Published by Diane Montagna, "'Apocalyptic': *Filial Correction* organizer warns of schism if errors aren't corrected," *LifeSiteNews*, September 29, 2017.

[2] "Prime riflessioni su un documento catastrofico," *Corrispondenza Romana*, April 10, 2016; published in English at *Rorate Caeli* on April 11.

the first open letter to the pope by Bishop Schneider, which were among the first and strongest reactions that appeared. I continued to investigate and read the many articles that continued to be published, so I have thought about it in an uninterrupted way ever since. Of course, up to that point, I was accustomed to thinking that this is not a matter for lay people to be involved with, because there are bishops and cardinals. But then I started to see that bishops and cardinals were not doing much, apart from Bishop Schneider, or afterwards, Cardinals Burke, Caffarra, Brandmüller, and Meisner. So I felt something had to be done.

In September I wrote my first article on the subject, drawing a parallel between the present situation and the Arian controversy, a parallel that had been suggested by Bishop Schneider. Since then, the thought has never left me. In April 2017, I was invited to participate in the international conference in Rome that featured lay speakers from five continents and called for clarity about *Amoris Laetitia*. There I spoke about the necessary link between Magisterium and Tradition, and about the case of the heresy of popes Liberius and Honorius. This was important in order that people might properly understand the doctrine of papal infallibility in the light of the history of the Church.[3] I felt very strongly that this contribution was a very important thing to do, because one of the main problems in this controversy has been the tendency of many Catholics to interpret the pope's personal ideas or accidental declarations as if they were necessarily a part of the Magisterium of the Church.

Some people said: what can you achieve with the "filial correction"? But I always thought that, by telling the truth, by stating it in a scholarly and well-founded way, you can achieve many things—just because you are telling the truth. It's not a question of human power, really. Of course, the truth must be spoken in a respectful way, the pope must be respected as the pope. And I think it should be clear that we consider him to be the pope, because some people might confuse this, suspecting that it is a sedevacantist position. That must be very clear, that we consider Francis to be the pope. That is precisely why we are insisting that he condemn these errors.

---

3   See chapter 6; cf. chapter 31.

Why has this step been taken if the cardinals, who are the pope's counsellors, are going to issue a formal correction?

The formal correction, as you remember, was already promised for January. But in April, when we had the Rome conference, there still was no hint that Cardinal Burke was going to issue a correction. So, in a little group, we started to think about a lay correction. Then, in July, when our correction was taking its final shape and had gained a certain number of signatures, we heard with great pleasure that Cardinal Burke was again thinking of a correction on his part. I also thought that, although the impact of a formal correction made by the cardinals would of course have a much greater impact—because to counsel the pope is their specific mission—there is not necessarily a *juridical* difference. We are inferior to the pope, but the cardinals are inferior as well. Some opponents of the "filial correction" argue that this is not a juridical act, that it has no juridical value. And I think they are right: properly speaking, it has no juridical value. The pope is above any juridical form of correction from a superior (as we state in our letter), because he has no superior on earth. But both in the case of the cardinals and of the scholars, a correction has great moral value. So the moral value is common to both.

You are right to say that that the job of the cardinals is to counsel the pope, but the duty of a correction belongs to anyone who has the knowledge to do it.

And I think, in this case, the cardinals need the support of scholars, because, in the first place, they are so few. If there were sixty cardinals that were also scholars, of course it would be useless. But given that they are now only two, I think they need lay and scholarly support. Perhaps people outside the Church think this is a political matter. But it is a theological, philosophical, historical matter that entails much scholarly work and needs much expertise. The kinds of problems this entails are wide-ranging. You need to have philosophers, historians, theologians.

It would be very easy for Pope Francis to answer your concerns and clarify matters, wouldn't it?

Yes, of course, in terms of practical action. But it would mean contradicting his main line of action and thought over many years—I believe not only during his years as pope but also previous years as well. It would be contradictory to a whole way of thinking, rather than just an error in part of the journey of life. I think that is why the reference to Modernism in our letter was especially important, for this current of thought has a long tradition in the twentieth century and has produced a very influential school and a way of thinking.

Do you think that Modernism is the root of the seven heretical propositions you have addressed in the Correction?

Yes, I think that Modernism is the basic root, even more than Lutheranism. Because Modernism is a more philosophically coherent system with definite presuppositions, whereas Lutheranism has different elements that are not always coherent with one another. For example, the basic presupposition of Modernism, which in the end is a derivation of German idealism, is that all being is history, so truth cannot be immutable, but must evolve. The basic presupposition is that there is not a really immutable God (an error condemned by the First Vatican Council), and therefore an immutable substance of truth, but somehow God identifies himself with creation (another error condemned by Vatican I) and so evolves with history. In that sense, something can be true in the fourth century and false in the twenty-first.

According to this view, today's magisterium doesn't need to be logically coherent with previous magisterium: it is enough to state that the same universal "Substance"—God, Reality, or Life—is speaking today through the present magisterium [as was speaking yesterday through the past], and there's no point in contrasting it with previous magisterium. That is the philosophical foundation of maxims such as "reality is superior to ideas" (cf. *Evangelii Gaudium*, 233). But, in the end, it is clear that this leads to abandoning the principle of non-contradiction: that's why you hear nowadays in Rome statements like Fr Spadaro's already (in)famous "two and two are five." Now I think this contradiction leads not only to heresy, but still more, to mental illness. It is no exaggeration what Cardinal Sarah stated during one of the Vatican synods of 2014–2015: "the divorce between doctrine and practice is a dangerous schizophrenic pathology."

Could you tell our readers more about what Modernism is?
I think that in Modernism there is a deep philosophical problem about the idea of God himself. In Modernism, God is conceived as changeable. Somehow the substance of God is immanent in the world in such a way that you cannot metaphysically distinguish being from becoming, being from change. If God is changing with reality, then you have a problem with the very notion of God, and nowadays this is a very strong school of thought. It is Hegelian in origin. I think it's much more ancient as a doctrine (you can trace it back to ancient Gnosticism), but Hegel is its most famous modern representative. And it's very strong in modern faculties of theology. So it's a very deep problem.

I think the immediate intention of the pope and his counsellors was to give an answer to the question of Communion for divorced and civilly remarried Catholics. But then, in order to give a theological and philosophical justification, they had to make explicit their own presuppositions, which are mistaken in a much more profound way. So the general view you get is very frightening and apocalyptic. Modernism, as Pope Pius X famously stated, is not just "one heresy," but the root and consummation of all heresies.

If the Correction were not issued, what did you fear might happen?
I think that if an error is not somehow corrected, then humanly speaking, the obvious prediction is that the error will continue to spread. At least, with a correction, many people may come to realize that there is a problem. I think to state clearly that what we have here is material heresy, and that it is directly contrary to the Faith, challenges anyone and obliges people to think.

You are also a Church historian. In what respect is the 1333 example (the correction of Pope John XXII) different from the present case?
I think the main difference is the sheer "volume" of heresy. One can make a mistake on one point, but I think one important characteristic of the statement we signed is that it provides a historical background, explaining how this kind of thought relates to Modernism and to Lutheranism. So you can see that it's not just one point on which a mistake has been made, but it's a whole school of thought that then comes out in heretical propositions. The situation today is much more complex and much more grave.

At the conference held in Rome last April, you described the current situation as "apocalyptic"...

Yes, and I still think it's apocalyptic, because you don't get the impression that the pope is making only one mistake. For example, during Pope John Paul II's pontificate there was a question about a "just war." He said, during the first war in Iraq, that all war was unjust. A friend of mine, Father Robert Dodaro, O. S. A., who later was director of the Augustinianum, published an article saying that tradition says there can be a just war. St. Augustine teaches this; St. Thomas Aquinas teaches this, based of course on Scripture. So, this doesn't seem orthodox. But no one thought John Paul II was a heretic. He made one mistake and one could correct him. But it's a very different situation when you have a completely different world vision that, theologically and philosophically, risks being opposed to the Catholic view—a modernist view that says that doctrine is basically changeable, so that something which is in Scripture means one thing in the first century, but another thing in the eleventh century, and another thing in the twenty-first century. One could ask, then, what's the use of having a Bible, or of having Tradition (the two sources of Divine Revelation)?

The Correction *has been presented in the media and elsewhere in terms of what* Amoris Laetitia *said about Communion for the divorced and remarried, but from what I understand you to be saying, other broader and deeper issues have emerged.*

And I think this is providential. Although it's frightening, I think it's providential that mistakes come out with their theological and philosophical presuppositions. Because otherwise, one could just say, "Do it. Give communion with no justification," as many priests have done before. But if you start trying to justify—rationally, theologically—the problem grows, because you show what the presuppositions are. So this exposure creates bigger problems in one sense, but it's also providential because one can see where the mistake really lies, what the basic mistake is that leads you to a certain conclusion. Conservative popes like Pope Benedict and Pope John Paul II tried to stop it, but this somehow obliged "progressive" theologians to hide their presuppositions and wait in secret. But now they have freedom to express themselves and so their train of thought is much clearer. You can know what they think, so it's much easier to understand how grave the situation is.

Is there a concern among the signatories—either priests or lay scholars—that they might suffer reprisals?

Yes, there is a concern about that. I have heard from many people in Catholic institutions (here in Santiago and elsewhere) who have been directly threatened with reprisal, and therefore they didn't sign. For example, I have heard from some people who signed the document of the forty-five that they were told not to sign anything else or they would lose their position. Of course, one is more at risk depending on the kind of institution. I have heard of people being threatened, not directly from Rome but by the local institution, sometimes striving to be "more Roman than the pope."

Are you personally concerned?

In my case, I work for a state university, so they are not so concerned. I also work for a Catholic institution, but there they mainly share the orthodox position, so they don't persecute people who hold an orthodox position. Of course, one always needs a certain degree of prudence in this, trying not to scandalize persons who are not prepared.

Is the group of signatories you have gathered representative of a much larger group then?

Oh yes, definitely. I sent it to ten people, for example, and seven out of ten told me they didn't want to sign it out of fear of reprisals. A few did not think they were prepared to make a direct correction of the pope, although they agreed with the content. I can tell you that many, many people basically agreed on the content, many more than those who signed. So I think it is an error to claim, as some have in the media, that this is a "marginal" or a "traditionalist" initiative. "Traditionalist" in the strict sense means someone who only goes to the Mass in the extraordinary form (i.e., the traditional Latin Mass), or who has a strong objection to Vatican II. But the positions contained in the document are very widely shared. In fact, some commentators said: "they have been very good about mentioning only seven heresies, because there are many more"—and these commentators were not traditionalists.

Of course one reason why they are calling it "ultra-traditionalist" is because of the presence of Bishop Fellay's signature.

Yes, well, it is true that there are a number of people among the signatories who come from a traditionalist way of thinking, but that does not mean that the position in itself is traditionalist. It's not a traditionalist position to mention these errors. I think many normal Catholics, when they start thinking, understand that there are grave errors. One could define the correction as "conservative," provided that one understands that "conservative," in the Church, is not the same as "conservative" in the British parliament. Conserving in politics can be discussed because one is dealing with human law, not absolute truth. But in the Church, conservative means to conserve what has been handed down from Christ himself, through the Apostolic tradition. In this sense, it is essential to a Catholic to be conservative.

It has been suggested that the correction might tear down the papacy, that the devil could be using this as a trick.

On the contrary, I think that in this enterprise that the pope and his counsellors have undertaken with *Amoris Laetitia* really lies the trick to tear down the papacy. The papacy came out immensely discredited after *Amoris Laetitia*. I have no doubts in saying that it is by far the worst document that has ever come out with a papal signature in the whole history of the Church. This explains why many people have now seriously started to doubt if Francis really is the pope. Many people, who rightly think the pope must be the defender of the tradition, thought: well, this can't be the pope. It has also led some people to doubt papal infallibility or the meaning of the papacy. My friend Prof. Josef Seifert was also accused by his archbishop in Granada of discrediting the papacy by pointing to one of the biggest problems in *AL*. But who is really discrediting the papacy? First we should decide if the problem he pointed out was real and serious.[4]

Finally, I think it's very evident that the pope is putting a lot of confidence in just one group of people, who are all of one school, theologically and politically; and that is not good for a pope. He should really try to listen to different people. In Italy, for example, but also in America and in many other places, he looks more and more every day like someone who is standing for a party (see the book *The Political Pope* [by George Neumayr]). *That* is what discredits the papacy.

---

4   See Dr Pierantoni's defense of Seifert in: http://aemaet.de/index.php/aemaet/article/view/46/pdf.

What do you think Leo XIII meant when he wrote, in the exorcism prayer he composed after his alleged vision of St. Michael: "In the Holy Place itself, where has been set up the See of the most holy Peter and the Chair of Truth for the light of the world, they have raised the throne of their abominable impiety, with the iniquitous design that when the Pastor has been struck, the sheep may be scattered"? Are you familiar with this passage?

Yes, I discovered it right after *Amoris Laetitia* came out, and it surprised me very much because, frightening as it was, it seemed to be a perfect picture of the situation. I think no fictional writer could have imagined this and it's a true prophecy which is unfolding now. No one could have imagined that this prophecy would really come true (at some moment that paragraph was thought so incredible that it was even deleted from the St. Michael Prayer in official texts), but I think what Leo XIII was describing is coming true. It is important to add that this is not a moral judgment about the pope. I think the pope and his counsellors — for example Fr Spadaro, whom I got to know when I was a young student in Rome — are in fact good people. I believe they are well-intentioned. Pope Francis is charismatic and has many human and Christian virtues, so of course many people tend to believe him. But this is precisely what creates more confusion and so behind all of this there is a truly diabolical trick.

What do you think will happen now that the Correction *has been made public?*

I think that now Cardinal Burke must proceed to issue his long-promised correction. If I were him, I would call it a "fraternal correction" (better than "formal"). He has in fact given us hints that he approves of our "filial" initiative and feels supported by it, and so I'm sure he now knows that very soon is his time to act. Perhaps two or three more cardinals, or half a dozen bishops, will join. Maybe more, maybe less. But even if he were the only one, I think he must soon issue a correction.

Are we therefore in a time similar to the Arian heresy and St. Athanasius?

Yes, very similar, because we have two schools of thought that are difficult to reconcile, and there is a sufficiently wide consensus among learned theologians in very influential academic institutions (above all in Germany) that what we consider the heretical school is in fact orthodox. So I think there is also in this case, as in ancient learned bishops of the Origenian school, a superiority complex among heretical (or semiheretical) thinkers: they tend to look on others as inferior, or stuck in the past, as happened during the Arian controversy with the attitude towards Occidental bishops. Sometimes a more modest academic training can be a better ally to orthodoxy, because usually clever people, who are raised in a famous or prestigious school, can be more easily misled, as they frequently judge theology on human academic standards, and tend to follow the trend of their time and their school (for example, Karl Rahner's school, which had in recent times a huge influence) more than Tradition and the Bible.

If a fraternal correction were made, what do you think the next step might be?

It's very difficult to say, but I believe they haven't issued it yet because they fear a schism. But I think the opposite is true: that if they don't do it, there will be a schism. To not speak of the true doctrine, to not correct errors, for fear of schism is a contradiction. Only truth can unite. If error spreads it will cause a split, from parish church to parish church, from bishop to bishop, from country to country. It would be a practical schism, which in fact already exists, but if the correction doesn't take place, it will get much worse.

Although the defenders of the pope may mock the initiative, and say the signatories are very few in number and ultraconservative, or traditionalists, in the end what's important is not who is saying it, but if what is being said is true, no matter whether it is said by famous or obscure people, whether it's Bishop Fellay or the president of the IOR. The news of the day passes, but the truth remains. I don't think it's the number that's important. St. Athanasius in his time was only one. There were some people supporting him, but they were very few. But what was maintained as orthodoxy remained.

What can the lay faithful do?

I think the lay people have a very important role, because they are freer. I think this document may help some people to reflect in a more comprehensive way. But I think there is much work still to be done. The laity need more formation. Many people can't react to this because they don't have basic formation. Scholars should try to take the occasion to teach what perhaps we suppose people know, but they don't know—about the nature of the Church, about the role of the pope, about infallibility, about moral doctrine.

Cardinal Müller has suggested holding a theological disputation. What do you think of his proposal?

I consider Cardinal Müller's proposal to be an excellent idea, and a wonderful occasion for dialogue and for the genuine pursuit of truth within the Church. It is vital for us, both as Catholics and as rational beings, that we concentrate on the intrinsic truth of the fundamental doctrines that are at stake in this controversy, and that we don't fall into the temptation of focusing on external arguments, based on the rank, prestige, or number of the counterpart. Rank, fame, or numbers are contingent realities that pass away: but the truth is that which IS (cf. Ex 3:14). The truth is God himself.

9

Response to Rocco Buttiglione's Latest Interview[1]

DR CLAUDIO PIERANTONI

AS "LOVERS OF THE PAPACY," THE CRITICS OF *Amoris Laetitia* wish to spare Pope Francis a fate worse than Honorius's, the only pope to have been formally condemned for heresy. But those who close their eyes to the present situation are only "encouraging him down that path." These remarks, by Italian philosopher and Church historian, Professor Claudio Pierantoni, have come in response to Rocco Buttiglione's latest interview with *Vatican Insider*.[2] Rocco Buttiglione is an Italian philosopher and politician, and author of the recent book *Risposte amichevoli ai critici di* Amoris Laetitia [*Friendly Responses to Critics of* Amoris Laetitia].

In the interview with Andrea Tornielli, one of Pope Francis's closest media advisors, Buttiglione said there are some cases when divorced Catholics who have not obtained an annulment and are living in a sexually-active second union "can be considered to be in God's grace" and so "deserve to receive the Sacraments." "It seems a shocking novelty," Buttiglione acknowledged, "but it is a doctrine that is entirely, and I dare say rock-solidly, traditional." In the interview, Buttiglione also accused critics of *Amoris Laetitia* of falling into "ethical objectivism" and said that those who have charged the pope with permitting the spread of heresy, at least by omission, are guilty of "calumny, schism, and heresy."

Cardinal Walter Kasper echoed Buttiglione's comments last Thursday in a commentary for Vatican Radio's German edition, saying: "The admission of remarried divorcees to the sacraments in individual cases is based on the teaching of tradition, especially of Thomas Aquinas and the Council of Trent." "It is not a novelty,

---

[1] Published by Diane Montagna, "Here's why every argument allowing Communion for 'remarried' ultimately fails," *LifeSiteNews*, December 12, 2017.

[2] "Here is the deviation in which *Amoris Laetitia*'s critics fall," *Vatican Insider*, November 20, 2017.

but a renewal of an old tradition," Cardinal Kasper said. The flaw in the critiques of *Amoris Laetitia*, he added, is "a unilateral moral objectivism that undervalues the importance of personal conscience in a moral act." In his commentary, Kasper praised Pope Francis's official endorsement of the Argentine bishops' guidelines (by publishing them in the *Acta Apostolicae Sedis*) and said he hopes it will end the "tiresome" debate over *Amoris Laetitia*.

Yet other high-ranking prelates, such as former prefect of the Congregation for the Doctrine of the Faith, Cardinal Gerhard Müller, have suggested Pope Francis appoint a group of cardinals to debate his critics in order to resolve the impasse.[3]

Claudio Pierantoni, one of the lay scholars who helped shape the *Filial Correction*, has been a chief contributor to theological debate on the topic over the past year. Born in Rome, Pierantoni is currently a professor of Medieval Philosophy in the Philosophy Faculty of the University of Chile (Santiago). He has two PhDs: in the History of Christianity and in Philosophy. Here Prof. Pierantoni responds to Rocco Buttiglione's latest interview in an exclusive report for LifeSiteNews.

* * *

The latest interview with Rocco Buttiglione on *Amoris Laetitia* strikes me as interesting and useful, as it expresses the philosopher's thought in a synthetic and linear way without undue complication and digressions. This makes it much easier to identify and respond briefly to the main fallacies that afflict it. Buttiglione begins by saying that, thanks to his book and Cardinal Müller's preface: "for the first time the critics have been forced to respond and cannot deny one point: there are mitigating circumstances in virtue of which a mortal sin (a sin that otherwise would be mortal) becomes a lighter sin, which is only venial."

Here, I would point out that critics have already responded, saying they have never denied the doctrine of extenuating circumstances taken in general: I myself had done so in all of my articles on *Amoris Laetitia*, beginning in September 2016, as well as in many private letters to Rocco Buttiglione. What Buttiglione says

---

3 Edward Pentin, "Cardinal Müller Suggests Pope Francis Appoint Group of Cardinals to Debate His Critics," *National Catholic Register*, September 26, 2017.

here is, therefore, demonstrably false. However, what I especially wish to point out here is the fallacy of the consequences Buttiglione draws from this statement, as though these conclusions were obvious. Buttiglione writes:

> There are therefore some cases in which remarried divorcees can (through their confessor and after suitable spiritual discernment) be considered to be in God's grace and therefore deserving of receiving the sacraments. It seems a shocking novelty, but it is a doctrine that is entirely, and I dare say rock-solidly, traditional.

Note the rush and superficiality (certainly not justified by the mitigating circumstance of a lack of intelligence) with which Buttiglione jumps to the twofold consequence: in the first passage, he draws from the general doctrine of extenuating circumstances the immediate consequence that "remarried divorces can be considered to be in God's grace." With this, he skips over the strong objections that we critics have raised without even responding to them.

The mitigating circumstances would be based, as *AL* states and Buttiglione reiterates, on an inadequate understanding of the norm. Now, *AL* proposes a "suitable spiritual discernment." But we would say that, for this spiritual discernment to be "suitable," it must necessarily lead to a proper understanding of the norm. A poor understanding of the norm could perhaps be invoked by those who, left to themselves, do not have access to a confessor or spiritual guide. But to suggest that it would be invoked by someone who has access to this spiritual formation is a contradiction. When someone confesses a sin, even if the confessor is able to assess that there have been mitigating circumstances in the past, the logical consequence is that the sinner renounces committing the sin in the future. If this were not the case, he would not be dealing with a sin, and so it wouldn't make sense to speak of mitigating circumstances. If the penitent thinks he can continue to act in this way, he is affirming that "given the situation" the action wasn't really, in fact, a sin, but rather the right thing to do. And this is precisely what situational ethics says, which in vain Buttiglione seeks to separate from *AL*. In this case, adultery wouldn't be intrinsically evil, as Catholic moral theology states, but would be so "according to the case."

Ultimately we are faced with a clear dilemma: either the irregular situation is sinful, or it isn't. If we say that it is sinful, then even though it might be mitigated by circumstances in the past, it must be forsaken in future. If instead, we say that it is not sinful, then we aren't talking about extenuating circumstances anymore, but rather we fall head-on into situational ethics, which states that adultery is not always evil, but only in certain cases. And if this is true for adultery, then there's no reason why it can't be true for other actions which are considered to be intrinsically evil in Catholic doctrine. This would be the "atomic bomb" effect of which Joseph Seifert spoke.

When the confessor determines that there have been extenuating circumstances for the sin committed, it doesn't follow, as Buttiglione claims, that the person "can be considered to be in God's grace." He may well be before God, and so we should never be so bold as to judge the inner life of a person, as Jesus teaches us. But it does not follow from this that the priest has the power to penetrate God's gaze and decide positively that a person is in the state of grace. That a person is actually in God's grace (in the secret of his mind and heart) is something completely different from the fact of being able to be considered such positively, in relation to ecclesiastical discipline. This creates enormous confusion, as pointed out by all the best critics of *AL*.

And here we come to the second point. In the second consequence Buttiglione states: "and therefore [the divorced and remarried] deserve to receive the sacraments." Now, were we actually to suppose that in some cases the priest, through a supernatural charism, had the power to penetrate the divine gaze in order to decide that a person is in God's grace — something which neither *AL* nor Buttiglione maintains — it does not follow that the divorced and remarried would deserve to receive the sacraments. Here, too, Buttiglione jumps to the conclusion without caring in the slightest about the objection that has repeatedly been raised over the past year and a half by dozens, if not hundreds, of critics. This objection is simple and consists in the fact that, according to the Magisterium of the Church, the reason why the divorced and remarried cannot be admitted to the Sacraments is *not* a presumed judgment about whether or not their soul is in a state of grace before God. No one would have dreamt of making such a judgment, either before or after *AL*.

The reason, instead, is their objective situation (= visible, verifiable), which stands in contrast with the objective situation for the reception of the Sacraments. The reception of the visible Sacraments of a visible Church has to correspond to an objective, visible situation. Otherwise, the visible order of the Church simply ceases to exist. We would no longer have a Catholic and apostolic Church, but a "pneumatic," pseudo-charismatic or gnostic church, a "church" whose external discipline, if one could still speak in this way, would be subject to the most absolute arbitrariness. It would be "the chaos erected into a system" that Robert Spaemann spoke of in referring to *AL*.

In fact, the declaration of the Pontifical Council for Legislative Texts ("Declaration concerning the admission to Holy Communion of faithful who are divorced and remarried," June 24, 2000), which is cited by *AL* precisely in reference to this point, in maintaining that "a negative judgment about an objective situation does not imply a judgment about the imputability or culpability of the person involved" (*AL* 302 and note 345), is the same declaration that denies access to the Sacrament, precisely because "the minister of Communion would not be able to judge from subjective imputability." The same declaration then adds with absolute clarity that "the prohibition found in the cited canon [CIC 915], by its nature, is derived from divine law and transcends the domain of positive ecclesiastical laws: the latter cannot introduce legislative changes which would oppose the doctrine of the Church."

On the basis of these observations, we may conclude that:

—Regarding moral theology, what Buttiglione states is false; namely, that what we would be dealing with is a harmless affirmation of the doctrine of extenuating circumstances rather than its perverse deformation, which is situational ethics.

—Regarding sacramental theology, what Buttiglione states is false; namely, that we are dealing with a development in continuity with the previous Magisterium, while in fact, they are claiming to change something that Pope St. John Paul II said belongs to the divine law.

—Regarding the accusation that we critics are guilty of falling into "objectivism," it seems abundantly clear to me that this is the fruit of Buttiglione's imagination. In fact, all our arguments necessarily presuppose, as we have seen, the distinction between the objective dimension and subjective imputability.

—Lastly, regarding the personal comments directed to critics of the texts, words, and actions of the pope, and, in particular, to the authors of the *Correctio filialis* [Filial Correction], claiming that we are "calumniators, schismatics," etc., because we have accused the pope of propagating heresy, I would point out that Buttiglione, in all of his interventions, has systematically defended the text of *Amoris Laetitia* in isolation from all of the pope's other statements, as if these are irrelevant because they are not "magisterium." But this sort of attitude is too easy: ultimately it's the attitude of the ostrich burying its head in the sand. In reality, all of the acts of the pope obviously have an extremely powerful impact on the Church and the whole world. Now, these statements not only confirm and make clear the heretical tendency present in *AL*, but also lend support to other numerous heresies: just think of the recent hagiographic exaltation of Luther by the Holy See, which in itself gives the green light to a whole host of errors. But they are not the only ones; for a more complete list see the recent article by the Anglican theologian Gerald McDermott: "Is Pope Francis a Liberal Protestant?"[4]

Pope Honorius was anathematized by the Third Ecumenical Council of Constantinople (680) for far less than this. The anathema was then confirmed by Pope Leo II, "for he [Honorius] did not extinguish immediately the flame of heretical teaching, as ought to be done by apostolic authority, but through his negligence he fostered it." (See my intervention at the recent conference in Rome on April 22, 2017.[5]) We critics, as sincere lovers of the papacy, wish to spare Francis Honorius's fate—or perhaps a fate even worse. Those instead who close their eyes to the present situation are encouraging him down that path. We do not presume to judge the internal forum of anyone. But unfortunately, from an objective point of view, we cannot seem to detect any extenuating circumstance in this behavior.

---

4 Published at *First Things*, November 15, 2017.
5 Chapter 6 in this volume.

10

The Worldwide Impact and Significance of the Correctio filialis[1]

DR ROBERTO DE MATTEI

THE "FILIAL CORRECTION" ADDRESSED TO Pope Francis by more than sixty priests and scholars of the Church has had an extraordinary impact all over the world. There was no lack of those who tried to minimize the initiative, declaring the number of signatories "to be limited and marginal." Yet if the initiative is irrelevant, why have its repercussions been so widespread in all the media outlets of the five continents, including countries like Russia and China? Steve Skojec of OnePeterFive reports that research on Google News resulted in more than 5,000 news articles, while there were 100,000 visits on the site www.correctiofilialis.org in a space of 48 hours. The adhesion on this site is still open, even if only some signatures will be made visible. It is essential to acknowledge that the reason for this worldwide echo is one only: the truth can be ignored or repressed, but when it is made manifest with clarity it has its own intrinsic power and is destined to spread by itself. The main enemy of truth is not error, but ambiguity. The cause of the diffusion of errors and heresies in the Church is due not to the strength of these errors, but to the culpable silence of those who should openly defend the truth of the Gospel.

The truth asserted by the "filial correction" is that Pope Francis, through a long series of words, acts, and omissions, "has upheld, by direct or indirect means (whether being aware or not, we do not know, neither do we want to judge him) at least seven false and heretical propositions, propagated in the Church through his public office as well as through private action." The signatories insist respectfully that the pope "condemn these propositions publicly, thus carrying out the mandate of Our Lord Jesus Christ given to

---

[1] Published at *Corrispondenza Romana* on September 27, 2017; translation by Francesca Romana published at *Rorate Caeli* on the same date.

Peter and through him to all his successors until the end of time: 'I have prayed for thee, that thy faith fail not: and thou, being once converted, confirm thy brethren.'"

No reply regarding the correction has yet arrived; only clumsy attempts at disqualifying or singling out the signatories, with particular aim at some of the most well-known, like the former President of the Vatican Bank, Ettore Gotti Tedeschi. In reality, as Gotti Tedeschi himself said in an interview to Marco Tosatti on September 24, the authors of the *Correctio* have acted out of love for the Church and the papacy. Gotti Tedeschi and another well-known signatory, the German writer Martin Mosebach, were both applauded last September 14 at the Angelicum by a public of over 400 priests and laypeople, comprising three cardinals and several bishops, on the occasion of the convention celebrating the tenth anniversary of the motu proprio *Summorum Pontificum*. Two other signatories, Professors Claudio Pierantoni and Anna Silvas, expressed the same ideas as those in the *Correctio* at a meeting on the theme "Seeking Clarity," organized on April 22 of this year by the *Nuova Bussola Quotidiana*, supported by other prelates, among whom was the late Cardinal Carlo Caffara. Many other signatories of the document occupy or have occupied prominent positions in ecclesiastical institutions. Others again are distinguished university professors. If the authors of the *Correctio* were isolated in the Catholic world, their document would not have had the resonance it attained.

A Filial Appeal to Pope Francis in 2015 was signed by around 900,000 people from all over the world, and a Declaration of Fidelity to the unchangeable teaching of the Church on matrimony, presented in 2015 by eighty Catholic personalities, gathered 35,000 signatures. A year ago, four Cardinals formulated their *Dubia* on the Exhortation *Amoris Laetitia*. In the meantime, scandals of an economic and moral nature are undermining Pope Francis's pontificate. The American vaticanist, John Allen, certainly not of a traditional bent, revealed on September 25 in *Crux* how difficult his position has become these days.

Among the most ridiculous accusations that are being made about the signatories of the document is that of being "Lefebvrists" on account of the signature of Bishop Bernard Fellay, Superior of the Fraternity of St. Pius X. Monsignor Fellay's adhesion to a document of this type is an historic act, which clarifies without the shadow of a doubt the Fraternity's position in regard to the new pontificate. However, "Lefebvrism" is a locution which has for the progressives the same role the word "fascism" had for the Communists in the 1970s: discredit the adversary without discussing the reasons. The presence of Monsignor Fellay is, moreover, reassuring for all the signatories of the *Correctio*. How can the pope not have the same comprehension and benevolence regarding them that he has shown over the last two years towards the Fraternity of St. Pius X?

The Archbishop of Chieti, Bruno Forte, previously special secretary to the Bishops' Synod on the Family, declared that the *Correctio* represents "a prejudicially closed stance towards the spirit of the Second Vatican Council which Pope Francis is incarnating so profoundly" (*Avvenire*, September 26, 2015). The spirit of Vatican II, incarnated by Pope Francis, writes Monsignor Lorizio, in turn, in the same Italian Bishops' newspaper, consists in the primacy of the pastoral over theology; in other words, in the subordination of the natural law to life experience, since, as he explains, "the pastoral comprises and includes theology" and not vice versa. Monsignor Lorizio teaches theology at the same Faculty of the Lateran University in which the Dean used to be Monsignor Brunero Gherardini, who died on September 22, on the eve of the *Correctio* he was unable to sign because of his precarious health conditions.

This great exponent of the Roman Theological School demonstrated in his most recent books what a deplorable landing-place we have been brought to by the primacy of the pastoral announced at Vatican II and propagated by its ultraprogressive interpreters, among whom may be classed the same Forte and the makeshift theologian Massimo Faggioli, along with Alberto Melloni, who are all distinguishing themselves with their flimsy attacks on the *Correctio*.

Monsignor Forte in *Avvenire* added that the document is an operation that cannot be shared by "those who are faithful to the successor of Peter in whom they recognize the Pastor the Lord has given to the Church as the guide of universal communion. Fidelity should always be directed to the living God, Who speaks to the Church today through the Pope." Now, we have come to the point of defining Pope Francis as a "living God," forgetting that the Church is founded on Jesus Christ, for Whom the pope is a representative on earth; the pope is not its divine owner. As Antonio Socci correctly wrote, the pope is not a "second Jesus" (*Libero*, September 24, 2017) but the 266th successor to Peter. His mandate is not that of changing or "improving" the words of Our Lord, but of guarding and transmitting them in the most faithful manner. If this doesn't happen, Catholics have the duty to reprove him in a filial way, following the example of St. Paul in regard to the Prince of the Apostles, Peter (Gal 2:11).

Lastly, there are those who are surprised that Cardinals Walter Brandmüller and Raymond Leo Burke didn't sign the document, ignoring, as *Rorate Caeli* underlined, that the *Correctio* of the sixty is of a purely theological nature, whereas the correction of the cardinals, when it comes, will have much more authority and importance, also on the canonical level. The correction of a fellow-man, foreseen by the Gospel and current Canon Law, in art. 212, par. 3, can take different forms. "This principle of fraternal correction inside the Church"—declared Bishop Athanasius Schneider in a recent interview with Maike Hickson—"has been valid for all time, even with regard to the pope, and so it should be valid also in our times. Unfortunately, these days anyone who dares speak the truth—even if he does so respectfully with regard to the Shepherds of the Church—is classified as an enemy of unity, as happened to St. Paul when he declared: 'Am I then become your enemy, because I tell you the truth?'" (Gal 4:16).

11

Correctio filialis: *A First Appraisal*[1]

DR ROBERTO DE MATTEI

ON SEPTEMBER 25, THE DAY AFTER THE PUBLIcation of the *Correctio filialis* to Pope Francis, Greg Burke, the spokesman for the Vatican Pressroom, with condescending irony, denied the news diffused by ANSA, which had reported that access to the site of the *Correctio* had been blocked by the Holy See: "Do you really think we would do this for a letter with sixty names?" The director of the Pressroom, who judges initiatives on the basis of the number of "followers," might be interested to know that the website www.correctiofilialis.org, eight days after being put online, had more than 180,000 individual visitors and 330,000 page visits.

The visits come from two hundred different countries of the five continents. Italy and the United States lead the number of accesses. Further, the letter of correction addressed to Pope Francis by sixty-two scholars was, by the date of October 3, cosigned by 216 theologians, priests, professors and scholars of all nationalities, whose signatures are visible on the site. Added to these, there are thousands of adherents who put their signature on the official site or on other Catholic sites which actively support the initiative, such as onepeterfive.com, lifesitenews.com, katholisches.info. Guido Mocellin, in *Avvenire* of September 27, had to admit that in "the ecclesial blogosphere," thanks to a "modern website in six languages," "the posts on the *Correctio filialis* directed to Pope Francis 'as a result of the propagation of heresies' have been the most present over the past few days: they constituted 30% of all those that I was able to consult between Saturday the 24th and Monday the 26th of September." If we want to stay with the numbers, the number of cardinals, bishops, and theologians who have risen up against the *Correctio*, in defence of *Amoris Laetitia*, is

---

[1] Published at *Corrispondenza Romana* on October 4, 2017; translation by Francesca Romana published at *Rorate Caeli* on October 5.

negligible. Even the cardinal closest to Pope Francis, the Secretary of State Pietro Parolin, took a position of equidistance, declaring that "people who disagree express their dissent, but on these things we have to reason, to try to understand one another."

What is missing most of all, beyond the numbers, is substance in the argumentation of the efforts to reply to the *Correctio*. The greatest effort done, which nearly arrives at the acrobatics of the Sophists, we owe to the Member of Parliament and philosopher Rocco Buttiglione on *Vatican Insider* of October 3. The central passage of *Amoris Laetitia* criticized by the signatories of the *Correctio*, according to Buttiglione, is "something absolutely traditional, which we all studied as children at catechism in the Catholic Church, not only in the new one by St. John Paul II, but also in the old one by Pius X." It's true—Buttiglione admits that there is "an absolute impossibility of giving Communion to those in a state of mortal sin (and this rule is of the divine law and thus unbreakable), but if, as a result of lack of instruction or deliberate consent, there is no mortal sin, Communion may be given, from the point of view of moral theology, even to a divorced and remarried [person]."

For Buttiglione, like Pope Bergoglio's trusted theologian, Monsignor Víctor Manuel Fernández, the basic problem would be that of the "imputability" of the acts—an imputability that would be absent in the great majority of *more uxorio* cohabitants, since the concrete situations they are living in mitigate their awareness and, above all, for them, render it practically impossible to observe the law of the Lord. With this claim the Council of Trent is, without any qualms, contradicted, the very Council that anathematizes those who say "that the commandments of God are impossible, even for a man who is justified and confirmed in grace" (*DH* 1568). "God, in fact, does not command the impossible; but when He commands He admonishes us to do what is possible and to ask for what is not possible, and He helps us to make it possible" (*DH* 1356).

On the other hand, the bishops who apply Pope Francis's teaching are inspired neither by Pius X's catechism nor by John Paul II's new one. In their dioceses, the divorced-remarried, perfectly aware of their situation, insist on Communion, and, according to *Amoris Laetitia*, Communion is permitted to them, as a legitimate right.

To justify this immoral practice, we have arrived at the falsification of St. Thomas Aquinas's thought. However, a valiant Italian moralist who signed the *Correctio*, Don Alfredo Morselli, demonstrated, on *Messainlatino*, October 3, the impossibility of harmonizing Pope Francis's Exhortation with the doctrine of St. Thomas. Don Morselli refers to some unequivocal passages by the Angelic Doctor that affirm the contrary of *Amoris Laetitia* 301: "A good intention is not sufficient to determine the goodness of an act: since an act can be in itself bad, and in no way can it become good" (*Super Sent.*, lib. 2, d. 40, q. 1, a. 2, co.). "There are some [human actions] that have a deformity inseparably belonging to them, like fornication, adultery, and other things of this kind, which cannot be considered morally good in any way whatsoever" (*Quodlibet* IX, q. 7, a. 2, co.). In coherence with authentic Thomism, Monsignor Fernando Ocáriz, presently an Opus Dei prelate, at a convention promoted to celebrate the twentieth anniversary of *Humanae Vitae*, recalled that "the existence of particular norms of natural morals, having universal and unconditional value, belongs to Catholic doctrine, and actually is a truth of the faith"[2] — among these, the prohibition of contraception and the prohibition of adultery. Has the teaching of the University of Santa Croce and Navarre (promoter of that convention along with the John Paul II Institute) changed, or will it change? One wonders, after the interview on September 30 at Infovaticana.com in which the present Vicar of Opus Dei, Mariano Fazio, censures other members of the prelature who signed the *Correctio*, accusing them of "scandalizing the entire Church."

The interview is strange: neither the Argentine bishops nor the Maltese bishops, who authorize adultery in their dioceses, are guilty of scandalizing the Church, but those who protest against these scandals are. The pope, according to Fazio, can be criticized, but only in private circles. In the avalanche of contrary comments that submerged the blog InfoVaticana, there is one that hits the nail on the head: "What about St. Paul?" Wasn't it precisely St. Paul who corrected St. Peter publicly (Gal 2:7–14)? The apostolic candour of St. Paul and the humility of the Prince of the Apostles have remained, since then, the model of the correct relationship between those who exercise authority and those who obey them with filial respect but not without discernment.

One of the most influential signatories of the *Correctio*, the theologian and philosopher of science, Don Alberto Strumia, prefers

---

2   *Humanae Vitae Twenty Years Later* (Milan: Edizioni Ares, 1989), 129.

discernment. In an interview on September 30 to the daily *Il Giornale*, he explained:

> The doctrine of the Church was not invented by theologians and not even by popes, but is founded in the Scriptures and rooted in the tradition of the Church. The pope is at its service, as guardian and guarantor of this continuity, and cannot break it, not even covertly, implying, with ambiguous formulations, that today one might think of doing the opposite of what has been taught until now by the Magisterium, regarding essential questions such as the doctrine of the Sacraments and family morality, with the motivation that times have changed and the world demands some adjustment. For this [reason] it is a duty of charity, which has the aim of "saving souls" (as it was said in the past), [and a duty of] the defense of the very dignity of the throne of Peter and of the one who sits there, to highlight these ambiguities with the greatest respect.... To dare address a doctrinal correction to the pope can be done and must be done only when the truth of the Faith is in danger and, thus, the salvation of the members of the people of God.

At a time when consciences are darkened, the *Correctio filialis* expresses the *sensus fidei* of tens of thousands of Catholics who remind their Supreme Pontiff with filial respect that the salvation of souls is the greatest good and that for no reasons in the world may one do evil or make compromises with it.

12

"True love may justly express itself in the form of a correction"[1]

AN INTERVIEW WITH
DR JOSEPH SHAW
ON THE *FILIAL CORRECTION*

ON SEPTEMBER 30, THE VICAR GENERAL OF THE Personal Prelature of Opus Dei, Msgr. Mariano Fazio of Argentina, accused the authors in an interview with *La Nación* of attacking the pope, sowing disunity and using the "totally wrong method." "If it is a filial relation, a son does not 'correct' his father in public," Msgr. Fazio said. The second in command of Opus Dei continued: "Any faithful, bishop, cardinal, lay person has the right to tell the pope what he sees fit for the good of the Church. But it seems to me that he has no right to do so publicly and to scandalize the whole Church with these manifestations of disunity." We spoke to Joseph Shaw, Fellow and Tutor in Philosophy at St. Benet's Hall, Oxford University. Professor Shaw, who serves as spokesman for the filial correction's authors, responded to charges that he and the other signatories are airing the Church's dirty laundry in public. We also discussed why it was necessary to make the *Correction* public, and in what sense Catholics are called to always "be with the pope."

Professor Shaw, Msgr. Fazio has accused the authors and signatories of the "filial correction"—particularly those who are members of Opus Dei—of attacking the pope and scandalizing the whole Church, saying that "a son should not 'correct' his father in public." In Genesis 9:23, we read about Noah's sons (Shem and Japheth) "covering the nakedness of their father" out of respect for him, and this was in a private setting. Does Msgr. Fazio have a point? Are the authors and organizers of the "filial correction" scandalizing the Church?

---

[1] Published by Diane Montagna, "Filial Correction an act of loyalty to Pope: organizer responds to Opus Dei leader," *LifeSiteNews*, October 4, 2017.

Dr Shaw: Scandal is a complex concept which should be used with care. Scandal is given when a person's words or actions cause others to sin. It can be deliberate — "formal scandal" — or inadvertent — "material scandal." It is also possible for people to "take scandal" without justification, such as the Pharisees who accused Our Lord of blaspheming, when in reality he merely spoke the truth.

As far as ordinary Catholics are concerned, when we see something which is apparently bad happening within the Church, we must be aware that knowledge of this bad thing by a wider audience may cause people to sin: it may undermine their faith, cause them to neglect their religious duties, or, if not Catholic, harden them to the truths of the Gospel. For this reason, we can say not only that it is a scandal if, say, a priest is too fond of drink, but also that a person revealing such a thing causes scandal. However, the situation is complicated by the fact that revealing a private vice is also wrong because it is detraction: it endangers the priest's good name, which is a very serious matter.

When the bad things happening in the Church are not so much private failings as serious injustices to others, and especially when they begin to be reported, there is an instinct to seek to protect the Church's reputation by denial, by seeking to explain them away, or by covering them up. What has become very evident in recent decades, however, is that, understandable as this instinct is, it should be resisted. First and foremost, it works against justice. Secondly, it actually *causes* scandal, because those who become aware of the reality of the situation and of Catholics' reactions to it are put off the Church because of our apparent indifference to justice. Thirdly, even in the narrowest terms of dealing with bad publicity, it is very often counterproductive, especially in the longer term. These are hard-learnt lessons of the clerical sex abuse crisis, perhaps the most expensive education Catholics have had in history.

Non-Catholics, especially serious-minded non-Catholic Christians suspicious of the role of the pope in the Church, will be scandalised very deeply by the impression that, when a pope speaks and writes in ways apparently at variance with the Church's earlier teaching, faithful Catholics remain silent. It will confirm for them the caricature of Catholics as brainwashed slaves of the pope.

Catholics who have respect for the papal office are vulnerable in a different way, since when they see what appears to be a pope offering a way out from difficult moral teachings, they will be tempted to ignore those teachings in their own lives—often, indeed, tempted to go much further than anything directly justified by the pope's words. These Catholics' scandal will be deepened by the silence of faithful Catholics, especially pastors and academics known for their earlier defence of these teachings.

There is no question, in this situation, of the signatories "revealing their father's nakedness": the fact to which they draw attention is evident to all. Indeed, the appearance of a discrepancy between Pope Francis's indications about the correct interpretation of *Amoris Laetitia* and the teaching of Pope St. John Paul II (and the tradition in general) is something emphasized above all by those who present themselves as supporters of Pope Francis! The only question which remains is whether Catholic pastors and academics would give the impression, in turn, of acting like weathervanes, and simply change their beliefs to suit the prevailing officially-sanctioned view: keeping ready to change back again under the next pope as necessary. It would certainly cause a scandal if no Catholics were prepared at least to ask some insistent questions about what is going on.

Perhaps critics of the signatories mean, however, that the *Correctio* causes scandal by revealing divisions in the Church, which would better be covered up. Again, however, these divisions have been emphasised by the pope's supposed partisans, who have criticised those still basing their views on the teaching of Pope St. John Paul II when, according to them, it has been overturned. What is needed, where there are divisions, is respectful dialogue and a resolution of differences.

If we are to speak of filial obligations, we should remember that the Father to whom ultimate loyalty is due is our heavenly Father. When it comes to popes, we also owe loyalty not only to the current holder of the papal office, but to all the popes who have carried out their office of teaching the faith given to them by that heavenly Father. The *Correctio* is an act of loyalty and duty towards our heavenly Father and our human fathers in the faith—most especially those popes who have transmitted the teaching on marriage and the Eucharist given by Jesus Christ Himself in obedience to His Father.

The "filial correction" has drawn considerable attention in both Catholic and secular media. Why did the authors and organizers of the correction go public with it? And why is it not a "display of disunity," as the Argentinian Vicar General of Opus Dei suggests?

Catholics concerned about the direction of the debate about remarriage and Communion, and related issues, have made repeated attempts to express these concerns in ways which would not create a public impression of opposition to the person of the pope. The *Filial Appeal*, signed by 800,000 people, was part of a debate called for by Pope Francis before he had composed *Amoris*. The letter of the "Thirteen Cardinals" and the "forty-five academics and pastors' appeal to Cardinals" were, alike, not intended to be public documents. Obviously, in this way these initiatives observed both the letter and the spirit of Matthew 18:15–17 on speaking first to one's brother in private. The *dubia* of the four cardinals, like the *Correction*, was made public only when Pope Francis declined to discuss the matter with the cardinals in any way. This is not the history of a group of Catholics who wish to attack either the person of the present pope or the papal office.

It should also be emphasised that Canon 212 permits and encourages lay Catholics not only to manifest their concerns to their superiors, but also to each other. The latter is necessary where there is a danger to the Faith and of scandal to ordinary Catholics which is not being addressed by the proper authorities—in this case, the Holy Father. This is clearly the case where the authorities have declined to respond to a non-public appeal.

Disunity is being displayed in a very public way by bishops' conferences, such as those of Germany and Poland, issuing contrasting guidelines for the application of *Amoris*, not by those who, concerned about this disunity, appeal for an act of the Magisterium which would bring it to an end.

It is true that the *Correction* is more strongly worded than previous initiatives: this reflects the escalating seriousness of the situation, and the absence of a response from Pope Francis to the earlier documents.

Can you point to a passage in Scripture, a Doctor or Father of the Church, or perhaps even a famous piece of literature, that illustrates your point?

Both Testaments of Scripture are replete with examples of subordinates criticising superiors in public. The criticism of the leaders of Israel by prophets and priests, from the public humiliation of

King Saul by Samuel, the denunciation of King Ahab by Elijah, and the attack on Herod the Tetrarch by St. John the Baptist, are in general the criticism of official, and usually divinely sanctioned, authority, by persons who may have been inspired by God but who lacked institutional standing. This pattern is taken to its logical extreme by the condemnation of the two elders by the prophet Daniel when only a child (Dan 13:45ff.). Our Lord made the situation clear when, while eviscerating the Chief Priests, Scribes, and Pharisees, he acknowledged nonetheless that they held "the seat of Moses," a position which meant that people should listen to them as speaking with authority, despite all their shortcomings (Mt 23:2–3).

Private remonstrations also take place, a notable example being the prophet Nathan's criticism of King David, but even this was not intended as a way to hush things up. Nathan speaks of God's coming punishment of David: "For thou didst it secretly: but I will do this thing in the sight of all Israel, and in the sight of the sun" (2 Sam 12:12). In the other cases, it is fair to assume that the prophets realised that the time for private discussion had passed (Mt 18:15–17). We may take it that this was also so in the famous confrontation of St. Peter by St. Paul (Gal 2:11–14). Commenting on that last passage, St. Thomas Aquinas wrote: "Where there is a proximate danger to the faith, prelates must be rebuked, even publicly, by subjects. Thus, St. Paul, who was subject to St. Peter, rebuked him publicly" (*Commentary on the Epistle to the Galatians* 2:14).

It should be emphasised that when an inferior criticises a superior, he takes a great risk, as demonstrated in a number of the cases mentioned. He makes his criticism not only out of zeal for justice, but out of love of the superior. This is a theme particularly developed by Shakespeare, in *The Winter's Tale*, and even more famously in *King Lear*. In the latter, Lear banishes Cordelia and the Duke of Kent for speaking of truth and justice when he wanted flattery. They alone, however, are later revealed as loyal subjects. It is not criticism which is most to be feared by those in positions of authority, but flattery. As Pope Francis expressed it: "The hypocrite is capable of destroying a community. While speaking gently, he ruinously judges a person. He is a killer." Again: "The hypocrite always uses language to flatter," "feeding into one's vanity."

Msgr. Fazio has said that Opus Dei, like all Catholics, "is always with the pope." Do you agree that it is always important to "be with the pope"?

Of course I agree that we Catholics must always be with the pope. But we must understand correctly what "to be with the pope" really means. "To be with," understood in a correct sense, means to *love*. That also implies to help and support, provided that our help and support are in favour of words and actions that are true and just. Now, not all words and actions that come from a pope are necessarily and absolutely true and just. So, in case they aren't, true love may justly express itself in the form of a correction. To correct someone who is wrong is a necessary part of human love. To omit a correction when it is necessary would indeed be a grave sin.

We know that, under certain conditions, the pope is infallible (this is noted in the *Correction*). But it is clear on a number of grounds that we are not dealing with infallible teaching in *Amoris* chapter eight, and indeed, early in *Amoris* Pope Francis distances what he is doing from a contribution to the Magisterium, writing (§3): "Since 'time is greater than space,' I would make it clear that not all discussions of doctrinal, moral or pastoral issues need to be settled by interventions of the magisterium" (in the official text: "Commemorantes tempus superius esse quam spatium, confirmare volumus non cunctas doctrinales, morales vel pastorales disputationes per magisterii declarationes esse absolvendas"). So it says that these questions are not now addressed with a magisterial kind of statement not only on the doctrinal level, but also on the moral and pastoral level. It is clear, then, that we have here, properly speaking, no new magisterium, either doctrinal or pastoral. It follows that we must go on giving our full assent and support, in these matters, to the really existing Magisterium, settled by the previous popes, and contest any kind of opposition to it, whether it comes from theologians or from the pope himself as a private doctor. It is not enough to say that his opinions are formally contained in a document of the magisterium, when the document itself states explicitly that it is renouncing the making of magisterial statements both on a doctrinal and pastoral level.

Is there anything else you would like to add?

Something profoundly worrying about criticisms of the signatories of the *Correction* specifically for speaking out about problems which every informed Catholic already knows about is the mindset it reveals—one focused not on the truth, but on appearances. It is strongly reminiscent of the mindset at work in abusive families, where children are taught to pretend things are all right, when they are not: certain topics are not to be broached, certain facts are not to be referred to. This attitude can be enforced not by the abusive parent directly, but by other family members who are trying to keep up appearances and hold the family together. It is nevertheless profoundly unhealthy, and indeed is linked to psychological disorders in the children. We should fear any such attitude, however well-intentioned, invading the Church. If there are problems, we should talk about them, and not pretend they do not exist.

13

Ratzinger's Rules for Faithful Theological Discourse[1]

ROBERT FASTIGGI, PH.D.,
AND
DAWN EDEN GOLDSTEIN, S.T.D.

IT SEEMS THAT THE CASE FOR THE *AMORIS Laetitia* critics' self-proclaimed "Filial Correction" of Pope Francis is weakening. Dr Joseph Shaw, one of the signers of the *Correctio filialis*, recently wrote: "It is not that we're saying that the text of *Amoris* cannot be bent into some kind of orthodoxy. What we are saying is that it has become clear that orthodoxy is not what Pope Francis wants us to find there."[2] Shaw's claim that Pope Francis doesn't want orthodoxy, however, is based on subjective impressions derived from mostly non-authoritative statements of the pope. This does not seem to be a very strong foundation for accusing the Roman Pontiff of promoting false teachings and heresies.

The supporters of the *Correctio* and other critics of *Amoris Laetitia* often try to contrast what Pope Francis says in this exhortation to teachings of St. John Paul II and Benedict XVI. It is interesting, therefore, to note that many of these same critics fail to follow the guidelines for theologians published by the Congregation for the Doctrine of the Faith in 1990 when John Paul II was pope and Joseph Cardinal Ratzinger, the future Benedict XVI, was prefect of the CDF. These guidelines are contained in the Instruction on

---

[1] Originally published apparently on October 4, 2017, under the title "Critics of *Amoris laetitia* ignore Ratzinger's rules for faithful theological discourse," at *Vatican Insider* of *La Stampa*, where, however, its original date is given as October 13, 2017 (impossible given how many replies were already published to it prior to October 13), and last modified July 5, 2019.
[2] Shaw made this comment in his article for the Latin Mass Society posted on *LifeSiteNews* September 29, 2017: https://www.lifesitenews.com/opinion/correctio-filialis-a-response-to-some-critics. Shaw was responding to a fine article by Prof. Jacob Wood: https://www.ncregister.com/daily-news/some-basic-questions-and-answers-on-the-filial-correction-of-the-pope.

the Ecclesial Vocation of the Theologian *Donum Veritatis*[3] — a document that traditionalist opponents of *Amoris Laetitia*, such as Dr Peter Kwasniewski,[4] ironically claim to hold in high esteem.

Donum Veritatis was issued to explain the need for Catholic theologians to maintain communion with the Magisterium of the Church. Building upon Vatican II's *Lumen gentium* §37 and Canon 212 §3 of the 1983 *Code of Canon Law*, *Donum Veritatis* does recognize that theologians might have problems with certain magisterial teachings.[5] If these problems persist, "the theologian has the duty to make known to the Magisterial authorities the problems raised by the teaching in itself, in the arguments proposed to justify it, or even in the manner in which it is presented."[6] The theologian, however, "should do this in an evangelical spirit and with a profound desire to resolve the difficulties."[7]

Critics of *Amoris Laetitia* might argue that, in making their petitions to the pope and signing the *Correctio filialis*, they are doing exactly what *Donum Veritatis* charges them to do. In what follows, we hope to show that the critics of *Amoris Laetitia* have not properly followed the guidelines set forth in that document.

Donum Veritatis §24 instructs theologians "to assess accurately the authoritativeness of the [magisterial] interventions." The *Correctio filialis* fails to do this. Instead, it catalogues comments made by Pope Francis in press conferences, private letters, etc., without taking into account the authoritativeness of these statements and their context.[8] It also cites statements by papal associates and appointees. In loading down their petition with cherry-picked statements bearing little or no magisterial authority, the *Correctio*

---

3   *AAS* 82 (1990) 1550–70; also available on the Vatican website: https://www.vatican.va/roman_curia/congregations/cfaith/documents/rc_con_cfaith_doc_19900524_theologian-vocation_en.html.
4   See this 2015 article of his: https://rorate-caeli.blogspot.com/2015/05/on-25th-anniversary-of-cdfs-instruction.html. Kwasniewski was one of the forty-five signatories of a summer 2016 letter to Pope Francis critical of *Amoris Laetitia*.
5   *Donum Veritatis* §30.
6   Ibid.
7   Ibid.
8   Cardinal Müller addressed the lack of magisterial authority of some of the very sources cited by the authors of the *Correctio* in his September 28, 2017 interview with Edward Pentin: https://www.ncregister.com/daily-news/cardinal-mller-discusses-the-cdf-the-curia-and-amoris-laetitia.

authors seem intent upon discrediting the Holy Father and his intentions. Can such an approach truly reflect "an evangelical spirit" and "a profound desire to resolve the difficulties" with *Amoris Laetitia*?⁹

Moreover, the *Correctio* authors omit any evidence that would invalidate their claim that Francis is operating out of a heretical mindset. They therefore make no mention of numerous unambiguously orthodox papal statements that are of a far higher level of magisterium than those that they cite. For example, the *Correctio* ignores the pope's January 2016 address to the Roman Rota, in which he affirmed the indissolubility of marriage and ruled out Walter Cardinal Kasper's proposal to readmit the divorced and civilly remarried to Communion without requiring continence:

> The Church... with a renewed sense of responsibility continues to propound marriage in its essential elements—offspring, the good of the spouses, unity, indissolubility and sacramentality—not as an ideal meant only for the few, notwithstanding modern models fixated on the ephemeral and the passing, but rather as a reality that in Christ's grace can be lived out by all baptized faithful.¹⁰

Donum Veritatis §26 admonishes theologians to safeguard not only the "unity of truth" (*unitas veritatis*) but also the "unity of charity" (*unitas caritatis*). Many prominent critics of *Amoris Laetitia*, however, are quite transparent in their intent to give the worst possible interpretations to statements and actions of Pope Francis.¹¹ This tendency violates not only the unity of charity but also goes against the need to avoid rash judgment. Such commentators would

---

9 Cf. *Donum Veritatis* §30.
10 "Address of His Holiness Pope Francis to the Officials of the Tribunal of the Roman Rota for the Inauguration of the Judicial Year," https://w2.vatican.va/content/francesco/en/speeches/2016/january/documents/papa-francesco_20160122_anno-giudiziario-rota-romana.html.
11 See the October 1, 2017 article in *The Remnant* by Christopher Ferrara, one of the signers of the *Correctio*: https://remnantnewspaper.com/web/index.php/articles/item/3450-wait-wait-it-s-all-a-mistranslation. In this article, he states: "This Pope's plan of promulgating a deliberately ambiguous document whose heterodox interpretation and application he would later approve with a series of sub-magisterial winks and nods, both oral and written, is the reason I signed on to the *Correctio filialis*."

do well to recall the teaching of St. Ignatius of Loyola cited in the *Catechism of the Catholic Church*: "Every good Christian ought to be more ready to give a favorable interpretation to another's statement than to condemn it" (CCC 2478).[12]

In *Donum Veritatis* §27, we find this instruction: "The theologian will not present his own opinions or divergent hypotheses as though they were non-arguable conclusions." The authors of the *Correctio filialis*, however, seem to present their opinions as if they are non-arguable facts rather than personal opinions. They boldly declare that "the words, deeds, and omissions" of Pope Francis, in conjunction with certain passages of *Amoris Laetitia*, "are serving to propagate heresies within the Church."[13]

Donum Veritatis §27 also warns theologians against giving "untimely public expression" to their opinions. This admonition is concerned about the effect of such expressions on the Catholic faithful.[14] This is why the theologians are warned against turning to the "mass media."[15] Instead, they should have recourse to the responsible authority, for it is not by seeking to exert the pressure of public opinion that one contributes to the clarification of doctrinal issues and renders service to the truth.[16] But supporters of the *Correctio filialis* have set up internet sites seeking signatures in support of the "correction" of Pope Francis for "propagating heresies."[17] *Donum Veritatis* §34 recognizes the danger of such a "parallel magisterium" of theologians, which "can cause great

---

[12] St. Ignatius of Loyola, *Spiritual Exercises* §22.
[13] "Correctio filialis de haeresibus propagatis."
[14] We only need to consider the effect on the faithful of the article by the philosopher, Josef Seifert, who claims that *Amoris Laetitia* 303 "has the logical consequence of destroying the entire Catholic moral teaching." See Josef Seifert, "Does Pure Logic Threaten to Destroy the Entire Moral Doctrine of the Catholic Church?" The excessive language of Seifert's article prompted us to write our previous article, which was published on Sept. 26, 2017: https://www.lastampa.it/2017/09/26/vaticaninsider/eng/documents/doesamoris-laetitia-really-undermine-catholic-moral-teaching-yom5rmEIfGPzsMDlS706eP/pagina.html.
[15] *Donum Veritatis* §30.
[16] Ibid.
[17] See *LifeSiteNews*, which has a link asking readers to sign the petition to "support the filial correction of Pope Francis for propagating heresies": https://www.lifesitenews.com/opinion/correctio-filialis-a-response-to-some-critics.

spiritual harm by opposing itself to the Magisterium of the Pastors. Indeed, when dissent succeeds in extending its influence to the point of shaping a common opinion, it tends to become the rule of conduct. This cannot but seriously trouble the People of God and lead to contempt for true authority."

Indeed, *Donum Veritatis* has strong words for those who promote "polling public opinion to determine the proper thing to think or do, opposing the Magisterium by exerting the pressure of public opinion, making the excuse of a 'consensus' among theologians, [or] maintaining that the theologian is the prophetical spokesman of a 'base' or autonomous community which would be the source of all truth" (§39). "All this," it says, "indicates a grave loss of the sense of truth and of the sense of the Church." Yet is this not precisely what the *Correctio* signatories are doing? They are presenting themselves as the spokesmen of an autonomous community that pits itself against an orthodox reading of Pope Francis's words in a document of high magisterial level. *Donum Veritatis*'s statement that such actions indicate "a grave loss of the sense of truth and of the sense of the Church" should serve as an admonition to these signatories: they are operating outside the *habitus* of theology.

Some commentators say that they have a right to speak out against *Amoris Laetitia* because the pope has not made his opinion clear enough to them. Such an attitude, however, stands in opposition to *Donum Veritatis* §28, which says that disagreement with the Magisterium "could not be justified if it were based solely upon the fact that the validity of the given teaching is not evident or upon the opinion that the opposite position would be the more probable. Nor, furthermore, would the judgment of the subjective conscience of the theologian justify it because conscience does not constitute an autonomous and exclusive authority for deciding the truth of a doctrine."

Critics of *Amoris Laetitia*, however, often claim that they are only expressing their difficulties with reconciling certain statements of the exhortation with previous Church teaching. To help overcome such difficulties, *Donum Veritatis* §29 provides this instruction: "The theologian will strive then to understand this teaching in its contents, arguments, and purposes. This will mean an intense and patient reflection on his part and a readiness, if need be, to revise his own opinions and examine the objections which his colleagues might offer him." Sending petitions that accuse the Holy Father of directly or indirectly promoting heresies, however, does not seem to reflect such an attitude of "intense and patient reflection" which is open to correction from theological colleagues. The critics of *Amoris Laetitia* don't often seem to welcome constructive criticisms of their assertions. Instead, they appear resolved to discredit any effort to challenge their position.[18]

In making these observations, we do not wish to impugn the sincerity of the critics of *Amoris Laetitia*. Perhaps in their own way they believe they are acting for the good of the Church. However, if they are to voice their concerns about Pope Francis's Apostolic Exhortation in a manner that is truly Catholic, it is their responsibility to do so in conformity with the instructions of *Donum Veritatis*, which even they agree form a vital part of the tradition they claim to value.

---

18   This is reflected in several articles on *LifeSiteNews* critical of our September 26 *La Stampa* article on *Amoris Laetitia* 303.

14

A Challenge for Fastiggi and Goldstein[1]

DR JOSEPH SHAW

YOU KNOW YOU'VE HAD AN INFLUENCE WHEN the *Vatican Insider* addresses you by name. Robert Fastiggi and Dawn Eden Goldstein write:

> It seems that the case for the *Amoris Laetitia* critics' self-proclaimed "Filial Correction" of Pope Francis is weakening. Dr Joseph Shaw, one of the signers of the *Correctio filialis*, recently wrote: "It is not that we're saying that the text of *Amoris* cannot be bent into some kind of orthodoxy. What we are saying is that it has become clear that orthodoxy is not what Pope Francis wants us to find there."
>
> Shaw's claim that Pope Francis doesn't want orthodoxy, however, is based on subjective impressions derived from mostly non-authoritative statements of the pope. This does not seem to be a very strong foundation for accusing the Roman Pontiff of promoting false teachings and heresies.

What interests me about this is less the attempt to suggest that the *Correction*'s signatories are shifting their position — we haven't in the least, although we are getting used to our critics calling us names and being economical with the truth — and more the second paragraph I quote. For the information of Fastiggi and Goldstein, "impressions" are always subjective, but they are our window onto the world. What we can determine about what is going on, based — obviously — on what we can see and hear ("impressions") is indeed that "Pope Francis doesn't want orthodoxy."

And I would go further than what Fastiggi and Goldstein say: our impression is not based "mostly" on non-authoritative statements, but based entirely upon non-authoritative statements by

---

[1] Published at *LMS Chairman*, October 5, 2017.

Pope Francis, plus his failures to speak. It should be obvious that it is impossible for the Supreme Pontiff to guide the Church away from the Deposit of Faith authoritatively, since his authority is given him to confirm the brethren in the Faith. What we find, indeed, is that Pope Francis has singled out modes of communication which cannot possibly be mistaken for authoritative statements, when he indicates the kind of interpretation he wishes people to have of *Amoris Laetitia*. These include his remark in a press conference that *Amoris* makes a "change"; a private letter to the bishops of Buenos Aires; the printing of the guidelines drawn up by the bishops of Malta in *L'Osservatore Romano*; and most eloquent of all, his refusal to answer the four cardinals' *dubia*. It is not our impression only: it is the impression gained by many theologians and bishops who regard themselves as loyal to the pope, who are taking the hints, the nods, and the winks, and are writing and promulgating guidelines for their flocks which are impossible to square with the constant practice and teaching of the Church, or indeed with canon law as it currently exists.

My challenge to Fastiggi and Goldstein is a simple one. What would they do if they thought that the pope of the day were doing this: indicating non-authoritatively that bishops and ordinary Catholics should act and believe in ways contrary to the teaching of the Church? What would they regard as the correct response to the situation we believe we are actually facing? This is clearly not an impossible situation. Even those with an exaggerated view of the authority of the pope must surely admit, unless they have left common sense entirely behind, that it is theoretically possible for a pope, who can after all teach non-infallibly, to say things about faith and morals, when not teaching authoritatively, which are not correct. What should the faithful—and particularly academics and pastors—do in this situation?

The answer which comes to mind, inspired by Canon 212, is that those who think that this is happening should make their concerns known to the proper authorities, without ruling out that they should make them known to their fellow Catholics. In light of Matthew 18:15, it makes sense to go public when private communications have had no effect.

What Fastiggi and Goldstein point to instead is the passage in *Donum Veritatis* which tells dissident theologians to talk to their superiors rather than to appeal to the mass media. Fastiggi and

Goldstein appear to imagine that this imposes silence on all educated Catholics whatever the situation might be. But *Donum Veritatis* cannot be read in this way. First, it speaks of theologians who reject the ordinary Magisterium, not of those who wish to uphold it. Secondly, it speaks of theologians who have (or easily could have) dialogue with their superiors. It would be a very different matter for *Donum Veritatis* to say that theologians should not publicly support the Magisterium, or for it to contradict Canon 212 by saying that lay Catholics in general should not make "concerns" clear to their fellow Catholics, or indeed to contradict Matthew 18:15–17 about making problems public when private admonitions have failed. For *Donum Veritatis* to have said any of those things would, obviously, have been insane.

It is not the signatories of the *Correction* who are ignoring the ordinary Magisterium: if it were not enough to cite Canon Law and *Familiaris Consortio*, we could cite canons and magisterial documents going back centuries—all the way, in fact, back to St. Paul in 1 Corinthians 11:27, and beyond. It is this teaching, the teaching of the infallible ordinary and universal Magisterium, which Fastiggi and Goldstein do not want us to reiterate in this moment of crisis.

15

Fastiggi and Goldstein versus Shaw: Responses[1]

ROBERT FASTIGGI AND DAWN EDEN GOLDSTEIN have done me the honour of a reply, at some length, to my post, in my comments box. I want to take this as seriously as possible, so I paste their reply in full below, in italics, followed by my reply to each point.

Dear Dr Shaw,

Dr Dawn Eden Goldstein and I wish to thank you for your tone of civility. We hope to reply with equal civility regarding your post: "A Challenge for Fastiggi and Goldstein."

Thank you.

Our points of response are the following:

1. You are correct that "impressions" are subjective. Our point, however, is that your subjective impressions regarding papal words and actions are not shared by all. In justice there is always a need to determine what people mean before making judgments of potential heresy. When the Congregation for the Doctrine of the Faith examines cases of possible heresy, it follows strict norms of procedure in order to insure justice for the one accused (see CDF, Regulations for Doctrinal Examination *"Ratio Agendi," May 30, 1997; AAS 89 [1997] 830–835). If so much care is given to the examination of individual theologians before making judgments of heresy, should not the same be extended to the Roman Pontiff? Canon law tells us: "The First See is judged by no one" (CIC [1983], canon 1404).*

Certainly the pope deserves the chance to clarify what exactly he means, in the context of disagreement about what that may be. That is why many people, including "the four cardinals," have been respectfully but urgently asking Pope Francis for such a clarification: as you know, they wrote to him in September 2016, more than a year ago. He has not responded formally, but meanwhile many of

---

[1] Published at *Rorate Caeli*, October 6, 2017.

his supporters have been telling us that various informal responses are clear enough, and have criticised strongly those unwilling to allow their interpretation of *Amoris* to be guided by these informal indications. In any case, other people have been guided by them, and Pope Francis has not intervened to put them right.

The *Correctio* makes it very clear that we are not judging the pope or accusing him of the sin of heresy.

2. You object to the word "mostly" when we say that your claim of Pope Francis not wanting orthodoxy is derived "mostly [from] non-authoritative statements of the pope" and not, as you assert, "entirely [from] non-authoritative statements." "Mostly" is correct because, in addition to citing references to non-authoritative sources, the Correctio filialis *speaks of "the propagation of heresies effected by the Apostolic Exhortation* Amoris Laetitia *and by other words, deeds, and omissions of Your Holiness." As a papal exhortation,* Amoris Laetitia *would carry the same authority of the ordinary papal Magisterium as St. John Paul II's* Familiaris Consortio *of 1981.*

Documents emanating from the Holy See or General Councils can contain both magisterial and non-magisterial statements. Non-magisterial statements would include, obviously, those not concerning faith and morals, such as historical claims. They also include statements which are unclear: there can be no obligation on Catholics to believe a statement if they cannot determine what the statement means. Yet another category of non-magisterial statements in official documents are those which go beyond or against the ordinary Magisterium.

An example of this last case which is not controversial is the claim of the Council of Florence-Ferrara that the sacramental "matter" in priestly ordination is not the laying-on of hands, but the handing over of the chalice. We commonly say that statements of General Councils other than anathemas have non-infallible teaching authority from the ordinary Magisterium. In such a case, however, it would be more accurate to say that this statement is not a statement of the ordinary Magisterium at all, since it contradicts the ordinary Magisterium, and the ordinary Magisterium cannot contradict itself.

The contention of the *Correctio filialis* is that the statements of *Amoris* which concern us are ambiguous: they can be read in accordance with the ordinary Magisterium, which we would obviously accept, or they can be read as contradicting the ordinary

Magisterium. Those who insist on the latter possibility cannot, of course, simultaneously claim that they are examples of the ordinary Magisterium and are therefore binding. You can't be bound by the ordinary Magisterium to reject the ordinary Magisterium.

3. *You mention the private letter of Pope Francis to the bishops of Buenos Aires as an example of something that is "impossible to square with the constant teaching of the Church." Cardinal Müller, however, in his September 28* National Catholic Register *interview with Edward Pentin, said: "[If] you look at what the Argentine bishops wrote in their directive, you can interpret this in an orthodox way." What you consider "impossible" to square with orthodoxy, others find possible.*

That no one disagrees with me is not part of what I am claiming. It would be interesting, though hardly decisive, to know what Cardinal Müller thinks of the guidelines of the bishops of Malta, which seem to go beyond those of the bishops of Buenos Aires in clearly contradicting Canon 915.

4. *You ask what we would do if we thought the pope of the day were indicating non-authoritatively that bishops and ordinary Catholics should act and believe in ways contrary to the teaching of the Church. This is something purely hypothetical. Neither of us believes Pope Francis is asking people to act or believe in ways contrary to the teaching of the Church. If, though, we thought we were facing such a situation, we would make our concerns known to our Ordinary first, and then, if need be, to the papal nuncio or the Holy See. We would not have recourse to the mass media.*

We and many others who have had concerns over *Amoris* and its interpretations have gone to considerable trouble to go through the proper channels. Grouping together to compose and sign a joint statement is an obvious way to maximise the "knowledge, competence, and position" mentioned in Canon 212 in relation to appeals by the faithful; it would also be impractical to expect the Holy See to respond to hundreds of individual petitions. Being an international group means that we do not have a single Ordinary or indeed a single papal nuncio. There is nothing in Canon Law which prohibits us from appealing directly to the pope, but as a matter of fact many of us first appealed to the College of Cardinals a year ago. Finally, we did not "have recourse to the mass media" until six weeks had passed, without response, from the time our petition was given personally to the Holy Father.

Ruling out "recourse to the mass media" in all circumstances clearly contradicts Canon 212 which notes that it can be an obligation to make concerns known to "others of Christ's faithful," and is therefore ruled out as a sensible reading of *Donum Veritatis*, from which you take the phrase.

I would suggest that were you facing that situation, and were you to respond as you suggest, you could very well find yourselves failing to discharge the duty which Canon 212 mentions, to make your concerns known to other members of the faithful. For myself, I feel subjectively obliged to act because it seems clear to me that, given the knowledge, competence, and position of my fellow signatories, and given that bishops and the Holy Father are not (or not all) acting to defend the Magisterium, we can and must warn the faithful about a proximate danger to the Faith.

5. Your point about Donum Veritatis *referring to theologians who reject the ordinary Magisterium begs the question because you have not established that Pope Francis is going against any teaching of the Magisterium. You cite canon 212 §3, but you fail to mention that it also requires manifesting opinions with reverence toward pastors and attention to "the common advantage and the dignity of persons." We question whether accusing Pope Francis of propagating heresies is really showing reverence, and we question whether this serves the common advantage of the Church and the dignity of persons. We also do not believe that the* Correctio *follows the guidelines of* Donum Veritatis, *as we explained in our article.*

The text of the *Correctio* makes the case in detail, and with copious documentation, for the view that, by his words, deeds, and omissions, Pope Francis is propagating views contrary to the Magisterium. A bald denial by you is hardly an adequate response.

We are very aware of the requirement of Canon 212 (and of common sense) for reverence, attention to the common advantage, and so on. Again, a bald assertion by you that we have failed to do this is no argument.

You appear to be missing what should be obvious: we believe that Pope Francis is doing what we claim he is doing. Given our subjective position, what is it we are obliged to do, in conscience, and how should we go about it? It is not an act of reverence or affection to fail to point out grave and urgent problems in a pope's government of the Church; to fail in this way is to act as a timeserving courtier, not a faithful member of the Mystical Body. Those who love the pope and respect his office should feel profoundly the duty to make clear exactly how serious the problem is, however much what they say is expressed in respectful terms, and however much they may wish to give the pope the chance to clarify his position privately and so on. I really cannot see how the *Correctio* can be faulted on these grounds.

6. You mention that Matthew 18:15–17 allows for making problems public when private admonitions fail. This text, though, advises taking a brother to the Church for correction. It does not advise correcting the head of the Church.

This seems a most surprising reading of Matthew 18:15–17, in light of Galatians 2:11, in which St. Paul recalls how he "opposed" St. Peter, the pope, "to his face," and the tradition of interpretation the latter text has had among the Fathers and Doctors of the Church. The most famous example of this tradition of interpretation is St. Thomas Aquinas, who notes two other scriptural passages: "Reverence not thy neighbour in his fall and refrain not to speak in the time of salvation" (Sir 4:27) and "Thou shalt not hate thy brother in thy heart: but reprove him openly, lest thou incur sin through him" (Lev 19:17). (We could also add Ezekiel 33:8: "If thou dost not speak to warn the wicked man from his way, that wicked man shall die in his iniquity, but I will require his blood at thy hand.") Aquinas continues: "Apropos of what is said in a certain Gloss — namely, that I withstood him as an adversary — the answer is that the Apostle opposed Peter in the exercise of authority, not in his authority of ruling. Therefore from the foregoing we have an example: prelates, indeed, [have] an example of humility, that they should not disdain corrections from those who are lower and subject to them; subjects have an example of zeal and freedom, that they should fear not to correct their prelates, particularly if their crime is public and verges upon danger to the multitude."

7. Like you, we wish to affirm the teachings of the infallible Ordinary and Universal Magisterium. We are not questioning your faith or sincerity; we are only questioning your methods.

Affirming the infallible ordinary and universal Magisterium requires of Catholics that they not only live by it, but as God's honour and the good of their neighbours requires, witness to it publicly.

16

On the Moral Liceity of Publicly Correcting the Pope[1]

DR MICHAEL SIRILLA

THERE IS A GOOD BIT OF CONFUSION CURrently among faithful Catholics about whether it was morally licit for the pastors and theologians to make public their filial correction of the Holy Father regarding portions of *Amoris Laetitia* [*AL*] and his actions that, in their estimation, propagate heresy; or the liceity of Prof. Seifert's public expression of grave concerns about the same. It is unfortunate that their actions and those of others such as Germain Grisez and John Finnis have been impugned by other theologians, Catholic pundits, and even some bishops who have claimed publicly and in Catholic media that these persons acted immorally and are causing damage to the unity of the Church, even inciting the faithful to disobedience to the Apostolic See. It seems as though more ink has been spilled over the fact that there *is* a filial correction than on the *content* of the correction itself. My sole intention in this article is to show that the public expression of these concerns and corrections of the Holy Father is morally licit, prescinding entirely from the question of whether any particular interpretation of *AL* or of the Holy Father's other words and deeds is correct.

St. Thomas Aquinas, drawing from the rich tradition of the Church's history, specifically from St. Paul's account of rebuking St. Peter in Galatians 2 as commented upon by St. Augustine, shows quite clearly that not only is it permissible for a subordinate to correct fraternally his prelate, but that it is also necessary for him to do so publicly in certain circumstances. And this, notwithstanding the alleged prohibition in *Donum Veritatis* (hereafter *DV*) a. 30 of theologians expressing their concerns in the mass media; below, it will be made clear that *DV* was not firmly prohibiting every instance of making concerns public. In his treatise on the theological virtue of charity, an act of which is "fraternal correction," a spiritual work of mercy, Aquinas argues that correcting the sinner

---

[1] Published at *OnePeterFive*, October 5, 2017.

is an act of love, helping to save one's brother from sin and for virtue. One may even be bound to correct one's superior in the Church because he is bound to him by charity; though he must do so "not with impudence and harshness, but with gentleness and respect" (*Summa Theologiae*, II-II, q. 33, a. 4, corp.). Under very specific conditions, this correction may have to be given to a prelate publicly. Aquinas argues:

> It must be observed, however, that if the faith were endangered, a subject ought to rebuke his prelate even publicly. Hence Paul, who was Peter's subject, rebuked him in public, on account of the imminent danger of scandal concerning faith, and, as the gloss of Augustine says on Galatians 2:11, "Peter gave an example to superiors, that if at any time they should happen to stray from the straight path, they should not disdain to be reproved by their subjects." (*Summa Theologiae*, II-II, q. 33, a. 4, ad 2)

The basis in divine revelation for the proper exercise of the duty of fraternal correction is found in St. Paul's narrative in Galatians 2:11 ("But when Cephas was come to Antioch, I withstood him to the face, because he was to be blamed") and more generally in Christ's words in Matthew 18:16–17 where He instructs the disciples to make known to the Church (i.e., publicly) the fraternal correction they gave to an errant brother, failing the first two attempts at private remonstration ("And if he will not hear thee, take with thee one or two more: that in the mouth of two or three witnesses every word may stand. And if he will not hear them: tell the church. And if he will not hear the church, let him be to thee as the heathen and publican"). While Christ's words form the basis for the dominical directive of proper fraternal correction, St. Paul's narrative constitutes the basis for the divinely-inspired directive of appropriate correction of superiors by subordinates.

The current Code of Canon Law recognizes that at certain times it is a duty, not just a right, for competent persons to make known to the faithful (again, that would be *publicly*) their opinion on matters pertaining to the good of the Church:

> §3. According to the knowledge, competence, and prestige which they possess, they have the right and *even at*

times the duty to manifest to the sacred pastors their opinion on matters which pertain to the good of the Church *and to make their opinion known to the rest of the Christian faithful*, without prejudice to the integrity of faith and morals, with reverence toward their pastors, and attentive to common advantage and the dignity of persons. (CIC, can. 212 §3, emphasis added)

Whether one agrees with the assessment found in any of the corrections or concerns made public so far (the "filial correction," Prof. Seifert's letters, etc.), a fair reading and plain interpretation of those texts — one that avoids groundless conspiracy theories — shows that they meet the criteria mentioned so far: 1) competent, knowledgeable persons; 2) matters pertaining to the good of the Church; 3) maintaining reverence towards their pastors and especially the Holy Father; 4) attentive to the common good and the dignity of persons. Along these same lines, it should be noted that canonist Dr Edward Peters recently published an essay on his blog, "On arguments that may be, and sometimes must be, made," arguing that the filial correction seems to fall within the boundaries of Canon 212, which states "in regard to persons with special knowledge, competence, and prestige in regard to ecclesiastical matters, that they 'have the right *and even at times the duty*' to express their views on matters impacting the well-being of the Church."

One canonical argument that has surfaced recently in the Catholic press *against* the filial correction is that it serves to incite animosity or malice among the faithful against the Pope. Canon 1373 has been cited to this effect:

> A person who publicly incites among subjects animosities or hatred [*simultates vel odia*] against the Apostolic See or an ordinary because of some act of power or ecclesiastical ministry or provokes subjects to disobey them is to be punished by an interdict or other just penalties.

The public corrections in question do not incite such odium, unless by "odium" here one means that it would be hateful to say, contrary to some alleged claims in *Amoris Laetitia*, that it is not permissible for divorced-and-remarried Catholic living *more uxorio* (i.e., as if they were husband and wife) to receive Communion. In other words, *it would be hateful to say that the Pope is wrong* to propose such a solution for those persons and that doing so would incite others to disregard the Pope's teaching. (What would that say about Paul correcting Peter?)

On the contrary, the authors of all the documents mentioned do not incite hatred but explicitly affirm that they are moved by love of Christ, the Holy Father, and the good of souls in expressing their corrections because, in their estimation, proposing Communion for those living *more uxorio*, some of them "knowing full well" that their situation is a problem (as *AL* rightly says), is a danger to the faith. The authors take great pains to demonstrate their love for the doctrine of Christ and the Church, for the current Holy Father himself, and for the good of souls. The souls of persons who are not instructed about the gravity of their actions, who are told to receive Communion without repentance are imperiled and the souls of pastors who fail in their regard are more gravely imperiled by committing scandal in the strict sense (i.e., proposing that someone commit a sin; see Matthew 18:6). The attempt to correct these errors is an act of charity to lead others, including our prelates, to divine truth and to a life of holiness in Christ.

Some intelligent and faithful Catholics think that *AL* and the Holy Father do not propose this pastoral approach. But others in the Church do, such as those bishops and episcopal conferences (such as Malta and Germany) who propose precisely this and who have the public support of the Pope. The diocese of Rome itself has adopted this policy. But if those who have publicly corrected the Pope are right, then the danger to the faith that this proposal presents is real and grave and thus their public correction is warranted. On the other hand, if the writers and signers misunderstood the Holy Father, it should not be impossible to clear this up and the Holy Father, whose principal duty as holder of the petrine office is to secure the unity of the Church, ought to do so or explain why doing so is not necessary. He is not bound to do so by any earthly authority since he holds supreme jurisdiction in the Church on earth. Rather, the Lord Himself binds Peter and his successors to instruct the errant in matters of faith and morals as a matter of charity (Jn 21:15ff., "Do you love me? . . . Feed my sheep"). It is hard to imagine a graver situation: to very many faithful Catholics it seems that we must choose to disregard either the Pope's apparent directives in *AL* or those of Christ and St. Paul, consistently upheld by the Church's magisterium up to the present. Christ teaches that divorce and remarriage is adultery (Mt 5:32) and St. Paul teaches that receiving Communion unworthily is condemnable (1 Cor 11:29). It is a matter of whether our Lord's teaching and that of St. Paul and the Church in this regard is being respected or spurned. The Holy Father seems to affirm Christ's teaching on divorce in *AL*; but the apparent pastoral proposal seems to fall afoul of St. Paul's teaching on worthy reception of Communion. And this is not a matter of private judgment regarding Mt 5 and 1 Cor 11 since the Church has *publicly* and *definitively* affirmed the interpretation that divorce and unworthy reception of Communion are gravely sinful (e.g., Trent, Vatican II, *Familiaris Consortio*, etc.).

Still, serious confusion persists among faithful Catholics about whether or not theologians and other competent persons in the Church are permitted publicly to express their grave concerns about a non-definitive magisterial teaching. In light of this dilemma and the one precipitated by various interpretations of *AL* (and whether or not one agrees with the assessment of the "correctors"), there is a way to judge between licit and illicit ways of going to the mass media, and the Church herself has given us at least some guidance on this.

A passage from the 1990 CDF document *Donum Veritatis* has been cited recently and mistakenly in the Catholic press in order to condemn the actions of the signatories of the filial correction. Speaking of situations in which faithful theologians find non-definitive magisterial teachings problematic or erroneous, *Donum Veritatis* 30 states:

> In cases like these, the theologian should avoid turning to the "mass media," but have recourse to the responsible authority, for it is not by seeking to exert the pressure of public opinion that one contributes to the clarification of doctrinal issues and renders service to the truth.

Going back a few articles to number 27 we read:

> The theologian will not present his own opinions or divergent hypotheses as though they were non-arguable conclusions. Respect for the truth as well as for the People of God requires this discretion (cf. Rom 14:1–15; 1 Cor 8; 10:23–33). For the same reasons, the theologian will refrain from giving untimely public expression to them.

These two articles make it clear that going public is not licit when the intention is to exert public pressure on the Church to change her teaching (especially teaching that cannot be changed) and when the theologian has not made known his concerns to the "responsible authority" *first*. It is also clear in this article that theologians must avoid "untimely" public expression of their concerns. Does this mean that there may be "timely" public expressions of concerns? The document does not give many explicit criteria for determining timeliness, but "exerting public pressure" (*DV*, a. 30) is certainly one criterion. As it stands, *DV* is arguably too vague to resolve this. However, in 1990, during the official press conference on the release of *DV*, then-Cardinal Ratzinger himself (the co-author of *DV*) publicly affirmed that there may be *licit* public expression of grave concerns made by theologians regarding problems in magisterial statements. When questioned about theologians going public with a criticism of non-definitive magisterial teaching, Ratzinger replied: "We have not excluded all kinds of publication, nor have we closed him up in suffering. The Vatican insists, however, that theologians must choose the proper place to expound their ideas." His comments are published in the July 5, 1990 edition of the journal *Origins* (p. 119), a publication of the USCCB documenting official acts of the Church's prelates and related articles. The issue here is not solely *which venue* is used to express public concerns, since, whether one shares them in a scholarly journal or a conference presentation or in a widely-read publication such as an op-ed section of a newspaper, the net result is similar: the concerns are made public. The issues are also *how* one expresses the concerns (e.g., with respect, cogency, and humility) and *to whom* one expresses them. On the latter point, different circumstances will dictate different approaches. For instance, while it could be scandalous to air concerns to non-experts on a matter understood mainly by theologians (such as the metaphysical status of Christ's Body in the Eucharist), it could be scandalous *not* to air concerns to non-experts on a fundamental matter easily understood (such as the sin of active divorce or the need to receive Communion in a state of grace).

Lacking further official guidelines for communicating problems with non-definitive magisterial teachings, the current state of the Church's directives may be summarized as follows: going to the media to put pressure on the Church to change or correct her unchangeable doctrine is clearly illicit. Going public with a concern about an error in non-infallible doctrine or praxis put forth by persons exercising the magisterium may be done licitly as long as charity and prudence are followed. Due to the constraints of space, it is not possible to cite all the other relevant portions of *DV* that ground this summary; the reader should consult the entire document, but especially aa. 24 through 31 (above all, note the section that begins with the words, "When it comes to the question of interventions in the prudential order, it could happen that some Magisterial documents might not be free from all deficiencies").

But, it is argued, are not the "correctors" illicitly expressing merely their "opinion" or "divergent hypotheses" as "non-arguable conclusions" (as prohibited by *DV*, a. 27, cited above)? On the contrary, they are reiterating what the Church has publicly, definitively, and consistently taught. It is not their private opinion that Christ says that divorce is gravely sinful (Mt 5); the Church publicly and consistently has taught this (Trent, *Gaudium et Spes*, *Familiaris Consortio*, the CCC, etc.). It is not their private opinion that Paul teaches that unworthy reception of Communion is gravely sinful (1 Cor 11), but the Church again has publicly and consistently taught this. It is also not merely their private opinion that the Holy Father has publicly supported those bishops and episcopal conferences who permit reception of Communion by those divorced and remarried Catholics living *more uxorio*. He has done so publicly. Where they may "diverge" at all is when they "diverge" from the implicit liceity of such permission arguably granted in *AL* and clearly granted by some episcopal conferences (Germany, Malta).

Neither do they fall afoul of the concluding formula of the *Professio Fidei* nor of the last part of the Oath of Fidelity since in this matter they are, in fact, *assenting* to a definitive public teaching of the Church (on divorce and Communion) and at most refusing to assent to the recent but ambiguous pastoral directives to the contrary. It is a well-known principle of theological hermeneutics that ambiguous claims are to be interpreted in light of the unambiguous, and non-definitive teaching in light of definitive teaching on the same matters of faith or morals. Of course, if *AL* is *not* giving that pastoral directive, then they are not even refusing to assent to *AL*.

Surely, the "correctors" have privately discussed and debated their concerns with each other and they first approached the Holy Father privately with their letter before releasing it publicly. They consistently maintain a position of respect and reverence for the

Pope. And the matter is timely, as discussed above. Great damage is already occurring in the Church, with particular churches and national episcopal conferences suffering a balkanization such that "what is permissible in Germany is gravely sinful in Poland." Thus, regardless of whether one concurs with their assessment, it should be easy to recognize that they acted morally licitly, if not heroically.

A final point of clarification: the filial correction does not accuse Pope Francis of heresy. Rather, it claims that Pope Francis has propagated heresy in his public approval and support of those bishops and episcopal conferences who are now permitting divorced and remarried persons living *more uxorio* to receive Communion. More precisely, the "correctors" are pointing out that they consider the Pope to be failing in his duty to preserve, defend, and explain divinely-revealed truth in the area of marriage and the Eucharist by supporting those bishops who are granting such permissions. There are ways to propagate heresy other than by teaching heresy; for instance, promoting and approving others who do so. This is not an act of heresy but of negligence. Pope Honorius was posthumously condemned by Constantinople III (AD 680–681) for *allowing* heretical teaching. This is truly distinct from actually teaching heresy.

This is a rather painful issue about which the brightest lights and authorities in the Church disagree. Many faithful Catholics hope and pray that the Holy Father, as our loving spiritual Father, would kindly reach out to these individuals and help them and all of us understand better and more clearly the deposit of faith and morals regarding marriage, divorce, and the proper dispositions for fruitful reception of the Eucharist. They implore him to secure the supernatural unity of the Church in faith, hope, and charity which is the principal duty of the petrine office. Those who have made public their concerns and corrections *with these precise intentions* have acted uprightly for the good of the Church and the honor of Christ.

17

Before Pope Francis Was Accused of Heresy, Catholics Reached Out to Him Numerous Times[1]

DR MAIKE HICKSON

THE APRIL 30 OPEN LETTER TO BISHOPS HAS caused much discussion in Catholic circles. The authors of the letter have appealed to the bishops of the world, for the sake of the salvation of souls, "as our spiritual fathers, vicars of Christ within your own jurisdictions and not vicars of the Roman pontiff, publicly to admonish Pope Francis to abjure the heresies that he has professed." Some of the heresies they name flow out of the pope's Post-synodal Apostolic Exhortation, *Amoris Laetitia*, on marriage and the family, which opened the path to many episcopal guidelines now allowing "remarried" divorcees to receive Holy Communion contrary to perennial Church teaching.

Some Catholic commentators have argued against this Open Letter with the claim that Pope Francis deserves the benefit of the doubt with regard to some of the papal quotations as they are presented by the Open Letter. As Father Thomas Petri, O. P., for example, stated: "I'm disappointed that a group of theologians, some of whom I admire, chose to express themselves by contributing to a letter calling the pope a heretic. Their citations of him can be all interpreted in a way that gives the Holy Father the benefit of the doubt, which we owe him." In a similar manner, other commentators have asked whether the authors have ever first contacted the pope privately, or whether they first went to their own bishops with their objections. For example, the Vice-President for the Center of Legal Studies at the Center for Family and Human Rights (C-Fam), Stefano Gennarini, stated on Twitter: "I only want to know one thing. Did any of the folks on this list even try to express their concerns with His Holiness privately, through their bishops, or even publicly, before inciting others to schism [sic]."

---

[1] Published at *LifeSiteNews*, May 7, 2019; updated May 21, 2019.

These are objections that should be faced and discussed. Since we are in the middle of an unprecedented situation in the history of the Catholic Church, reasonable people can come to different conclusions here. It must be remembered that during the time of the fourteenth-century antipopes, there were saints on both sides.

Leila Marie Lawler, wife of Catholic commentator and book author Phil Lawler, commented on this ongoing discussion on Twitter, saying: "Worst take: 'Give Pope Francis the benefit of the doubt' — as if criticism is personal and not about objective issues, [in] the defense of which he has ultimate responsibility. Instead, protect those 'little ones' exposed to error and its corrosions," adding in her follow-up tweet: "The 'benefit of the doubt' defense has been used from Day One of this pontificate. Where is charity for the little ones?" In light of this piercing comment, it is worthwhile bringing to mind just how many Catholics, as children of God, have called out to the pope for clarifications, corrections, and help, and how many learned Catholics — cardinals, bishops, priests, and laymen alike — have issued, during the last six years, pleas to Pope Francis himself.

This list of initiatives taken under Pope Francis's pontificate was started on Twitter by the present author, and then substantially enriched by others, such as Leila Lawler and Julia Meloni. The list is now very long, and it will prove how many chances Pope Francis has received to respond to accusations of his allegedly heterodox teachings.

In March of 2013, Pope Francis was elected. In February of 2014, he asked Cardinal Walter Kasper to give a speech to the College of Cardinals, in which he presented his idea to give Holy Communion to some "remarried" divorcees. This speech was hotly discussed at the consistory, with perhaps about 85% of the attending cardinals opposing Kasper's progressive ideas, according to a report by Marco Tosatti. This event — together with Pope Francis's announcement of a twofold Synod of Bishops on Marriage and the Family in 2014 and 2015 — inspired the first public attempts at preserving the Church's traditional teaching. What follows is a non-exhaustive list of twenty direct attempts by clergy and laity to reach Pope Francis for clarification. Following this is a list of indirect attempts.

DIRECT ATTEMPTS BY CLERGY AND LAITY TO REACH POPE FRANCIS

In October of 2014, a large U. S. Catholic parish—St. John the Baptist, in Front Royal, Virginia—issued an "Affirmation of Faith Concerning Marriage and the Family" that gained more than 1,000 signatures from parishioners and was sent to Pope Francis.

On April 16, 2015, the Catholic newspaper *The Wanderer* published an Open Letter to Pope Francis, in which the signatories asked Pope Francis to "celebrate the conclusion of the Synod of the Family with a clear and strong reaffirmation of the Church's timeless teachings on the indissolubility of marriage, the nuptial nature and definition of marriage and conjugal love, and the virtue of chastity, as presented in the *Catechism of the Catholic Church*."

After the first troubling synod, in December of 2014, the author of this article herself made her own small attempt to defend the Church's teaching on marriage by writing an Open Letter to Pope Francis (published December 10, 2014), arguing on the basis of her own experience as a child of divorce. This letter was sent to Pope Francis, but was never responded to. It was also sent to the Secretariat of the Synod of Bishops, but was not responded to, either.

In October of 2015, at the beginning of the second synod on the family, thirteen cardinals wrote a letter to Pope Francis, asking the pope for a fair procedure during the synod and pointed to the danger of adapting the Church's teaching on marriage to the current secular culture.

In November of 2015, Prof. Paolo Pasqualucci published an Open Letter to Pope Francis, asking him not to permit Communion for the "remarried" divorcees and not to make laxer the Church's canonical process of declaring a marriage null.

On April 24, 2016, very shortly after the publication of the papal document, Bishop Athanasius Schneider published a charitable and clear critique of *Amoris Laetitia*, speaking about the confusion and "contradictory interpretations even among the episcopate" flowing from this papal text, and calling upon the Church's hierarchy and the laity to beg the pope for a clarification and an official interpretation of *Amoris Laetitia* in line with the constant teaching of the Church.

On July 13, 2016, in a spirit of love, humility, and faithfulness, sixteen international life and family advocates asked Pope Francis in a powerful "Plea to the Pope" to unambiguously speak the truth of the Catholic faith, to end doctrinal confusion, to restore clarity, and to be the Holy Father that Catholics need.

In July of 2016, forty-five clergy and scholars published a letter to the cardinals of the Catholic Church[2] in which they "request that the Cardinals and Patriarchs petition the Holy Father to condemn the errors listed in the document [attached to the letter] in a definitive and final manner, and to authoritatively state that *Amoris Laetitia* does not require any of them to be believed or considered as possibly true." The letter contains a very detailed list of potentially heretical or heterodox statements that could be drawn out of *Amoris Laetitia*.

On August 3, 2016, Professor Josef Seifert published a detailed critique of *Amoris Laetitia*, listing several errors in the document that could be heretical, and asking the pope to "revoke them himself." Seifert was later, in August of 2017, to issue a second text on *Amoris Laetitia*, with a question addressed "to Pope Francis and to all Catholic cardinals, bishops, philosophers, and theologians. It deals with a *dubium* about a purely logical consequence of an affirmation in *Amoris Laetitia*, and ends with a plea to Pope Francis to retract at least one affirmation of *AL*." That question pertains to *AL*'s claim "that we can know with 'a certain moral security' that God himself asks us to continue to commit intrinsically wrong acts, such as adultery or active homosexuality."

On November 14, 2016, four cardinals published a letter to Pope Francis[3] that they had sent to him privately on September 19 and that had remained unanswered, which is very unusual. The letter contained the now-famous five *dubia* concerning *Amoris Laetitia*, for example as to whether those who live in a second "marriage" after a divorce may now receive the Sacraments and as to whether there still exist intrinsically evil acts, that is to say acts that are under all conditions to be regarded as evil. The cardinals requested a papal audience but were never received. The four *dubia* cardinals are Cardinals Joachim Meisner, Raymond Burke, Carlo Caffarra, and Walter Brandmüller. (Two of the four have since died.) Subsequently, fifteen cardinals, archbishops, and bishops individually expressed their support for the *dubia*, among them Cardinals Joseph Zen and Willem Eijk, Archbishop Charles Chaput and Archbishop Luigi Negri.

At the end of 2016, two scholars, Professor John Finnis and Professor Germain Grisez, published an Open Letter to Pope Francis,

---

2   See the first document in Part II of this volume.
3   See Part I.

asking him "to condemn eight positions against the Catholic faith that are being supported, or likely will be, by the misuse of his Apostolic Exhortation *Amoris Laetitia*." They also called upon the bishops to join this request.

On September 23, 2017, more than a year after the publication of *Amoris Laetitia*, sixty-two clergy and scholars issued a *Filial Correction* of Pope Francis,[4] in which they stated: "We are compelled to address a correction to Your Holiness on account of the propagation of heresies effected by the Apostolic Exhortation *Amoris Laetitia* and by other words, deeds, and omissions of Your Holiness."

On November 1, 2017, Father Thomas Weinandy published a letter that he had sent to Pope Francis in July of that year. In that letter, Weinandy says that Francis's pontificate is marked by "chronic confusion," and he warns the pope that a "seemingly intentional lack of clarity [of teaching] risks sinning against the Holy Spirit."

On January 2, 2018, three Kazakh bishops—among them Bishop Schneider—issued a profession of the immutable truths about sacramental marriage in light of *Amoris Laetitia*, and especially in light of the many episcopal pastoral guidelines permitting Communion for "remarried" divorcees. These prelates reaffirm the traditional teaching of the Church on marriage and the family. Subsequently, one cardinal and six bishops—among them Cardinal Janis Pujats and Archbishop Carlo Maria Viganò—signed this statement.

Also in January of 2018, Cardinal Willem Eijk asked Pope Francis publicly to clarify questions about *Amoris Laetitia* and to clear the confusion stemming from the document. Eijk proposed that the pope write an additional document in which doubts should be removed. On May 7, 2018, Cardinal Eijk once more raised his voice and asked Pope Francis to clarify questions arising from the discussion among German bishops to give Holy Communion to Protestant spouses of Catholics. He observed that "the bishops and, above all, the Successor of Peter fail to maintain and transmit faithfully and in unity the deposit of faith contained in Sacred Tradition and Sacred Scripture."

Pope Francis, over the course of several years, made statements against the death penalty. He finally decided, in August of 2018, to change the *Catechism of the Catholic Church*, declaring the death penalty to be immoral in all cases. Two weeks later, a group of 75

---

4   See the second document in Part II.

prominent clergy and scholars issued a public letter to cardinals, published in *First Things*, asking them to urge Pope Francis to recant and rescind this change in the *Catechism*.[5]

In August of 2018, Archbishop Carlo Maria Viganò published a testimony in which he claims, among many other things, that Pope Francis was aware of the moral corruption of then-Cardinal Theodore McCarrick and of the fact that Pope Benedict XVI had placed certain restrictions upon him, but that he chose to ignore them. The Archbishop called upon the pope to resign. When Pope Francis was asked about this document, he answered that he would later respond to it ("When some time passes and you have drawn your conclusions, I may speak"), but then he never made any response. In August of 2018, 47,000 Catholic women worldwide called upon Pope Francis to answer the question as to whether Archbishop Viganò's claim is true. The U. S. website *Church Militant*—which up to then had been careful not to criticize Pope Francis for his teaching on marriage and the family—called upon Pope Francis to resign, in light of his complicity with McCarrick's sins.

In 2019, Pope Francis signed the controversial Abu Dhabi Statement which says that the "diversity of religions" is "willed by God." Both Bishop Athanasius Schneider and Professor Josef Seifert strongly opposed this formulation and called upon Pope Francis to rescind it. Bishop Schneider, on March 1, was able to receive from the pope in a private conversation a sort of correction that this formulation really meant the "permissive will of God," yet both he and Professor Seifert maintain that a public and definite correction is needed.

INDIRECT ATTEMPTS BY CLERGY AND LAITY TO REACH POPE FRANCIS

Cardinal Gerhard Müller—then the Prefect of the Congregation for the Doctrine of the Faith—published a book *The Hope of the Family*, in which he maintains the indissolubility of marriage, adding that "not even an ecumenical council can change the doctrine of the Church."

The Voice of the Family, an international coalition of pro-life and pro-family organizations, was founded ahead of the first family synod in 2014, establishing a website and organizing conferences in Rome in order to protect marriage and family from perceived threats.

---

5 See the fourth document in Part II.

Five cardinals—Walter Brandmüller, Gerhard Müller, Carlo Caffarra, Raymond Burke, and Velasio De Paolis—wrote, together with other authors such as Professor John Rist (one of the signatories of the Open Letter to the Bishops), a book in defense of the sacrament of marriage, called *Remaining in the Truth of Christ*.

At the first Synod of Bishops on the Family, in October of 2014, there was a group of bishops who strongly opposed introducing heterodox statements concerning homosexuality and "remarried" divorcees into the Synod document; subsequently, neither the Kasper proposal nor a change of the Church's teaching on homosexuality was included in the final document.

In 2016, before the publication of Pope Francis's *Amoris Laetitia*, tens of thousands of Catholics signed a Filial Appeal, a Declaration of Fidelity to the Church's unchangeable teaching on marriage. This appeal had also been signed by Cardinal Burke, Cardinal Caffarra, Cardinal Pujats, and Bishop Athanasius Schneider.

Also before the second family synod, Father José Granados—at the time Vice-president of the John Paul II Institute for Studies on Marriage and Family in Rome—published a book in defense of the indissolubility of marriage.

In May of 2015, before the second Synod of Bishops on Marriage and the Family, nearly 1,000 priests from the United States issued a statement asking the synod to affirm the Church's teaching on marriage and the family.[6]

In August of 2015, Ignatius Press published the "eleven cardinals book," called *Eleven Cardinals Speak on Marriage and the Family: Essays from a Pastoral Viewpoint*. The authors—among them Cardinals Paul Josef Cordes, Dominik Duka, O.P, and John Onaiyekan, but also Robert Sarah and Carlo Caffarra—once more defended the Church's teaching on marriage and published proposals for good pastoral care for marriages.

In September of 2015, just before the second synod, eleven African prelates—among them Cardinal Robert Sarah and Cardinal Barthélemy Adoukonou—published a book, *Christ's New*

---

6   See "Hundreds of US priests ask Synod to stand firm on Church teaching," *Catholic News Agency*, May 16, 2015. This document was nearly identical to that which was published in March of the same year in the U.K., signed by 500 Britsh clergy (see "In open letter, 500 British priests ask Synod to stand firm on Church teaching," *Catholic News Agency*, March 30, 2015).

Homeland: Africa, in which they analyzed and sharply criticized the essential preparatory Vatican documents for the upcoming synod, once more defending the Church's teaching on marriage and the family.

In February of 2019, just before the beginning of the Abuse Summit in Rome from February 21–24, the two remaining *dubia* cardinals—Raymond Burke and Walter Brandmüller—wrote an Open Letter to the Presidents of the Conferences of Bishops encouraging them "to raise your voice to safeguard and proclaim the integrity of the doctrine of the Church" and also to address the protracted problem of homosexual networks in the Catholic Church.

At the same time, the Swiss lay organization Pro Ecclesia and *LifeSiteNews* launched a petition to "Stop homosexual networks in the Church" that aimed at tightening the Church's law in order clearly to punish the priests who violate the Sixth Commandment by homosexual acts and those who abuse minors and vulnerable adults such as seminarians.

Also in 2019, Cardinal Gerhard Müller published his *Manifesto of Faith*, in which he restated the main tenets of Catholic faith and morals as they have always been taught and as they can be found in the *Catechism of the Catholic Church*. He did so expressly referring to the many clergy and laymen who have asked him for such a doctrinal clarification in the middle of grave confusion in the Church.

In April of 2019, Pope Emeritus Benedict XVI published a letter on the sex abuse crisis, in which he pointed to the moral and doctrinal laxity that has entered the Catholic Church in the wake of the cultural revolution of the 1960s. Here thereby tried to help to point to deeper explanations of the current sex abuse crisis than the mere references to "abuse of power and spiritual abuse" and "clericalism," as they had been presented at the February 2019 Sex Abuse Summit in Rome.

Throughout these years, there have been many individuals who have raised their voices. Among the first papal critics were the now-deceased Mario Palmaro and Alessandro Gnocchi ("We do not like this Pope"[7]) and Professor Roberto de Mattei, who accompanied this papacy with numerous articles and commentaries. Then there

---

7 For a translation, see Christopher Ferrara, "Confusion Mounts, Pope Acknowledges Critics," *The Remnant*, January 16, 2014.

were also Father Brian Harrison[8] and the internationally renowned Catholic philosopher Professor Robert Spaemann, now deceased.[9]

Later on, several books were written that describe in a critical manner Pope Francis's leadership and doctrinally confusing actions and words. Among them are *The Political Pope* by George Neumayr, *The Dictator Pope* by Henry Sire, *The Lost Shepherd* by Phil Lawler (who subsequently also authored *The Smoke of Satan* dealing with the sex abuse crisis), and José Antonio Ureta's book *Pope Francis's Paradigm Shift: Continuity or Rupture in the Mission of the Church?—An Assessment of His Pontificate's First Five Years*.

POPE FRANCIS HAS NOT RESPONDED

This written record of some of the major charitable and urgent initiatives taken by prelates, priests, academics, and earnest laymen is by far not exhaustive, but it sheds light on the many beautiful manifestations of a loyal witness to the Faith that were meant to be pleas both to Pope Francis to amend his ways and to cardinals and bishops to help him to act decisively in this regard. However, Pope Francis has not responded in any visible and clear way to all of these initiatives, nor met with those who have called upon him (not even with the four *dubia* cardinals), except for the recent meeting with Bishop Schneider, which, nonetheless, was finally without any clear and unequivocal results. Despite these pleas, Pope Francis appears to be continuing his course of obstinately revolutionizing the Catholic Church at the cost of doctrinal orthodoxy and her moral clarity.

---

8   See Maike Hickson, "Priest: I'll never 'profane' the sacraments by following Kasper's proposal, no matter who tells me to do it," *LifeSiteNews*, April 24, 2015; Brian Harrison, "Authentic confusion over Pope Francis's 'authentic magisterium,'" *LifeSiteNews*, December 19, 2017.

9   See Maike Hickson, "Famed German Catholic philosopher makes waves for criticizing Pope Francis's 'autocratic' style," *LifeSiteNews*, April 27, 2015.

18

The Heresy Letter Is Intelligent, but Doesn't Quite Convince[1]

DR EDWARD PETERS

THE OPEN LETTER "ACCUSING POPE FRANCIS of the canonical delict of heresy" raises several canonical questions. It is generally recognised, subject to important qualifications, that a pope can commit material, formal, or obstinate heresy, triggering thereby, for himself and the Church, canonical consequences running from the almost non-existent to the catastrophic.

Academics have speculated on procedures for assessing allegations of papal heresy but have concluded little except that a pope cannot be put on trial (can. 1404). Given the gravity of obstinate heresy in a pope, however, it is accepted that some mechanism for assessing and, if demonstrated, proclaiming such heresy must exist.

The right of the letter's signatories to publish their contentious opinions is protected by Canon 212 §3 and they correctly recite the elements of a heresy case (can. 751, can. 1364). But, as an outline of a canonical case against a pope for heresy, the letter stumbles in several crucial respects. Most seriously, it fails to grapple with the "principle of benignity" in the interpretation of law and evidence.

For many centuries canon law has expressly demanded that "in penal matters, the more benign interpretation must be followed" (*Regula Iuris* 49), meaning, in brief, that the benefit of the doubt is to be accorded the accused in a criminal case. This interpretive principle goes beyond canon law: it is fundamental to the Western legal tradition.

The principle of benignity demands that, in every facet of the penal process, one must, for example, construe penal norms as narrowly as is reasonably possible (can. 18) and judge the accused only and strictly in accord with law (can. 221 §3). But the letter consistently fails to appreciate, or even allude to, the principle of benignity as it impacts any penal matter, let alone one involving a pope.

---

[1] Published at *The Catholic Herald* [UK ed.], May 9, 2019.

The letter claims, for example, after reciting several statements by Francis, that "understood in their most obvious sense, the statements listed above are heretical." But that assertion, even if it were factually correct, is canonically irrelevant for, per the principle of benignity, if an orthodox interpretation exists for an ambiguous theological assertion, that benign interpretation must be ascribed to the words of the accused — regardless of whether the accused actually intended such an interpretation. To adapt a phrase from *A Man for All Seasons*, the world may construe words according to its wits, but courts must construe according to law.

Again, the letter correctly notes that behavior can be taken as evidence of heresy. A traditional example is mentioned in the letter: a man's failure to kneel before the Blessed Sacrament could be evidence of his heretical denial of the Real Presence. But such behavior could be also explained on other grounds ranging from mere physical disability to intentional disrespect for the Real Presence. Thus a man's failure to kneel, even if it indicates an offence, would not necessarily be evidence of heresy.

Ironically, the principle of benignity also protects the signatories: there is talk of their being sanctioned, but I would reject that. The letter, though wrongheaded, can, and thus should, be taken in an ecclesially acceptable sense.

Heresy cases are not impossible under canon law, but they are, and are meant to be, very difficult. As a brief against the pope for, say, chronic misuse of his office (can. 1389, a crime for which a pope cannot be tried), I find the letter thought-provoking; as an admonition to His Holiness that his words and actions have attracted serious, unprecedented, negative attention, I find the text instructive. But as a canonical brief for a papal heresy case, I find it unconvincing.

19

The Right and the Not-so-right in the Open Letter Accusing Pope Francis of Heresy[1]

DR EDWARD FESER

WHAT SHOULD WE THINK OF THE RECENT open letter accusing Pope Francis of heresy, signed by Fr Aidan Nichols, Prof. John Rist, and other priests and academics (and for which Prof. Josef Seifert has now expressed his support)? Like others who have commented on it, I think the letter overstates things in its main charge and makes some bad arguments, but that it also makes many correct and important points that cannot reasonably be dismissed merely because the letter is seriously deficient in other respects.

As to the main charge, it is true that a pope can fall into doctrinal error, even material heresy, when not speaking *ex cathedra*. However, whether and how a pope can be charged with *formal* heresy, and what the consequences would be if he were guilty of it, are simply much less clear-cut canonically and theologically than the letter implies. Some of the Church's greatest theologians have speculated about the matter, and while there are serious arguments for various possible positions, there is no theological consensus and no magisterial teaching that resolves the issue. Moreover, a pope falling into formal heresy would be about as grave a crisis for the Church as can be imagined. So, maximum caution is called for before making such a charge, and in my opinion it is simply rash flatly to accuse the pope of "the canonical delict of heresy," as the letter does.

Some of the arguments deployed are also ill-advised, to say the least. For example, it was foolish to appeal to the allegedly sinister shape of the staff that the pope used in a particular Mass as evidence of heretical intent. To be sure, the open letter does not make much of this, but it is a bad argument, and the letter's critics have understandably pounced on it.

---

[1] Published at *LifeSiteNews*, May 8, 2019.

I would guess that these serious problems with the letter are one reason that it did not gather more signatures, though it is certainly significant that it attracted signatories as formidable as Nichols and Rist. (This is not meant in any way as a slight against the other signatories, some of whom are also formidable scholars. But most of them have signed several other public statements critical of Pope Francis, so the fact that they signed this one is less noteworthy than the fact that Nichols and Rist signed it.) Another reason, I suspect, is that by now it seems that there is little point to further public letters and petitions critical of Pope Francis, when several others have already been issued and simply ignored by the pope, the cardinals, and the bishops. (I signed one of them myself.) I realize that the signatories to this latest open letter do not suppose they are likely to move the bishops to action, but merely want to get into the historical record a summary of the problems with some of Pope Francis's words and actions and the fact that there were faithful Catholic scholars who criticized them. But there is a point to doing even that much only if the letter adds something new and significant to the previous letters and petitions, and the main thing this one adds is a charge that is, as I say, rashly made.

Having said all that, it simply will not do for critics of the letter to point to its deficiencies and then roll over and go back to sleep. The letter, however problematic, is a response to statements and actions of the pope that are also seriously problematic. And if its rashness reflects a kind of exasperation on the part of the signatories, it cannot reasonably be denied that the pope can indeed be exasperating. For example, Pope Francis has made many statements that at least seem to contradict traditional Catholic teaching on divorce and remarriage, conscience, grace, the diversity of religions, contraception, capital punishment, and a variety of other topics. The open letter is right about that. Indeed, at least where the number of problematic statements from Pope Francis is concerned, the open letter actually understates the case, because it does not address the pope's remarks about contraception, capital punishment, or certain other issues. The sheer volume of these problematic statements is alarming in itself, whatever one thinks of any one of them considered in isolation. You can find previous popes who have made a theologically problematic statement here or there. You cannot find a previous pope who has made so many theologically problematic statements.

It is true that the pope's defenders have come up with ways to read some of these statements so as to reconcile them with traditional doctrine. But there are two general problems with such attempts, even apart from the fact that not all of the proposed readings are terribly plausible.

First, and as I have pointed out before, when defending the doctrinal soundness of a statement, it does not suffice to come up with some strained or unnatural interpretation that avoids strict heresy. That is a much lower standard than the Church herself has applied historically, and would rule out very little. To take an example I have used in the past, even the statement "God does not exist" could be given an orthodox interpretation if you strain hard enough. You could say: "What I mean when I say that is that God does not 'exist' in the sense of merely having or participating in existence, the way other things do. Rather, he just is Subsistent Being Itself and the source of the existence of other things." The trouble is that the average person would not understand such a highfalutin interpretation even if it occurred to him. The average person would naturally hear the statement in question as an expression of atheism. He would be especially likely to do so if the statement was addressed to a mass audience rather than to an audience of academics, and if the person who made the statement did not himself clarify things by explicitly giving a non-atheistic interpretation.

A theological statement—especially when made by a churchman to a mass audience—should be clearly orthodox on a natural reading, not merely arguably orthodox on some creative reading. This is why the Church has traditionally held that being strictly heretical is only one of several ways that a statement can be doctrinally objectionable. Even a statement that is not explicitly heretical might still be erroneous, or proximate to heresy, or rash, or ambiguous, or "offensive to pious ears," or subject to one of the other theological censures with which the Church has in the past condemned various theological opinions.

Where the question of problematic papal statements is concerned, we might consider the cases of Pope Honorius I and Pope John XXII, who are frequently cited as the two clearest examples of popes who arguably were guilty of heresy. Their defenders have argued that the precise wording of the statements that got them into trouble could be construed as strictly heretical only in light of later dogmatic definitions rather than in light of definitions already on the books in their day. Even if that is the case, however, the fact remains that John XXII, who had denied that the blessed in heaven immediately enjoy the beatific vision after death, recanted this error in the face of vigorous criticism from the theologians of his day. The fact remains that Honorius was condemned by two later popes for statements of his that at least gave aid and comfort to the Monothelite heresy. Pope St. Leo II declared: "We anathematize... Honorius, who did not attempt to sanctify this Apostolic Church with the teaching of Apostolic tradition, but by profane treachery permitted its purity to be polluted." And: "Honorius... did not, as became the Apostolic authority, extinguish the flame of heretical teaching in its first beginning, but fostered it by his negligence." So, whether or not Honorius and John XXII were guilty of strict heresy, they were undeniably guilty of making statements that fell under one or more of the lesser theological censures cited above. Similarly, even if Pope Francis's problematic statements can be given readings that avoid strict heresy, it doesn't follow that they can avoid falling under one or more of the lesser theological censures.

The second problem with the proposed explanations of Pope Francis's remarks is that it is the pope himself, and not his defenders, who should be providing them—and he has persistently refused to do so. The open letter is right to complain about this. For one thing, upholding traditional teaching and resolving doctrinal disputes is the main job of a pope. Hence, that he has still not responded to the now famous *dubia* (to take just one example) is indefensible. He has in this regard clearly failed to do his duty, and it is intellectually dishonest for his defenders to pretend otherwise. Had the pope simply reaffirmed traditional teaching in response to these straightforward and respectfully presented questions from several of his cardinals, the main doctrinal controversy that has roiled his pontificate would have been swiftly resolved.

For another thing, what a person fails to say, and how he acts, can "send a message" no less than what he does explicitly say. The open letter is also right to emphasize that. Suppose, to return to my example, that I not only publicly stated "God does not exist," but also refused to say one way or the other whether I myself endorsed the non-atheistic interpretation of this utterance proposed by some of my defenders on my behalf. Suppose also that I frequently praised atheist thinkers like Nietzsche, Marx, Sartre, et al., and frequently criticized theistic religions and thinkers. But suppose too that, for all that, I still denied that I was an atheist. People would naturally be confused, and many would suspect that I was simply engaging in double-talk—that I really *was* an atheist but didn't want to be entirely frank about it.

Similarly, when the pope not only makes theologically ambiguous statements about divorce and remarriage, conscience, etc., but refuses to clarify those statements, and promotes and praises people with a reputation for departing from traditional teaching in these areas while criticizing and sidelining people with a reputation for upholding traditional teaching, it is hardly surprising if many people worry—whether correctly or not—that he does not agree with traditional teaching, but doesn't want to say so directly.

Suppose that the open letter had alleged, not that the pope is guilty of the canonical delict of heresy, but rather that the pope's words and actions have, even if inadvertently, encouraged doctrinal error, or perhaps that the pope has been negligent in his duty to uphold sound doctrine. It would be much harder to defend the pope against these milder charges, as the evidence adduced in the open letter clearly shows. These milder charges also would not raise the question of the loss of the papal office, with all of its unresolved canonical and theological difficulties and horrific practical implications. And it would also (unlike the prospect of a formally heretical pope) have clear precedents in the cases of Honorius and John XXII.

The Church famously teaches that the salvation of souls is the supreme law. She does not teach that defending the pope at all costs is the supreme law. Some of the pope's defenders seem not to know the difference. But as the precedents of St. Paul's rebuke of St. Peter, the condemnation of Pope Honorius, and the fourteenth-century theologians' criticism of Pope John XXII all show—and as the Church herself has always acknowledged—it can happen, albeit very rarely, that what the salvation of souls requires is precisely the correction rather than defense of a pope. The open letter is right about that too. However, such correction must be carried out with filial reverence, and with extreme caution.

20

Why I Signed the Papal Heresy Open Letter[1]

INTERVIEW WITH DR JOHN RIST

AN OPEN LETTER ACCUSING POPE FRANCIS OF heresy and calling the world's bishops to investigate has been signed by eighty-six people as of May 10, among them some prominent theologians and other academics. One of the most notable of the initial nineteen to sign the missive is Professor John Rist, a respected British scholar of patristics best known for his contributions to the history of metaphysics and ethics. The author of detailed studies on such subjects as Plato, Aristotle, and St. Augustine of Hippo, Rist held the Father Kurt Pritzl, O.P., Chair in Philosophy at The Catholic University of America and is a life member of Clare Hall at the University of Cambridge, England. He was also one of the contributors to *Remaining in the Truth of Christ*, a book upholding the Church's teaching on divorce and remarriage published ahead of the 2014 Synod on the Family. Cardinal Gerhard Müller, who was then serving as prefect of the Vatican's Congregation for the Doctrine of the Faith, was another contributor to that 2014 collection of essays.

In this May 13 email interview with *Register* Rome correspondent Edward Pentin, Professor Rist responds to a number of criticisms that the open letter has drawn, including that it is "extreme" and "intemperate" and "overstates" its case. In response, he says he put his name to the initiative chiefly because he believes that what he sees as ambiguous statements from Pope Francis are designed to try to change the Church's doctrine "by stealth." He says the letter is aimed at preventing "further massive confusion among Catholics" and to "expose papal double talk," which he believes is a deliberate effort by the pope for "evading charges of heresy."

---

[1] Published by Edward Pentin, *National Catholic Register*, May 15, 2019.

Professor Rist, what were your own motives for signing the open letter?

My chief motive for signing was that I had come to the conclusion that so many vain attempts have been made to get the pope to "clarify" his ambiguities and correct his seeming errors that there was no useful alternative to an outright "charge." By his wholly unreasonable unwillingness, in particular to answer the *dubia*, Pope Francis has brought this upon himself.

How far has the letter achieved its goal?

I do not think the letter has achieved its goal—nor did I think there was much chance that it would, at least in the short run. That is because the pope can always shelter behind silence, and there is a servile mentality among the episcopate (and many others, even conservative commentators), which is squeamish about criticizing a pope. Such commentators approximate too closely to reducing the sacred and unchallengeable dogmatic teachings of the Church to the utterances of a pope: the Father [Thomas] Rosica theory of the present papacy![2]

Why release the letter now, what prompted its publication, and how many people were asked to sign it?

I did not organize the letter so I cannot answer your questions. But I do know that there was considerable debate about the content. I was only involved relatively late on and agreed to sign because I thought the general approach was essential at this time. I doubt whether a document could be written in which everyone would agree with all the wording: that is, unless it were so bland as to be pointless.

---

2   A reference to Fr Thomas Rosica's article "The Ignatian Qualities of the Petrine Ministry of Pope Francis," *Zenit*, July 31, 2018, in which he stated: "Pope Francis breaks Catholic traditions whenever he wants, because he is 'free from disordered attachments.' Our Church has indeed entered a new phase: with the advent of this first Jesuit pope, it is openly ruled by an individual rather than by the authority of Scripture alone or even its own dictates of tradition plus Scripture." The full text as published by *Zenit* was preserved at *Rorate Caeli* under the heading: "Member of Francis' Inner Circle in Article: 'Church in New Phase, beyond Scripture and Tradition' (Updated)," August 13, 2018. Due to the worldwide controversy generated by these words, they were quickly removed from their original location.

What do you say to the various criticisms of the letter: that it represents an "extreme" and "intemperate" approach which "overstates" the case—as some see it—and that this makes further criticism of this pontificate harder?

Criticisms of intemperance, etc., whatever their intent, can only have the effect of diverting attention from the main concerns: that the pope is deliberately using ambiguity to change doctrine and that the attitude he adopts over appointments indicates that he is out of sympathy (to put it mildly) with traditional Catholic teachings on a whole range of subjects. Fussing about "extremism," etc., seems like fiddling while Rome burns. What it shows is that even many conservatives do not want to grasp the gravity of a situation where the pope seems bent on turning the Church into a vaguely spiritually-flavored NGO.

Another criticism is that the signatories are not in a position to accuse the pope of heresy, that only bishops can hold him to account for such a charge, and that the letter would have been better just calling on bishops to investigate the alleged heresies rather than accusing the pope of them. What is your response to this view?

But calling on the bishops is precisely what the letter does! The signatories are not in a position to convict a pope of heresy; they are in a position to "prosecute" the charge, and we judged it was our duty to do so. The letter is primarily and immediately a challenge to the bishops to act rather than ignore or wring hands only.

What is your view of the critique that it's not yet possible to accuse Pope Francis of specific formal heresy, but he can be accused of deliberate ambiguity and confusion, or "drift" toward heresy, and that that might have made a better critique?

See my answer above. I am not a canonist, nor (see above) a judge. What I am is someone who believes he can recognize intended heresy in word [and] also how the words are confirmed by the actions.

Others have said it would have been better to omit aspects which they believe are not strictly suspected of being heretical, such as supposed dubious episcopal appointments, protecting bishops who have covered up or committed abuse, and the pope's use of what some thought was a "stang" for a staff. What do you say to the criticism, that these are too extraneous to the accusation of heresy?

The list of "misdeeds" is cumulative. One or two could be ignored, but this number...? I fail to see how someone who, for example, calls abortion activist (and abortionist) Emma Bonino a "forgotten great" can possibly believe the truth of Catholic teaching (going back to the *Didache*) on such an important matter, involving the deaths of millions by abortion.

What is your response to Jimmy Akin's criticism that none of the signatories are specialists in ecclesiology and that the letter fails to show that Pope Francis obstinately doubts or denies dogmas?

Someone pointed out to me that Catherine of Siena has only an "honorary 'doctorate' of the Church" and that, to the best of our knowledge, the apostles had no degrees at all!

Some of the criticism in this letter—including charges of syncretism, indifferentism, and questionable appointments—has been raised to some extent about Pope St. John Paul II, as well. Are there any parallels here, and should his legacy be given greater scrutiny along these lines?

This is now a merely historical matter. John Paul's theatrical talents, and his comparative indifference to curial reform, have not been helpful. The former encouraged the disastrous practice, which we now see in spades, of assuming that if you want the answer to any question, you go to the pope as a talking oracle. The media took (and takes) advantage of that, often to the detriment of the Church.

Are you concerned that in accusing the pope of heresy, and especially if this accusation goes unheeded, you might be leading others to a sedevacantist position and disunity?

Some may, unfortunately, resort to sedevacantism. That would be sad but cannot be advanced as an excuse for inaction. Francis's election does seem to have some uncanonical features (recognizable in the activities of the "St. Gallen mafia"), but elections in the past have also been dodgy. That is no justification for sedevacantism.

Which period of Church history do the troubles of our own time most remind you of?

At first sight there might seem particular similarities between the present situation and the rebellion of Luther. In both cases we had an overemphasis on a tendentious version of traditional teaching. Luther talked misleadingly about *sola fides* (saved by faith alone)—rather than the traditional *fides caritate formata* (faith expressed through love)—while the present German and Roman theologians seem to deal in *sola misericordia* (saved by mercy alone) without attention to Jesus's call to reform one's ways. But in our present case, a deliberate disregard of the recorded teachings of Jesus over "remarriage" while a spouse is still living implies either that Jesus did not really say what is reported of him or that his teachings have passed their sell-by date. This would accord with some Hegelian account of truth; however, that scenario implies a denial of his teaching authority and thus of his divinity.

Which brings us to the most obvious parallel with the present situation: the Arian conflict of the fourth century. Insofar as current German-Roman theology implies or suggests the diminished authority of Christ, it is Arian, not in the sense of a direct "subordinationism," since now the subordination arises not from dogmatic theologizing but indirectly out of moral theology. Furthermore, while Luther was soon expelled from the Church, in our case, as with the Arians, it is an internal matter: bishop against bishop, bishop against pope (as Liberius was for a while in Arian times). As Newman observed, the world woke up and found itself Arian. What are we going to find when we wake up?

Some noted that the letter was released not only on the traditional feast of St. Catherine of Siena, famous for her criticism of a pope, but also on the (postponed because of Easter) feast of St. George, the pope's name day. Do you see this letter not as a hostile attack on the pope, as many have suggested, but as an act of fraternal charity? If so, do you think that that could have been made clearer in the letter, to avoid such criticism of hostility?

Some will see it as "fraternal charity"; others as an attack on the pope. My own sole concern is to act, after the failure of others to elicit responses from the pope, to help to prevent any further massive confusion among Catholics. The job of a pope is to encourage unity, not to become the leader of a faction.

What other concerns do you have that prompted you to sign the letter?

I am concerned above all else to expose double-talk, which is how the present pope has been evading charges of heresy. Uttering ambiguous and/or contradictory remarks on important issues must ultimately be viewed as a planned attempt to change doctrine by stealth. Had such ambiguities/contradictions been occasional, they could be attributed—in accord with the canonical principle of benignity—to "mere" muddle. Prolonged ambiguity on this scale requires that a sadder conclusion be drawn: that there is a design to achieve by stealth what could not be achieved by openly and unambiguously un-Catholic decrees.

I end with a quotation from the greatest of Catholic doctors: "We tend culpably to evade our responsibility when we ought to instruct and admonish [evildoers], sometimes even with sharp reproof and censure, either because the task is irksome or because we are afraid of giving offense, or it may be that we shrink from incurring their enmity, for fear that they may hinder and harm us in worldly matters, in respect either of what we eagerly seek to attain, or of what we weakly dread to lose" (Augustine, *City of God*, I.9).

21

Why I Signed the Open Letter Accusing Pope Francis of Heresy[1]

DR PETER A. KWASNIEWSKI

CATHOLICS WHO HAVE BEEN PAYING ANY attention to the words and deeds of Pope Francis over the past six years are aware of the mounting problems of this pontificate. It is hardly necessary to go into details here; those who care to know either already know or can easily find out. The Open Letter to the Bishops of the Catholic Church that was signed by a number of scholars and pastors, including me, furnishes clear evidence of heretical (not just erroneous) statements that may be found in the approved writings of Pope Francis, as well as evidence—in the form of repeated acts and omissions of governance—that he is fully aware of what he is promoting.

Many people have been asking: What's the good of taking a step like this? Will it not further polarize the situation? Will it not offer excuses to the Bergoglio party to intensify their confinement and persecution of Catholics? Is it not overwhelmingly likely to be ignored? Can anyone do anything about a wayward pope—mustn't we just wait until God sorts it out for us? And besides, aren't the signatories lacking in sufficient theological qualifications?

This document is good and valuable for three reasons.

First, it documents instances of heresy that cannot be denied, taking the textual evidence together with supportive actions. The truths at stake are not minor ones, nor are they hazy, debatable propositions. We are dealing with truths taught directly by Sacred Scripture, confirmed in *de fide* pronouncements of popes and ecumenical councils. Saying so may not help take away the scales from the eyes of those who refuse to see, but it seems like the next logical step after the *Correctio filialis*, which had argued that Francis supported or did not oppose heresies. This new document goes a step further: he is "guilty of the crime of heresy" and can be

---

[1] Published as "Catholic philosopher: Why I signed the open letter accusing Pope Francis of heresy," *LifeSiteNews*, May 2, 2019.

judged as such by those who are competent to govern the Church of God, namely, the bishops, who are not vicars of the pope, but true and proper rulers of their own portion of the Lord's flock, with (as Vatican II teaches) a responsibility for the well-being of the entire Church.

Second, it is a step that we are taking for the historical record, for posterity. It will be seen clearly that Catholics in our day were willing to call out not only sins of clerical abuse, but also sins of heresy, which are worse in kind because they more directly oppose God Himself. The worst sin, teaches St. Thomas Aquinas, is that of infidelity or lack of faith; and this lack of faith is manifested in a denial of any truth of the Catholic Faith.

Third, it is a step we take before God, as a testimony of our conscience. Perhaps there are others who can sleep like babes without raising a voice of protest to the autodemolition of the Faith and the misleading of countless souls; who see what the pope is saying and doing, but who shrug their shoulders and figure that it won't redound to lasting damage. I am not such a person, and I think the same is true of the other signatories.

Those who have dismissed this document (and other documents like it, such as the *Correctio filialis*) have shown an astonishing lack of seriousness in engaging the numerous grave issues the authors have brought forward, preferring to take refuge in comforting sentiments of papal allegiance and boilerplate generalities recycled from scholastic manuals. In this way, although they believe themselves to be putting out fires and calming irrational fears, they are in reality paving a broad path for the triumph of the modernist-narcissist despots who currently dominate high ecclesiastical offices. In the end, those who clear away obstacles from the progress of despots will be no less liable to judgment. Battles are won not by generals only, nor by soldiers only, but also by the cowardice, obliviousness, and complicity of their opponents.

The signatories have been taunted as "lacking in sufficient theological qualifications." This is false, since several signatories are highly trained theologians of good reputation. But it is also somewhat irrelevant. One does not have to be a medical doctor in order to recognize a compound fracture or a bleeding jugular vein; in like manner, one does not have to be a professional theologian to know when basic truths of the Faith are being contradicted outright. The fool who says "there is no God" is a fool and can be identified as such. Similarly, the man, no matter who he is, who says that those who are already married but living *more uxorio* with another partner may be admitted to Holy Communion is denying truths of natural law, divine law, and ecclesiastical law, established in both Scripture and Tradition. Such a one is dissenting from the truth of the Faith.

As the last three pages of the Letter explain — and I highly recommend that those who have not yet read the Letter to the end read these last pages without delay — a broad consensus of Catholic authors allow for the possibility of the pope being confronted by his fellow bishops and then, if he persists in heresy, to be declared deposed in the sight of God and the faithful by the very fact of his having fallen into heresy. As canonists teach, a heretical pope is deposed through the simple fact of being recognized as a public formal heretic by those who are competent *ex officio* to identify and proscribe heresy. This position was argued without demur by the recent and well-respected ecclesiologist Cardinal Charles Journet:

> The action of the Church [towards the wayward pope] is simply declarative; she manifests that there is an incorrigible sin of heresy: then the authoritative action of God is exerted to sever the papacy from a subject who, persisting in heresy after admonition, becomes, according to Divine Law, unfit to hold the office any longer. So by virtue of the Scripture, the Church designates and God deposes. (*L'Église du Verbe incarné. Essai de théologie spéculative*, 2:266)

Finally, the despairing and cynical comment: "What good is it?" deserves a response.

The fact that God is ultimately in charge of everything has never been taken as an excuse to do nothing. Would the Roman world have been converted to Christianity if no one had ever preached? Would the pagan world have come to know Christ without missionaries journeying to the ends of the earth? The quietists among us would seem to think that it is enough to "leave it to God." Let *Him* preach if He wants the adherence of the world to His message; let *Him* journey to its remotest corners if He seeks their salvation. Obviously that view is absurd. We must do all that we can for Christ and the Church, in whatever station we occupy, knowing that God will bless with fruitfulness any efforts that derive from His inspiration, correspond to His will, and promote His glory.

The question "What good is it?" sounds eerily like Pontius Pilate's "What is truth?" True Christians have never been proportionalists or consequentialists. Their motto has been Mother Teresa's famous remark: "God does not ask us to be successful; He asks us to be faithful." Even so, we find supernatural success only among those who are faithful. David did not take a look at Goliath and say: "Forget about it; outclassed by a few cubits." He whipped out his little slingshot, picked up the five smooth stones, and let fly into the Philistine's forehead. The giant was ultimately despatched with his own sword, to show that evil consumes itself—but only when human valor is at hand.

From those to whom more has been given, more will be expected. If we have been given to see a wolf in shepherd's clothing, we are expected to do something about it. We will cry "Wolf!" to the vulnerable sheep, and pray fervently that other true shepherds will come to the rescue, in ways that we cannot. If they fail to do so, that is not our problem, but theirs to answer for.

22

Why I Didn't Sign the Open Letter Accusing the Pope of Heresy[1]

FR BRIAN W. HARRISON, O.S.

I WAS ONE OF THOSE INVITED TO SIGN THIS new statement publicly denouncing Pope Francis to the world's Catholic bishops as a formal heretic. However, I declined, because I don't think you can judge someone—especially a pope!—to be a formal (i.e., pertinacious or obstinate) heretic without first hearing what he might have to say in his self-defense. That's an elementary question of due process! The Church (via the Congregation for the Doctrine of the Faith) always does this with any theologian suspected of heresy, so how much more should the pope himself be given a chance to explain himself before being publicly branded as formally heretical!

To be a formal heretic, you not only have to hold a certain opinion that contradicts what the Church has declared is revealed truth, to be believed with Divine and Catholic Faith; you also have to know that the Church condemns your opinion for that reason, and yet still stubbornly refuse to admit your mistake and retract it.

Pope Francis has indeed said some things I believe to be heretical, and I suspect he may well be formally heretical, but I would not be so rash to assert that he definitely is, much less publicly. The authors of this document just presume that he knows these statements/actions are heretical because he's had a good theological education. But the Vatican never acts on a mere presumption with a suspect theologian. They always listen to what he/she might have to say in reply. That can often clarify certain things.

First, there's the question of fact: Did the person really say or do what he was reported to have said or done? Francis was reported in 2017 as saying to a newspaper interviewer that nobody goes to Hell, and that those who die with unrepented mortal sin are just annihilated. The Vatican neither confirmed nor denied the substantial

---

[1] Published at *The Wanderer*, May 3, 2019.

truth of this report—only that these were not the exact words of the pope. Of course, if it was false, there was a grave duty for the pope to tell the whole Church and the world immediately that he never said this and doesn't believe it. So you have to suspect strongly that he said and holds this heretical doctrine of annihilation. But a suspicion isn't enough to convict anyone of heresy—or of any other offense or crime, for that matter.

Next, supposing the heretical statement has in fact been reported accurately, there's still the question of whether the person expressed his/her own thinking accurately on that occasion. We often say things hurriedly, which means we sometimes say things we don't really mean, or that we wouldn't have said if we'd stopped to think a little more carefully. And Francis is notorious for frequently speaking "off the cuff" even in his homilies. (E.g., I strongly suspect that when he in effect denied the dogma of the Immaculate Conception in a homily of a few months ago, saying "no one, not even Joseph or Mary, is born as a saint," he just didn't carefully think through the implications of his words. I'd be willing to bet that if he were asked, "Holy Father, in saying Our Lady wasn't 'born as a saint,' did you mean to teach that she was born with the stain of original sin like all the rest of us, even though the Church has solemnly defined that she was conceived without sin?," he would probably reply that, No, he didn't mean to say that; rather, what he had in mind was something to the effect that Our Lady faced temptations, as even Jesus did in the desert, and sometimes had to struggle against them. In other words, holiness wasn't just a "cakewalk" for her, and in some ways she grew spiritually throughout her life as she matured as a human being and as a believer.)

Next, even when conversation or correspondence between Church authority and the person suspected of heresy establishes that he/she was accurately reported and really did mean what he/she said, the question still remains as to whether the controversial opinion in question really does contradict something the Church has taught as revealed truth, to be believed with Divine and Catholic Faith. When it's a question of a truth that has never been solemnly defined by a pope or council, but has been taught rather by the universal and ordinary Magisterium, establishing the heretical character of its denial can often be tricky. It might be the kind of error which is only proximate to heresy, or one on which different approved theologians have different opinions regarding its degree of gravity.

Finally, supposing all this has been clarified and a really heretical opinion has been shown to have been taught by the suspect, it has to be seen if he/she still remains stubborn and obstinately refuses to retract and correct said opinion. Only if he/she remains obstinate can the Church then declare him/her to be a formal heretic, earning the canonical penalty for this crime. But with Pope Francis, certainly, no such critical discussion has ever taken place with regard to nearly all the shocking statements that he has made. So I think it's very premature, unfair, and disrespectful to the Supreme Pontiff for these nineteen Catholic scholars to jump straight to the conclusion that he's a formal heretic, and urge the world's bishops to treat him as such.

Indeed, in the one instance I know of when Pope Francis replied personally to a direct question about the meaning of one of his shocking statements — the Abu Dhabi document saying that the existing pluralism and diversity of religions is something "willed by God" — he eventually explained it to Bishop Schneider, face to face, in a doctrinally acceptable way that I had already suspected was what he quite likely meant.[2] Yet the scholars who are now calling Francis a formal heretic ignore this clarification given by the pope himself, and include the Abu Dhabi statement as the last of the seven heresies of which they say Francis is formally guilty.

Is that fair?

---

2 See first the article I wrote for *The Wanderer* (February 14, 2019, p. 5A) immediately after the Abu Dhabi statement came out; then look at the *LifeSiteNews* report (March 7, 2019) about what the pope told Bishop Schneider some weeks later about what he meant to say.

23

Theologian Responds to Criticisms of Letter to Bishops Concerning Heresies of Pope Francis[1]

DR JOHN R.T. LAMONT

IN THE RECENT "OPEN LETTER TO THE BISHops of the Catholic Church," a number of Catholics accused Pope Francis of the canonical delict of heresy and asked the bishops to take action to address this situation. The letter has not surprisingly been the target of a number of criticisms.

These criticisms are not always easy for the general Catholic reader to assess, because the document is long, precisely rather than accessibly formulated, and sometimes technical in its language. These features of the letter are required by its purpose; a legal accusation against a pope must be careful, detailed, and sometimes technical in its facts and arguments. It may, therefore, be helpful to offer an explanation of some of the aspects of the letter that its critics have attacked. As a signatory of the letter, and a theologian who had some input into its drafting, I offer the remarks below with the intention of indicating why these criticisms lack any force.

WHAT IS THE CRIME THAT POPE FRANCIS IS BEING ACCUSED OF?

The letter accuses Pope Francis of having committed the canonical delict of heresy. A delict is a crime in canon law; an external violation of a law or precept that is gravely imputable by reason of malice or negligence. The canonical delict of heresy is not the same as the personal sin of heresy. A Catholic can commit the personal sin of heresy by deliberate, obstinate, but purely internal doubt or disbelief of a truth of the Catholic faith. If this doubt or disbelief is never shown by word or deed, the canonical crime of heresy is not committed. Canon law deals only with sins that are outwardly

---

[1] Published at *LifeSiteNews*, May 24, 2019.

manifested and that can be established through publicly available evidence. The canonical crime of heresy requires public manifestation of doubt or disbelief in some teaching of the Catholic faith, in circumstances where it is clear that the person expressing disbelief knows that the teaching he is rejecting is a part of the Catholic faith. One can reasonably suppose that when the canonical crime of heresy is committed, the personal sin of heresy has been committed as well; but a condemnation for the canonical crime of heresy is not in itself a condemnation for the personal sin of heresy. The two offenses are dealt with by different tribunals. The canonical crime of heresy is judged by a canonical, non-sacramental act of ecclesiastical authority; the personal sin of heresy is judged (if it is ever presented for judgment) in the sacrament of penance.

ARE THE VIEWS THAT POPE FRANCIS IS ACCUSED OF MAINTAINING REALLY HERESIES?

Some opponents of the letter have denied that the positions listed as heretical are in fact heresies. The letter's explanation of the canonical crime of heresy contains an account of the nature of heresy:

> For the canonical delict of heresy to be committed, two things must occur: the person in question must doubt or deny, by public words and/or actions, some divinely revealed truth of the Catholic faith that must be believed with the assent of divine and Catholic faith; and this doubt or denial must be pertinacious, that is, it must be made with the knowledge that the truth being doubted or denied has been taught by the Catholic Church as a divinely revealed truth which must be believed with the assent of faith, and the doubt or denial must be persistent.

According to this passage, a heresy is a proposition that contradicts a truth that is divinely revealed, and that has been taught by the Catholic Church as a divinely revealed truth that must be believed with the assent of faith. This is the generally agreed definition of a heresy that is offered by canonists and theologians. The question is thus whether the propositions that are given in the letter as heresies satisfy this definition. These propositions are the following:

I. A justified person has not the strength with God's grace to carry out the objective demands of the divine law, as though any of the commandments of God are impossible for the justified; or as meaning that God's grace, when it produces justification in an individual, does not invariably and of its nature produce conversion from all serious sin, or is not sufficient for conversion from all serious sin.

II. A Christian believer can have full knowledge of a divine law and voluntarily choose to break it in a serious matter, but not be in a state of mortal sin as a result of this action.

III. A person is able, while he obeys a divine prohibition, to sin against God by that very act of obedience.

IV. Conscience can truly and rightly judge that sexual acts between persons who have contracted a civil marriage with each other, although one or both of them is sacramentally married to another person, can sometimes be morally right, or requested or even commanded by God.

V. It is false that the only sexual acts that are good of their kind and morally licit are acts between husband and wife.

VI. Moral principles and moral truths contained in divine revelation and in the natural law do not include negative prohibitions that absolutely forbid particular kinds of action, inasmuch as these are always gravely unlawful on account of their object.

VII. God not only permits, but positively wills, the pluralism and diversity of religions, both Christian and non-Christian.

The only proposition in these seven that involves some sort of theological sophistication is the first one. It describes theses concerning justification that were asserted by some Protestants. It was condemned as heretical by the Council of Trent. All of the other six propositions concern fundamental aspects of Christian life and morals. They are denials of things that most adult Catholics need to explicitly grasp, believe, and practice in order to lead Christian lives and get to heaven.

So the fact that these propositions are false, and that they must be held to be false by Catholics, cannot reasonably be denied. The question is whether they are not just false, but heretical; that is, whether their contradictories are truths that have been taught by the Church as being divinely revealed, and as calling for the assent of faith. For each one of these propositions, the open letter provides texts of the divinely revealed Scriptures that condemn them, and magisterial texts that condemn them as contrary to the faith. They thus satisfy the conditions for being heresies.

There is a further point to be made about the Catholic teachings denied by I to VII. They are so fundamental that if you accept IV and V, you will be left with no true moral principles about sexual behavior at all; if you accept VI, you will be left with no true moral principles, full stop; if you accept I, II, and III, you will be left with no connection between acting rightly and eternal salvation; and if you accept VII, you will be left with no true worship of God and no true religion. So if the claims described by the letter as heresies are accepted, every other teaching of divine revelation will be either falsified, or made pointless and powerless to redeem. As a result, if we hold that the contradictories of I to VII are not divinely revealed and proposed by the Church for belief, we will have to conclude that what is divinely revealed and taught as such by the Church is, on its own, useless for salvation. But this consequence is absurd.

HAS POPE FRANCIS IN FACT COMMITTED THE CRIME OF HERESY?

The evidence for Pope Francis having maintained the heresies listed above is set out in the letter. It is not a complete description of the evidence for his heresy, and does not claim to be one. It simply claims to be sufficient to establish that he has publicly maintained these heresies. Catholics must judge for themselves in reading the letter whether this evidence is sufficient or not.

To assist Catholics in making this judgment, it can be pointed out that although much of the evidence consists of statements or actions that could individually be given a Catholic interpretation, for each of the numerous pieces of evidence a Catholic interpretation would be strained or improbable to a greater or lesser degree. From this it follows that it is beyond a reasonable doubt that *all* of this evidence *taken together* cannot be given a Catholic interpretation. One should keep in mind a principle of the probability calculus: if the probability of event A is .25 (25%), and the probability of event B is .25 (25%), then the probability of A and B together is .25 multiplied by .25 = .0625 (6.25%). If the probability of event C is .25 (25%), then the probability of A, B, and C together is (.25 times .25 times .25) = .015625 (1.5625%); and so on. So even if there is a 25 percent chance of a given word or action by Pope Francis not being heretical, the probability that three words or actions with this chance of being Catholic will all have an orthodox meaning is 1.5625%. Since he is the pope, we should make every effort to understand the words and actions of Pope Francis in an orthodox sense. But even with the most strained, charitable, and generous interpretation of the words and actions listed in the letter, after a certain point the weight of probability in favor of his being a heretic becomes overwhelming. Only a prior decision never to accept the conclusion that Pope Francis is a heretic can resist this weight of evidence.

We should therefore accept that Pope Francis has publicly and persistently upheld the heresies listed above. It cannot be seriously questioned that Pope Francis knows that these heresies are contrary to the teachings of the Catholic Church. He is the pope. The charism of office given to him as pope has the specific purpose of ensuring that he knows what the Catholic faith contains. He taught Catholic theology for many years, as the letter documents. The heresies are not arcane or remote ones — it is not a question of his advancing the Monothelite heresy, or the Christological positions of Theodore of Mopsuestia. The heresies in question have been at the heart of theological debate—a debate in which he has taken part—for decades.

At this point, the ambiguity of most of Pope Francis's heretical actions can be seen as a strategy rather than an excuse. Pope Francis is following the method of Arius, Nestorius, and other heretics in advancing his heretical views. He expresses himself in a plethora of words, confessing Catholic doctrine and the need for adherence to it in a general way, while undermining or denying it with other, more specific expressions and actions. Thus he will couch his heretical utterances in words which are naturally understood to express heresy, while admitting of an orthodox meaning if they are given a strained and non-natural interpretation. He will allow others to take the lead at times in promoting heresy and show his approval of their views without necessarily endorsing their statements explicitly. These tactical oscillations are a most effective way for him to promote the heresies in which he manifests his belief. If he were to repudiate the Catholic faith in an open and straightforward manner, he would lose the power and the opportunity to exercise influence that stems from his office; his ability to advance his heretical views would be largely eliminated.

IS THE COURSE OF ACTION THAT THE BISHOPS ARE REQUESTED TO TAKE A REASONABLE OR LEGITIMATE ONE?

To address this question, we must specify what exactly is being requested of the bishops. When a crime is committed and then dealt with by the law, three things occur. There is the commission of the offense itself; the judgment that the offender is guilty of the offense; and the punishment imposed for the offense by a legal sentence.

The signatories of the letter are not attempting to pass a judgment or a sentence on the crime of heresy. They are reporting to the responsible authorities—the bishops of the Catholic Church—that a crime has been committed. They assert that there is sufficient evidence to show that the crime has been committed, but they are not asking these authorities to rule that Pope Francis is a heretic on the basis of this evidence alone, strong as it is. They ask the bishops to take further steps to determine with complete certainty whether or not Pope Francis is a heretic. This determination, following the canonical tradition of the Church, is to be done by the bishops formally requesting Pope Francis three times to abjure these heresies and withdraw the words and actions that indicate his belief in them.

If these steps are taken and Pope Francis persists in his heresy, the bishops will then have both the right and the duty to judge that Pope Francis is a heretic, and to announce their judgment to the faithful. This judgment would not be an exercise of superior jurisdiction, but the recognition of a public fact. The role of this judgment would be to give the public fact a juridical force; it would not be an exercise of authority that would create this fact or its consequences.

The sentencing for this crime can be done only by Pope Francis's superior. This superior is God. We cannot expect a direct divine intervention to carry out this sentencing, but we do not need such an intervention, because God has made His will concerning heretics known to us through His law. The divine law concerning heretics is given in the Holy Scriptures: "But though we, or an angel from heaven, preach a gospel to you besides that which we have preached to you, let him be anathema. As we said before, so now I say again: If anyone preach to you a gospel, besides that which you have received, let him be anathema" (Gal 1:8–9). "A man that is a heretic, after the first and second admonition, avoid: knowing that he that is such an one, is subverted, and sinneth, being condemned by his own judgment" (Tit 3:10–11). A heretic is thus separated from the Church, and *a fortiori* from any office in the Church. If Pope Francis chooses to persist in heresy in such as way as to make this persistence a juridical fact, through the decree of the divine law he separates himself from the Church and from the papal office. The letter is not intended to bring about this lamentable result. It is issued in the hope that the legal punishment that is due for the crime of Pope Francis will exercise its medicinal purpose of withdrawing a sinner from his sin through anticipation, rather than through actual infliction.

24

Is Pope Francis a Heretic?[1]

FR THOMAS WEINANDY, O.F.M. CAP.

NINETEEN THEOLOGIANS AND ACADEMICS recently released a letter to all Catholic bishops throughout the world, accusing Pope Francis of being a heretic and urging the bishops to take action, even canonical, in order to rectify this dire state of affairs.

There is no need to repeat the concerns expressed within that letter. They are well known, and have already been critiqued by many theologians, academics, priests, bishops, and even cardinals. What makes this open letter unique is its formal charge of heresy. This is an extreme position to take, as the authors themselves admit, but they believe that, given the critical situation that has developed in the Church, such a position is merited.

Undoubtedly, many of the statements Pope Francis has made are ambiguous, and therefore troubling—for they can be interpreted in both an orthodox and a heterodox manner. What is most disconcerting is that erroneous interpretations, those contrary to the Church's doctrinal and moral tradition, are often propounded by bishops and cardinals—those who want to implement misguided teaching within their dioceses and urge that they become the norm within their national jurisdictions.

In view of this, many of the concerns addressed in the open letter are valid, some more than others. However, the fact that Pope Francis articulates these positions in an ambiguous manner makes it almost impossible to accuse him rightly of heresy. (This is, in a sense, a saving grace.) Those who interpret his ambiguous teaching in a manner not in keeping with the Catholic faith may be heretical, but the pope is not, even if the pope appears to give silent approval to their erroneous interpretations. Thus, I think that the letter's authors have gone beyond what is objectively warranted. Yes, there are grave concerns and important doctrinal and moral issues at stake—ultimately the truth of the gospel itself.

---

1 Published at *First Things* web exclusives, May 7, 2019.

But the manner in which they were presented, the conclusions drawn, and the actions proposed will not help rectify the present crisis within the Church. Actually, the open letter makes it more difficult for others to appropriately critique the ongoing doctrinal and moral chaos within the Church, a disorder that will continue to intensify as this pontificate progresses.

Why do I say that? First, let me speak of the bishops to whom the letter is addressed. Yes, it is disheartening, especially for the laity, that the bishops do not speak out more forthrightly in defense of the Church's authentic doctrinal and moral tradition. Yet, if bishops do maintain the integrity of the gospel within their own dioceses, this in itself is a major achievement, given today's oppressive and fearful ecclesial atmosphere. Their silence, then, may be a guarded expression of their displeasure with the present pontificate.

Nonetheless, because the open letter is extreme in its appraisal and intemperate in its approach, more than likely it will make it more difficult for bishops, and even cardinals, to address present concerns. While they may be displeased, and even annoyed, with Pope Francis's ambiguity and the manner in which he conducts his Petrine ministry, yet they rightly are nowhere near judging Francis a heretic and will remain silent about the letter. Moreover, if a bishop does attempt to comment on the present serious concerns, he will now be labeled as one who agrees with and promotes the "extremist" cause of the letter's authors. Thus, this letter, while it may have been well-intentioned, has made it even more difficult for bishops to address the crisis within today's Church.

Second, if we focus on whether or not the pope is heretical, the more pressing issue confronting the Church is pushed to the background: the doctrinal and moral chaos this pontificate has nurtured, regarding such issues as the sacramental nature of marriage, the intrinsic evil of homosexual acts, and whether Judaism and Christianity are merely two of the many religions that God willed. This doctrinal and moral chaos is where the real battle must be fought. There are many theologians and academics, as well as many priests and laity, who have taken up this good fight of faith. They have done so through articles in academic journals and more serious periodicals, blogs, and websites. They have also done so in academic conferences and general public forums. The fruit is an ever-growing community of ardent believers, from all walks of life, academic backgrounds, and ecclesial vocations — united in the truth that there is but one, holy, catholic, and apostolic Church, which cannot be destroyed or superseded by a new church, even if such is the aim of some in high ecclesial positions.

Yet the open letter throws this work of the Spirit into jeopardy, for now those who have undertaken this battle will more easily be tarred with the brush of extremism. The wisdom, the forthrightness, the prudence, the respect, and the love with which they have worked to proclaim and defend the truth of the gospel could easily be lost in the clamor for anathematizing the pope or the ensuing uproar in his defense. What are lost are measured, intelligent, nuanced responses to the present ecclesial crisis and a rational Spirit-filled fortitude to bring truth to light in the midst of deceitful darkness.

So, while the open letter hopes to be a clarion call to rectify a grievous situation within the Church, it may have unintentionally contributed to making the victory of faith even more difficult.

25

"We uphold the dignity of the Apostolic See by desiring that its occupant be free of heresy"[1]

INTERVIEW WITH DR CLAUDIO PIERANTONI ON THE *OPEN LETTER*

THE RECENT OPEN LETTER TO ALL CATHOLIC bishops accusing Pope Francis of heresy and urging the world's episcopate to investigate these charges has provoked admiration and opposition among leading Catholics and drawn considerable attention in the secular media. Notable responses to the letter have come from Fr Joseph Fessio, S.J., Fr Brian Harrison, O.S., and Fr Thomas Weinandy, O.F.M. Capuchin.[2] The letter has also left many Catholics with questions: are the signatories accusing Pope Francis of being a formal heretic? Are they contravening canon law? What will the effect be now that the word "heresy" has been used openly in reference to Pope Francis? And why did they not first seek to address their concerns with him privately, before taking this historic step?

LifeSite spoke with Professor Claudio Pierantoni, one of the lay scholars who helped to draft the open letter. Professor Pierantoni, who was born in Rome, is a professor of Medieval Philosophy in the Philosophy Faculty of the University of Chile (Santiago). He has two PhDs: in the History of Christianity and in Philosophy. In this wide-ranging interview, Pierantoni addresses these questions, responds to critics of the open letter, and explains why he believes the Church is now passing through "the most serious crisis not only since the Protestant Reformation, but in all of her history."

---

1 Published by Diane Montagna, "Scholar defends letter accusing Pope of heresy: Church is facing 'most serious crisis' in history," *LifeSiteNews*, May 7, 2019.
2 For Fr Harrison's response, see chapter 22; for Fr Weinandy's, see chapter 24.

Professor Pierantoni, what motivated you to sign the open letter accusing Pope Francis of the crime of heresy and calling the bishops of the Catholic Church to investigate the charges?

Prof. Pierantoni: First, a duty in conscience as a Catholic. As the Letter notes, this act follows the publication of a document on *Amoris Laetitia* (*AL*), signed by forty-five scholars in 2016 that highlighted the serious ambiguity of many passages which, in their most obvious and natural sense, seemed heretical. Then, in 2017, with a larger group of 250 scholars, we published the *Correctio filialis de haeresibus propagatis* (Filial Correction about the Propagation of Heresies), when it was clear from various statements made by the pope that the ambiguous passages of *AL* were certainly to be understood in a heretical sense. Finally, during the last period, the pope's will to impose a certain line of revolutionary change in sexual and matrimonial ethics has been widely confirmed, especially through the appointment of prelates favoring such a revolution to important places of the government in the Church. Therefore, we have now reached the point of affirming the heresy which is appropriate to call "obstinate" or "pertinacious." Hence the need to have recourse to the bishops to remedy this tragic situation for the faith: the situation of a pope who falls into heresy.

Were you also involved in the drafting of the document?

Yes, I was a member of the discussion group from which the final version (laboriously) emerged. The letter was initially written by a single author but was then widely discussed in a small group for about four months, with numerous amendments made.

The summary reads: "The present Open Letter *to the Bishops of the Catholic Church goes a stage further [than the* Filial Correction*] in claiming that Pope Francis is guilty of the crime of heresy." Many Catholics might find this language new or strange. In what sense is heresy a "crime"? And how can the pope be guilty of heresy, given the Lord's promise to always be with His Church?*

A delict (or crime) is an action that undermines the rights of others. The Catholic faithful have the right to have bishops publicly guard and teach the correct doctrine of the Church without ambiguity, change, or novelty. The concept of Tradition, of the *depositum fidei* [deposit of faith], is very precise in the Catholic Church: it is not a generic love of the past or respect for the wisdom of one's forefathers, but a much more specific commitment. Just as in a deposit agreement, the depositary is required to return to the depositor exactly what he received, neither more nor less, so in the Church a bishop must deliver intact to the faithful what he has received as a deposit from the Apostles, who have received it directly from Christ. He has the further duty of ensuring that no one else alters or contaminates it with strange doctrines. This duty belongs most especially to the bishop of Rome, to whom Christ himself gave the primacy in this action of feeding and tending his flock. The words of Jesus Christ to Peter reported by the beloved disciple: "Feed my sheep," and repeated three times (Jn 21:15–19), are inscribed in enormous gold letters along the base of the inner frame of the dome of St. Peter's Basilica. For the pope to fail in this duty is therefore not only "a" crime but the most serious of crimes, because it endangers the salvation of souls. It empties of meaning his very essence as Shepherd, and that is why in doing so he renounces his role as such. The bishops who recognize this fact do not "depose" the pope, because the pope cannot be deposed: they only take note of the fact that the pope has spontaneously renounced his office. In juridical language, we say that the act of the bishops would have a purely declarative nature.

What heresies is Pope Francis accused of in the letter? Which to your mind is the most serious?

There are seven statements contained in the letter: the first six are distilled from passages of *AL* and the famous dispute over Communion for divorced persons who are living together in a new union *more uxorio*. Two roads can be taken to affirm that it is licit to give Communion to this category of people. The first would be to deny the indissolubility of marriage. This road was tried in several studies that preceded and accompanied the two synods on the Family (2014–2015), but it was effectively refuted and this strategy was abandoned. The other road is to state that, while marriage remains indissoluble, there are cases in which sexual relations outside a legitimate marriage would still be lawful.

To sum up, therefore, I would say that the main heresy resides precisely in the doctrine — today called "situation ethics" — which denies that there are acts that by their very nature are intrinsically evil, and therefore cannot in any case be considered lawful. Once this doctrine is accepted, not only is the doctrine of the indissolubility of marriage at risk but the whole of Christian ethics — and not only it, but the whole of natural ethics. In fact, on the basis of this doctrine we could say, for example, that abortion is indeed a crime, but in some cases it is lawful; that the murder of an innocent person is wrong, but not in some cases; that torture is immoral, but in particular circumstances it could be lawful; that active homosexual relationships are sinful, but not in certain cases, and so on. It is therefore a real "atomic bomb," which entirely destroys ethics, as Prof. Josef Seifert fittingly called it in a brief but, it must be said, explosive article.[3]

It is important to underline that the battle against this error (i.e., "situation ethics") was one of the absolute priorities of Pope John Paul II's pontificate. To it he dedicated one of his most important encyclicals, *Veritatis Splendor*. This is why many thousands of the most serious and committed Catholics — and not just a "tiny fringe of extremists" or "ultraconservatives," as some would have us believe — have felt betrayed by this new direction inaugurated by Bergoglio, which threatens to frustrate precisely one of the most important legacies of the saintly Polish pope. That is why Benedict XVI, in the Notes he published just a few weeks ago, also strongly emphasized that this was one of the chief errors of moral theology in the last sixty years. It is certainly a providential coincidence that these Notes came out at almost the same time as our letter.

Many people might wonder what authority a group of clergy and scholars has to accuse the pope — the Vicar of Christ — of heresy. How do you respond?

We do not claim any particular authority, except the theological competence necessary to carry out this study to highlight a factual situation which undermines a fundamental right of all Catholic faithful. The *Code of Canon Law* attributes to all the faithful, in proportion to their competence, the right to speak in so far as they deem it necessary to do so in order to point out a difficulty or problem in the Church.[4] Nor, as some have said (e.g., Fr Thomas

---

3   See Josef Seifert, "Does pure Logic threaten to destroy the entire moral Doctrine of the Catholic Church?," *AEMAET: Wissenschaftliche Zeitschrift für Philosophie und Theologi*e, 6.2 (2017): 2–9.

4   Can. 212 §3 reads: "According to the knowledge, competence, and prestige which they possess, they [the laity] have the right and even at times the duty to manifest to the sacred pastors their opinion on matters which pertain to the good of the Church and to make their opinion

Petri, O. P.), do we run into the prohibition, also recorded in the *Code of Canon Law*, of "mak[ing] recourse against an act of the Roman Pontiff to an ecumenical council or the college of bishops" (can. 1372). In fact, here it is not a matter of making recourse to the bishops to overrule an act of the Pontiff in the governance of the Church as if they were a higher authority, which is what is forbidden by the canon, but of the very serious situation in which one must take note of the fact that the Pontiff himself has fallen into heresy, which is expressly indicated by canonical tradition as one of the three causes of loss of the papal office. As we explain in the appendix on the loss of the papal office, it is not a matter of deposing the pope, but only of declaring that he has spontaneously renounced the papacy through his adherence to heresy. Much less do we contravene Canon 1373, which punishes those who "publicly incite animosities or hatred against the Apostolic See ... because of some act of power or ecclesiastical ministry or provokes subjects to disobey." On the contrary we are upholding the dignity of the Apostolic See by desiring that its occupant be free of heresy.

Are the signatories of the open letter accusing Pope Francis of being a formal heretic? If so, why did you not first present the charges to him privately, giving him a chance to respond (even if a response is unlikely)? Isn't it a part of due process to do so? The Congregation for the Doctrine of the Faith does so with any theologian suspected of heresy, so why shouldn't the pope be given a chance to explain himself?

First of all, I would like to distinguish between the accusation of heresy, and the formal declaration of someone being a heretic by the competent authority. The accusation of being a heretic is one thing, the sentence that formally declares him such is another; the latter is not up to us to issue, but precisely to the bishops, to whom we have addressed the open letter. Now, if we use the term "formal heresy," as distinguished from "material heresy," in the sense that the person upholding it is conscious that it is a proposition opposed to a teaching of the Catholic faith, and does not uphold it out of mere ignorance of the faith, then we claim that we are speaking of "formal" heresy in this sense. However, this must still be distinguished from the situation of a person who has already been admonished by

---

known to the rest of the Christian faithful, without prejudice to the integrity of faith and morals, with reverence toward their pastors, and attentive to common advantage and the dignity of persons."

the competent authority about the incompatibility of his doctrine with the Catholic faith: this has not, of course, yet happened with the pope, as no one with authority has formally admonished him: so, in this sense his position is not that of "formal heresy," and such an admonition is precisely what we are asking of the bishops.

Now, we are presenting these accusations after a great number of warnings have already been presented privately to the pope, many more than would have been sufficient and fair. In fact, this was already done in the theological censures presented to him by a number of us in 2016 (first privately)[5]; then with the *dubia* (also previously presented in private),[6] then with the *Correctio filialis* (2017),[7] which was also put directly into his hands a full month before it was published. But this is only a part of the story. Pope Francis was already warned of these errors by many bishops and cardinals and even lay scholars during the Synods on the family; then, after the drafting of *AL*, by the many corrections that came from the Congregation for the Doctrine of the Faith, which were all rejected. Then by a series of articles, books, and open letters by important authors.[8] Faced with all these warnings, questions, books, articles, letters, and corrections, the pope had all the time and material to reflect and eventually to respond. But instead, he clearly and consciously chose the path of ignoring them altogether. In an answer given during a meeting with the Jesuits last year here in Chile, he stated verbatim regarding these critics that he "does not read them" because he does not find in them "spiritual goodness," and limits himself to "praying for them."[9] It remains to be explained how he knows that the critics do not have spiritual goodness, since he does not read them.

However, for our part we thank him for his prayers, which we reciprocate. But we are sadly forced to record that it is therefore a matter of a voluntary and stubborn closure to listen to these criticisms, which fully justifies our accusation of "fully conscious and pertinacious" heresy, although in the limited sense that can be applied to a person who has not yet been formally admonished, as I explained before. So, as I have already said, this does not mean at all that we

---

5 See the first document in Part II.
6 See Part I.
7 See the second document in Part II.
8 See the list compiled by Maike Hickson in chapter 17.
9 "Pope says he prays for those who call him a heretic," *Catholic News Agency*, February 15, 2018.

claim the authority necessary to issue a sentence and thus formally declare the heresy of any person, and therefore not the pope either; indeed, although it is already obvious in itself, we have taken care to expressly state the contrary. So it isn't at all true—as, for example, Father Brian Harrison said in his recent article (among other inaccuracies)—that we "jump straight to the conclusion that he's a formal heretic, and urge the world's bishops to treat him as such."[10] This is very inaccurate. What we are doing is simply presenting an accusation, accompanied by the evidence that we consider necessary and sufficient: it will then be up to the competent authority, in this case the bishops, to examine the evidence, admonish the pope in an appropriate manner, give him the possibility of a retraction, and only after that, to issue the sentence. And we are not presenting these accusations lightly at all, but, as I have already said, we are doing so after having waited several years in which a long series of prior notices, letters, and corrections have already been presented.

In any case, whether the judgment actually takes place during the pope's lifetime or not, an accusation that is based on a conspicuous series of evidence and testimonies is yet worthy of consideration by any serious person who cares about the good of the Church, beginning with the chief interested party.

What effect do you think it will have now that the word "heresy" has been openly used in reference to Pope Francis? What effect did you anticipate it would have before you decided to sign the open letter?

Well, we had foreseen that quite a few people, even among people who are sympathetic to our views and are, so to say, on our side in this wide controversy, would find this accusation overstated. So, many have argued that this was counterproductive, because it makes our own cause more vulnerable to attack. Many good theologians still argue that Francis's texts, although very problematic, cannot be convicted of heresy because they are too ambiguous.

I challenge this claim. In fact, I maintain that Francis's texts, in particular those contained in *AL* chapter VIII, are tortuous and meandering, but their aim is clear: he wanted to permit irregularly married couples to receive Communion in certain cases. And he officially confirmed his intention with his response to the Argentinian bishops, which he ordered to be included in the *Acta Apostolicae Sedis*. This is an historical fact and, moreover, one that is

---

10 See chapter 22.

in perfect consonance with too many elements in his record to be reasonably called into question.

Now, in order to find a justification for this step, he was bound to affirm a contradiction to Catholic teaching: either to the doctrine of indissolubility of marriage, or to the doctrine that some actions are always and in all cases prohibited, because they are intrinsically evil (*intrinsece mala*). Since he rejected the first path, he was bound to go down the other. It was a logical necessity, and so he ran headlong into a fatal contradiction with the doctrine solemnly confirmed by *Veritatis Splendor*. This is a position expressed with more than sufficient clarity in *AL*, as many theologians have already shown in their analyses of the document. The first six of our propositions are necessarily related to this error. (On the seventh we have already commented.) So, it is wholly incorrect to affirm that our case is "overstated." It is not a rational refutation of our position (which has not been given) but only a psychological fear of the terrible consequences of admitting papal heresy that prevents many good theologians from facing the hard truth.

The signatories allege a link between Pope Francis's rejection of Catholic teaching and the favor he has shown to bishops and other clergy who have either been guilty of sexual sins and crimes or covered them up. Can you give the most striking example?

Probably the most disturbing case is that of Cardinal Óscar Rodríguez Maradiaga. In the letter it is noted, among other things, that "Maradiaga refused to investigate complaints made by 48 out of 180 seminarians about homosexual misbehavior at the Honduras seminary, and attacked the complainants. Pope Francis named Maradiaga as a member and coordinator of the council of nine cardinals that he set up in 2013 to advise him in the government of the universal church." In this single case, the decidedly criminal inclination of a person whom the pope insists on keeping among his closest collaborators is clear.

But, even more than a single person, what's disturbing is the number of prelates who, having concealed or even personally committed serious crimes, have been promoted by the pope to positions of the highest responsibility in the Church. As Archbishop Viganò aptly said, only *one* of these scandalous promotions would suffice to justify the pope's resignation. However, in the case of our letter, we use them mainly as evidence that the pope doesn't seem to consider these shortcomings particularly serious, and only proceeds to necessary censures when he is obliged to do so by circumstances, especially by pressure from civil authorities.

Is the Church in the worst crisis since the Reformation?

I believe that the Church is going through the most serious crisis not only since the Protestant Reformation, but in all of her history. One only need observe that it is the first time in history that a pope is accused of heresy in such a massive way, about a whole series of doctrines as important as these.

As I have already noted in previous talks and interviews, comparisons with the examples of the past, such as that of Pope Liberius, Honorius, or John XXII, don't stand up at all. In the case of Liberius, the issue was a formula of Trinitarian faith that the pope was forced to sign by the pro-Arian imperial party, at a time when the Trinitarian formula itself was not yet definitively established, and therefore there were still many terminological uncertainties. In the case of Honorius, it was a question of a single doctrinal formula on the problem of the two wills of Christ, a problem that was debated at the time and therefore also suffered a margin of terminological uncertainty. In the case of John XXII, it was a question of the denial of the doctrine of the immediate beatific vision of the blessed after death: an important doctrine to be sure, but not as vital and central as the doctrines that we are discussing here.

In the case of Francis, one has the clear impression that he wants to relativize the whole of Catholic doctrine, especially on the issues of marriage and family ethics, as we said, but also on the very important issue of the relationship of Catholicism with other religions, as we state in our seventh proposition. This came to light in the recent Abu Dhabi document, but perhaps even more dramatically, in the continuous affirmation that Catholics should not "proselytize," in the sense that they should not worry in any way about convincing or converting non-Catholics to the true faith. It is a position that, in practice, is very close to religious indifferentism. Many committed Catholics and even outside observers have the impression that the pope — while certainly affirming some Catholic doctrines — deep down isn't really Catholic. It's interesting that Reuters, at the end of its article on our letter, in speaking about this subject, states: "Conservatives say the Roman Catholic Church is the only true one and that members are called to convert others to it." Evidently Reuters doesn't classify Francis as a "conservative," so it agrees with us in saying that the pope rejects this doctrine.

On this topic, too, Father Harrison unjustly accuses us of ignoring the verbal clarification of his statement that the pope gave in a conversation with Bishop Athanasius Schneider, and in a public audience. In fact, in a special note of our letter, which we ask Fr Harrison to read, we make reference to these informal clarifications, and we explain why we consider them to be totally insufficient. I would add to the reasons presented there, that it should already be self-evident that merely verbal clarifications can never be sufficient to eliminate the meaning of a statement present in an official document signed by the pope that is clearly incompatible with the Catholic faith.

Would the signatories consider themselves "in communion with the pope" or are you taking a sedevacantist position?

The answer can be deduced from previous answers. Since we have no authority to formally declare the pope's heresy, of course we cannot declare his loss of office. Besides, we have explicitly excluded the sedevacantist position in the appendix about the loss of papal office.

The open letter was published on the traditional feast of St. Catherine of Siena, and the feast of Pope St. Pius V in the new calendar. What symbolic value do you see in this?

It was an intentional choice to publish the open letter on the feast of St. Catherine of Siena. In fact, the letter was supposed to be published on April 29, then there was a brief delay. But the release still fell on the traditional liturgical feast of the saint, who lived in a time of deep crisis for the Church, as well as schism. A humble virgin, she was not afraid to speak up in order to tell the truth about the urgent reforms that the Church needed. We trust in her intercession to exit from today's crisis, which in my opinion is even more serious and profound. We also trust in the intercession of Pope St. Pius V, who was able to defend the Catholic Church, and the whole of Christian civilization, against the terrible assault from the Turks.

You've issued the open letter to the Bishops of the Catholic Church. What happens next?

It's difficult to say what's going to happen. I personally believe that the Catholic episcopate in general is still far from becoming truly aware of the gravity of the situation. After all, to become aware is also very uncomfortable and even dangerous: it's much more convenient to take a sleeping pill and continue to sleep, dreaming that everything is just fine. Therefore, I believe that this is one step in what is still a long journey. There is still a good deal of work to be done to raise awareness among the hierarchy, so that it can counter the heretical drift which, even if it had already been going on for a long time in the Church, has been accentuated in alarming proportions in the last six years.

I believe it is imperative that the few cardinals and bishops who have woken up to the gravity of the situation, such as Burke, Brandmüller, Eijk, Müller, Sarah, Woelki, Schneider, Chaput, Laun, Viganò, and others, could and should begin to form a network of relationships and communication across the various countries and continents, to begin to raise awareness among the portion of the episcopate that is still healthy and would be ready to work to encourage resistance to the heretical drift that is spreading. This healthy, orthodox part of the episcopate certainly exists, and it's not the tiny minority that some would try to make us believe it is, by taking advantage of the fact that it is less noisy and less scheming, let us say less astute than the heretical faction. The children of darkness are more cunning than the children of light. In short, this orthodox portion of the episcopate needs to come together, to get to know and communicate with one another, to be animated and organized in order to work effectively for a true reform of the Church.

Is there anything you wish to add?

To wrap up, I would like to respond to those critics who now, as with the previous documents we have published, punctually repeat the usual script according to which we are "ultraconservatives," or a "tiny fringe of extremists," as Prof. Massimo Faggioli put it. I'll leave aside (because it's so blatantly obvious to any reader) the fact that it's very convenient to slap a nice prepackaged label on us instead of taking the trouble to refute us, which is a bit more difficult.

I would like to underline two things, which perhaps escape our critics. The first is that they too naively let themselves be fooled by a trivial error of perspective: they are convinced that we are few, because those who dare to come out with a signature are few (although not so few, as the number of signatures has already more than tripled in a few days, today reaching 81). But a look at history is enough to recall that it has always been this way: in the year 360, when it was politically correct to be pro-Arian, how many bishops dared to refuse to sign the pro-Arian formula? Perhaps a dozen. Those who didn't sign it lost their position. Just like now.

Their second and even more serious and fatal mistake is to confuse quantity with quality. Let's go ahead and admit that we are a minority (even if much less sparse than they would have us believe): I say that we are in good company. For example, we are in the company of Josef Seifert, one of the philosophers closest to Pope John Paul II in the fight against situation ethics, who in more recent interventions has expressed himself in ways very similar to our document, and for this reason has been harshly punished; he has now signed the petition in favor of our letter, and has publicly stated he agrees with us on the bulk of our letter; Robert Spaemann, who called *Amoris Laetitia* "chaos elevated to a system"; Cardinals Burke, Caffarra, Brandmüller and Meisner, the authors of the *dubia*; Cardinal Müller, the man chosen by Benedict XVI to lead the Congregation for the Doctrine of the Faith, who recently stated that a bishop who changes the discipline of the Church to grant the Holy Eucharist to persons not in full communion with the Church "is a heretic and a schismatic"; with Cardinal Sarah, who already in 2014 said that dividing doctrine from the discipline of the Eucharist "is a dangerous schizophrenic disease"; finally, with the Pope Emeritus himself, who in his recently published Notes, as I have already said, explained how situation ethics has been the most serious error in moral theology in the last 60 years. And the list could go on. In short, with a "small minority" of this caliber, we feel we are in good company.

In conclusion, I would like to recall that, beyond the impact on the episcopate—for which we hope but which will certainly still require a wait—we are convinced that the clear denunciation of the errors being spread today is a strong reason for hope for many thousands of Catholic faithful who are deeply concerned about a situation that many describe not only as heresy and schism, but even as apostasy, who hope and pray in silence that Christ will come soon to redeem his Church. This document seeks to give voice to so many who have no voice, to send the message that, even when heresy and corruption seem to prevail, the Holy Spirit always raises up an immune response, antibodies, often in humble people who do not occupy positions of power, but who, even against human predictions, preserve the faith and commit themselves to fighting the good fight to which we are all called.

26

When Creeping Normalcy Bias Protects a Chaotic Pope[1]

DR PETER A. KWASNIEWSKI

REACTIONS TO THE OPEN LETTER ACCUSING Pope Francis of holding seven heretical propositions—a letter that now bears the signatures of 81 clergy, religious, and scholars—have ranged from strong support[2] to sympathetic critiques[3] to undisguised hostility.[4]

The authors in the "sympathetic critiques" category make some good points worthy of further consideration. I am all the more inclined to listen to them because they agree, right off, that Pope Francis is a colossal problem, that his pontificate has left a wreckage of errors and scandals, and that we are in full meltdown mode. In other words, they have eyes to see and ears to hear, so their disagreements with the Open Letter have more to do with the nature of the arguments to be made, the forum in which to make them, and the ramifications for future steps. Such critics are not in denial.

---

1 Published at *OnePeterFive*, May 8, 2019.
2 See John Zmirak, "Catholic Scholars Accuse Pope Francis of Heresy for Promoting Lax Sexual Ethics and Acclaiming Islam," *The Stream*, May 2, 2019; interview with Charles Coulombe, Tumblar House, May 2, 2019, available on YouTube; Louie Verrecchio, "Jimmy Akin v. Open Letter: A way forward," *aka Catholic*, May 6, 2019.
3 See Phil Lawler, "Is the Pope a heretic? The danger of asking the wrong question," *Catholic Culture*, May 3, 2019; Edward Feser, "Some comments on the open letter," May 6, 2019 (cf. chapter 19); Thomas G. Weinandy, O. F. M. Cap., "Is Pope Francis a Heretic?," *First Things*, May 7, 2019 (see chapter 24); Joseph Shaw, "Can Pope Francis really be accused of committing heresy?," *LifeSiteNews*, May 7, 2019.
4 See Jimmy Akin, "On Charging a Pope with Heresy," *National Catholic Register*, May 2, 2019; David Armstrong, "Reactionary Signees of Easter 'Heresy' Letter (13 of 19), *Biblical Evidence for Catholicism*, May 6, 2019; Ed Condon, "Analysis: Serious and unserious allegations of papal heresy," *Catholic News Agency*, May 2, 2019. For a general roundup of reactions, see Dorothy Cummings McLean, "Leading Catholics react to Open Letter accusing Pope Francis of heresy," *LifeSiteNews*, May 6, 2019.

Our disagreements are like those among the Allied Powers as to the best strategy for resisting the Axis.

They complain, incidentally, that we have made the work of orthodox Catholics and especially bishops harder by supercharging the atmosphere, but the irony is that we have already helped them to be seen as *moderates* in the conversation, when what they are saying would have sounded extreme a year ago. "We don't hold that the pope is a formal heretic. We just hold that he has introduced massive confusion, has led bishops and episcopal conferences widely astray, refuses to do his duty as vicar of Christ by upholding traditional doctrine, fails to respond to reasonable petitions, and threatens to drive the Church into schism. That's all."

Meanwhile, one of the signatories, Professor Claudio Pierantoni, has entered the ring with a formidable defense of the Open Letter.[5] Pierantoni brings clarity without embellishment. I highly recommend this interview as a substantive response to our critics.

However, what has really surprised me in the past week — though perhaps it should not have — is the extent of the insensibility that has descended upon the so-called "conservatives" in the mainstream.[6] Much criticism I have read serves only to confirm the gravity of the situation the letter addresses. The general lack of alarm at the seven manifestly heretical propositions, or the contortionist glosses of papal texts to exonerate their author from said heresies, in spite of all words and deeds converging upon them, proves at least this much: Francis's battle of theological attrition has been successful beyond the St. Gallen Mafia's wildest dreams and is poised for new conquests.

Just a few short years ago, everyone who considered himself a conservative was up in arms about *Amoris Laetitia* and skeptical of the elaborate rabbinical apparatus that attempted to square it with the Church's perennial teaching. Now it's as if they've given up; they shrug their shoulders and say, "I'm sure it'll all be fine someday. It'll come out in the wash. Put credentialed theologians and canonists on the case, and everything Francis says and does can be justified." We strain the canonical gnats and swallow the doctrinal camel.

---

5   The preceding item in this volume.
6   See my article "Why Conservatism Is Part of the Problem, Not Part of the Solution," *OnePeterFive*, September 25, 2018.

It seems that many simply do not wish to confront the weighty and ever mounting evidence of the pope's errors and reprehensible actions, of which the letter provided only a sample sufficient to make the case.[7] This is not to say that Francis altogether lacks true words and admirable actions. It would be nearly impossible for someone to say false things or do bad things all the time. That is beside the point. It is enough for a pope to assert a doctrinal error only *once* or *twice* in a pontifical document, or to perform really bad acts (or omissions) of governance a *few* times, in order to merit rebuke from the College of Cardinals or the body of bishops, sharers in the same apostolic ministry. With Francis, however, there is a lengthy catalogue, with no sign of coming to an end. If this does not galvanize the conservatives into concerted action, one has to wonder — what *would*? Do they have a line in the sand? Or has papal loyalism dethroned faith and neutered reason?

Things that made everyone anxious just a few years ago are now taken in stride: today we all live in a post-Bergoglian Catholic Church, where you can make exceptions about formerly exceptionless moral norms, give Communion to those living in adultery, and say God wills many religions as He wills two sexes, or — a point not addressed in the Open Letter — dismiss the witness of Scripture, Tradition, and Magisterium (trifecta!) on the death penalty. The frogs have grown accustomed to floating in ever hotter water and have decided to call it a spa.

It may therefore be concluded that the pope's strategy of dismantling the Catholic Faith plank by plank in slow motion is working. He ignored the *dubia* on *Amoris Laetitia* because he knew he could not answer them in an orthodox sense without undermining his entire double-synod Kasperian project. He has ignored over thirty attempts to reach out to him, whether by the mighty or by the lowly, by small groups of reputable scholars or by petitions with hundreds of thousands of signatures.[8] The Open Letter simply draws the final conclusions.

I admire and appreciate the work being done by our assiduous Catholic apologists, who beaver away, day after day, to refute Protestant Fundamentalists, militant atheists, homosexual and feminist

---

7   See my article "Six years in, Francis has shown himself to be the most troubling pope in history," *LifeSiteNews*, March 19, 2019.
8   See Maike Hickson, "Before Pope Francis Was Accused of Heresy, Catholics Reached Out to Him Numerous Times" (chapter 17 above).

agitators, and other such opponents. But to think the current crisis of Pope Francis can be contained by means of a few pat "Catholic Answers" is like trying to extinguish the flames of Notre Dame with a squirt gun.

Frankly, it is a world-class scandal for a pope even to *seem* to be lending support to only *one* heretical proposition, let alone showing textual and behavioral adherence to (at least) seven such propositions. It is, moreover, no defense of the pope to say his statements are "ambiguous" and can be taken several different ways. Even if the sum total of evidence did not adequately resolve our doubts, such vagueness about grave matters would be no less reprehensible in a pope than outright error. The pope is given to the Church to *clarify* Christ's teaching, not to obscure it; to instruct in the truth, not to make room for fashionable theories that leave the faithful confused as to what they should believe and how they should live.

Let us not forget that Pope St. Leo II condemned his predecessor Pope Honorius for *negligence* in upholding the orthodox faith. A teacher wrote to me:

> If my students don't understand something I've taught, if they have a concern about the content (or their parents do), or think I'm contradicting myself, I stop and explain it clearly, and I apologize for causing any confusion. I've never read Francis say anything like that, ever. There's an old story of a man who never lied. A stranger to the village came to meet him and question him. He realized he never lied because all he did was talk in circles.

This is why people—accurately—call the Argentinean pontiff a Peronist.[9] He speaks out of both sides of his mouth so that the progressives will get the encouragement they need to carry on, while the ultramontanists can hear a comforting reassurance to go back to sleep.

The open letter has stirred conservatives to a frenzy because they can't bear the thought of a heretic on the throne of Peter. Well, as parents say to children, "guess again." The third Council of Constantinople judged Honorius after his death to have "confirmed the wicked dogmas" of Monothelitism and anathematized

---

9   See Steve Skojec, "The Perón Rule," *OnePeterFive*, June 22, 2018.

him. Outside infallible *ex cathedra* pronouncements, it *is* possible for a pope to deviate from the Faith. It *can* happen. And Francis runs circles around Honorius. Francis is an unprecedented trial for the Church of God.

A friend of mine wrote me these sobering words, with which I entirely agree:

> Paragraph 675 of the *Catechism* speaks of a final trial of the Church. We are entering some sort of arrest, scourging, mocking, and crucifixion of the Church that is going to be very difficult for people who love the Church to understand. Just as Christ's disciples had their faith shaken — "this can't be happening if he really is the Messiah" — so it is happening now for the sons and daughters of the Church: "this can't be happening if the Church really is infallible and indefectible and the gates of hell will not prevail." We are headed for a vast purification that will leave much of the Catholic landscape utterly unrecognizable, washing away the petrified filth of vice and error and restoring her to her lost beauty. But it is going to be very difficult to make sense of it as it happens, and, as Our Lord ominously warns, many will lose their faith.

In this modern-day Passion of the Church of Christ — replete with temptations all the more dangerous for their more than human subtlety, cloaked in garments of sophistry and pushed by figures of authority — let us hold fast to the Catholic Faith as taught through the ages, and pray for perseverance more fervently than ever. In this way, Our Lord's haunting question "When the Son of man comes, will he find faith on earth?" (Lk 18:8) will be able to be answered: Yes.

27

Cardinal Müller: Open Letter Accusing Pope of Heresy Deserves a Response[1]

DR MAIKE HICKSON

CARDINAL GERHARD MÜLLER, FORMER PREfect of the Congregation for the Doctrine of the Faith, said that while he believes Pope Francis is not a heretic, the April 30 Open Letter from prominent clergymen and scholars accusing the pope of committing heresy, nevertheless, deserves a "response" from Rome.

The German prelate said in an interview with *Die Tagespost*'s Regina Einig that the authors of the letter are "renowned theologians." Therefore, he says, "it would be important that the Holy Father makes the Congregation for the Faith issue a response, and not the Secretary of State or any of his friendly journalists or theologians." Cardinal Müller said that the accusation of heresy that has now been addressed to Pope Francis in the Open Letter to Bishops "is the worst thing" that "can happen" in the Catholic Church, since "the pope is, as bishop of Rome, the successor of Saint Peter, upon whom Our Lord has built His Church." "As much as one can understand the concerns of these theologians [who criticize the pope], one also has to say that one has to choose the right means for the justified aim of a greater clarity of some statements of Pope Francis," he commented later in the interview.

Responding to the argument that there have been in the past some popes who taught, in individual points, heresy, the German cardinal stated: "Here [with the Open Letter], the accusation goes much deeper, that is to say, that the whole edifice of the Catholic Faith in its principles of knowledge and in some of its essential contents is being uprooted. I do not agree with this." For Cardinal Müller, the "problems arise rather, in my view, with the help

---

1 Published by Maike Hickson as "Vatican's former doctrine chief: open letter accusing pope of heresy deserves 'response,'" *LifeSiteNews*, May 16, 2019.

of a wrong approach [according to which] the Church is said to have been left behind, and [consequently] the Faith is in need of a modernization so that the contradiction in moral questions with regard to the leading forces of the Western world is not so glaring." "In the camp of the 'friends' of the pope," the prelate continued, "one mixes up the Faith with a neo-marxist, neo-liberal ideology." Catholics are left to wonder, however, why Pope Francis chooses such friends in the first place.

The prelate called upon Pope Francis for help to clear up the problems: "Here, it is time that Pope Francis speaks a clear word for the sake of the unity of all Catholics in the revealed Faith. Not a blind obedience toward a command of the party line of the moment is asked, but trust in the pope and the bishops who themselves also know of the limits and characteristics of ecclesial authority."

"A teaching is not true—nor is a Catholic called to obey blindly—just because a bishop gives a command (simply out of his own formal authority), but because the instructions of the Church authorities are rooted in Holy Scripture, Tradition, and in the defined doctrinal teaching of the Church." As an example, Cardinal Müller mentioned here Communion for Protestant spouses of Catholics, as it has been introduced last year by many German bishops. Müller states: "The command of a bishop to give Holy Communion to non-Catholic faithful is against the Faith and may not be obeyed. The sanctions that he [the bishop] would order because of this [disobedience] are invalid and need to be lifted by the pope and his tribunals."

Cardinal Müller outlined the threat facing the Church: "The Church indeed finds herself inwardly and outwardly in one of the gravest crises of her whole history. She will not continue to exist when she is being turned into a religious-political NGO and when the teaching on faith and morals, as it has been revealed to us by Christ, is being relativized or fully abandoned." The German prelate also strongly criticized the newly promoted principle of "synodality" when he says: "We will soon not recognize the Church anymore, when the adaptation to the decline of morality is being presented as a synodal process. Only she will not be different; she will cease to exist—at least in those regions where false prophets are setting the tone." Cardinal Müller may have been alluding to the "synodal path" as it has been launched by the German bishops this March, during which matters such as celibacy and the Church's sexual morality are under scrutiny.

At another point in the interview, the Cardinal referred to the German bishops—or, more specifically, to Cardinal Reinhard Marx—when he commented: "It cannot be that, in passing, a counselor [of the pope] can extract from the pope the concession that each bishop decides that Christians who are not in full communion with the Catholic Church—except in danger of death and in the presence of required spiritual preconditions—may receive Holy Communion." The prelate insists that "the individual bishop cannot rescind the binding doctrinal teaching, case by case; he can only determine whether the conditions are met."

Cardinal Müller also said in the interview that while he has "defended" Pope Francis's Apostolic Exhortation on Marriage and the Family, *Amoris Laetitia*, he nevertheless considers "some reformulations of the Church's teaching to be in need of clarification." "I have also, after my time as the Prefect of the Congregation for the Doctrine of the Faith, defended *Amoris Laetitia*," he said, adding: "I welcome [the fact] that the pope approaches also Catholics in irregular marital relationships in a pastoral manner, but I consider some reformulations of the Church's teaching to be in need of clarification." Further attempting to explain the nature of Pope Francis's documents, he said: "It is often with his documents that those people who prepare them might be his confidants, but they do not have the expertise either by virtue of their office or theologically, and they burden themselves with a grave guilt by causing irritations which very much damage the pope and the papacy." In a striking sentence, Cardinal Müller commented: "It is a sign of intellectual and moral decay when those who confess the Catholic Faith are being accused—by those who disfigure it [the Faith]—of disobedience toward the pope and the bishops and of instigation of strife and schism."

Finally, the interviewer Regina Einig raised the question of Pope Francis's Abu Dhabi statement, which contains the phrase that the "diversity of religions" is "willed by God." Although Cardinal Müller supports Pope Francis's work for a "peaceful living together" among people with different religions, he states: "It must, however, be clear that we agree with the Muslims *de facto* in the faith in one single God. But, with the supernatural Faith, which exists due to revelation and grace, we Christians also believe in the one and true God in the name of the Father, and the Son, and the Holy Ghost." Here, the Holy Trinity is not just an "accidental addition to the general monotheism," the prelate adds, "but is the substance of the salvific Faith of the Christians in the One God and Creator of the world and of man." Religion itself as a "moral virtue," he explains, is part of "human nature that is oriented toward the adoration of God. But the concrete myths and their rites of the historic 'religions' are not willed by the God of Abraham and by the God and Father of Jesus Christ as an expression of His self-revelation for the salvation of man, but, at the most, only as a preparation for Christ's gospel," he added.

The German prelate added: "A better theological preparation surely would have avoided many misunderstandings here." Such a declaration of agreement with "a non-Catholic authority" is also "not part of the Magisterium's mandate to faithfully preserve the Catholic Faith."

"A Catholic professor who academically examines this joint declaration [of Abu Dhabi] and who criticizes it—justly or unjustly—may by no means be censured. That would be a stretching of the Church's authority and a glaring example of clerical abuse of power," he said.

28

Pope Francis and Schism[1]

FR THOMAS G. WEINANDY, O.F.M. CAP.

THE CHURCH, IN HER LONG HISTORY, HAS never been confronted with the situation like the one in which she now finds herself. Pope Francis recently spoke of a possible schism within the Church, a schism that does not frighten him. We have had many schisms in the past, he says, and there will be schisms in the future. So, there is nothing to fear in the present. However, it is the nature of the present possible schism that is new, and this unprecedented new schism *is* frightening.

One cannot help but think that Francis is referring to members of the Church in the United States. Francis receives, from America, his most theologically challenging and pastorally concerned criticism, which centers on a questionable remaking of the faith and of the Church. Such censure, it is believed by Francis's cohort, originates from within a conservative intellectual elite who are politically motivated, and many of whom are wealthy. Francis thinks that they are unwilling to change, and so refuse to accept the new work of the Spirit in our day. Ultimately, one discerns that he believes his critics are psychologically and emotionally impaired, and so must be dealt with gently (though that gentleness is yet to be experienced by those who fall under his vindictive abuse). He himself has called those who oppose him many insulting names.

What Francis does not realize (and his close associates fail to grasp) is that the overwhelming majority of his American critics would never initiate a schism. They recognize that he is the pope and thus the successor of Peter, and that to remain within the Catholic Church is to remain faithful to the pope, even if it entails being critical of the pope in one's faithfulness to him.

Some may wish that an actual schism will take place in America in order to get rid of the obdurate conservative element and so demonstrate that they were not really Catholic all along. But that is not going to happen, because those critical bishops, priests, theologians,

---

[1] Published at *The Catholic Thing*, October 8, 2019.

commentators, and laity (more laity than Francis will admit) know that what they believe and uphold is in accord with Scripture, the Church councils, the ever-living magisterium, and the saints.

As has been often noted, Pope Francis and his cohort never engage in theological dialogue, despite their constant claim that such dialogue is necessary. The reason is that they know they cannot win on that front. Thus, they are forced to resort to name-calling, psychological intimidation, and sheer will-to-power.

Now, as many commentators have already pointed out, the German church is more likely to go into schism. The German bishops are proposing a two-year "binding" synod that, if what is proposed is enacted, would introduce beliefs and practices contrary to the universal tradition of the Church.

I believe, however, that such a German schism will not formally happen either, for two reasons. First, many within the German hierarchy know that by becoming schismatic they would lose their Catholic voice and identity. This they cannot afford. They need to be in fellowship with Pope Francis, for he is the very one who has fostered a notion of synodality that they are now attempting to implement. He, therefore, is their ultimate protector. Second, while Pope Francis may stop them from doing something egregiously contrary to the Church's teaching, he will allow them to do things that are ambiguously contrary, for such ambiguous teaching and pastoral practice would be in accord with Francis's own. It is in this that the Church finds herself in a situation that she never expected.

It's important to bear in mind that the German situation must be viewed within a broader context: the theological ambiguity within *Amoris Laetitia*; the not-so-subtle advancing of the homosexual agenda; the "re-foundation" of the (Roman) John Paul II Institute on Marriage and Family, i.e., the undermining of the Church's consistent teaching on moral and sacramental absolutes, especially with regard to the indissolubility of marriage, homosexuality, contraception, and abortion. Similarly, there is the Abu Dhabi statement, which directly contradicts the will of the Father and so undermines the primacy of Jesus Christ His Son as the definitive Lord and universal Savior. Moreover, the present Amazon Synod is teeming with participants sympathetic to and supportive of all of the above. One must likewise take into account the many theologically dubious cardinals, bishops, priests, and theologians whom Francis supports and promotes to high ecclesial positions.

With all of this in mind, we perceive a situation, ever-growing in intensity, in which, on the one hand, a majority of the world's faithful—clergy and laity alike—are loyal and faithful to the pope, for he is their pontiff, while critical of his pontificate, and, on the other hand, a large contingent of the world's faithful—clergy and laity alike—enthusiastically support Francis precisely because he allows and fosters their ambiguous teaching and ecclesial practice. What the Church will end up with, then, is a pope who is the pope of the Catholic Church and, simultaneously, the *de facto* leader, for all practical purposes, of a schismatic church. Because he is the head of both, the appearance of one church remains, while in fact there are two.

The only phrase that I can find to describe this situation is "internal papal schism," for the pope, even as pope, will effectively be the leader of a segment of the Church that through its doctrine, moral teaching, and ecclesial structure, is for all practical purposes schismatic. This is the real schism that is in our midst and must be faced, but I do not believe Pope Francis is in any way afraid of this schism. As long as he is in control, he will, I fear, welcome it, for he sees the schismatic element as the new "paradigm" for the future Church.

Thus, in fear and trembling, we need to pray that Jesus, as the head of His body, the Church, will deliver us from this trial. Then again, He may want us to endure it, for it may be that only by enduring it can the Church be freed from all the sin and corruption that now lies within her, and be made holy and pure.

On a more hopeful note, I believe it will be the laity who bring about the needed purification. Pope Francis has himself stated that this is the age of the laity. Lay people see themselves as helpless, having no ecclesial power. Yet if the laity raise their voices, they will be heard. More specifically, I believe it will depend mostly on faithful and courageous Catholic women. They are the living icons of the Church, the bride of Christ, and they, in union with Mary, the Mother of God and the Mother of the Church, will birth anew, in the Holy Spirit, a holy Body of Christ.

29

The SSPX, the Open Letter, and the Heresies of Pope Francis[1]

DR JOHN R.T. LAMONT

ARCHBISHOP MARCEL LEFEBVRE DISTINguished himself during and after the Second Vatican Council by his public combat against the modernist heresies of the day, and by his willingness to publicly oppose the reigning popes when he considered that they were tolerating or even fostering these heresies. This opposition culminated in his ordination of four bishops in 1988 in defiance of the will of Pope John Paul II, an action that led to him dying excommunicate.

One would therefore expect that the priestly fraternity that he founded and that claims to carry on his mission would follow his example of resistance when confronted by the overtly heretical behavior of the current pontiff. The Society of St. Pius X ought to be at the forefront of opposition to Pope Francis's attacks on the Faith and the Church. This expectation has been disappointed — a development that is not the least of the unpleasant surprises of this pontificate. The Society has not been vocal or active in opposing these attacks. The important opposition to Pope Francis has come from clerics and laity outside of the Society.

In reaction to the recent publication of the Open Letter to the Bishops of the Catholic Church, the Society has taken another step away from combating the heresies of Pope Francis. This Open Letter accused Pope Francis of the canonical crime of heresy and asked the bishops of the Catholic Church to admonish him for this crime. If he failed to abjure these heresies after being asked to do so on three occasions, it further requested that the bishops declare that he had forfeited the papal office on account of his heresy. The General House of the Society of Saint Pius X issued a statement in response to this letter, condemning it in strong terms: "This Open Letter is a waste of time — an action producing little effect, the fruit

---

[1] Published at *OnePeterFive*, October 23, 2019.

of a legitimate indignation but which falls into excess." Here we have not only a failure to oppose Pope Francis's promotion of heresy, but an attack on those who do oppose him. As a signatory of the Open Letter, I think it necessary to address this attack.

The statement of the General House does not give reasons for rejecting the content of the Open Letter. It offers a criticism of the approach of the Letter:

> We risk being captivated by the present evil, forgetting that it has roots, that it is a logical result of a tainted process at its origin. Like a pendulum, some believe they can magnify the recent past to better denounce the present, including counting on the magisterium of the popes of the Council—from Paul VI to Benedict XVI—to oppose Francis. This is the position of many conservatives, who forget that Pope Francis is only drawing out the consequences of the teachings of the Council and his predecessors.

This criticism does not have much weight. The letter is specifically aimed at addressing the actions of Pope Francis. It is not pertinent to object that it does not consider the faults of his predecessors or the historical and ideological roots of his deviations. It is not entirely accurate to raise this objection, either; the Open Letter was presented as a continuation of a process that began with a letter sent to the cardinals and patriarchs of the Church assigning theological censures to certain propositions of the Apostolic Exhortation *Amoris Laetitia* and that continued with a filial correction sent to Pope Francis himself. This filial correction identified the modernist heresy as a source of Pope Francis's aberrations and gave a detailed exposition and condemnation of this heresy.

Moreover, even a cursory investigation into the signatories of these documents will reveal that many of them have written extensively on the evils of modernism, the Novus Ordo, and the Second Vatican Council and have criticized Popes John XXIII, Paul VI, John Paul II, and Benedict XVI for words and actions that are harmful to the faith. Many of the leading critics of these evils can be found among the signatories. Indeed, this was presented as a reason for dismissing these documents when they were made public. The Society's characterization of the signatories of these documents as "conservatives" in the sense given above is absurd.

The statement of the General House further criticizes the initiative of the Open Letter:

> [W]e have to question what results are expected from such an action. Is this way of doing things prudent? Does it have a chance to succeed? Let's ask about the recipients. Who are they? What formation have they received? What theology has been taught to them? How were they chosen? Given the way in which the incriminating texts have been received by the various episcopates in the world, it is highly probable, even certain, that the vast majority of bishops will not react.

But what answers could Archbishop Lefebvre have given to these questions when he set up the SSPX? What answers, indeed, could the SSPX give to these questions today, if it were asked how likely it is that the bishops of the world will consider and accept any of the positions that the Society exists to uphold?

An attempt to substantiate this rejection of the Open Letter has been made by Fr Jean-Michel Gleize, FSSPX in two articles in the May 2019 issue of the traditionalist monthly *Courrier de Rome* ("Si Papa" and "Fidelis servus et prudens"). Fr Gleize is the professor of ecclesiology at the Society's seminary in École, and he took part in the Society's doctrinal discussions with the Congregation for the Doctrine of the Faith. We may take it that his arguments offer the best case that can be made by the SSPX against the Open Letter, and that their contents are found acceptable by the leadership of the Society. He offers two lines of criticism. In one article, he attacks the canonical basis of the Open Letter, and in another, he criticizes the prudential wisdom of the initiative.

CANONICAL OBJECTIONS TO THE OPEN LETTER

Before considering Fr Gleize's canonical arguments, we should clarify the question at stake. The Open Letter states that it is accusing Pope Francis of the canonical crime of heresy. This expression is used in order to prevent misunderstanding of the accusation against the pope. The term "heresy" is used to refer to the personal sin of heresy as well as to the public crime of heresy. The personal sin of heresy is a sin against the theological virtue of faith. It occurs when a person rejects the faith, by doubting or disbelieving a proposition he knows to be taught by the Catholic Church as being a divinely revealed truth contained in the deposit of faith. No public manifestation of this disbelief is necessary in order to commit the personal sin of heresy. An inner refusal to believe is sufficient. The public crime of heresy, on the other hand, involves a pertinacious public doubt or denial of such a divinely revealed truth. Doubt or denial of a divinely revealed truth is pertinacious when there are publicly available facts that establish that the person doubting or denying the truth has been presented with the fact that it is taught by the Catholic Church as divinely revealed.

The canon law of the Church punishes the public crime of heresy. Hence, this public crime is rightly described as a canonical crime. However, it is not constituted as a crime by the law of the Church or defined by the law of the Church. It can be compared to murder in the civil law, as opposed to tax evasion in the civil law. The nature of tax evasion, and its character as a crime, are both defined by the civil law. We could imagine a society where there were no taxes (perhaps the state would function by demanding military and labour service from its citizens, not monetary payments). In such a society, there would be no such thing as tax evasion, and there could be no crime of tax evasion. Murder, however, is identified and punished as a crime by the civil law, but it is not made a crime or defined in its nature as a crime by the civil law. It is a crime prior to its condemnation by the civil law, which only recognizes it as a crime and specifies the legal treatment it receives.

Heresy is like murder in this respect. Its nature and character as a crime are specified by the divine law; ecclesiastical law simply recognizes it as a crime and specifies the means of identifying, judging, and punishing it. The public crime of heresy can be taken to indicate the personal sin of heresy, but it is a crime not just because it indicates the existence of this personal sin. Its criminal nature goes farther. It is an attack on the Church and the faith of Catholics, as well as an individual sin against God.

Since this attack is a public and deliberate rejection of the faith of the Church, the person who commits it voluntarily separates himself from the Church. This separation happens not because the Church inflicts it as a punishment for the crime. It is an intrinsic consequence of the crime of heresy in itself. "Not every sin, however grave it may be, is such as of its own nature to sever a man from the Body of the Church, *as does schism or heresy or apostasy*" (Pius XII, *Mystici Corporis* 23). The penal sanctions for heresy inflicted by canon law recognize and enforce this separation, rather than causing it.

Fr Gleize's criticism of the content of the Open Letter is directed at its assertion that the canon law of the Church supports the view that a pope who is guilty of heresy must lose the papal office. He does not deny that there is a theological consensus in favor of this view, nor does he deny the truth of the view itself. He simply rejects the claim that this consensus has any canonical force and asserts that the view is no more than a theological opinion.

There is an important inconsistency in his characterization of the position of the Open Letter. In some passages, he describes the letter as maintaining that a pope can be deposed for heresy ("l'hypothèse théologique qui voudrait légitimer la déposition du Pape tombé dans l'hérésie"). In other passages, he describes the letter as simply asserting that a pope who is guilty of heresy must lose the papal office ("un pape coupable d'hérésie et qui s'obstine dans ses vues hérétiques ne peut continuer d'être Pape"). These positions are quite different. There are three views that have been advanced on how a pope loses the papal office as a result of heresy. The conciliarist view holds that a heretical pope must be deposed by an ecumenical council that exercises a superior jurisdiction over him. The view of St. Robert Bellarmine is that a manifestly heretical pope loses the papacy *ipso facto*, with no need or possibility for an intervention of the Church. The view of Cajetan and John of St. Thomas is that the Church must act in order for a heretical pope to fall from the papacy.

The conciliarist position has been condemned by the Church. No choice has been made by the Church concerning the positions of Bellarmine and Cajetan, both of which are supported by reputable Catholic scholars up to the present day. The Open Letter rejects the conciliarist view, but it does not take a position on the choice between Cajetan and Bellarmine. It states:

> The Church does not have jurisdiction over the pope, and hence the Church cannot remove a pope from office by an exercise of superior authority, even for the crime of heresy.... There are some lesser differences of opinion between Catholic theologians concerning the measures that the Church must take in dealing with a heretical pope. The school of Cajetan and John of St. Thomas asserts that in order for the papal office to be lost, the Church, after ascertaining and pronouncing

that the pope is a heretic, must also command the faithful to avoid him for his heresy. The school of St. Robert Bellarmine does not reject the step of commanding the faithful to avoid the pope as a heretic, but it does not consider it a necessary precondition for the pope's losing office for heresy. Both these schools have adherents, up to and including the present day. We do not take a position on these disputed questions, whose resolution is a matter for the bishops of the Church.

The letter limits itself to maintaining the general view, common to both Cajetan and Bellarmine, that a pope who pertinaciously denies a truth of the Faith must lose the papal office. There is no insuperable opposition between these two views when it comes to the practical steps that must be taken in order for a heretical pope to fall from the papacy. The position of Cajetan holds that certain measures are necessary in order for this to happen; the position of Bellarmine states that these steps are not necessary but accepts that they are permissible. The practical recommendations of the Open Letter are acceptable to both positions. Fr Gleize's references to the Open Letter as calling for the deposition of the pope are thus inaccurate.

Fr Gleize offers two lines of argument that attempt to refute the position of the Open Letter concerning the canonical basis for the deposition of a pope. In the first line of argument, he appeals to Fr Claeys Bouuaert's article "Déposition" in Raoul Naz's *Dictionnaire de droit canonique*. This article, he points out, states that "the question of the deposition of a pope does not arise in canon law." He quotes Fr Bouuaert's article in more detail on this issue:

> Let us sum up, by way of conclusion, the explanation that the best theologians and canonists have given for this difficulty… There can be no judgment and deposition of a pope in the strict and proper sense of these words. The vicar of Jesus Christ is not subject to any human jurisdiction. God alone is his direct and immediate judge. If, therefore, some ancient conciliar or doctrinal texts seem to admit that a pope can be deposed, the meaning of their assertions must be properly distinguished and rectified. On the assumption (a most improbable one) that a pope should have fallen into public and formal heresy, he would be deprived of his

papal office not by a human judgment, but by his own action, since formal adherence to heresy would exclude him from the Church.[2]

Fr Gleize presents this article as supporting the conclusion that the only canonical principle that is relevant to the question of a heretical pope is the one stated in canon 1556 of the 1917 *Code* and canon 1404 of the 1983 *Code*, "Prima sedes a nemine judicatur," "the Apostolic See is judged by no one." The view that a heretical pope must lose the papal office he qualifies as a mere theological opinion that has no canonical weight. It is a mystery how Fr Gleize draws this conclusion from the article of Fr Bouuaert. The passage from the article cited above is a straightforward assertion of the position of St. Robert Bellarmine concerning the situation of a heretical pope, and it says the pope loses his office if he is a heretic. This assertion is not qualified as an opinion, but given as a statement of fact about canon law.

In addition to this appeal to the authority of Fr Bouuaert, Fr Gleize offers arguments of his own against the Open Letter's claim that the canonical tradition of the Church holds that a heretical pope must lose the papal office. He points out that the Open Letter cites a text from the *Decretals* of Gratian in support of its claim. The *Decretals* of Gratian is a collection of canonical texts from the twelfth century that was later incorporated into the *Corpus iuris canonici*, the collection of legislative texts that served as the basis for the Latin Church's canon law until the promulgation of the first *Code of Canon Law* in 1917. The text in question states that the pope can be judged by no one unless he is found to have deviated from the Faith ("Hujus culpas redarguere præsumit mortalium nullus, quia cunctos ipse judicaturus a nemine est judicandus, nisi

---

[2] "Il ne peut être question de jugement et de déposition d'un Pape dans le sens propre et strict des mots. Le vicaire de Jésus Christ n'est soumis à aucune juridiction humaine. Son juge direct et immédiat est Dieu seul. Si donc d'anciens textes conciliaires ou doctrinaux semblent admettre que le pape puisse être déposé, ils sont sujets à distinction et rectification. Dans l'hypothèse, invraisemblable d'ailleurs, où le Pape tomberait dans une hérésie publique et formelle, il ne serait pas privé de sa charge par un jugement des hommes, mais de par son propre fait, puisque l'adhésion formelle à une hérésie l'exclurait du sein de l'Église." Fr Clayes Bouuaert, 'Déposition,' in Raoul Naz, ed., *Dictionnaire de droit canonique*, vol. IV: Condition-Droits acquis (Paris: Letouzey et Ané, 1949), col. 1159.

deprehendatur a fide devius": dist. XL, C. 6). Fr Gleize asserts that this text has no authority on two grounds: i) the *Decretals* of Gratian are a private collection rather than an official text of the Church and ii) the entire *Corpus iuris canonici*, including this text, was in any case suppressed with the promulgation of the 1917 *Code of Canon Law*, unless its contents were explicitly or implicitly included in that code or were statements of divine positive law or natural law.

Fr Gleize's first argument for rejecting the content of this text of the *Decretals* is clearly invalid. From the premise that not all texts in the *Decretals* of Gratian have legal force, it does not follow that no text in the *Decretals* states a law of the Church. This line of argument would provide a basis for rejecting the legal principle that the Apostolic See is judged by no one, since that principle is stated in the *Decretals*, and is indeed stated in the very text from the *Decretals* that Fr Gleize objects to.

Fr Gleize's second argument begs the question. It assumes that the content of this text from Gratian is not based on divine positive law or natural law. But the canonists and theologians who have cited this text in support of the claim that a heretical pope must lose office have maintained that this claim is based on divine positive law and even on natural law. St. Robert Bellarmine makes this point clearly, in arguing for his thesis that a heretical pope must fall from the papacy:

> There is no basis for that which some respond to this: that these Fathers based themselves on ancient law, while nowadays, by decree of the Council of Constance, they alone lose their jurisdiction who are excommunicated by name or who assault clerics. This argument, I say, has no value at all, for those Fathers, in affirming that heretics lose jurisdiction, did not cite any human law, which furthermore perhaps did not exist in relation to the matter, but argued on the basis of the very nature of heresy. The Council of Constance deals only with the excommunicated, that is, those who have lost jurisdiction by sentence of the Church, while heretics already before being excommunicated are outside the Church and deprived of all jurisdiction. For they have already been condemned by their own sentence, as the Apostle teaches.[3]

---

3   *De Romano Pontifice*, lib. II, cap. 30.

John of St. Thomas appeals to the natural law to support the claim that a heretical pope can lose his office for heresy:

> In addition, as the heretic is an enemy of the Church, natural law provides protection against such a pope according to the rules of self-defense, because she can defend herself against an enemy, as is a heretical pope; therefore, she can act (in justice) against him.[4]

The argument from divine positive law is based on the following Scriptural texts:

> "And we charge you, brethren, in the name of our Lord Jesus Christ, that you withdraw yourselves from every brother walking disorderly and not according to the tradition which they have received of us." (2 Thess 3:6)

> "If any man come to you and bring not this doctrine, receive him not into the house nor say to him: God speed you." (2 Jn 1:10)

> "A man that is a heretic, after the first and second admonition, avoid: knowing that he, that is such an one, is subverted, and sinneth, being condemned by his own judgment." (Tit 3:10–11)

> "But though we, or an angel from heaven, preach a gospel to you besides that which we have preached to you, let him be anathema. As we said before, so now I say again: If any one preach to you a gospel, besides that which you have received, let him be anathema." (Gal 1:8–9)

These scriptural arguments are supported by magisterial teachings. The content of the text of Gratian is supported by the teaching of Gregory the Great, *Moralia* XXV, c. 16; the allocution of Pope Hadrian II to the Roman Council in 869, which was incorporated into the acts of the Fourth Council of Constantinople (869–870); and the teaching of Pope Innocent III, who asserted that only for heresy could he be judged by the Church ("propter solum peccatum quod in fide committitur possem ab Ecclesia judicari"). The text from Gratian is usually cited by canonists and theologians simply as expressing the conclusion established by these

---

4 *In Secunda Secundae*, q. 1, a. 7, disp. II, a. III.

arguments from Scripture and magisterial teaching. This text is seen as deriving from and expressing the contents of divine positive law and Church teaching, rather than as the origin of the legal principle that a heretical pope must lose the papacy.

The justification given by theologians and canonists for the text in Gratian entails that Fr Gleize is wrong in supposing that this text can have been abrogated by the 1917 or 1983 codes of canon law. The 1917 *Code* states that it does not abrogate earlier laws derived from natural law or divine positive law.[5] It also states that if there is a doubt about whether an older law differs from the new code, the old law is not to be rejected.[6] The 1983 Code states that "insofar as they repeat former law, the canons of this Code must be assessed also in accord with canonical tradition" (can. 6 §2). The 1983 *Code* does not change any canons of the 1917 *Code* that are pertinent to the issue of a heretical pope, so the content of the 1983 *Code* in relation to this issue is the same as the content of the 1917 *Code*.

In earlier writings on the question of a heretical pope,[7] Fr Gleize has argued that these scriptural passages do not require that a heretical pope lose the papacy. He claims that they simply require that a heretical pope be avoided, and that this can be done while the pope in question retains the papal office. But this argument is absurd. The pope is the head of the Church, and the Church cannot avoid her head. Nor can a person who has been anathematized by the Church retain the papal office, or any office in the Church.

Fr Gleize's arguments against the consensus of canonists and theologians thus lack any force. His own view on the canonical situation with respect to a heretical pope is not tenable. He asserts that the only law relevant to this situation is the traditional principle asserted in canon 1556 of the 1917 *Code* and canon 1404 of the 1983 *Code*, "the Apostolic See is judged by no one." But if this claim is to be used to support his position concerning a heretical pope, we

---

5   Can. 6 §6: "Si qua ex ceteris disciplinaribus legibus, quae usque adhuc viguerunt, nec explicite nec implicite in Codice contineatur, ea vim omnem amisisse dicenda est, nisi in probatis liturgicis libris reperiatur, aut lex sit iuris divini sive positivi sive naturalis."
6   Can. 6 §4: "In dubio num aliquod canonum praescriptum cum veteri iure discrepet, a veteri iure non est recedendum."
7   "Le pape qui tombe dans l'hérésie perd-il l'investiture dans le Primat?," *Courrier de Rome*, no. 595, January 2017. This can be found at laportelatine.org/publications/presse/courrier_de_rome/2017/1701cdr595.pdf.

must refrain from asking what canon 1404 means and how it is to be interpreted. We cannot ask how the occupant of the Apostolic See is determined, and in particular, we cannot ask if heresy does or does not lead to the loss of the papal office. However, it is obvious that these questions must be asked if we are to know how to obey the canon. If we do ask them, we find that the answer offered by canonists is the one given in the authoritative *New Commentary on the Code of Canon Law*:

> "Canon 1404—The First See is judged by no one."
>
> Canon 1404 is not a statement about the personal impeccability or inerrancy of the Holy Father. Should, indeed, the pope fall into heresy, it is understood that he would lose his office. To fall from Peter's faith is to fall from his chair.[8]

The same answer is given by all commentators on the 1917 *Code* concerning canon 1557 §1.

Fr Gleize's position betrays a misunderstanding of the nature of the 1917 and 1983 codes. The structure of these codes is influenced by the European codes of civil law—the Napoleonic Code and the later codes that were inspired by it. The codification of canon law produced a result that was much smaller and more organized than the previous mass of legislation in the *Corpus iuris canonici*. This brevity and organization is not achieved without a cost. The cost is that the laws in such a code are generally not self-explanatory, and indeed often cannot be understood without reference to a mass of legal material that they necessarily presume. This material includes the definitions of standard terms, the history of previous legislation, magisterial teaching concerning the content of the laws, and the consensus of canonists about the scope and meaning of the laws. The dependence of the 1917 and 1983 codes on this material is acknowledged in the codes themselves, as the references above indicate. Such material is not made up of theological opinions independent of the law itself, to be accepted or rejected according to the judgment one forms of the strength of the theological case made. They are an essential part of the law. When this material agrees on an interpretation of the law, that interpretation is what

---

8 *New Commentary on the Code of Canon Law*, Beal, Coriden, and Green, 1618.

Catholics should take the law to mean. They are not free to reject it. But in the case of a heretical pope, this agreement exists. It asserts that a heretical pope cannot retain the papal office. Fr Gleize is wrong in dismissing this agreement as a theological opinion that he is free to reject. It is the law of the Church.

Fr Gleize's dismissal of this law is mysterious in light of the position taken on this question by other authorities of the SSPX. In 2015, John Salza and Robert Siscoe published the book *True or False Pope? Refuting Sedevacantism and Other Modern Errors*. This book was published by STAS Editions, the publishing arm of the SSPX's St. Thomas Aquinas Seminary in Winona, Minnesota. The book provides a good overview of the theological debates concerning heretical popes and is worth reading and even purchasing. Salza and Siscoe describe the positions of Cajetan, Bellarmine, Suárez, and John of St. Thomas on the situation of a heretical pope and conclude that John of St. Thomas advances the correct view. The book has a laudatory foreword by Bishop Bernard Fellay, then superior general of the SSPX, who stated: "We thus pray that *True or False Pope?* finds its way to many Catholics of good will." It receives enthusiastic endorsements from other high-ranking priests and scholars of the SSPX:

> "It will give light to all its readers." — Fr François Laisney, SSPX, former district superior, USA
>
> "This clear exposé [sic] of Catholic doctrine will nourish the faith of all Catholics of good will." — Fr Steven Reuter, SSPX, professor, St. Thomas Aquinas Seminary, Winona
>
> "Siscoe and Salza communicate to their readers another great benefit; they patiently and clearly present the constant teaching of the Church on her own nature." — Fr Paul Robinson, SSPX, professor of dogmatic theology, Holy Cross Seminary, Australia

One would not want to calumniate these clerics by accusing them of agreeing with John of St. Thomas when they are opposing sedevacantism but dismissing his position as unfounded when it comes to accusing Pope Francis of heresy. One must therefore count them as agreeing with the position of the Open Letter on this topic and rejecting the view of Fr Gleize.

Bishop Fellay's support of the position of the Open Letter has not been limited to his endorsement of Salza's and Siscoe's book. He also signed the *Correctio filialis* addressed to Pope Francis, which reproached the pope for upholding heresy and asked him to repudiate his heretical words and deeds.

It is true that Bishop Fellay is no longer the superior general of the SSPX. The character of the new leadership of the Society may give a clue to the position that the SSPX has taken toward the Open Letter. The current superior general of the Society is Fr Davide Pagliarini, who was the superior of the SSPX seminary in La Reja, Argentina from 2012 until his election in 2018. The new assistants to the superior general are Bishop Alfonso de Galarreta and Fr Christian Bouchacourt. Bishop de Galarreta was also a rector of the Society's seminary in Argentina. Fr Bouchacourt served as the district superior of the Society in Latin America from 2003 until 2014 and is known to have enjoyed good relations with the then-archbishop of Buenos Aires, Jorge Bergoglio. The new leadership of the SSPX thus seems to have been chosen in order to promote better relations with Pope Francis. Pursuit of this policy requires rejection of the Open Letter. It explains why the Society has chosen to attack the letter, regardless of the badness of the reasons it provides for rejecting it.

PRACTICAL OBJECTION TO THE OPEN LETTER

Fr Gleize's attack on the canonical basis of the Open Letter has required a detailed discussion because of the complexity of the subject matter. His criticism of the prudential wisdom of the initiative can be dealt with more briefly. Fr Gleize observes that although Archbishop Lefebvre thought Paul VI and John Paul II promoted heresy, and could on occasion have been taken to have expressed it, he nonetheless never accused them of being heretics and always accepted them as legitimate popes. Fr Gleize states that this policy should be changed only if there were a change in circumstances. He acknowledges that some people allege that circumstances have in fact changed, because Pope Francis has crossed lines that his predecessors respected. However, Fr Gleize denies that there is a significant difference between Pope Francis and his predecessors. He argues for this conclusion as follows:

> In fact, circumstances have not changed substantially. On the one hand, Rome continues to have distanced herself from doctrinal tradition because of the errors of the Council, errors which have not changed, even if some concessions have been made in order to tolerate some aspects of Tradition in disciplinary or liturgical matters. On the other hand, this distancing, although it has increased as a result of having been extended from doctrine to morals, conserves the same root, which is the false idea of freedom of conscience.[9]

The premise of this argument is dubious. A false idea of freedom of conscience is no doubt one of the roots of the theological errors that can be attributed to Popes Paul VI, John Paul II, and Francis, but it is not the only one. The *Correctio filialis* described some of the other intellectual sources of Pope Francis's heresies, including modernism and the ideas of Martin Luther. In any case, Fr Gleize's argument is a *non sequitur*. Let us concede for the sake of argument that the questionable ideas and statements of Paul VI, John Paul II, and Francis have some of the same sources, or even exactly the same source. This would not prevent Francis from taking these ideas farther than his predecessors did, and doing so in a way that means he is a formal heretic where they were not.

The conclusion for which Fr Gleize is arguing is also obviously false. Any informed person can cite several respects in which Francis has shown himself far more hostile to the Faith than his predecessors. For example, Paul VI and John Paul II both made strong magisterial statements in defense of truths of the faith that were being widely questioned—Paul VI in *Mysterium Fidei*, for example, and John Paul II in *Veritatis Splendor* and *Fides et Ratio*. Francis has never done this. On the contrary, he has deliberately repudiated the teaching of many of the documents of John Paul II concerning divinely revealed moral truths. His episcopal appointments show a

---

[9] "En effet, les circonstances n'ont pas substantiellement changé : d'une part, Rome reste toujours aussi éloignée de la Tradition en matière doctrinale, à cause des erreurs inchangées du Concile, même si quelques concessions ont pu être faites, pour tolérer une certaine part de Tradition en matière de discipline ou de liturgie ; d'autre part cet éloignement, pour s'aggraver en étendue, du fait qu'il s'étend du plan dogmatique au plan moral, reste toujours le même dans sa racine, qui est l'idée fausse de la liberté de conscience."

deliberate policy of appointing only heretics and excluding orthodox believers as far as is possible, which Paul VI and John Paul II did not do. The Open Letter provides a detailed case for Francis's heterodoxy, to which readers can be referred.

CONCLUSION

The General House of the SSPX concludes its criticism of the Open Letter with this exhortation: "'What to do?,' some ask. Without parochialism or misplaced pride, we can say there is an example to follow, that of the Athanasius of modern times—Archbishop Marcel Lefebvre." This conclusion can be heartily accepted by those who endorse the Open Letter. The relevant part of Archbishop Lefebvre's example is that when faced with an unparalleled crisis he did something to address it. This is what the Open Letter has done in the case of Pope Francis.

30

On Bishop Voderholzer's Dissociation from the "Protest"[1]

DR CLAUDIO PIERANTONI

IN A STATEMENT[2] ORIGINALLY SIGNED BY ONE hundred Catholic scholars, priests, and laity—now almost two hundred—to protest against the idolatrous acts that took place in the Vatican, we referred to the criticisms or condemnations that had already come from seven prominent prelates, as, for example, Cardinal Müller and Bishop Schneider. Among these, we mentioned Bishop Voderholzer of Regensburg, for a homily he gave on October 31 (Feast of St. Wolfgang) in which he criticized what was happening in the Vatican.[3] Once our statement was published (November 12), however, Bishop Voderholzer disassociated himself from it.[4] He did that, he said, especially because he disagreed with the statement's "reproaches, accusations, or even condemnations of the Holy Father."

First of all, we wish to note that he incorrectly affirms that we are "condemning" the Holy Father ("Verurteilungen des Heiligen Vaters"). This is absolutely not the case: we are protesting against and condemning certain specific actions objectively considered, and make no judgement of any person. We do say that such actions violate objectively the First Commandment, and are as such both sinful and scandalous, "independently of the subjective culpability, which only God can judge." In consequence, we are asking all Catholic bishops to fraternally correct the Holy Father. Thus, it is certainly true that we are protesting, and asking the pope to repent of this sin and of the scandal that has been caused by these actions. More exactly, we are asking the bishops of the Catholic Church, and

---

1 Published as "Catholic prof defends initiative calling Pope Francis to repent for Pachamama idolatry," *LifeSiteNews*, November 19, 2019.
2 The text is the fifth document in Part II.
3 See www.bistum-regensburg.de/news/wolfgangspredigt-2019-7073 and www.kath.net/news/69615, with Maike Hickson's report: www.lifesitenews.com/blogs/german-bishop-criticizes-use-of-pachamama-statues-at-amazon-synod.
4 www.kath.net/news/69724.

therefore also Bishop Voderholzer, to fraternally correct Pope Francis in this aspect. This is not because we have already passed judgement on the pope, but simply because he was *expressly* involved in these actions which took place in the Vatican — in the context, moreover, of inaugurating a synod of the Catholic Church. His explicit involvement makes legitimate, and even obligatory, a fraternal correction of all involved. If these kinds of objective assumptions are not possible or licit, no kind of correction or human exhortation to repent of any sin would ever be possible. Accordingly, there is nothing wrong in itself in reproaching or asking someone to repent on the basis of an objective involvement of that person in a specific misdeed. Moreover, this is all the more applicable to certain categories of people in relation to others: to parents, for example, with respect to their children, to teachers with respect to their pupils; to the pope with respect to bishops and all Christ's faithful; and in fraternal reciprocity, to the bishops (and if necessary, to all competent Catholic faithful) with respect to the pope.

Allowing that reproach and correction are not wrong in themselves, it would be necessary to establish that in this specific case, the reproach is wrong: (a) either because the facts under consideration are innocent, (b) or because the person was not involved in the facts. But Bishop Voderholzer makes none of these claims. To start with, claim (a) is certainly untenable, on the basis of what Voderholzer himself stated in his own homily. Thus we note that the bishop does not really give any reasons for his disassociation, but says simply that we are "missing the point" ("gehen an der Sache vorbei") and that "this is not my way." In his statement, he does make references to his own homily of October 31; but, all too significantly, he omits everything related to all the criticisms he had expressed against the actions that took place in the Vatican Gardens and Saint Peter's Basilica, which are the very object of our protest.

So, it will be good to remind the bishop at least of some of his own words, which we appreciated. We choose only two important remarks.[5]

First, in his homily Bishop Voderholzer asked whether it is the right thing to "carry into the realm of the Church pagan statues" without their being transformed into Christian symbols — as happened, for example, with the Oak of Thor that St. Boniface chopped down and carved into a cross. Bishop Voderholzer referred

---

[5] See the link above to Maike Hickson's report.

concretely to "the veneration of natural fertility in the form of the personified Mother Earth, the 'Pachamama.'" St. Boniface' example, of course, was far from an isolated case. It was common practice in the process of Christianization to destroy pagan idols, and, if possible, to transform the raw material into Christian symbols. Secondly, with regard to the Pachamama statues, before which people prostrated themselves during the October 4 ceremony in the Vatican Gardens at which Pope Francis was present in the lead-up to the Amazon Synod, the bishop stated that: "It was not apparent that the figures that we are talking about had undergone the transformation and purification—from a natural piety toward a Marian devotion in light of the history of salvation—as earlier Catholic missionaries had done it."

Some comments. Although the first remark is expressed in the form of a question, it is clearly a rhetorical question: "Was it right?" "Of course not" is the natural answer. So much so, that in the very question it is assumed that these are "pagan statues" that represent "personified Mother Earth, the Pachamama." This being so, how can it be right to prostrate before the personified Mother Earth? The bodily gesture used, it should be emphasized, was *proskynesis*, which was often translated in Latin as *adoratio*, that is, adoration. The bishop's second remark also assumed that "it is not apparent that these figures had undergone the transformation and purification—from a natural piety toward a Marian devotion in light of the history of salvation." In other words, there was no hint, in the appearance of these figures, that they are now used in a different sense than the pagan one, for example as representations of Mary. That said, given that in an image, especially if used in public prayer, *the "appearance" is precisely the essential matter*, it must be admitted that this action has all the appearance of a prostration to a pagan goddess. People are praying and prostrating around a "mandala" representative of the Amazonian land,[6] in the center

---

6   It is worth noting that, in the theological background of this Amazon synod, specifically in the famous *Instrumentum laboris* ("Working document") that preceded it, the Amazonian land is itself granted a sacred status as "a particular source of God's revelation," and even an "epiphanic place" where "the caresses of God become manifest and *incarnate* in history" (my emphasis). See IL 19: "Thus territory is a theological place where faith is lived, and also a particular source of God's revelation: epiphanic places where the reserve of life and wisdom for the planet is manifest, a

of which is an out-of-scale image of a naked, pregnant woman, universal personification of fertility, not only in South America, but all over the planet.

Now, this is more than enough to explain the critical remarks of the bishop. Less understandable is his unwillingness to stand by his own words and to be consistent. If he maintains that we are wrong in protesting against idolatry, then he must explain why he thinks so. Have the images suddenly ceased to be "representations of personified fertility," as he himself had stated? Has a hint emerged that this pagan personification has been fittingly reinterpreted, purified, "baptized" in the way he himself had deemed to be necessary? No, there is no hint of it, by his own admission. There were no indications of anything Christian and Catholic in the mandala around which the people prayed. As we stated in the document, even if there was no idolatrous *intention* behind it — which we do not judge — the mere bodily gesture of prostrating oneself before something which, to all appearances, is a pagan personification of natural forces is more than sufficient to produce an *objective* scandal. Let us remember that the Christian martyrs of ancient and modern times chose rather to die than to give even the *appearance* of burning incense to the pagan gods, which they could have done in a merely external way, without the internal consent of their hearts.

In conclusion: if the bishop wished to refute us, he would be obliged to retract and correct what he himself had earlier said. But he does not do that. He simply omits quoting his own original remarks, which objectively support our criticism and protest.

As to (b), the second possible claim — that there is no connection between these events and the pope — the bishop does not make the claim, and of course it is even less tenable. In fact, these events took place inside the Vatican, in the context of a synod organized under the pope, and were personally attended by the pope. And here comes our most important reflection: we can see that Voderholzer certainly is an orthodox bishop, who felt it necessary to protest against this idolatry that took place within the Vatican. However, in his homily he did not relate the incident to the pope. And when a statement came out, which *did* make that reference,

---

life and wisdom that speaks of God. In the Amazon, the 'caresses of God' become manifest and become incarnate in history."

he steps back, as if he were thinking: "I am against what the pope is doing, but because he is the pope, I cannot tell him; moreover, I must hasten to dissociate myself from people who do that." Now we ask: what kind of assumption could lead a bishop to such an illogical conclusion?

Let us suggest that there are, roughly speaking, four kinds of bishops in the way they relate to the pope in doctrinal matters. One is the "progressive" bishop, who maintains positions more or less at variance with the traditional teaching of the Church's faith, and who, in the present pontificate, now feels much freer to express his views. The second is the more orthodox-minded bishop, who is also something of a political opportunist; he will not criticize the pope out of simple fear of incurring some disadvantage to his ecclesiastical career. We know that Voderholzer does not belong to either of these two categories.

But there is also the sincerely orthodox-minded bishop who has the will to oppose heresy as such, but who unfortunately believes in an implicitly assumed doctrine according to which no reproach, no kind of fraternal correction, is to be deemed appropriate, or even licit, if the one responsible for some bad behavior is the pope himself. If anyone dares to make or to propose such a correction, the attempt is immediately and irrationally quashed as "an attack against the pope." Such an ingenuous doctrine, of course, has never existed in Catholic teaching: it is either a fruit of this-worldly human respect, or else a complete misconstrual of the doctrine of papal infallibility, when it is arbitrarily extended to anything and *everything* a pope happens to think or say or do. Now, this false and dangerous doctrine is fervently and contagiously at work: it is, in the disastrous situation of the present pontificate, like a paralyzing virus, immobilizing irrationally a great many orthodox bishops, who could and should help the pope with a just fraternal correction concerning many aspects of his recent action. We fear that Bishop Voderholzer, who began well with an orthodox critique of these idolatrous acts, has now fallen a victim to this doctrinal illness, and is thereby losing a splendid opportunity to help the present successor of Peter.[7]

---

[7] We make these comments also in light of the fact that other people, like Princess Gloria von Thurn und Taxis and Father Dreher FSSP, unfortunately followed his example. See www.lifesitenews.com/news/german-princess-withdraws-signature-from-statement-urging-pope-to-repent-for-pachamama-idolatry; www.kath.net/news/69762.

But Voderholzer might very well change his course, and decide to inscribe himself in a fourth and best category of bishops: those who are neither heretics, nor time-serving opportunists, nor subscribers to a distorted doctrine of papal infallibility, but are so personally kindled with the love of our Lord Jesus Christ, that, leaving aside all kinds of human respect, they decide to speak a word of truth to Pope Francis, for the benefit of his own soul and the benefit of the universal Church. And the same counsel could also serve many other bishops, each lending a strong pastoral arm to help cure the present, dreadful wounds of Christ's Bride upon earth.

One final observation: we are not urging Bishop Voderholzer, or any other bishop, to sign our protest. We are simply asking them to truly help the pope with their own fraternal correction, in the words that the Holy Spirit is certainly available to suggest to them.

31

Papal Infallibility After One Hundred and Fifty Years[1]

PAUPER PEREGRINUS

SATURDAY, JULY 18, 2020, MARKED THE 150TH anniversary of the definition of papal infallibility by the First Vatican Council in the constitution *Pastor Aeternus*, as a dogma of the Catholic faith, to be held by all Catholics under pain of losing their eternal salvation. On the same occasion, the same Vatican Council, under the headship of Pope Pius IX, also defined as a dogma the universal jurisdiction of the pope over all the baptized — that is, the fact that the pope is by divine law the vicar of Christ and pastor of all Christians.

As the assembled fathers cast their votes in favor of the definition of infallibility, a great thunderstorm raged over St. Peter's and across a large part of Europe, and the sky grew so dark that candles had to be lit in the daytime. John Henry Newman, not yet a cardinal, who though believing in the two papal dogmas had thought it "inopportune" to define them, wondered whether these extraordinary phenomena were a sign that "our great Lord was angry at us." Presumably, he was speculating that the bishops were committing the sin of tempting God by invoking the Church's power to define dogma without (as he supposed) true need. Yet when one remembers how Scripture and the saints attribute to the evil spirits a power to stir up storms, one may believe, on the contrary, that it was the enemy of mankind who was enraged to see so magnificent a declaration made, on that far-off summer's day, of the prerogatives of Christ's universal vicar.

After all, a dogmatic definition by the Church, duly accompanied with anathema against those who deny it, is always, in itself, a splendid thing: a monument to the truthfulness of God, who can neither deceive nor be deceived, and who has communicated some portion of His infallibility to men. Even on the natural level, such a definition stands, against all the skeptical philosophies, as

---

[1] Published at *OnePeterFive*, July 20, 2020.

a reminder of the capacity of the human mind to know *what is*, and to express it in words that will never need to be reformed or corrected. On the supernatural level, a definition of dogma reassures us that we are not in this world like children adrift on a sea of uncertainty, and that God has told us what we need to find our way home.

What is the meaning of papal infallibility? It does not mean that a pope can never err when speaking about religion. Nor even, contrary to the opinion of some who publish their thoughts on theological matters today, does it mean that a pope can never commit the sin of heresy. This last point was expressly touched on at the Council of 1870 by Bishop Vincent Gasser, the *Relator* charged by Pope Pius IX with answering any questions and objections raised by the conciliar fathers about the text on which they had to vote. In a speech to the assembled bishops, Gasser described as "extreme" the opinion put forward by the 16th-century author Albert Pigghe, that a pope could never fall into heresy. Pigghe, sometimes known by the Latinized form of his name, Pighius, had argued that while a pope could err as a private person, and could from ignorance teach something incorrect while acting as a "private doctor" — for example, in a book published under his pre-papal name — he would never fall into heresy or teach a heresy. Gasser noted that some of the council Fathers were upset with the proposed dogma, since they were under the impression that it was identical to Pigghe's view. Gasser, however, repudiated this suggestion and stated that the document on which they were being asked to vote by no means taught this "extreme" position:

> The Deputation [that is, the group of bishops charged with drafting the document] is unjustly criticised, as if it wished to raise an extreme opinion, that of Albert Pigghe, to the rank of a dogma. The opinion of Albert Pigghe, which Bellarmine indeed describes as "pious and having some plausibility," was that while a pope as an individual man or a private teacher could err from some kind of ignorance, he could never fall into heresy or teach heresy.... It is obvious that the doctrine contained in the schema is not that of Albert Pigghe.[2]

---

2   *Acta et decreta sacrosancti oecumenici concilii Vaticani* (Coll. Lacensis, VII, 405–6): "Deputatio iniuste traducitur ac si voluisset extremam

In other words, the dogma of papal infallibility leaves unresolved the question of whether a pope can fall into heresy privately or even express heresy in some public statement.

Later in the same speech, Bishop Gasser considered the latter point in more detail. The proposed dogma does not mean that a pope would be infallible, he explained, whenever he is speaking about faith or morals in a context in which only a pope could speak. As examples of such a context, we might mention papal Christmas messages *Urbi et Orbi*, or even encyclicals or apostolic exhortations addressed to all the bishops of the world. Gasser told the conciliar fathers:

> Not just any way of proposing doctrine is sufficient, even when the Pontiff is exercising his supreme office of shepherd and teacher. It is necessary that the intention of defining doctrine be manifest, and of putting an end to uncertainty about some doctrine or matter to be defined, by giving a definitive judgement and proposing that doctrine as something that the universal Church must hold.[3]

It is not sufficient, therefore, that a pope show a desire to make Catholics favor this or that position: he must make it clear that all the faithful are obliged to assent to some clearly articulated doctrine, if they want to remain "Catholics in good standing." This is what it means to speak *ex cathedra*, "from the throne." And in the history of the Church, the Roman pontiffs have done this often, as anyone may see for himself by consulting a copy of Denzinger.

---

opinionem, scilicet illam Alberti Pighii, ad dignitatem dogmatis evehere. Nam opinio Alberti Pighii, quam Belllarminus vocat piam quidem et probabilem, erat quod Papa qua persona singularis seu doctor privatus ex ignorantia quadam possit errare, sed nequaquam in haeresim incidere vel haeresim docere.... Apparet doctrinam quae habetur in schemate non esse illam Alberti Pighii." Note that the scholastic term *probabilis,* when used to describe an opinion, does not mean "probable," but "having some plausibility." Contradictory statements may therefore both be *probabilis.*
3 Ibid., 414: "Non sufficit quivis modus proponendi doctrinam, etiam dum Pontifex fungitur munere supremi pastoris et doctoris, sed requiritur intentio manifestata definiendi doctrinam, seu fluctuationi finem imponendi circa doctrinam quamdam seu rem definiendam, dando definitivam sententiam, et doctrinam illam proponendo tenendam ab Ecclesia universali."

Gasser went so far as to say that thousands of definitive judgements have been issued by the apostolic see.[4]

The definition of papal infallibility marked the final, happy triumph of the Church over the "conciliarist" movement that had begun in the later Middle Ages, and which had sought to subject popes to ecumenical councils. Why, then, did a man of the moral and intellectual stature of Newman think it would be inopportune to define the dogma? He feared that at that particular point in history, such a definition would upset the delicate balance among the different organs by which truth is taught within the Church—the papacy and the episcopacy and, in dependence on them, theologians and parish priests. He feared a hypertrophy of the papacy at the expense of other parts of the mystical body.

Newman had a point. Human beings find it hard to keep a firm grasp of complementary truths or fine distinctions. Once the papal prerogatives had been put into so bright a light, it was perhaps inevitable that many Catholics would tend in practice to act as if a pope's every word were an oracle, or as if the wisdom of his policies could not be questioned without disloyalty. One may wonder, also, whether the atmosphere fostered by the definitions of 1870 may not have led the popes themselves to act as if their monarchy were more absolute, or their infallibility more extensive, than they really are, to the point that Paul VI could seek to give the Church a whole new liturgy, and Francis can laugh when accused of heresy. Did Paul VI, as he sought to "reform" the Roman rite beyond recognition, unconsciously reassure himself: "This may seem like a bad idea, but I'm the pope, so nothing can go really wrong"?

Has the episcopacy, too, suffered in the long wake of Vatican I? It was not Pius IX's desire to turn the world's bishops into his vicars, and he repudiated Bismarck's claim that the council had done so. Yet, given human weakness, there was always a danger that this might happen, at least to some extent—that bishops might imagine, perhaps unconsciously again, that they were vicars not of Jesus Christ, but of the pope, charged with making his policies and preferences their own. Hence, surely, the deplorable lack of reaction among the bishops to the novelties of Paul VI and to the modernism of Francis.

---

4   Ibid., 401: "Iam millena et millena iudicia dogmatica a Sede apostolica emanarunt."

Was it also from being thus weakened in their sense of their own prerogatives that orthodox bishops came to depend too much on Rome to teach the unpopular doctrines, for example on sexual morality? While we were blessed with many fine papal encyclicals in the 19th and 20th centuries, it is not a healthy sign when letters from the Roman pontiff to the universal Church become the usual means by which orthodoxy is maintained among Catholics. The episcopacy is the normal means for doing this; the papacy exists to scotch errors that episcopal teaching has not been able to defeat. Whether the massive increase, in modern times, of papal documents directed to the universal Church is related as cause or as effect to a dearth of good episcopal teaching is a nice question.

Without embracing Adrian Fortescue's ironical suggestion that a pope should not open his mouth at all unless he is doing so infallibly, one may reasonably expect that teaching documents sent by a pope to the whole Church will principally intend to settle definitively some doctrinal crisis. Otherwise, why bother? *Ordinatio Sacerdotalis,* Pope John Paul II's brief letter excluding the priestly ordination of women, is a good example of this. Papal documents offering only "non-infallible" teaching are another sign that the functions of the episcopacy have become partially absorbed into the papacy.

None of this means that Newman was right. Things could well have gone worse had the "inopportunists" triumphed a century and a half ago. Even armed with the two papal definitions, St. Pius X could hardly keep modernism at bay; how much less if they had been refused him? And would belief in the Assumption of the Blessed Virgin Mary have survived the modern decay of faith if Pius XII had not been able to rely on the defined prerogatives of his office to declare it as dogma?

On the whole, I think we may be not only proud of these two definitions in themselves, but grateful to God that they were defined when they were. Newman was a great man, but as Chesterton remarked in his biography of St. Francis, the great men can be wrong when the little men are right. We groan inwardly at the present humiliation of the apostolic see, but at least we know whence the remedy must come. Just as Pope Honorius I was condemned for heresy after his death by the 3rd Council of Constantinople, and Pope St. Leo II ratified this conciliar act, so it seems impossible that Pope Francis should not one day be condemned for the same crime (unless the Lord returns first), by one of his successors speaking from the throne. When that day comes, it will be a splendid example of what Vatican I meant, and of what it didn't mean, by the infallibility of the pope.

THE CONTRIBUTORS

CLAIRE CHRETIEN is a journalist and editor for *LifeSiteNews* who writes on life issues and abortion, human dignity, bioethics, the Catholic Church, and politics.

ROBERT DE MATTEI, a student of philosopher Augusto del Noce and historian Armando Saitta and a disciple of Professor Plinio Corrêa de Oliveira, served as chair of Modern History in the Faculty of Letters at the University of Cassino (1985–2009), and is currently Professor of Modern History and History of Christianity at the European University of Rome. He is President of the Lepanto Foundation, as well as Founder and Director of the Lepanto Cultural Centre (1986–2006). De Mattei directs the magazine *Radici Cristiane* and the *Corrispondenza Romana* News Agency. Between 2003 and 2011 he was Vice President of the Italian National Research Council (CNR). He is the author of many books, which have been translated into several languages—most recently in English, *Love for the Papacy and Filial Resistance to the Pope in the History of the Church* (Angelico, 2019).

ROBERT FASTIGGI (A. B. in Religion, Dartmouth College; M. A. in Theology, Fordham University; Ph.D. in Historical Theology, Fordham) holds the Bishop Kevin M. Britt Chair of Dogmatic Theology and Christology at Sacred Heart Major Seminary, where has taught since 1999. Dr Fastiggi teaches ecclesiology, Christology, Mariology, church history, sacramental theology, and moral theology. He served as co-editor of the English translation of the 43rd edition of the Denzinger-Hünermann *Enchiridion* (2012), and revised the translation of Ludwig Ott's *Fundamentals of Catholic Dogma* (2018).

EDWARD FESER is a writer and philosopher living in Los Angeles. He teaches philosophy at Pasadena City College. His primary academic research interests are in the philosophy of mind, moral and political philosophy, and philosophy of religion; he also writes on politics, from a conservative point of view; and on religion, from a traditional Roman Catholic perspective. His books include *Five Proofs of the Existence of God*, *The Last Superstition: A Refutation of the New Atheism*, *Scholastic Metaphysics: A Contemporary Introduction*, and (with Joseph Bessette) *By Man Shall His Blood Be Shed: A Catholic Defense of Capital Punishment*.

DAWN EDEN GOLDSTEIN (S. T. D., University of St. Mary of the Lake), from a reformed Jewish background, worked as a rock journalist in New York City and held editorial positions at the *New York Post* and the *Daily News*. In 2006, after five years as a Protestant, she was received into full communion with the Catholic Church. She has taught at universities and seminaries in the United States, England, and India. Her books include *Sunday Will Never Be the Same*, *The Thrill of the Chaste*, and *My Peace I Give You: Healing Sexual Wounds with the Help of the Saints*.

BRIAN W. HARRISON, O. S. (M. A.; S. T. L., Angelicum; S. T. D. in Systematic Theology, Pontifical University of the Holy Cross) was ordained a priest for the Society of the Oblates of Wisdom by Pope John Paul II in 1985 at St. Peter's Basilica. He is an emeritus Professor of Theology of the Pontifical Catholic University of Puerto Rico in Ponce, where he also worked as a Defender of the Bond for the marriage tribunals. Since 2007, Fr Harrison has been scholar-in-residence at the Oblates of Wisdom house of studies in St. Louis, Missouri. He is the author of two books and many articles on theological and liturgical matters, upholding a "hermeneutic of continuity" between the teachings of Vatican Council II and the bimillennial heritage of Catholic Tradition.

MAIKE HICKSON, born and raised in Germany, studied History and French Literature at the University of Hannover and lived for several years in Switzerland where she wrote her doctoral dissertation. She writes for *LifeSiteNews*. Her articles have also appeared at *OnePeterFive*, *Catholicism.org*, *The Wanderer*, *Culture Wars*, *Catholic Family News*, *Christian Order*, *Apropos*, and *Zeit-Fragen*. Dr Hickson has edited two books since living in the United States: *A Catholic Witness in our Time: A Festschrift in Honor of Dr Robert Hickson* (Loreto Publications, 2015) and Robert Hickson's *Gratitude, Contemplation, and the Sacramental Worth of Catholic Literature* (Loreto Publications, 2020).

JOHN HUNWICKE, a priest of the Personal Ordinariate of Our Lady of Walsingham, was for nearly three decades at Lancing College, where he taught Latin and Greek language and literature, and was Head of Theology, and Assistant Chaplain. He has served three curacies, been a parish priest, and Senior Research Fellow at Pusey House in Oxford. Since 2011, he has been in full communion with the See of St. Peter.

The Contributors

PETER A. KWASNIEWSKI (B. A. in Liberal Arts, Thomas Aquinas College; M. A. and Ph.D. in Philosophy, Catholic University of America) is an author and speaker on Catholic Tradition, especially in its liturgical dimension. After teaching at the International Theological Institute in Austria and the Franciscan University of Steubenville's Austrian Program, he joined the founding team of Wyoming Catholic College in 2006, where he taught theology, philosophy, music, and art history, and directed the choir and schola, until his departure in 2018. He has published over a thousand articles on Thomistic thought, sacramental and liturgical theology, the history and aesthetics of music, Catholic Social Teaching, and issues in the contemporary Church, and has written or edited twelve books, including most recently *Reclaiming Our Roman Catholic Birthright* (Angelico, 2020) and *The Holy Bread of Eternal Life* (Sophia, 2020).

JOHN R. T. LAMONT is a Canadian Catholic philosopher and theologian. He studied philosophy and theology at the Dominican College in Ottawa and at Oxford University, and has taught philosophy and theology in Catholic universities and seminaries. He is the author of *Divine Faith* (Ashgate, 2004) and of a number of academic papers.

EDWARD PETERS (B. A. in Political Science, St. Louis University; J. D., University of Missouri at Columbia; J. C. L. and J. C. D., Catholic University of America) is the Edmund Cardinal Szoka Chair of Faculty Development at Sacred Heart Major Seminary. Dr Peters has served the Church in many capacities: as diocesan Vice-Chancellor and Chancellor, Director of the Office for Canonical Affairs, Defender of the Bond, and Collegial Judge, and as a canonical consultant to numerous ecclesiastical institutions and persons. He has taught canon law at numerous institutions and has published extensively on the subject, including an edition of the 1917 *Pio-Benedictine Code of Canon Law* and a textual history of the 1983 *Code*, both works winning international acclaim.

CLAUDIO PIERANTONI (Ph.D. in History of Christianity, Rome University La Sapienza; Ph.D. in Philosophy, Universidad de Los Andes, Santiago) studied classical philology and then specialized in patristics and history of Christianity at the Institutum Patristicum Augustinianum. He has served as professor of history of the ancient Church and patrology at the Faculty of Theology in Santiago, Chile and at present teaches medieval philosophy at the University of

Chile. His main lines of investigation are the Christological and Trinitarian controversies of the ancient Church, St. Augustine, the philosophical problem of Truth, and natural theology.

JOHN RIST (M. A. in Classics, University of Cambridge) holds the Father Kurt Pritzl, O. P., Chair in Philosophy at the Catholic University of America. His areas of expertise include ancient philosophy, Neoplatonism, Patristics, and ethics. Rist is the author of numerous books, such as *Plato's Moral Realism: The Discovery of the Presuppositions of Ethics* (2012), *What is Truth? From the Academy to the Vatican* (2008), *Real Ethics: Reconsidering the Foundations of Morality* (2001), and *Augustine: Ancient Thought Baptized* (1994). He previously taught at the University College, Toronto; University of Aberdeen; Institutum Patristicum Augustinianum; and University of Toronto, where he is professor emeritus.

JOSEPH SHAW is a British academic and the current chairman of the Latin Mass Society of England and Wales. Educated at Ampleforth College and the University of Oxford, he is currently a tutorial fellow in philosophy at St Benet's Hall, Oxford. His main areas of interest are practical ethics, the philosophy of religion, and medieval philosophy. In 2015, he was elected a fellow of the Royal Society of Arts. His publications include *The Case for Liturgical Restoration: Una Voce Studies on the Traditional Latin Mass* (Angelico, 2019) and *How to Attend the Extraordinary Form* (Catholic Truth Society, 2020). He blogs at *LMS Chairman* and *LifeSiteNews*.

ANNA M. SILVAS resides in Armidale, New South Wales, Australia, and is a member of the Romanian Greek Catholic Church, in union with Rome. She is an Adjunct Senior Research Fellow in the School of Humanities at the University of New England, Australia, and a Fellow of the Australian Academy of the Humanities. Her undergraduate studies were in Greek, Latin, Hebrew, and Aramaic/Syriac. Her research has concentrated on late antiquity, particularly on the Cappadocian Fathers, the development of Christian monasticism, and the spirituality of ascetic women in early and medieval Christianity. Her published works include translations of ancient literature as well as monographs. Her *magnum opus* was a first critical edition of the Syriac *Questions of the Brothers*. She has also been associated with the John Paul II Institute for Marriage and Family in Melbourne.

The Contributors

MICHAEL SIRILLA has served as a professor of systematic theology at Franciscan University of Steubenville since 2002. He earned his Ph.D. in systematic and historical theology from The Catholic University of America and has researched and written in the areas of ecclesiology and moral theology. He is the author of the book *The Ideal Bishop: Aquinas's Commentaries on the Pastoral Epistles* (CUA Press, 2017), as well as numerous academic and popular articles.

ROBERT SPAEMANN (1927–2018) was a German Roman Catholic philosopher, considered a member of the Ritter School, whose work in Christian ethics, particularly bioethics, ecology, and human rights, was influential and highly praised. Spaemann studied at the University of Münster, where, in 1962, he was awarded his Habilitation. He was Professor of Philosophy at the Universities of Stuttgart until 1968, Heidelberg until 1972, and Munich, where he worked until he was made Emeritus Professor in 1992. He was also Honorary Professor at the University of Salzburg and was awarded an honorary doctorate by the Catholic University of Lublin in 2012. His books include *Glück und Wohlwollen* (1989) and *Personen* (1996).

THOMAS WEINANDY, O. F. M. CAP. entered the Franciscan Capuchin Order (Pittsburgh Province) in 1968 and was ordained to the priesthood in 1972. He earned a Doctorate in Historical Theology at King's College, University of London in 1975. He has taught in a number of Catholic universities in the United States and for twelve years was the Warden (President) of Greyfriars, Oxford and taught History and Doctrine within the Faculty of Theology at the University of Oxford. He has written or edited twenty books and published numerous articles in academic journals and edited books of essays. For nine years he was the Executive Director of the Secretariat for Doctrine at the United States Conference of Catholic Bishops. He has given retreats and parish missions in the United States, Canada, Ireland, and Great Britain. He is a former member of the Vatican's International Theological Commission. Pope Francis conferred upon him the Pro Ecclesiae et Pontificae medal in 2013. His latest book is *Jesus Becoming Jesus: A Theological Interpretation of the Synoptic Gospels*.

PAUPER PEREGRINUS is the *nom de plume* of a priest in good standing with a doctorate in sacred theology.

INDEX

OF PERSONS AND SUBJECTS

The sheer number of ecclesiastical documents and sources cited would make a comprehensive index onerous. Included below are some of the most notable; others will be discovered in connection with their subject matter.

abortion: 143–46, 182, 344, 370, 390

absolution (sacramental): 39–42, 65, 70, 80, 83, 88, 90, 135, 181, 185, 189, 196, 217–18, extenuating circumstances and, 279–80; "hard cases" and, 220–22

Abu Dhabi, see *Document on Human Fraternity*

Adoukonou, Cardinal Barthélemy: 329

adultery: according to situation ethics, 222, 279–80; authorized by certain bishops, 85, 289, and by Pope Francis, xii, 18, 120, 122, 217–18; commandments of God and, 41, 180, 227; Council of Trent on, 63–64, 130; Holy Communion and, 70, 85, 136, 140–41, 182, 226, 228–30, 381 and *passim*; intrinsic evil, 43–44, 183, 228, 289; places person in grave sin, 29, 43–44; Scriptural teaching on, 17–18, 61, 86–88, 130, 179–80, 223–25, 319; whether may be requested by God, 326

African bishops: 329

Ahmad Al-Tayyeb: 18, 137, 168

Amazon rain-forest, source of divine revelation: 411

"Amazonian Synod": 390; idolatry at 3, 31, 167–70, 390, requiring fraternal correction, 409–11

American neo-conservatives, allegation of funding by: 4, 389

Amoris Laetitia (Francis), authority of, 53–55, 179, 219, 231, 233, 296, 310; balkanization of Church by, 294, 322; establishes clerical tyranny, 218; meaning of clarified by Pope Francis, authoritatively, 12, 136, 216–17. *See also* adultery; capital punishment; justification; moral law; sacrilege; situation ethics; Synod on the Family in 2015; virginity; and *passim*

annihilation of souls: belief in encouraged by Pope Francis, 351–52

Appeal to the Cardinals of the Catholic Church: 161–62

Aquinas, St Thomas: 43, 52, 64, 75, 80, 134, 161–62, 185, 195–96, 259, 270, 277, 288, 295, 313, 315–16, 348; misuse of, 158, 195–96

Arian crisis, parallel with: 239–42, 266, 273–74, 345, 375, 378

Augustine, St, 75, 155, 162, 189, 270, 315–16, 341, 346

Barros-Madrid, Bishop Juan: 143

Bellarmine, St Robert: 154–55, 157, 397–400, 404, 416

Biggar, Nigel: 144

bishops: depositaries, 369; duties of in present crisis, 12–15, 148–49, 188, 232–33, 250, 360, 376–78; "immune system" of Church, 232; in relation to pope, four categories of, 413–14; influence of Vatican I on, 418–19

Bonino, Emma, greatness of: 144, 344

Brandmüller, Cardinal Walter: 37–38, 167, 286, 329–30, 377–78

Buenos Aires, bishops of: 12, 82–84, 135–36, 215–18, 306, 311

427

Burke, Cardinal Raymond: 37–38, 168, 231, 261, 286, 326, 329–330, 377–78; and "formal correction," 11–13, 267, 273
Buttiglione, Rocco: 277–82, 288

Caffarra, Cardinal Carlo: 37–38, 148, 329, 378; on ontological nature of marriage, 244
Cajetan: 154, 157, 397–98, 404
Calcagno, Cardinal Domenico: 140
canon law: and correction of superiors, 161, 286, 294, 306–7, 311–12, 316–17, 333, 370–71; on heretical pope, 153–157, 349, 395–99; principles of interpretation of, 138–39, 333, 346, 402–4
capital punishment: xii, 2, 15, 57, 161–62, 327–28, 336, 381
cardinals: book by eleven, 329; duties of in present crisis, 10, 26, 250, 381; letter of thirteen, 294, 325; orthodox statements by, 147–48;
Catechism of the Catholic Church: 2–3, 58, 60, 64, 66, 68, 71–72, 88–89, 130, 161–62, 183, 288, 302, 325, 327–28, 330, 383
Catechism of the Council of Trent: 58
censures, *see* theological censures
Chaput, Archbishop Charles: 326, 377
China: 142, 146
Chiodi, Fr Maurizio: 145
clerical celibacy: xii, 59, 386
Coccopalmerio, Cardinal Francesco: 140
codification of canon law: 403
cognitive dissonance: *see* irrational responses to crisis
commandments: *see* moral law
confession *see* absolution (sacramental)
conscience: in *Amoris Laetitia*, 63, 68, 71–72, 78–79; moral norms and, 39,
44–46, 89, 129, 278, 357, 406; of theologian, 303, 312
Contra recentia sacrilegia: 167–70
contraception: 145–46, 187, 289, 336, 390
Cordes, Cardinal Paul Josef: 329
Correctio Filialis: summary of, 119–23; text of, 75–119
correction: right of subjects to issue, 75, even in public, 286, 289, 291–97, 311–13, 315–22; St Augustine on, 346. See also *Correctio Filialis*; Formal Correction
Cupich, Cardinal Blaise: 140

Danneels, Cardinal Godfried: 125, 140–41
Decretals: 399–400
Delpini, Archbishop Mario Enrico: 143
Dew, Cardinal John: 141
divorce and "remarriage": see *Amoris Laetitia*, and *passim*
Document on Human Fraternity: 137–38, 328, 353, 375, 390; Cardinal Muller on, 387–88; idolatry and, 168; to be distributed as widely as possible, 168–69
dogmatic relativism: 108
Donum Veritatis (CDF): 73, 300–304, 306–7, 312, 315, 319
Dubia of cardinals: 35–46; deaths of authors while waiting for reply to, 326; supported by other cardinals and bishops, 326
Duka, Cardinal Dominik: 329

Eijk, Cardinal Willem: 148, 326–27, 377
Exorcism of Pope Leo XIII: 24, 273

faith, Catholic notion of: 104–9
Familiaris Consortio (John Paul II): 3, 39, 41, 53, 65, 68, 70, 81, 88, 103, 136,

147, 180, 193–94, 213, 219, 221–23, 225, 230, 232, 307, 310, 319, 321
Farrell, Cardinal Kevin: 85, 141, 201
Fazio, Mgr Mariano: 289, 291, 296
Fellay, Bishop Bernard: 122, 233, 271, 274, 284–85, 404–5
Fernández, Archbishop Victor Manuel: 202–3, 288
Filial Appeal to Pope Francis: 284, 294, 329
Filial Correction: see *Correctio Filialis*
Finnis, John: 315, 326
"Formal Correction": 11–13, 267
Forte, Archbishop Bruno: on Pope Francis, 258; on the *Correctio Filialis*, 285
Francis, Pope: accused of sevenfold delict of heresy, 128–31; actions as bishop in Buenos Aires, 4, 29, 186–87, 256–67, 259, 405; actions as pope relevant to charge of heresy, 125–26, 138–47; agrees with Luther about justification, 114, 137; aims of, 16, 202–3, 258; as superseding gospel, 200, 206–8, 285; compared to his recent predecessors, 405–6; corrected for propagating seven heresies, 86–87, aware of correction, 13–14; "Creed on behalf of Pope Francis," 200; cumulative nature of case against, 344, 358–59; does not find spiritual goodness in his critics, whom he does not read, 372; *Dubia* of cardinals and, 81, 306, 342; extenuating factors, absence of, 242–43, 282; gratitude for Reformation, 137; guidelines for diocese of Rome issued by, 145; has ignored twenty direct appeals for clear teaching, 325–28, and many indirect ones, 325–31; homosexuality and, 132; independence of from scripture and tradition, praised, 342; not frightened by possible schism, 389; orthodox faithful, how treated by, 139; Peronism and, 16, 382; pertinacity of, 147, 368, 372; positions of recognised by outside observers, 375; praise and promotion of criminal or heretical clergy, 139–45; praise of B. Häring, 257; reaction to popular campaigns against abortion and homosexuality, 146; refusal to teach, 146–47, 162, 338–39, 380, 382; Society of St Pius X and, 405; unprecedented nature of errors of, 1, 148, 179, 232, 249–50, 269, 282, 375, 382–83; vagueness and ambiguity, strategic use of, 301, 339, 343, 345–46, 359–60, said to make charge of heresy almost impossible, 363, this claim disputed, 373–74

Gasser, Bishop Vincenzo: 416–18
Gaudium et Spes (Vatican II): 64, 69, 88, 107, 130, 181, 184, 256, 321; misuse of: 69, 184, 256
German idealism: 268
Gleize, Fr Jean-Michel: 395, 398–400, 402, 404–6
Gozo, Bishop of: 85
Gracias, Cardinal Oswald: 141
Gracida, Bishop Henry: 233
Granados, Fr José: 329
Grassi, Fr Julio: 16–17, 144
Gratian: 33, 112, 155–56, 399–402
Gregory I, Pope: 32–33, 155, 401
Grisez, Germain: 315, 326

Hadrian II, Pope: 401
Häring, Bernard: 257, 269
Hegel, Georg Wilhelm: 258, 260, 269, 345
hell: 60, 66, 351–52; for offences against First Commandment, 170
heresy, canonical crime of: 2, 112–13, 125, 149, 355–56, 368–69, 393, 395–96; jurisdiction and, 154, 334, 349,

396–97; manner of establishing, 231–33, 352–53, 358; post-mortem condemnation for, 19

heresy, sin of: 112, 355–56, 395–96; pertinacity in, 112–13, 127–28, 349, 372; prevalence of, 18–19, 22–23, 273–74; superiority complex and, 274. *See also* modernism; papal heresy

Higher Committee for Human Fraternity: 168

Holy Eucharist, conditions for reception of: 39, 41, 70, 85, 136–7, 140–41, 145, 182, 217–18 228–30, 381 and *passim*; according to Scriptures, 223–26; Cardinal Sarah on 268; duty of minister to enforce, 229–30, even against command of a bishop, 386

Holy Spirit: appeals to 202; blasphemy against, 209, 327; does not teach the Church new doctrines, 76, 111, 205, 208–9; relation to pope, xii, 202–5, 260

homosexuality: xii, 130–132, 329–30, 390; and clerics promoted by Pope Francis, 140–45

Honorius I, Pope: 235–39, 242, 282, 322, 337–39, 419

ideals: as replacing commandments, 180, 184

idolatry: *see* Amazonian Synod

indifferentism: 14, 146, 344, 375

infallibility: xii, 53, 57, 200, 383; definition by Vatican I, 76, 415–20; exaggerations of, 413–14; Fathers of the Church and, 238; of ordinary and universal magisterium, 307, 313; Pope Francis and, 77, 120, 128, 257–58

Innocent III, Pope: 33, 112, 156, 401

Inzoli, Maurice: 144

irrational responses to present crisis: xii–xiii, 9, 16, 255, 292, 296–97, 342–43, 374, 380–81, 413

Jesus Christ, absence of in *Amoris Laetitia*: 182

John XXII, Pope: 121, 261, 269, 337–38, 375

John Paul II, Pope: conditions for Holy Communion, 70; distortion of his teaching, 183–86, 193–94; on universal commandments, 64–65. *See also Familiaris Consortio; Reconciliatio et Paenitentia; Veritatis Splendor*

John Paul II Institutes: Australian, closed, 262; Roman, "re-founded," 390

justification: in *Amoris Laetitia*, 59–60, 86, 89, 128, 132; Luther said by Pope Francis to be correct about, 114–16, 137; Lutheran doctrine of 118–19

Kasper, Cardinal Walter: 257, 277–78; on *Amoris Laetitia,* 221–22; on *Familiaris Consortio,* 194; innovation and, 205; his proposal, 183, 324. *See also* adultery

de Kesel, Cardinal Jozef: 141

"Law of gradualness": according to Pope John Paul II, 183–84; in *Amoris Laetitia,* 59, 66,78, 83

Lefebvre, Archbishop Marcel: 393, 395, 405, 407

Leo II, Pope: 153, 237–38, 282, 338

Liberius, Pope: 239–42, 345, 375

liturgy: of Paul VI, 27, 418; traditional Latin, xii, 4

Lumen Gentium (Vatican II): 14–15, 76, 106, 215, 300; duties of bishops, 14–15; limits to papal powers, 76

Luther, Martin: apparent influence on Pope Francis, 113–19, 121–22, 132, 137, 406; his followers given Holy Communion in St Peter's, 119. *See also* justification

Maccarone, Bishop Juan Carlos: 143
magisterium: authentic, conditions for, 54–55, and consequences of 215–16; how exercised from 16th to 18th centuries, 7; Modernism and 232, 268; relation to power of governance, 53; theologians and 300–303, 307, 319–21, 388; undivided, 111
Malta, archbishop of: and reception of Holy Communion, 85; importance of not consulting past popes, 205
Maradiaga, Cardinal Oscar Rodriguez: 141–42, 374; on car of Church, whether has reverse gear, 202
marriage: cohabitating couples said often to have grace of, 137; Council of Trent on 63–64, 87–88, 130; headship of husband in, 58; notion of dissolved by Pope Francis, 213; practical denial of indissolubility of, 42–43, 65, 70, 136, 220–21, 244–45, 250;. *See also* adultery; *Amoris Laetitia*; and *passim*
Martin, Fr James: 144
de Mattei, Roberto: 23, 330
McCarrick, Theodore: 142, 328
Meisner, Cardinal Joachim: 37–38
Mendonça, Bishop José Tolentino: 143
mercy: 67, 194, 196, 207, 259, 345
Modernism: 4, 21, 103–13, 120–22, 141, 393–94, 419; consummation of all heresies, 269; mental illness, 268; Pharisees as Jewish modernists, 183; Pope Francis and, 232, 268–70, 406, 418; theological censures and, 10
modernity: 253–54, 260
moral law: idolatry and, 169–70, 409; objectivity and universality of, 41, 64–65, 88, 131, 226–27, 247, 289; obligation to observe, 62–63, 69, 71; Pope Francis and, 18, 76, 122, 125, 132, 250; possibility of observing, 59–60, 62, 221, 288

moral theology: 72, 195, 279; and casuistry, 187. *See also* situation ethics
Müller, Cardinal Gerhard: on Amazonian synod, 167–68; on Argentine bishops, 311; asks for response to *Open Letter to Bishops*, 385; asks for theological disputation, 275; defender of *Amoris Laetitia*, 387; on giving Holy Communion to non-Catholics, 137–37; *Manifesto of Faith*, 330

Negri, Archbishop Luigi: 326
New Commentary on the Code of Canon Law: 34, 403
Newman, Cardinal John Henry: on development, 260; papal infallibility and, 415–19; on Roman church, 208
Nichols, Cardinal Vincent: 203–4

obsequium religiosum: *see* magisterium
Onaiyekan, Cardinal John: 329
Open Letter to Bishops: 125–59; probability calculus and, 359; references in not exhaustive, 128, 139; report of crime committed, 360; whether due process followed by, 351–53, 370–73
Opus Dei (personal prelature): theological position of, 289
Order of Preachers: 5
ordination of women: xii, 419
Osservatore Romano: 85
Oxford University: 4–5

Pachamama: *see* "Amazonian Synod"
Paglia, Archbishop Vincenzo: 85
Panormo, Antonio de: 7
Paolis, Cardinal Velasio de: 329
papacy: "first see is judged by no one," 9, 309–10, 403; not an "oracle," 292, 344, 418; subject to apostolic tradition, 238

papal heresy: Bellarmine on, 154–55, 157, 397–400, 404, 416; Cajetan on, 154, 157, 397–98, 404; canon law concerning, 401–4, based on divine law, 155, 349, 360–61, 401; consequence of, 154, 396–98; declaration versus deposition, 397–99; due process and, 351, 371–73; John of St Thomas on, 154, 157, 397, 401, 404; Journet on, 154, 349; Juan de Torquemada on, 33, 156; natural law and, 491; possibility of, 155, 416–17; sedevacantism, 157; various authorities on, 154; wrongness of tolerating, 154

Parolin, Cardinal Pietro: 14, 215–16, 288

Paul VI, Pope: defence of revealed truths by, 108, 406

Penance (sacrament): *see* Absolution (sacramental)

pertinacity: 112–13, 127, 356, 396. *See also* Francis, Pope; heresy, crime of

Peters, Edward: legitimacy of the *Correctio filialis*, 317

Petrine ministry, purpose of: 37, 76–77, 318, 322. *See also* papacy

Pigghe, Albert: 416

Pio, Mgr Vito Pinto: 204

Pius IX, Pope: defines papal prerogatives, 415; denies that pope is absolute sovereign, 76

Pius X, Pope: 120, 122, 269, 419

Pius XII, Pope: 199–200, 396, 419

polemics: 15–16

Pontifical Academy for Life: 144–45

principle of benignity: 333–34, 346

principle of non-contradiction: xiii, 249, 268

"*probabilis*": 417

processional cross: *see* "stang"

Professio Fidei: 321

proportionalism: 226

Protestant Reformation: Pope Francis's gratitude for, 137

Pujats, Cardinal Janis: 147, 327, 329

Radcliffe, Fr Timothy: 144

rainbow-cross: 146

Reconciliatio et Paenitentia (John Paul II), 39, 41, 53, 60, 62, 86–87, 128–29

Remaining in the Truth of Christ: 329, 341

Ricca, Mgr Mario Salvatore Battista: 144

Rosica, Fr Thomas: 342

rule of law: 8, 218

Sacramentum Caritatis (Benedict XVI): 39, 41, 71–72

sacrilege: and Holy Communion, 85, 228–30. *See also* Amazonian Synod and *Contra recentia sacrilegia*

same-sex "unions": 182–83

Sarah, Cardinal Robert: 268, 329, 378

scandal: 76, 289, 291–94, 318, 320; generalized, 250; independence of intention, 412; St Thomas Aquinas on, 75, 162, 316

schism, "internal papal": 391

Schneider, Bishop Athanasius: 26, 167–68, 266, 325, 409; on *Document on Human Fraternity*, 328; on fraternal correction, 286

Schönborn, Cardinal Christoph: 14, 81–82, 204

sedevacantism: 157, 344, 376

Seifert, Josef: 24–25, 272, 328, 378; description of *Amoris Laetitia* as "atomic bomb," 302, 370

Sire, Henry: 16, 331

situation ethics: 183, 195, 369, 378; and *Amoris Laetitia*, 188, 213, 279–81; John Paul II, on 196, 370; Pius XII on, 64

Society of Jesus: casuistry and, 187–88, 195; unreliability of gospels according to General of, 248–49

Sodano, Cardinal Angelo: 1

Sosa, Fr Arturo: *see* Society of Jesus

Spadaro, Fr Antonio: 205, 248, 273; arithmetic and, 268
"stang": 146, 343
Strumia, Don Alberto: 289–90
Synod on the Family in 2014: 3, 81, 145, 341; how directed by Pope Francis, 257
Synod on the Family in 2015: 3–4, 140–41, 325, 329
"synodal path": xi, 386

Theologians: as authors of documents collected here, how characterised, 4–5, 21–22, 25–27, 394; duties of, 10
Theological censures: concept and history of, 6–9; twofold, of content and effect, 56; usefulness of, 10–11
Theological censures of Amoris Laetitia: 49–73; not intended to be exhaustive, 56; not made public by its authors, 1, 212
Thiel, Marie-Jo: 145
Thomasset, Fr Alain: 145

Time, its superiority to space: 257–60
Trent, Council of: 58–63, 66, 68, 72, 86–87, 89, 112, 128–30, 277, 288, 319, 321, 357

ultramontanism: 8–9

Vatican Council, First: *see* infallibility
Veritatis Splendor (John Paul II), 3, 39, 42–45, 60, 61–66, 69, 71, 73, 86–88, 128–31, 147, 186, 188, 196, 226, 247, 370, 374, 406
Viganò, Archbishop Carlo Maria: xi–xiv, 142, 168, 327–28, 374
virginity: 58–59, 212
Voderholzer, Bishop Rudolf: 168, 409–14

Weinandy, Fr Thomas: 327
Wuerl, Cardinal Donald: 142–43

Yanez, Fr Humberto Miguel: 145

Zanchetta, Bishop Gustavo Óscar: 143
Zen, Cardinal Joseph: 326